T0185895

Lecture Notes in Computer Science   11535

Commenced Publication in 1973
Founding and Former Series Editors:
Gerhard Goos, Juris Hartmanis, and Jan van Leeuwen

More information about this series at http://www.springer.com/series/7408

Jorge A. Pérez · Nobuko Yoshida (Eds.)

Formal Techniques for Distributed Objects, Components, and Systems

39th IFIP WG 6.1 International Conference, FORTE 2019
Held as Part of the 14th International Federated Conference
on Distributed Computing Techniques, DisCoTec 2019
Kongens Lyngby, Denmark, June 17–21, 2019
Proceedings

Springer

Editors
Jorge A. Pérez ⓘ
University of Groningen
Groningen, The Netherlands

Nobuko Yoshida ⓘ
Imperial College London
London, UK

ISSN 0302-9743   ISSN 1611-3349   (electronic)
Lecture Notes in Computer Science
ISBN 978-3-030-21758-7   ISBN 978-3-030-21759-4   (eBook)
https://doi.org/10.1007/978-3-030-21759-4

LNCS Sublibrary: SL2 – Programming and Software Engineering

This Springer imprint is published by the registered company Springer Nature Switzerland AG
The registered company address is: Gewerbestrasse 11, 6330 Cham, Switzerland

Foreword

The 14th International Federated Conference on Distributed Computing Techniques (DisCoTec) took place in Kongens Lyngby, Denmark, during June 17–21, 2019. It was organized by the Department of Applied Mathematics and Computer Science at the Technical University of Denmark.

The DisCoTec series is one of the major events sponsored by the International Federation for Information Processing (IFIP). It comprised three conferences:

- COORDINATION, the IFIP WG 6.1 21st International Conference on Coordination Models and Languages
- DAIS, the IFIP WG 6.1 19th International Conference on Distributed Applications and Interoperable Systems
- FORTE, the IFIP WG 6.1 39th International Conference on Formal Techniques for Distributed Objects, Components and Systems

Together, these conferences cover a broad spectrum of distributed computing subjects, ranging from theoretical foundations and formal description techniques to systems research issues.

In addition to the individual sessions of each conference, the event included several plenary sessions that gathered attendants from the three conferences. This year, the general chair and the DisCoTec Steering Committee joined the three DisCoTec conferences in the selection and nomination of the plenary keynote speakers, whose number was accordingly increased from the traditional three to five. The five keynote speakers and the title of their talks are listed below:

- Prof. David Basin (ETH Zürich, Switzerland) – "Security Protocols: Model Checking Standards"
- Dr. Anne-Marie Kermarrec (Inria Rennes, France) – "Making Sense of Fast Big Data"
- Prof. Marta Kwiatkowska (University of Oxford, UK) – "Versatile Quantitative Modelling: Verification, Synthesis and Data Inference for Cyber-Physical Systems"
- Prof. Silvio Micali (MIT, USA)—"ALGORAND—The Distributed Ledger for the Borderless Economy"
- Prof. Martin Wirsing (LMU, Germany) – "Toward Formally Designing Collective Adaptive Systems"

As is traditional in DisCoTec, an additional joint session with the best papers from each conference was organized. The best papers were:

- "Representing Dependencies in Event Structures" by G. Michele Pinna (Coordination)
- "FOUGERE: User-Centric Location Privacy in Mobile Crowdsourcing Apps" by Lakhdar Meftah, Romain Rouvoy and Isabelle Chrisment (DAIS)

- "Psi-Calculi Revisited: Connectivity and Compositionality" by Johannes Åman Pohjola (FORTE)

Associated with the federated event were also two satellite events that took place:

- ICE, the 12th International Workshop on Interaction and Concurrency Experience
- DisCoRail, the First International Workshop on Distributed Computing in Future Railway Systems

I would like to thank the Program Committee chairs of the different events for their help and cooperation during the preparation of the conference, and the Steering Committee and Advisory Boards of DisCoTec and their conferences for their guidance and support. The organization of DisCoTec 2019 was only possible thanks to the dedicated work of the Organizing Committee, including Francisco "Kiko" Fernández Reyes and Francesco Tiezzi (publicity chairs), Maurice ter Beek, Valerio Schiavoni, and Andrea Vandin (workshop chairs), Ann-Cathrin Dunker (logistics and finances), as well as all the students and colleagues who volunteered their time to help. Finally, I would like to thank IFIP WG 6.1 for sponsoring this event, Springer's *Lecture Notes in Computer Science* team for their support and sponsorship, EasyChair for providing the reviewing infrastructure, the Nordic IoT Hub for their sponsorship, and the Technical University of Denmark for providing meeting rooms and additional support.

June 2019   Alberto Lluch Lafuente

Preface

This volume contains the papers presented at FORTE 2019: the 39th IFIP WG 6.1 International Conference on Formal Techniques for Distributed Objects, Components, and Systems. FORTE 2019 was held as one of three main conferences of the 14th International Federated Conference on Distributed Computing Techniques (DisCoTec), during June 17–21, 2019 in Lyngby, Denmark.

FORTE is a well-established forum for fundamental research on theory, models, tools, and applications for distributed systems, with special interest in:

- Software quality, reliability, availability, and safety
- Security, privacy, and trust in distributed and/or communicating systems
- Service-oriented, ubiquitous, and cloud computing systems
- Component- and model-based design
- Object technology, modularity, software adaptation
- Self-stabilization and self-healing/organizing
- Verification, validation, formal analysis, and testing of the above

The Program Committee received a total of 42 quality submissions, written by authors from 21 different countries. Of these, 18 papers were selected for inclusion in the scientific program: 15 full papers, one short paper, and two "journal first" papers—a new submission category we introduced this year. Each submission was reviewed by at least three Program Committee members with the help of external reviewers in selected cases. There was one submission with which both of us declared ourselves in conflict; Uwe Nestmann kindly agreed to oversee and lead the discussion for this submission, which was eventually accepted.

The selection of accepted submissions was based on electronic discussions via the EasyChair conference management system. Toward the end of this electronic discussion, there was a two-day physical meeting in which we discussed the referee reports for each submission with the relevant Program Committee members. We found this combination of electronic and physical discussion highly effective.

As program chairs, we actively contributed to the selection of the five keynote speakers of DisCoTec 2019:

- Prof. David Basin (ETH Zürich, Switzerland)
- Dr. Anne-Marie Kermarrec (Inria Rennes, France)
- Prof. Marta Kwiatkowska (University of Oxford, UK)
- Prof. Silvio Micali (MIT, USA)
- Prof. Martin Wirsing (LMU, Germany)

We are most grateful to Prof. Basin for accepting our invitation as FORTE-related keynote speaker. This volume includes the abstract of his keynote talk: "Security Protocols: Model Checking Standards."

As is traditional in DisCoTec, a joint session with the best papers from each main conference was organized. The best paper of FORTE 2019 was "Psi-Calculi Revisited: Connectivity and Compositionality" by Johannes Åman Pohjola (Data61/CSIRO, University of New South Wales, Australia).

We wish to thank all the authors of submitted papers, all the members of the Program Committee for their thorough evaluations of the submissions, and the 26 external reviewers who assisted the evaluation process. We are also indebted to the Steering Committee of FORTE for their advice and suggestions. Last but not least, we thank the DisCoTec general chair, Alberto Lluch Lafuente, and his organization team for their hard, effective work on providing an excellent environment for FORTE 2019 and all other conferences and workshops.

April 2019   Jorge A. Pérez
                                                               Nobuko Yoshida

Organization

Program Committee

Samik Basu	Iowa State University, USA
Annette Bieniusa	University of Kaiserslautern, Germany
Stefano Calzavara	Università Ca' Foscari Venezia, Italy
Natalia Chechina	Bournemouth University, UK
Mila Dalla Preda	University of Verona, Italy
Rayna Dimitrova	University of Leicester, UK
Patrick Eugster	University of Lugano (USI), Switzerland
Ichiro Hasuo	National Institute of Informatics, Japan
Thomas Hildebrandt	University of Copenhagen, Denmark
Sophia Knight	University of Minnesota, USA
Etienne Lozes	I3S, University of Nice and CNRS, France
Emanuela Merelli	University of Camerino, Italy
Roland Meyer	TU Braunschweig, Germany
Uwe Nestmann	TU Berlin, Germany
Gustavo Petri	IRIF, Paris Diderot, Paris 7, France
Jorge A. Pérez	University of Groningen, The Netherlands
Willard Rafnsson	IT University of Copenhagen, Denmark
Anne Remke	WWU Münster, Germany
Guido Salvaneschi	TU Darmstadt, Germany
Cesar Sanchez	IMDEA Software Institute, Spain
Ana Sokolova	University of Salzburg, Austria
Alexander J. Summers	ETH Zurich, Switzerland
Peter Thiemann	Universität Freiburg, Germany
Jaco van de Pol	Aarhus University, Denmark
Tim Willemse	Eindhoven University of Technology, The Netherlands
Nobuko Yoshida	Imperial College London, UK
Lukasz Ziarek	SUNY Buffalo, USA

Additional Reviewers

Aldini, Alessandro	Keiren, Jeroen	Sasse, Ralf
Alvim, Mario S.	Madiot, Jean Marie	Savvides, Savvas
Åman Pohjola, Johannes	Maestri, Stefano	Schweizer, Sebastian
Back, Christoffer Olling	Maubert, Bastien	Sedwards, Sean
Chini, Peter	Menikkumbura, Danushka	Tesei, Luca
Courtieu, Pierre	Neumann, Elisabeth	Wolff, Sebastian
Dubut, Jérémy	Otoni, Rodrigo	Yamada, Akihisa
Francalanza, Adrian	Pilch, Carina	Zeller, Peter
Inverso, Omar	Radanne, Gabriel	

Security Protocols: Model Checking Standards (Invited Talk)

David Basin

Department of Computer Science, ETH Zurich, Switzerland

The design of security protocols is typically approached as an art, rather than a science, and often with disastrous consequences. But this need not be so! I have been working for ca. 20 years on foundations, methods, and tools, both for developing protocols that are correct by construction [9, 10] and for the post-hoc verification of existing designs [1–4, 8]. In this talk I will introduce my work in this area and describe my experience analyzing, improving, and contributing to different industry standards, both existing and upcoming [5–7].

References

1. Basin, D.: Lazy infinite-state analysis of security protocols. In: Secure Networking — CQRE [Secure] 1999. CQRE. LNCS, vol. 1740, pp. 30–42. Springer, Heidelberg (1999)
2. Basin, D., Cremers, C., Dreier, J., Sasse, R.: Symbolically analyzing security protocols using tamarin. SIGLOG News **4**(4), 19–30 (2017). https://doi.org/10.1145/3157831.3157835
3. Basin, D., Cremers, C., Meadows, C.: Model checking security protocols. In: Clarke, E., Henzinger, T., Veith, H., Bloem, R. (eds.) Handbook of Model Checking, pp. 727–762. Springer, Cham (2018)
4. Basin, D., Mödersheim, S., Viganò, L.: OFMC: a symbolic model checker for security protocols. Int. J. Inf. Secur. **4**(3), 181–208 (2005). published online December 2004
5. Basin, D.A., Cremers, C., Meier, S.: Provably repairing the ISO/IEC 9798 standard for entity authentication. J. Comput. Secur. **21**(6), 817–846 (2013)
6. Basin, D.A., Cremers, C.J.F., Miyazaki, K., Radomirovic, S., Watanabe, D.: Improving the security of cryptographic protocol standards. IEEE Secur. Priv. **13**(3), 24–31 (2015). https://doi.org/10.1109/MSP.2013.162, http://dx.doi.org/10.1109/MSP.2013.162
7. Basin, D.A., Dreier, J., Hirschi, L., Radomirovic, S., Sasse, R., Stettler, V.: Formal analysis of 5G authentication. CoRR **abs/1806.10360** (2018). http://arxiv.org/abs/1806.10360
8. Schmidt, B., Meier, S., Cremers, C., Basin, D.: Automated analysis of Diffie-Hellman protocols and advanced security properties. In: Proceedings of the 25th IEEE Computer Security Foundations Symposium (CSF), pp. 78–94 (2012)
9. Sprenger, C., Basin, D.: Refining key establishment. In: Proceedings of the 25th IEEE Computer Security Foundations Symposium (CSF), pp. 230–246 (2012)
10. Sprenger, C., Basin, D.: Refining security protocols. J. Comput. Secur. **26**(1), 71–120 (2018). https://doi.org/10.3233/JCS-16814, http://dx.doi.org/10.3233/JCS-16814

Contents

Full Papers

Psi-Calculi Revisited: Connectivity and Compositionality............... 3
   Johannes Åman Pohjola

Squeezing Streams and Composition of Self-stabilizing Algorithms........ 21
   Karine Altisen, Pierre Corbineau, and Stéphane Devismes

Parametric Updates in Parametric Timed Automata.................... 39
   Étienne André, Didier Lime, and Mathias Ramparison

Parametric Statistical Model Checking of UAV Flight Plan 57
   Ran Bao, Christian Attiogbe, Benoît Delahaye, Paulin Fournier,
   and Didier Lime

Only Connect, Securely...................................... 75
   Chandrika Bhardwaj and Sanjiva Prasad

Output-Sensitive Information Flow Analysis....................... 93
   Cristian Ene, Laurent Mounier, and Marie-Laure Potet

Component-aware Input-Output Conformance...................... 111
   Alexander Graf-Brill and Holger Hermanns

Declarative Choreographies and Liveness......................... 129
   Thomas T. Hildebrandt, Tijs Slaats, Hugo A. López, Søren Debois,
   and Marco Carbone

Model Checking HPnGs in Multiple Dimensions: Representing State Sets
as Convex Polytopes... 148
   Jannik Hüls and Anne Remke

Causal-Consistent Replay Debugging for Message Passing Programs....... 167
   Ivan Lanese, Adrián Palacios, and Germán Vidal

Correct and Efficient Antichain Algorithms for Refinement Checking 185
   Maurice Laveaux, Jan Friso Groote, and Tim A. C. Willemse

Towards Verified Blockchain Architectures: A Case Study on Interactive
Architecture Verification 204
   Diego Marmsoler

Unfolding-Based Dynamic Partial Order Reduction of Asynchronous
Distributed Programs   224
   The Anh Pham, Thierry Jéron, and Martin Quinson

Encapsulation and Sharing in Dynamic Software Architectures:
The Hypercell Framework   242
   Jean-Bernard Stefani and Martin Vassor

Decentralized Real-Time Safety Verification for Distributed
Cyber-Physical Systems   261
   Hoang-Dung Tran, Luan Viet Nguyen, Patrick Musau, Weiming Xiang,
   and Taylor T. Johnson

Short and "Journal First" Papers

On Certifying Distributed Algorithms: Problem of Local Correctness   281
   Kim Völlinger

On a Higher-Order Calculus of Computational Fields   289
   Giorgio Audrito, Mirko Viroli, Ferruccio Damiani, Danilo Pianini,
   and Jacob Beal

Semantically Sound Analysis of Content Security Policies   293
   Stefano Calzavara, Alvise Rabitti, and Michele Bugliesi

Author Index   299

Full Papers

Psi-Calculi Revisited: Connectivity and Compositionality

Johannes Åman Pohjola[1,2]([✉]) [iD]

[1] Data61/CSIRO, Sydney, Australia
johannes.amanpohjola@data61.csiro.au
[2] University of New South Wales, Sydney, Australia

Abstract. Psi-calculi is a parametric framework for process calculi similar to popular pi-calculus extensions such as the explicit fusion calculus, the applied pi-calculus and the spi calculus. Mechanised proofs of standard algebraic and congruence properties of bisimilarity apply to all calculi within the framework.

A limitation of psi-calculi is that communication channels must be symmetric and transitive. In this paper, we give a new operational semantics to psi-calculi that allows us to lift these restrictions and simplify some of the proofs. The key technical innovation is to annotate transitions with a *provenance*—a description of the scope and channel they originate from.

We give mechanised proofs that our extension is conservative, and that the standard algebraic and congruence properties of bisimilarity are maintained. We show correspondence with a reduction semantics and barbed bisimulation. We show how a pi-calculus with preorders that was previously beyond the scope of psi-calculi can be captured, and how to encode mixed choice under very strong quality criteria.

Keywords: Process algebra · Psi-calculi · Nominal logic · Interactive theorem proving · Bisimulation

1 Introduction

This paper is mainly concerned with *channel connectivity*, by which we mean the relationship that describes which input channels are connected to which output channels in a setting with message-passing concurrency. In the pi-calculus [18], channel connectivity is syntactic identity: in the process

$$\underline{a}(x).P \mid \overline{b}\,y.Q$$

where one parallel component is waiting to receive on channel a and the other is waiting to send on channel b, interaction is possible only if $a = b$.

© IFIP International Federation for Information Processing 2019
Published by Springer Nature Switzerland AG 2019
J. A. Pérez and N. Yoshida (Eds.): FORTE 2019, LNCS 11535, pp. 3–20, 2019.
https://doi.org/10.1007/978-3-030-21759-4_1

Variants of the pi-calculus may have more interesting channel connectivity. The explicit fusion calculus pi-F [9] extends the pi-calculus with a primitive for *fusing* names; once fused, they are treated as being for all purposes one and the same. Channel connectivity is then given by the equivalence closure of the name fusions. For example, if we extend the above example with the fusion $(a = b)$

$$\underline{a}(x).P \mid \overline{b}\,y.Q \mid (a = b)$$

then communication is possible. Other examples may be found in e.g. calculi for wireless communication [19], where channel connectivity can be used to directly model the network's topology.

Psi-calculi [2] is a family of applied process calculi, where standard meta-theoretical results, such as the algebraic laws and congruence properties of bisimulation, have been established once and for all through mechanised proofs [3] for all members of the family. Psi-calculi generalises e.g. the pi-calculus and the explicit fusion calculus in several ways. In place of atomic names it allows channels and messages to be taken from an (almost) freely chosen term language. In place of fusions, it admits the formulas of an (almost) freely chosen logic as first-class processes. Channel connectivity is determined by judgements of said logic, with one restriction: the connectivity thus induced must be symmetric and transitive.

The main contribution of the present paper is a new way to define the semantics of psi-calculi that lets us lift this restriction, without sacrificing any of the algebraic laws and compositionality properties. It is worth noting that this was previously believed to be impossible: Bengtson et al. [2, p. 14] even offer counterexamples to the effect that without symmetry and transitivity, scope extension is unsound. However, a close reading reveals that these counterexamples apply only to their particular choice of labelled semantics, and do not rule out the possibility that the counterexamples could be invalidated by a rephrasing of the labelled semantics such as ours.

The price we pay for this increased generality is more complicated transition labels: we decorate input and output labels with a *provenance* that keeps track of which prefix a transition originates from. The idea is that if I am an input label and you are an output label, we can communicate if my subject is your provenance, and vice versa. This is offset by other simplifications of the semantics and associated proofs that provenances enable.

Contributions. This paper makes the following specific technical contributions:

- We define a new semantics of psi-calculi that lifts the requirement that channel connectivity must be symmetric and transitive, using the novel technical device of provenances (Sect. 2).
- We prove that strong bisimulation is a congruence and satisfies the usual algebraic laws such as scope extension. Interestingly, provenances can be ignored for the purpose of bisimulation. These proofs are machine-checked[1] in Nominal Isabelle [24] (Sect. 3.1).

---

[1] Isabelle proofs are available at https://github.com/IlmariReissumies/newpsi.

- We prove, again using Nominal Isabelle, that this paper's developments constitute a conservative extension of the original psi-calculi (Sect. 3.2).
- We further validate our semantics by defining a reduction semantics and strong barbed congruence, and showing that they agree with their labelled counterparts (Sect. 3.2).
- We capture a pi-calculus with preorders by Hirschkoff et al. [11], that was previously beyond the scope of psi-calculi because of its non-transitive channel connectivity. The bisimilarity we obtain turns out to coincide with that of Hirschkoff et al. (Sect. 4.1).
- We exploit non-transitive connectivity to show that mixed choice is a derived operator of psi-calculi in a very strong sense: its encoding is fully abstract and satisfies strong operational correspondence (Sect. 4.2).

For lack of space we elide proofs; please see the associated technical report [1].

2 Definitions

This section introduces core definitions such as syntax and semantics. Many definitions are shared with the original presentation of psi-calculi, so this section also functions as a recapitulation of [2]. We will highlight the places where the two differ.

We assume a countable set of *names* $\mathcal{N}$ ranged over by $a, b, c, \ldots, x, y, z$. A *nominal set* [8] is a set equipped with a permutation action $\cdot$; intuitively, if $X \in \mathbf{X}$ and $\mathbf{X}$ is a nominal set, then $(x\ y) \cdot X$, which denotes X with all occurrences of the name x swapped for y and vice versa, is also an element of $\mathbf{X}$. $\mathsf{n}(X)$ (the *support* of X) is, intuitively, the set of names such that swapping them changes X. We write $a\#X$ ("a is fresh in X) for $a \notin \mathsf{n}(X)$. A nominal set $\mathbf{X}$ has *finite support* if for every $X \in \mathbf{X}$, $\mathsf{n}(X)$ is finite. A function symbol f is *equivariant* if $p \cdot f(x) = f(p \cdot x)$; this generalises to n-ary function symbols in the obvious way. Whenever we define inductive syntax with names, it is implicitly quotiented by permutation of bound names, so e.g. $(\nu x)\overline{a}\langle x \rangle = (\nu y)\overline{a}\langle y \rangle$ if $x, y\#a$.

Psi-calculi is parameterised on an arbitrary term language and a logic of environmental assertions:

Definition 1 (Parameters). *A* psi-calculus *is a 7-tuple* $(\mathbf{T}, \mathbf{A}, \mathbf{C}, \vdash, \otimes, \mathbf{1}, \dot{\rightarrow})$ *with three finitely supported nominal sets:*

1. $\mathbf{T}$, *the* terms, *ranged over by* M, N, K, L, T;
2. $\mathbf{A}$, *the* assertions, *ranged over by* Ψ; *and*
3. $\mathbf{C}$, *the* conditions, *ranged over by* φ.

We assume each of the above is equipped with a substitution function $[\_ := \_]$ *that substitutes (sequences of) terms for names. The remaining three parameters are equivariant function symbols written in infix:*

$$\vdash : \mathbf{A} \times \mathbf{C} \Rightarrow \mathbf{bool}\ (entailment) \qquad \otimes : \mathbf{A} \times \mathbf{A} \Rightarrow \mathbf{A}\ (composition)$$
$$\mathbf{1} : \mathbf{A} \qquad\qquad (unit) \qquad \dot{\rightarrow} : \mathbf{T} \times \mathbf{T} \Rightarrow \mathbf{C}\ (channel\ connectivity)$$

Intuitively, $M \dashrightarrow K$ means the prefix M can send a message to the prefix K. The substitution functions must satisfy certain natural criteria wrt. their treatment of names; see [2] for the details.

Definition 2 (Static equivalence). *Two assertions Ψ, Ψ' are statically equivalent, written $\Psi \simeq \Psi'$, if $\forall \varphi. \Psi \vdash \varphi \Leftrightarrow \Psi' \vdash \varphi$.*

Definition 3 (Valid parameters). *A psi-calculus is valid if $(\mathbf{A}/\simeq, \otimes, \mathbf{1})$ form an abelian monoid.*

Note that since the abelian monoid is closed, static equivalence is preserved by composition. Henceforth we will only consider valid psi-calculi. The original presentation of psi-calculi had $\leftrightarrow$ for channel equivalence in place of our $\dashrightarrow$, and required that channel equivalence be symmetric (formally, $\Psi \vdash M \leftrightarrow K$ iff $\Psi \vdash K \leftrightarrow M$) and transitive.

Definition 4 (Process syntax). *The* processes *(or* agents*) $\mathbf{P}$, ranged over by P, Q, R, are inductively defined by the grammar*

$$
\begin{array}{llll}
P := \mathbf{0} & (nil) & (\!|\Psi|\!) & (assertion) \\
\overline{M} \, N.P & (output) & \underline{M}(\lambda\widetilde{x})N.P & (input) \\
\mathbf{case} \; \widetilde{\varphi} : \widetilde{P} & (case) & P \mid Q & (parallel \; composition) \\
(\nu x)P & (restriction) & !P & (replication)
\end{array}
$$

A process is assertion guarded *(*guarded *for short) if all assertions occur underneath an input or output prefix. We require that in $!P$, P is guarded; that in $\mathbf{case} \; \widetilde{\varphi} : \widetilde{P}$, all $\widetilde{P}$ are guarded; and that in $\underline{M}(\lambda\widetilde{x})N . P$ it holds that $\widetilde{x} \subseteq \mathsf{n}(N)$. We will use P_G, Q_G to range over guarded processes.*

Restriction, replication and parallel composition are standard. $\overline{M} \, N.P$ is a process ready to send the message N on channel M, and then continue as P. Similarly, $\underline{M}(\lambda\widetilde{x})N.P$ is a process ready to receive a message on channel M that matches the pattern $(\lambda\widetilde{x})N$. The process $(\!|\Psi|\!)$ asserts a fact Ψ about the environment. Intuitively, $(\!|\Psi|\!) \mid P$ means that P executes in an environment where all conditions entailed by Ψ hold. P may itself contain assertions that add or retract conditions. Environments can evolve dynamically: as a process reduces, assertions may become unguarded and thus added to the environment. $\mathbf{case} \; \widetilde{\varphi} : \widetilde{P}$ is a process that may act as any P_i whose guard φ_i is entailed by the environment. For discussion of why replication and case must be guarded we refer to [2,15].

The assertion environment of a process is described by its *frame*:

Definition 5 (Frames). *The* frame *of P, written $\mathcal{F}(P) = (\nu\widetilde{b}_P)\Psi_P$ where $\widetilde{b}_P$ bind into Ψ_P, is defined as*

$$
\mathcal{F}((\!|\Psi|\!)) = (\nu\epsilon)\Psi \qquad \mathcal{F}(P \mid Q) = \mathcal{F}(P) \otimes \mathcal{F}(Q) \qquad \mathcal{F}((\nu x)P) = (\nu x)\mathcal{F}(P)
$$

$$
\mathcal{F}(P) = \mathbf{1} \; otherwise
$$

where name-binding and composition of frames is defined as $(\nu x)(\nu \tilde{b}_P)\Psi_P = (\nu x, \tilde{b}_P)\Psi_P$, *and, if* $\tilde{b}_P \# \tilde{b}_Q, \Psi_Q$ *and* $\tilde{b}_Q \# \Psi_P$,

$$(\nu \tilde{b}_P)\Psi_P \otimes (\nu \tilde{b}_Q)\Psi_Q = (\nu \tilde{b}_P, \tilde{b}_Q)\Psi_P \otimes \Psi_Q.$$

We extend entailment to frames as follows: $\mathcal{F}(P) \vdash \varphi$ holds if, for some $\tilde{b}_P, \Psi_P$ such that $\mathcal{F}(P) = (\nu \tilde{b}_P)\Psi_P$ and $\tilde{b}_P \# \varphi$, $\Psi_P \vdash \varphi$. The freshness side-condition $\tilde{b}_P \# \varphi$ is important because it allows assertions to be used for representing local state. By default, the assertion environment is effectively a form of global non-monotonic state, which is not always appropriate for modelling distributed processes. With ν-binding we recover locality by writing e.g. $(\nu x)((\!| x = M |\!) \mid P)$ for a process P with a local variable x.

The notion of *provenance* is the main novelty of our semantics. It is the key technical device used to make our semantics compositional:

Definition 6 (Provenances). *The* provenances Π, *ranged over by* π, *are either* $\bot$ *or of form* $(\nu \tilde{x}; \tilde{y})M$, *where* M *is a term, and* $\tilde{x}, \tilde{y}$ *bind into* M.

We write M for $(\nu \epsilon; \epsilon)M$. When $\tilde{x}, \tilde{y} \# \tilde{x}', \tilde{y}'$ and $\tilde{x} \# \tilde{y}$, we interpret the expression $(\nu \tilde{x}; \tilde{y})(\nu \tilde{x}'; \tilde{y}')M$ as $(\nu \tilde{x}\,\tilde{x}'; \tilde{y}\,\tilde{y}')M$. Furthermore, we identify $(\nu \tilde{x}; \tilde{y})\bot$ and $\bot$. Let $\pi \downarrow$ denote the result of moving all binders from the outermost binding sequence to the innermost; that is, $(\nu \tilde{x}; \tilde{y})M \downarrow = (\nu \epsilon; \tilde{x}, \tilde{y})M$. Similarly, $\pi \downarrow \tilde{z}$ denotes the result of inserting $\tilde{z}$ at the end of the outermost binding sequence: formally, $(\nu \tilde{x}; \tilde{y})M \downarrow \tilde{z} = (\nu \tilde{x}, \tilde{z}; \tilde{y})M$.

Intuitively, a provenance describes the origin of an input or output transition. For example, if an output transition is annotated with $(\nu \tilde{x}; \tilde{y})M$, the sender is an output prefix with subject M that occurs underneath the ν-binders $\tilde{x}, \tilde{y}$. For technical reasons, these binders are partitioned into two distinct sequences. The intention is that $\tilde{x}$ are the frame binders, while $\tilde{y}$ contains binders that occur underneath case and replication; these are not part of the frame, but may nonetheless bind into M. We prefer to keep them separate because the $\tilde{x}$ binders are used for deriving $\vdash$ judgements, but $\tilde{y}$ are not (cf. Definition 5).

Definition 7 (Labels). *The* labels **L**, *ranged over by* α, β, *are:*

$$\overline{M}\,(\nu \tilde{x})N \text{ (output)} \qquad \underline{M}\,N \text{ (input)} \qquad \tau \text{ (silent)}$$

The bound names *of* α, *written* bn(alpha), *is* $\tilde{x}$ *if* $\alpha = \overline{M}\,(\nu \tilde{x})N$ *and* ϵ *otherwise. The* subject *of* α, *written* subj(α), *is* M *if* $\alpha = \overline{M}\,(\nu \tilde{x})N$ *or* $\alpha = \underline{M}\,N$. *Analogously, the* object *of* α, *written* obj(α), *is* N *if* $\alpha = \overline{M}\,(\nu \tilde{x})N$ *or* $\alpha = \underline{M}\,N$.

While the provenance describes the origin of a transition, a label describes how it can interact. For example, a transition labelled with $\underline{M}\,N$ indicates readiness to receive a message N from an output prefix with subject M.

Table 1. Structured operational semantics. A symmetric version of COM is elided. In the rule COM we assume that $\mathcal{F}(P) = (\nu\widetilde{b}_P)\Psi_P$ and $\mathcal{F}(Q) = (\nu\widetilde{b}_Q)\Psi_Q$ where $\widetilde{b}_P$ is fresh for Ψ and Q, $\widetilde{x}$ is fresh for Ψ, Ψ_Q, P, and $\widetilde{b}_Q, \widetilde{y}$ are similarly fresh. In rule PARL we assume that $\mathcal{F}(Q) = (\nu\widetilde{b}_Q)\Psi_Q$ where $\widetilde{b}_Q$ is fresh for Ψ, P, π and α. PARR has the same freshness conditions but with the roles of P, Q swapped. In OPEN the expression $\widetilde{a} \cup \{b\}$ means the sequence $\widetilde{a}$ with b inserted anywhere.

$$\text{IN} \ \frac{\Psi \vdash K \stackrel{.}{\to} M}{\Psi \rhd \underline{M}(\lambda\widetilde{y})N \,.\, P \xrightarrow[M]{K\,N[\widetilde{y}:=\widetilde{L}]} P[\widetilde{y} := \widetilde{L}]} \qquad\qquad \text{OUT} \ \frac{\Psi \vdash M \stackrel{.}{\to} K}{\Psi \rhd \overline{M}\,N \,.\, P \xrightarrow[M]{\overline{K}N} P}$$

$$\text{PARL} \ \frac{\Psi_Q \otimes \Psi \rhd P \xrightarrow[\pi]{\alpha} P'}{\Psi \rhd P \mid Q \xrightarrow[\pi\downarrow\widetilde{b}_Q]{\alpha} P' \mid Q} \ \text{bn}(\alpha)\#Q$$

$$\text{PARR} \ \frac{\Psi_P \otimes \Psi \rhd Q \xrightarrow[\pi]{\alpha} Q'}{\Psi \rhd P \mid Q \xrightarrow[(\nu\widetilde{b}_P)\pi]{\alpha} P \mid Q'} \ \text{bn}(\alpha)\#P$$

$$\text{COM} \ \frac{\Psi_Q \otimes \Psi \rhd P \xrightarrow[(\nu\widetilde{b}_P;\widetilde{x})K]{\overline{M}(\nu\widetilde{a})N} P' \qquad \Psi_P \otimes \Psi \rhd Q \xrightarrow[(\nu\widetilde{b}_Q;\widetilde{y})M]{K\,N} Q'}{\Psi \rhd P \mid Q \xrightarrow[\perp]{\tau} (\nu\widetilde{a})(P' \mid Q')} \ \widetilde{a}\#Q$$

$$\text{CASE} \ \frac{\Psi \rhd P_i \xrightarrow[\pi]{\alpha} P' \qquad \Psi \vdash \varphi_i}{\Psi \rhd \mathbf{case} \ \widetilde{\varphi} : \widetilde{P} \xrightarrow[\pi\downarrow]{\alpha} P'} \qquad\qquad \text{SCOPE} \ \frac{\Psi \rhd P \xrightarrow[\pi]{\alpha} P'}{\Psi \rhd (\nu b)P \xrightarrow[(\nu b)\pi]{\alpha} (\nu b)P'} \ b\#\alpha, \Psi$$

$$\text{OPEN} \ \frac{\Psi \rhd P \xrightarrow[\pi]{\overline{M}(\nu\widetilde{a})N} P'}{\Psi \rhd (\nu b)P \xrightarrow[(\nu b)\pi]{\overline{M}(\nu\widetilde{a}\cup\{b\})N} P'} \ \substack{b\#\widetilde{a},\Psi,M \\ b \in \text{n}(N)} \qquad\qquad \text{REP} \ \frac{\Psi \rhd P \mid \,!P \xrightarrow[\pi]{\alpha} P'}{\Psi \rhd \,!P \xrightarrow[\pi\downarrow]{\alpha} P'}$$

Definition 8 (Operational semantics). *The transition relation* $\longrightarrow \subseteq \mathbf{A} \times \mathbf{P} \times \mathbf{L} \times \Pi \times \mathbf{P}$ *is inductively defined by the rules in Table 1. We write* $\Psi \rhd P \xrightarrow{\alpha}_{\pi} P'$ *for* $(\Psi, P, \alpha, \pi, P') \in \longrightarrow$. *In transitions,* $\text{bn}(\alpha)$ *binds into* $\text{obj}(\alpha)$ *and* P'.

The operational semantics differs from [2] mainly by the inclusion of provenances: anything underneath the transition arrows is novel.

The OUT rule states that in an environment where M is connected to K, the prefix $\overline{M}\,N$ may send a message N from M to K. The IN rule is dual to OUT, but also features pattern-matching. If the message is an instance of the pattern, as witnessed by a substitution, that substitution is applied to the continuation P.

In the COM rule, we see how provenances are used to determine when two processes can interact. Specifically, a communication between P and Q can be derived if P can send a message to M using prefix K, and if Q can receive a message from K using prefix M. Because names occuring in M and K may be local to P and Q respectively, we must be careful not to conflate the local names of one with the other; this is why the provenance records all binding names that occur above M, K in the process syntax. Note that even though we identify frames and provenances up-to alpha, the COM rule insists that we consider alpha-variants such that the frame binders and the outermost provenance binders coincide. This ensures that the K on Q's label really is the same as the K in the provenance.

It is instructive to compare our COM rule with the original:

$$\Psi_Q \otimes \Psi \rhd P \xrightarrow{\overline{M}\,(\nu\tilde{a})N} P'$$

$$\text{COM-OLD} \;\; \frac{\Psi_P \otimes \Psi \rhd Q \xrightarrow{K\,N} Q' \qquad \Psi \otimes \Psi_P \otimes \Psi_Q \vdash M \leftrightarrow K}{\Psi \rhd P \mid Q \xrightarrow{\tau} (\nu\tilde{a})(P' \mid Q')} \;\; \tilde{a}\#Q$$

where $\mathcal{F}(P) = (\nu\tilde{b}_P)\Psi_P$ and $\mathcal{F}(Q) = (\nu\tilde{b}_Q)\Psi_Q$ and $\tilde{b}_P\#\Psi, \tilde{b}_Q, Q, M, P$ and $\tilde{b}_Q\#\Psi, \tilde{b}_Q, Q, K, P$. Here we have no way of knowing if M and K are able to synchronise other than making a channel equivalence judgement. Hence any derivation involving COM-OLD makes three channel equivalence judgements: once each in IN, OUT and COM-OLD. With COM we only make one—or more accurately, we make the exact same judgement twice, in IN resp. OUT. Eliminating the redundant judgements is crucial: the reason COM-OLD needs associativity and commutativity is to stitch these three judgements together, particularly when one end of a communication is swapped for a bisimilar process that allows the same interaction via different prefixes.

Note also that COM has fewer freshness side-conditions. A particularly unintuitive aspect of COM-OLD is that it requires $\tilde{b}_P\#M$ and $\tilde{b}_Q\#K$, but not $\tilde{b}_P\#K$ and $\tilde{b}_Q\#M$: we would expect that all bound names can be chosen to be distinct from all free names, but adding the missing freshness conditions makes scope extension unsound [14, pp. 56–57]. With COM, it becomes clear why: because $\tilde{b}_Q$ binds into M.

All the other rules can fire independently of what the provenance of the premise is. They manipulate the provenance, but only for bookkeeping purposes: in order for the COM rule to be sound, we maintain the invariant that if $\Psi \rhd P \xrightarrow[\pi]{\alpha} P'$, the outer binders of π are precisely the binders of $\mathcal{F}(P)$. Otherwise, the rules are exactly the same as in the original psi-calculi.

The reader may notice a curious asymmetry between the treatment of provenance binders in the PARL and PARR rules. This is to ensure that the order of the provenance binders coincides with the order of the frame binders, and in the frame $\mathcal{F}(P \mid Q)$, the binders of P occur syntactically outside the binders of Q (cf. Definition 5).

3   Meta-theory

In this section, we will derive the standard algebraic and congruence laws of strong bisimulation, develop an alternative formulation of strong bisimulation in terms of a reduction relation and barbed congruence, and show that our extension of psi-calculi is conservative. While weak equivalences are beyond the scope of the present paper, we believe it is possible (if tedious) to adapt the results about weak bisimilarity from [15] to our setting.

3.1   Bisimulation

We write $\Psi \rhd P \xrightarrow{\alpha} P'$ as shorthand for $\exists \pi. \ \Psi \rhd P \xrightarrow[\pi]{\alpha} P'$. Bisimulation is then defined exactly as in the original psi-calculi:

Definition 9 (Strong bisimulation). *A symmetric relation* $\mathcal{R} \subseteq \mathbf{A} \times \mathbf{P} \times \mathbf{P}$ *is a* strong bisimulation *iff for every* $(\Psi, P, Q) \in \mathcal{R}$

1. $\Psi \otimes \mathcal{F}(P) \simeq \Psi \otimes \mathcal{F}(Q)$ *(static equivalence)*
2. $\forall \Psi'.(\Psi \otimes \Psi', P, Q) \in \mathcal{R}$ *(extension of arbitrary assertion)*
3. *If* $\Psi \rhd P \xrightarrow{\alpha} P'$ *and* $bn(\alpha) \# \Psi, Q$, *then there exists* Q' *such that* $\Psi \rhd Q \xrightarrow{\alpha} Q'$ *and* $(\Psi, P', Q') \in \mathcal{R}$ *(simulation)*

We let bisimilarity $\overset{\cdot}{\sim}$ *be the largest bisimulation. We write* $P \overset{\cdot}{\sim}_\Psi Q$ *to mean* $(\Psi, P, Q) \in \overset{\cdot}{\sim}$, *and* $P \overset{\cdot}{\sim} Q$ *for* $P \overset{\cdot}{\sim}_1 Q$.

Clause 3 is the same as for pi-calculus bisimulation. Clause 1 requires that two bisimilar processes expose statically equivalent assertion environments. Clause 2 states that if two processes are bisimilar in an environment, they must be bisimilar in every extension of that environment. Without this clause, bisimulation is not preserved by parallel composition.

This definition might raise some red flags for the experienced concurrency theorist. We allow the matching transition from Q to have any provenance, irrespectively of what P's provenance is. Hence the COM rule uses information that is ignored for the purposes of bisimulation, which in most cases would result in a bisimilarity that is not preserved by the parallel operator.

Before showing that bisimilarity is nonetheless compositional, we will argue that bisimilarity would be too strong if Clause 4 required transitions with matching provenances. Consider two distinct terms M, N that are connected to the same channels; that is, for all Ψ, K we have $\Psi \vdash M \overset{\cdot}{\to} K$ iff $\Psi \vdash N \overset{\cdot}{\to} K$. We would expect $\overline{M}.0$ and $\overline{N}.0$ to be bisimilar because they offer the same interaction possibilities. With our definition, they are. But if bisimulation cared about provenance they would be distinguished, because transitions originating from $\overline{M}.0$ will have provenance M while those from $\overline{N}.0$ will have N.

The key intuition is that what matters is not which provenance a transition has, but which channels the provenance is connected to. The latter is preserved by Clause 3, as this key technical lemma—formally proven in Isabelle, by a routine induction—hints at:

Lemma 1. *(Find connected provenance)*

1. *If* $\Psi \rhd P \xrightarrow[\pi]{M\,N} P'$ *and* C *is finitely supported, then there exists* $\widetilde{b}_P, \Psi_P, \widetilde{x}, K$ *such that* $\mathcal{F}(P) = (\nu\widetilde{b}_P)\Psi_P$ *and* $\pi = (\nu\widetilde{b}_P; \widetilde{x})K$ *and* $\widetilde{b}_P \# \Psi, P, M, N, P', C, \widetilde{x}$ *and* $\widetilde{x} \# \Psi, P, N, P', C$ *and* $\Psi \otimes \Psi_P \vdash M \xrightarrow{\cdot} K$.
2. *A similar property for output transitions (elided).*

In words, the provenance of a transition is always connected to its subject, and the frame binders can always be chosen sufficiently fresh for any context. This simplifies the proof that bisimilarity is preserved by parallel: in the original psi-calculi, one of the more challenging aspects of this proof is finding sufficiently fresh subjects to use in the COM-OLD rule, and then using associativity and symmetry to connect them (cf. [2, Lemma 5.11]). By Lemma 1 we already have a sufficiently fresh subject: our communication partner's provenance.

Theorem 1 (Congruence properties of strong bisimulation).

1. $P \overset{\cdot}{\sim}_\Psi Q \quad \Rightarrow \quad P \mid R \overset{\cdot}{\sim}_\Psi Q \mid R$
2. $P \overset{\cdot}{\sim}_\Psi Q \quad \Rightarrow \quad (\nu x)P \overset{\cdot}{\sim}_\Psi (\nu x)Q \text{ if } x \# \Psi$
3. $P_G \overset{\cdot}{\sim}_\Psi Q_G \quad \Rightarrow \quad !P_G \overset{\cdot}{\sim}_\Psi !Q_G$
4. $\forall i.P_i \overset{\cdot}{\sim}_\Psi Q_i \quad \Rightarrow \quad \textbf{\textit{case }} \widetilde{\varphi} : \widetilde{P} \overset{\cdot}{\sim}_\Psi \textbf{\textit{case }} \widetilde{\varphi} : \widetilde{Q} \text{ if } \widetilde{P}, \widetilde{Q} \text{ are guarded}$
5. $P \overset{\cdot}{\sim}_\Psi Q \quad \Rightarrow \quad \overline{M}\,N.P \overset{\cdot}{\sim}_\Psi \overline{M}\,N.Q$

Theorem 2 (Algebraic laws of strong bisimulation).

$$P \overset{\cdot}{\sim}_\Psi P \mid \mathbf{0} \qquad P \mid (Q \mid R) \overset{\cdot}{\sim}_\Psi (P \mid Q) \mid R \qquad P \mid Q \overset{\cdot}{\sim}_\Psi Q \mid P \qquad (\nu a)\mathbf{0} \overset{\cdot}{\sim}_\Psi \mathbf{0}$$

$$P \mid (\nu a)Q \overset{\cdot}{\sim}_\Psi (\nu a)(P \mid Q) \text{ if } a \# P \qquad \overline{M}\,N.(\nu a)P \overset{\cdot}{\sim}_\Psi (\nu a)\overline{M}\,N.P \text{ if } a \# M, N$$

$$\underline{M}(\lambda\widetilde{x})N.(\nu a)P \overset{\cdot}{\sim}_\Psi (\nu a)\underline{M}(\lambda\widetilde{x})N.P \text{ if } a \# \widetilde{x}, M, N \qquad !P \overset{\cdot}{\sim}_\Psi P \mid !P$$

$$\textbf{\textit{case }} \widetilde{\varphi} : \widetilde{(\nu a)P} \overset{\cdot}{\sim}_\Psi (\nu a)\textbf{\textit{case }} \widetilde{\varphi} : \widetilde{P} \text{ if } a \# \widetilde{\varphi} \qquad (\nu a)(\nu b)P \overset{\cdot}{\sim}_\Psi (\nu b)(\nu a)P$$

The proofs of Theorems 1 and 2 have been mechanised in Nominal Isabelle. Note that bisimilarity is not preserved by input, for the same reasons as the pi-calculus. As in the pi-calculus, we can define *bisimulation congruence* as the substitution closure of bisimilarity, and thus obtain a true congruence which satisfies all the algebraic laws above. We have verified this in Nominal Isabelle, following [2].

The fact that bisimilarity is compositional yet ignores provenances suggests that the semantics could be reformulated without provenance annotations on labels. To achieve this, what is needed is a side-condition S for the COM rule which, given an input and an output with subjects M, K, determines if the input transition could have been derived from prefix K, and vice versa:

$$\frac{\Psi_Q \otimes \Psi \rhd P \xrightarrow{\overline{M}\,(\nu\widetilde{a})N} P' \qquad \Psi_P \otimes \Psi \rhd Q \xrightarrow{K\,N} Q' \qquad S}{\Psi \rhd P \mid Q \xrightarrow{\tau} (\nu\widetilde{a})(P' \mid Q')}$$

But we already have such an S: the semantics *with* provenances! So we can let

$$S = \Psi_Q \otimes \Psi \,\triangleright\, P \xrightarrow[(\nu\tilde{b}_P;\tilde{x})K]{\overline{M}(\nu\tilde{a})N} P' \wedge \Psi_P \otimes \Psi \,\triangleright\, Q \xrightarrow[(\nu\tilde{b}_Q;\tilde{y})M]{K\,N} Q'$$

Of course, this definition is not satisfactory: the provenances are still there, just swept under the carpet. Worse, we significantly complicate the definitions by effectively introducing a stratified semantics. Thus the interesting question is not whether such an S exists (it does), but whether S can be formulated in a way that is significantly simpler than the semantics with provenances. The author believes the answer is negative: S is a property about the roots of the proof trees used to derive the transitions from P and Q. The provenance records just enough information about the proof trees to show that M and K are connected; with no provenances, it is not clear how this information could be obtained without essentially reconstructing the proof tree.

3.2   Validation

We have defined semantics and bisimulation, and showed that bisimilarity satisfies the expected laws. But how do we know that they are the right semantics, and the right bisimilarity? This section provides two answers to this question. First, we show that our developments constitute a conservative extension of the original psi-calculi. Second, we define a reduction semantics and barbed bisimulation that are in agreement with our (labelled) semantics and (labelled) bisimilarity.

Let $\longrightarrow_o$ and $\dot{\sim}_o$ denote semantics and bisimilarity as defined by Bengtson et al. [2], i.e., without provenances and with the COM-OLD rule discussed in Sect. 2. The following result has been mechanised in Nominal Isabelle:

Theorem 3 (Conservativity). *When $\dot{\rightarrow}$ is symmetric and transitive we have* $\dot{\sim}_o = \dot{\sim}$ *and* $\longrightarrow_o = \longrightarrow$.

Our reduction semantics departs from standard designs [4,17] by relying on reduction contexts [7] instead of structural rules, for two reasons. First, standard formulations tend to include rules like these:

$$\frac{P \longrightarrow P'}{P \mid Q \longrightarrow P' \mid Q} \qquad \qquad \frac{}{\alpha.P + Q \mid \overline{\alpha}.R + S \longrightarrow P \mid R}$$

A parallel rule like the above would be unsound because Q might contain assertions that retract some conditions needed to derive P's reduction. The reduction axiom assumes prefix-guarded choice. We want our semantics to apply to the full calculus, without limiting the syntax to prefix-guarded **case** statements.

But first, a few auxiliary definitions. The *reduction contexts* are the contexts in which communicating processes may occur:

Table 2. Reduction semantics. Here $\widetilde{\Psi}$ abbreviates the composition $\Psi_1 \otimes \Psi_2 \otimes \ldots$, and $\widetilde{(\Psi)}$ abbreviates the parallel composition $(\!|\Psi_1|\!) \mid (\!|\Psi_2|\!) \mid \ldots$ —for empty sequences they are taken to be $\mathbf{1}$ and $\mathbf{0}$ respectively.

$$\textsc{Struct} \; \frac{P \equiv Q \quad Q \longrightarrow Q' \quad Q' \equiv P'}{P \longrightarrow P'} \qquad\qquad \textsc{Scope} \; \frac{P \longrightarrow Q}{(\nu a)P \longrightarrow (\nu a)Q}$$

$$\textsc{Ctxt} \; \frac{\widetilde{\Psi} \vdash M \overset{\cdot}{\leftrightarrow} N \quad K = L[\widetilde{x} := \widetilde{T}] \quad \forall \varphi \in \mathrm{conds}(C).\, \widetilde{\Psi} \vdash \varphi}{\widetilde{(\Psi)} \mid C[\overline{M}\,K.P, \; \underline{N}(\lambda\widetilde{x})L.Q] \longrightarrow \widetilde{(\Psi)} \mid P \mid Q[\widetilde{x} := \widetilde{T}] \mid \mathrm{ppr}(C)}$$

Definition 10 (Reduction contexts). *The* reduction contexts, *ranged over by C, are generated by the grammar*

$$\begin{aligned} C := &\; P_G \quad (\textit{process}) \quad [\,] \quad\quad\quad\quad\quad\quad\quad\quad\quad\quad\quad (\textit{hole}) \\ &\; C \mid C \; (\textit{parallel}) \quad \mathbf{case}\; \widetilde{\varphi} : \widetilde{P_G} \; [\!] \; \varphi' : C \; [\!] \; \widetilde{\varphi''} : \widetilde{Q_G} \; (\textit{case}) \end{aligned}$$

Let $H(C)$ denote the number of holes in C. $C[\widetilde{P_G}]$ denotes the process that results from filling each hole of C with the corresponding element of $\widetilde{P_G}$, where holes are numbered from left to right; if $H(C) \neq |\widetilde{P_G}|$, $C[\widetilde{P_G}]$ is undefined.

We let *structural congruence* $\equiv$ be the smallest equivalence relation on processes derivable using Theorems 1 and 2. The *conditions* $\mathrm{conds}(C)$ and *parallel processes* $\mathrm{ppr}(C)$ of a context C are, respectively, the conditions in C that guard the holes, and the processes of C that are parallel to the holes:

$$\mathrm{ppr}(P_G) = P_G \qquad \mathrm{ppr}([\,]) = \mathbf{0} \qquad \mathrm{ppr}(C_1 \mid C_2) = \mathrm{ppr}(C_1) \mid \mathrm{ppr}(C_2)$$

$$\mathrm{ppr}(\mathbf{case}\; \widetilde{\varphi} : \widetilde{P_G} \; [\!] \; \varphi' : C \; [\!] \; \widetilde{\varphi''} : \widetilde{Q_G}) = \mathrm{ppr}(C) \qquad \mathrm{conds}(P_G) = \emptyset$$

$$\mathrm{conds}([\,]) = \emptyset \qquad\quad \mathrm{conds}(C_1 \mid C_2) = \mathrm{conds}(C_1) \cup \mathrm{conds}(C_2)$$

$$\mathrm{conds}(\mathbf{case}\; \widetilde{\varphi} : \widetilde{P_G} \; [\!] \; \varphi' : C \; [\!] \; \widetilde{\varphi''} : \widetilde{Q_G}) = \{\varphi'\} \cup \mathrm{conds}(C)$$

Definition 11 (Reduction semantics). *The reduction relation $\longrightarrow\, \subseteq \mathbf{P} \times \mathbf{P}$ is defined inductively by the rules of Table 2.*

In words, Ctxt states that if an input and output prefix occur in a reduction context, we may derive a reduction if the following holds: the prefixes are connected in the current assertion environment, the message matches the input pattern, and all conditions guarding the prefixes are entailed by the environment. The $\mathrm{ppr}(C)$ in the reduct makes sure any processes in parallel to the holes are preserved.

Theorem 4. $P \longrightarrow P'$ iff there is P'' such that $1 \rhd P \xrightarrow{\tau} P''$ and $P'' \equiv P'$

For barbed bisimulation, we need to define what the observables are, and what contexts an observer may use. We follow previous work by Johansson et al. [15] on weak barbed bisimilarity for the original psi-calculi on both counts. First, we take the barbs to be the output labels a process can exhibit: we define $P \downarrow_{\overline{M}(\nu\widetilde{a})N}$ (P exposes $\overline{M}(\nu\widetilde{a})N$) to mean $\exists P'.\ 1 \rhd P \xrightarrow{\overline{M}(\nu\widetilde{a})N} P'$. We write $P \downarrow_{\overline{M}}$ for $\exists\widetilde{a}, N.P \downarrow_{\overline{M}(\nu\widetilde{A})N}$, and $P \Downarrow_\alpha$ for $P \xrightarrow{\tau}^* \downarrow_\alpha$. Second, we let observers use *static* contexts, i.e. ones built from parallel and restriction.

Definition 12 (Barbed bisimilarity). Barbed bisimilarity, *written* $\underset{\text{barb}}{\overset{\cdot}{\sim}}$, *is the largest equivalence on processes such that* $P \underset{\text{barb}}{\overset{\cdot}{\sim}} Q$ *implies*

1. *If* $P \downarrow_{\overline{M}(\nu\widetilde{a})N}$ *and* $\widetilde{a}\#Q$ *then* $Q \downarrow_{\overline{M}(\nu\widetilde{a})N}$ *(barb similarity)*
2. *If* $P \longrightarrow P'$ *then there exists* Q' *such that* $Q \longrightarrow Q'$ *and* $P' \underset{\text{barb}}{\overset{\cdot}{\sim}} Q'$ *(reduction simulation)*
3. $(\nu\widetilde{a})(P \mid R) \underset{\text{barb}}{\overset{\cdot}{\sim}} (\nu\widetilde{a})(Q \mid R)$ *(closure under static contexts)*

Our proof that barbed and labelled bisimilarity coincides only considers psi-calculi with a certain minimum of sanity and expressiveness. This rules out some degenerate cases: psi-calculi where there are messages that can be sent but not received, and psi-calculi where no transitions whatsoever are possible.

Definition 13. *A psi-calculus is* observational *if:*

1. *For all P there are M_P, K_P such that $\mathcal{F}(P) \vdash M_P \dot{\leftrightarrow} K_P$ and not $P \Downarrow_{\overline{K_P}}$.*
2. *If $N = (\widetilde{x}\ \widetilde{y}) \cdot M$ and $\widetilde{y}\#M$ and $\widetilde{x}, \widetilde{y}$ are distinct then $M[\widetilde{x} := \widetilde{y}] = N$.*

The first clause means that no process can exhaust the set of barbs. Hence observing contexts can signal success or failure without interference from the process under observation. For example, in the pi-calculus M_P, K_P can be any name x such that $x\#P$. The second clause states that for swapping of distinct names, substitution and permutation have the same behaviour. Any standard definition of simultaneous substitution should satisfy this requirement. These assumptions are present, explicitly or implicitly, in the work of Johansson et al. [15]. Ours are given a slightly weaker formulation.

We can now state the main result of this section:

Theorem 5. *In all observational psi-calculi,* $P \underset{\text{barb}}{\overset{\cdot}{\sim}} Q$ *iff* $P \overset{\cdot}{\sim}_1 Q$.

4   Expressiveness

In this section, we study two examples of the expressiveness gained by dropping symmetry and transitivity.

4.1   Pi-Calculus with Preorders

Recall that pi-F [25] extends the pi-calculus with name equalities $(x = y)$ as first-class processes. Communication in pi-F gives rise to equalities rather than substitutions, so e.g. $xy.P \mid \overline{x}z.Q$ reduces to $y = z \mid P \mid Q$: the input and output objects are fused. Hirschkoff et al. [11] observed that fusion and subtyping are fundamentally incompatible, and propose a generalisation of pi-F called the *pi-calculus with preorders* or πP to resolve the issue.

We are interested in πP because its channel connectivity is not transitive. The equalities of pi-F are replaced with *arcs* a/b ("a is above b") which act as one-way fusions: anything that can be done with b can be done with a, but not the other way around. The effect of a communication is to create an arc with the output subject above the input subject, so $x(y).P \mid \overline{x}(z).Q$ reduces to $(\nu xy)(z/y \mid P \mid Q)$. We write $\prec$ for the reflexive and transitive closure of the "is above" relation. Two names x, y are considered *joinable* for the purposes of synchronisation if some name z is above both of them: formally, we write $x \curlyvee y$ for $\exists z.x \prec z \wedge y \prec z$.

Hirschkoff et al. conclude by saying that "[it] could also be interesting to study the representation of πP into Psi-calculi. This may not be immediate because the latter make use of on an equivalence relation on channels, while the former uses a preorder" [11, p. 387]. Having lifted the constraint that channels form an equivalence relation, we happily accept the challenge. We write ΨP for the psi-calculus we use to embed πP. We follow the presentation of πP from [12,13], where the behavioural theory is most developed.

Definition 14. *The psi-calculus ΨP is defined with the following parameters:*

$$\mathbf{T} \triangleq \mathcal{N} \qquad \mathbf{C} \triangleq \{x \prec y : x, y \in \mathcal{N}\} \cup \{x \curlyvee y : x, y \in \mathcal{N}\}$$

$$\mathbf{A} \triangleq \mathcal{P}_{fin}(\{x \prec y : x, y \in \mathcal{N}\}) \qquad \mathbf{1} \triangleq \{\} \qquad\qquad \otimes \triangleq \cup$$

$$\overset{\cdot}{\to} \triangleq \curlyvee \qquad\qquad \vdash \triangleq \text{ the relation denoted } \vdash \text{ in [13].}$$

The prefix operators of πP are different from those of psi-calculi: objects are always bound, communication gives rise to an arc rather than a substitution, and a conditional silent prefix $[\varphi]\tau.P$ is included.[2] These are encodable as follows:

Definition 15 (Encoding of prefixes). *The encoding $[\![\_]\!]$ from πP to ΨP is homomorphic on all operators except prefixes and arcs, where it is defined by*

$$[\![a/b]\!] = (\!| b \prec a |\!) \qquad [\![\overline{a}(y).P]\!] = (\nu xy)(\overline{a}x.(\!(|x \prec y|\!) \mid [\![P]\!])) \text{ where } x\#y, P$$

$$[\![a(y).P]\!] = (\nu y)(\underline{a}(\lambda x)x.(\!(|y \prec x|\!) \mid [\![P]\!])) \text{ where } x\#y, P$$

$$[\![[\varphi]\tau.P]\!] = \mathbf{case}\ \varphi : (\nu x)(\underline{x}(\lambda x)x.0 \mid \overline{x}x.[\![P]\!]) \text{ where } x\#P$$

---

[2] We ignore protected prefixes because they are redundant, cf. Remark 1 of [12].

This embedding of πP in psi-calculi comes with a notion of bisimilarity per Definition 9. We show that it coincides with the labelled bisimilarity for πP (written $\sim$) introduced in [12,13].

Theorem 6. $P \sim Q$ iff $[\![P]\!] \stackrel{.}{\sim} [\![Q]\!]$

Thus our encoding validates the behavioural theory of πP by connecting it to our fully mechanised proofs, while also showing that a substantially different design of the LTS yields the same bisimilarity. We will briefly compare these designs. While we do rewriting of subjects in the prefix rules, Hirschkoff et al. instead use relabelling rules like this one (mildly edited to match our notation):

$$\frac{P \xrightarrow{a(x)} P' \qquad \mathcal{F}(P) \vdash a \prec b}{P \xrightarrow{b(x)} P'}$$

An advantage of this rule is that it allows input and output labels to be as simple as pi-calculus labels. A comparative disadvantage is that it is not syntax-directed, and that the LTS has more rules in total. Note that this rule would not be a viable alternative to provenances in psi-calculi: since it can be applied more than once in a derivation, its inclusion assumes that the channels form a preorder wrt. connectivity.

πP also has labels $[\varphi]\tau$, meaning that a silent transition is allowed in environments where φ is true. A rule for rewriting φ to a weaker condition, similar to the above rule for subject rewriting, is included. Psi-calculi does not need this because the PAR rules take the assertion environment into account. πP transitions of kind $P \xrightarrow{[\varphi]\tau} P'$ correspond to ΨP transitions of kind $\{\varphi\} \rhd P \xrightarrow{\tau} P'$.

Interestingly, the analogous full abstraction result fails to hold for the embedding of pi-F in psi-calculi by Bengtson et al. [2], because outputs that emit distinct but fused names are distinguished by psi-calculus bisimilarity. This issue does not arise here because πP objects are always bound; however, we believe the encoding of Bengtson et al. can be made fully abstract by encoding free output with bound output, exploiting the pi-F law $a\,y.Q \sim a(x)(Q \mid x = y)$.

4.2 Mixed Choice

This section will argue that because we allow non-transitive channel connectivity, the **case** operator of psi-calculi becomes superfluous. The formal results here will focus on encoding the special case of mixed choice. We will then briefly discuss how to generalise these results to the full **case** operator.

Choice, written $P + Q$, is a process that behaves as either P or Q. In psi-calculi we consider $P + Q$ to abbreviate **case** $\top : P \parallel \top : Q$ for some condition $\top$ that is always entailed. *Mixed choice* means that in $P + Q$, P and Q must be prefix-guarded; that is, the outermost operators of P, Q must be input or output prefixes. In particular, mixed choice allows choice between an input and an output. There is a straightforward generalisation to n-ary sums that, in order to simplify the presentation, we will not consider here.

Fix a psi-calculus $\mathcal{P} = (\mathbf{T}, \mathbf{A}, \mathbf{C}, \vdash, \otimes, \mathbf{1}, \dot{\rightarrow})$ with mixed choice; this will be our source language. We will construct a target psi-calculus and an encoding such that the target terms make no use of the **case** operator. The target language $\mathcal{E}(\mathcal{P})$ adds to $\mathbf{T}$ the ability to tag a term M with a name x; we write M_x for the tagged term. We write α_x for tagging the subject of the prefix α with x. Tags are used to uniquely identify which choice statement a prefix is a summand of. As the assertions of $\mathcal{E}(\mathcal{P})$ we use $\mathbf{A} \times \mathcal{P}_{\text{fin}}(\mathcal{N})$, where $\mathcal{P}_{\text{fin}}(\mathcal{N})$ are the *disabled tags*.

The encoding $[\![\_]\!]$ from $\mathcal{P}$ to $\mathcal{E}(\mathcal{P})$ is homomorphic on all operators except assertion and choice, where it is defined as follows:

$$[\![(\!|\Psi|\!)]\!] = (\!|(\Psi, \emptyset)|\!) \qquad [\![\alpha.P + \beta.Q]\!] = (\nu x)(\alpha_x.([\![P]\!] \mid (\!|(\mathbf{1}, \{x\})|\!)) \mid \beta_x.([\![Q]\!] \mid (\!|(\mathbf{1}, \{x\})|\!))$$

where $x \# \alpha, \beta, P, Q$. If we disregard the tag x, we see that the encoding simply offers up both summands in parallel. This clearly allows all behaviours of $\alpha.P + \beta.Q$, but there are two additional behaviours we must prevent: (1) communication between the summands, and (2) lingering summands firing after the other branch has already been taken. The tagging mechanism prevents both, as a consequence of how we define channel equivalence on tagged terms in $\mathcal{E}(\mathcal{P})$:

$$(\Psi, \mathbf{N}) \vdash M_x \dot{\rightarrow} N_y \quad \text{if } \Psi \vdash M \dot{\rightarrow} N \text{ and } x \neq y \text{ and } x, y \notin \mathbf{N}$$

That is, tagged channels are connected if the underlying channel is connected. To prevent (1) we require the tags to be different, and to prevent (2) we require that the tags are not disabled. Note that this channel connectivity is not transitive, not reflexive, and not monotonic wrt. assertion composition—not even if the source language connectivity is.

Theorem 7 (Correctness of choice encoding).

1. *If $\Psi \rhd P \xrightarrow{\alpha} P'$ then there is P'' such that $(\Psi, \emptyset) \rhd [\![P]\!] \xrightarrow{\alpha} P''$ and $P'' \dot{\sim}_{(\Psi, \emptyset)} [\![P']\!]$.*
2. *If $(\Psi, \emptyset) \rhd [\![P]\!] \xrightarrow{\alpha} P'$ then there is P'' such that $\Psi \rhd P \xrightarrow{\alpha_\perp} P''$ and $P' \dot{\sim}_{(\Psi, \emptyset)} [\![P'']\!]$.*
3. *$P \dot{\sim}_1 Q$ iff $[\![P]\!] \dot{\sim}_{(1, \emptyset)} [\![Q]\!]$.*

Here $\alpha_\perp$ denote the label α with all tags removed. It is immediate from Theorem 7 and the definition of $[\![\_]\!]$ that our encoding also satisfies the other standard quality criteria [10]: it is compositional, it is name invariant, and it preserves and reflects barbs and divergence.

In the original psi-calculi, our target language is invalid because of non-transitive connectivity. If we remove the requirement that tags are distinct, and only allow *separate* choice (where either both summands are inputs or both summands are outputs), the encoding is correct for the original psi-calculi.

These results generalise in a straightforward way to mixed CASE statements **case** $\varphi_1 : \alpha.P \,[\!]\, \varphi_2 : \beta.Q$ by additionally tagging terms with a condition, i.e. M_{x,φ_1}, that must be entailed in order to derive connectivity judgements involving the term. The generalisation to free choice, i.e. $P + Q$ where P, Q can be anything, is more involved and sacrifices some compositionality. The idea is to use sequences of tags, representing which branches of which (possibly nested) case statements a prefix can be found in, and disallowing communication between prefixes in distinct branches of the same CASE operator.

5   Conclusion and Related Work

We have seen how psi-calculi can be conservatively extended to allow asymmetric and non-transitive communication topologies, sacrificing none of the bisimulation meta-theory. This confers enough expressiveness to capture a pi-calculus with preorders, and makes mixed choice a derived operator.

The work of Hirschkoff et al. [11] is closely related in that it uses non-transitive connectivity; see Sect. 4.1 for an extensive discussion.

Broadcast psi-calculi [5] extend psi-calculi with broadcast communication in addition to point-to-point communication. There, point-to-point channels must still be symmetric and transitive, but for broadcast channels this condition is lifted, at the cost of introducing other side-conditions on how names are used: broadcast prefixes must be connected via intermediate *broadcast channels* which have no greater support than either of the prefixes it connects, precluding language features such as name fusion. We believe provenances could be used to define a version of broadcast psi-calculi that does not need this side-condition.

Kouzapas et al. [16] define a similar reduction context semantics for (broadcast) psi-calculi. Their reduction contexts requires three kinds of numbered holes with complicated side-conditions on how the holes may be filled; we have attempted to simplify the presentation by having only one kind of hole. While (weak) barbed congruence for psi-calculi has been studied before [15] (see Sect. 3.2), barbed congruence was defined in terms of the labelled semantics rather than a reduction semantics, thus weakening its claim to independent confirmation slightly.

There is a rich literature on choice encodings for the pi-calculus [10, 20–23], with many separation and encodability results under different quality criteria for different flavours of choice. Encodings typically require complicated protocols and tradeoffs between quality criteria. Thanks to the greater expressive power of psi-calculi, our encoding is simpler and satisfies stronger quality criteria than any choice encoding for the pi-calculus. Closest to ours is the choice encoding of CCS into the DiX calculus by Busi and Gorrieri [6]. DiX introduces a primitive for annotating processes with *conflict sets*, that are intended as a generalisation of choice. Processes with overlapping conflict sets cannot interact, and when a process acts, every process with an overlapping conflict set is killed. These conflict sets perform the same role in the encoding as our tags do. We believe the tagging scheme used in our choice encoding also captures DiX-style conflict sets.

Acknowledgements. These ideas have benefited from discussions with many people at Uppsala University, ITU Copenhagen, the University of Oslo and Data61/CSIRO, including Jesper Bengtson, Christian Johansen, Magnus Johansson and Joachim Parrow. I would also like to thank Jean-Marie Madiot and the anonymous reviewers for valuable comments on earlier versions of the paper.

References

1. Åman Pohjola, J.: Psi-calculi revisited: connectivity and compositionality. Technical report, EP192416, CSIRO, Canberra, Australia (2019). https://publications. csiro.au/rpr/pub?pid=csiro:EP192416

2. Bengtson, J., Johansson, M., Parrow, J., Victor, B.: Psi-calculi: a framework for mobile processes with nominal data and logic. Logical Methods Comput. Sci. **7**(1) (2011). https://doi.org/10.2168/LMCS-7(1:11)2011

3. Bengtson, J., Parrow, J., Weber, T.: Psi-calculi in Isabelle. J. Autom. Reasoning **56**(1), 1–47 (2016). https://doi.org/10.1007/s10817-015-9336-2

4. Berry, G., Boudol, G.: The chemical abstract machine. In: Proceedings of the 17th ACM SIGPLAN-SIGACT Symposium on Principles of Programming Languages, POPL 1990, pp. 81–94. ACM, New York (1990). https://doi.org/10.1145/96709. 96717

5. Borgström, J., et al.: Broadcast psi-calculi with an application to wireless protocols. Softw. Syst. Model. **14**(1), 201–216 (2015). https://doi.org/10.1007/s10270-013-0375-z

6. Busi, N., Gorrieri, R.: Distributed conflicts in communicating systems. In: Ciancarini, P., Nierstrasz, O., Yonezawa, A. (eds.) ECOOP 1994. LNCS, vol. 924, pp. 49–65. Springer, Heidelberg (1995). https://doi.org/10.1007/3-540-59450-7_4

7. Felleisen, M., Hieb, R.: The revised report on the syntactic theories of sequential control and state. Theor. Comput. Sci. **103**(2), 235–271 (1992). https://doi.org/ 10.1016/0304-3975(92)90014-7

8. Gabbay, M.J., Pitts, A.M.: A new approach to abstract syntax with variable binding. Formal Aspects Comput. **13**, 341–363 (2002). https://doi.org/10.1007/ s001650200016

9. Gardner, P., Wischik, L.: Explicit fusions. In: Nielsen, M., Rovan, B. (eds.) MFCS 2000. LNCS, vol. 1893, pp. 373–382. Springer, Heidelberg (2000). https://doi.org/ 10.1007/3-540-44612-5_33

10. Gorla, D.: Towards a unified approach to encodability and separation results for process calculi. Inf. Comput. **208**(9), 1031–1053 (2010). https://doi.org/10.1016/ j.ic.2010.05.002

11. Hirschkoff, D., Madiot, J., Sangiorgi, D.: Name-passing calculi: from fusions to preorders and types. In: 28th Annual ACM/IEEE Symposium on Logic in Computer Science, LICS 2013, New Orleans, LA, USA, 25–28 June 2013, pp. 378–387. IEEE Computer Society (2013). https://doi.org/10.1109/LICS.2013.44

12. Hirschkoff, D., Madiot, J., Xu, X.: A behavioural theory for a π-calculus with preorders. J. Log. Algebr. Meth. Program. **84**(6), 806–825 (2015). https://doi.org/ 10.1016/j.jlamp.2015.07.001

13. Hirschkoff, D., Madiot, J.-M., Xu, X.: A behavioural theory for a π-calculus with preorders. In: Dastani, M., Sirjani, M. (eds.) FSEN 2015. LNCS, vol. 9392, pp. 143–158. Springer, Cham (2015). https://doi.org/10.1007/978-3-319-24644-4_10

14. Johansson, M.: Psi-calculi: a framework for mobile process calculi: cook your own correct process calculus - just add data and logic. Ph.D. thesis, Uppsala University, Division of Computer Systems (2010)

15. Johansson, M., Bengtson, J., Parrow, J., Victor, B.: Weak equivalences in psi-calculi. In: LICS, pp. 322–331. IEEE Computer Society (2010). https://doi.org/10.1109/LICS.2010.30

16. Kouzapas, D., Gutkovas, R., Gay, S.J.: Session types for broadcasting. In: Donaldson, A.F., Vasconcelos, V.T. (eds.) Proceedings 7th Workshop on Programming Language Approaches to Concurrency and Communication-cEntric Software, PLACES 2014, Grenoble, France, 12 April 2014. EPTCS, vol. 155, pp. 25–31 (2014). https://doi.org/10.4204/EPTCS.155.4

17. Milner, R.: Functions as processes. In: Paterson, M.S. (ed.) ICALP 1990. LNCS, vol. 443, pp. 167–180. Springer, Heidelberg (1990). https://doi.org/10.1007/BFb0032030

18. Milner, R., Parrow, J., Walker, D.: A calculus of mobile processes, part I/II. Inf. Comput. 100(1), 1–77 (1992). https://doi.org/10.1016/0890-5401(92)90008-4

19. Nanz, S., Hankin, C.: A framework for security analysis of mobile wireless networks. Theor. Comput. Sci. 367(1–2), 203–227 (2006)

20. Nestmann, U., Pierce, B.C.: Decoding choice encodings. Inf. Comput. 163(1), 1–59 (2000). https://doi.org/10.1006/inco.2000.2868

21. Palamidessi, C.: Comparing the expressive power of the synchronous and the asynchronous pi-calculus. In: Lee, P., Henglein, F., Jones, N.D. (eds.) Conference Record of POPL 1997: The 24th ACM SIGPLAN-SIGACT Symposium on Principles of Programming Languages, Papers Presented at the Symposium, Paris, France, 15–17 January 1997, pp. 256–265. ACM Press (1997). https://doi.org/10.1145/263699.263731

22. Peters, K., Nestmann, U.: Is it a "good" encoding of mixed choice? In: Birkedal, L. (ed.) FoSSaCS 2012. LNCS, vol. 7213, pp. 210–224. Springer, Heidelberg (2012). https://doi.org/10.1007/978-3-642-28729-9_14

23. Peters, K., Nestmann, U., Goltz, U.: On distributability in process calculi. In: Felleisen, M., Gardner, P. (eds.) ESOP 2013. LNCS, vol. 7792, pp. 310–329. Springer, Heidelberg (2013). https://doi.org/10.1007/978-3-642-37036-6_18

24. Urban, C.: Nominal techniques in Isabelle/HOL. J. Autom. Reason. 40(4), 327–356 (2008). https://doi.org/10.1007/s10817-008-9097-2

25. Wischik, L., Gardner, P.: Explicit fusions. Theor. Comput. Sci. 304(3), 606–630 (2005). https://doi.org/10.1016/j.tcs.2005.03.017

Squeezing Streams and Composition of Self-stabilizing Algorithms

Karine Altisen[⊠], Pierre Corbineau, and Stéphane Devismes

Univ. Grenoble Alpes, CNRS,
Grenoble INP (Institute of Engineering Univ. Grenoble Alpes), VERIMAG,
38000 Grenoble, France
Karine.Altisen@univ-grenoble-alpes.fr

Abstract. Composition is a fundamental tool when dealing with complex systems. We study the hierarchical collateral composition which is used to combine self-stabilizing distributed algorithms. The PADEC library is a framework developed with the Coq proof assistant and dedicated to the certification of self-stabilizing algorithms. We enrich PADEC with the composition operator and a sufficient condition to show its correctness. The formal proof of the condition leads us to develop new tools and methods on potentially infinite streams, these latter ones being used to model the algorithms' executions. The cornerstone has been the definition of the function Squeeze which removes duplicates from streams.

Keywords: Coq proof assistant · Streams · Coinduction · Composition · Distributed algorithm · Self-stabilization

1 Introduction

In computer science, *separation of concerns* is a standard design principle which consists of decomposing a complex problem into several simpler ones. These sub-problems are then solved independently, and finally, glued together to obtain a global solution to the initial problem. With this in mind, *composition* is a natural tool that simplifies both the design and proof of complex algorithms. For example, the sequential composition of two algorithms "$\mathcal{A}_1$; $\mathcal{A}_2$" enforces $\mathcal{A}_1$ and $\mathcal{A}_2$ to be executed in sequence, *i.e.*, $\mathcal{A}_2$ is initiated only after $\mathcal{A}_1$'s completion. Composition methods are widely used in distributed systems [4, 10, 25].

Self-stabilization [21] is a versatile fault-tolerant paradigm of distributed computing. Indeed, a self-stabilizing distributed algorithm resumes a correct behavior within finite time, regardless the initial state of the system, and therefore also after a finite number of transient faults hit the system and place it in some arbitrary global state. The ability to implement sequential composition

This study has been partially supported by the ANR projects DESCARTES (ANR-16-CE40-0023) and ESTATE (ANR-16-CE25-0009).

J. A. Pérez and N. Yoshida (Eds.): FORTE 2019, LNCS 11535, pp. 21–38, 2019.
https://doi.org/10.1007/978-3-030-21759-4_2

in a distributed system mainly relies on the ability to locally detect the termination. Now, termination detection is inherently impossible for self-stabilizing algorithms [34]. Indeed, since the system may suffer from faults such as memory corruption, the nodes cannot trust their local memory. To circumvent such an issue, several other composition operators devoted to self-stabilizing algorithms have been proposed, *e.g.*, the fair [23] and cross-over [6] compositions. We are more particularly interested in the *hierarchical collateral composition* [20], a simple and widely used variant of the collateral composition [27]. This composition actually emulates the sequential composition "$\mathcal{A}_1$; $\mathcal{A}_2$" by providing the same output despite $\mathcal{A}_1$ and $\mathcal{A}_2$ being executed (more or less) concurrently.

The PADEC framework [2, 3] consists in a library for *certifying* self-stabilizing algorithms. The certification of an algorithm means proving its correctness *formally* using a proof assistant, here Coq [9, 35], *i.e.*, a tool which allows to develop formal proofs interactively and *mechanically check* them. The framework includes tools to model self-stabilizing algorithms, certified general statements that can be used to build certified correctness proofs of such algorithms, and case studies that validate them. In PADEC, the semantics of self-stabilizing algorithms' executions is defined as potentially infinite streams and properties, such as algorithm specifications, are defined using temporal logic on those streams. Hence, the definitions and proofs presented in PADEC as well as this paper, make an intensive use of streams and thus of coinductive definitions and proofs.

Overview of the Contributions. The first contribution of this paper consists of new general tools for streams, in particular a squeezing operator. This latter is actually a productive filter on streams that uses both inductive and coinductive mechanisms. Our second contribution is a case study: we apply the squeezing operator to certify the hierarchical collateral composition of self-stabilizing algorithms. To our knowledge, our proposal is the first work on the certification of a composition operator for self-stabilization.

Detailed Contributions. We develop many tools for streams. Our streams are potentially infinite sequences of at least one element and require to be defined over a partial setoid, *i.e.*, over a type endowed with a partial equivalence relation that models equality; thus justifying this new development. Apart from usual tools required by developments on streams, such as temporal logic operators, we also provide tools specific for PADEC. In particular, the *squeezing toolbox* provides a filter to remove any duplicated value from a given stream that may contain an infinite suffix of duplicates. We study the conditions under which such a squeezed stream can be computed and provide a function that actually builds it. This filter can be viewed as an extension of a work by Bertot [8]. Indeed, although Bertot's filter relies on a general predicate (ours simply uses the equality between two consecutive elements), the squeezing operator is designed for more complex streams (that can be finite or infinite) and allows to remove an infinite suffix. In his paper, Bertot clearly explains the difficulty to formally define such a filter since this latter mixes both coinduction and induction mechanisms. The definition of squeezing is even more difficult since it requires to decide at each step whether the filtering of new elements should continue or be given up because a constant, potentially infinite, suffix has been reached.

As an application, we use these tools to enrich the PADEC library with a formalization of the hierarchical collateral composition operator $\oplus$ and a sufficient condition to show its correctness. By correctness, we mean that if $\mathcal{A}_1$ and $\mathcal{A}_2$ are self-stabilizing *w.r.t.* their specification, then $\mathcal{A}_1 \oplus \mathcal{A}_2$ is also self-stabilizing *w.r.t.* both specifications. Executions of self-stabilizing algorithms and their compositions are modeled as streams, and the squeezing toolbox has been the cornerstone to solve the major locks in the correctness proof of the composition operator.

Related Work. Previous work dealing with PADEC [3] only considered *terminating* algorithms that did not require any scheduling assumption, consequently their proofs were only induction-based. Here, $\mathcal{A}_2$ may be a *non-terminating* algorithm (*e.g.*, a token circulation). Moreover, the sufficient condition to show the correctness of the composition assumes a weakly fair scheduling, which requires a coinductive definition. Coinductive objects and proofs allow to reason on potentially infinite objects. They are supported by major proof assistants such as Coq [26], Isabelle [32], and Agda [1]. Coinductive constructions are commonly used to represent potentially infinite behaviors of programs and systems (see, for example, [31] for sequential programs and [17] for distributed systems) but also for modeling lazy programs such as the prime number sieve [8].

Proofs in distributed algorithms are commonly written by hand, based on informal reasoning. This potentially leads to errors when arguments are not perfectly clear, as explained by Lamport in his position paper [30]. As a matter of facts, several studies [7,22] reveal, using formal methods, some bugs in existing literature. Hence, certification of distributed algorithms is a powerful tool to prevent bugs in their proofs, and so, to increase confidence in their correctness. Certification of non fault-tolerant distributed algorithms is addressed in [13,14,17]; and certification in the context of fault-tolerant, yet non self-stabilizing, distributed computing is addressed in [5,28]. Up to now, only few *simple* self-stabilizing algorithms have been certified, *e.g.*, [29] (in PVS) and [3,16] (in Coq). By simple, we mean non-composed algorithms working on particular topologies (*i.e.*, rings, lines, or trees) and/or assuming restrictions on possible interleaving (*e.g.*, in [29], only sequential executions are considered). Now, progress in self-stabilization has led to consider more and more complex distributed systems running in increasingly more adversarial environments. As an illustrative example, the three first algorithms proposed by Dijkstra in 1974 [21] were designed for oriented ring topologies and assuming sequential executions only, while nowadays most self-stabilizing algorithms are designed for fully asynchronous arbitrary connected networks, *e.g.*, [12,19], and even for networks, such as peer-to-peer systems, where the topology (frequently) varies over the time, *e.g.*, [11]. Consequently, the design of self-stabilizing algorithms becomes more and more intricate, and accordingly, their proofs of correctness and complexity. To handle such difficulties, designers must adopt a modular approach, *e.g.*, using composition operators. Consequently, a preliminary necessary step to certify present-day self-stabilizing algorithms is the certification of a composition operator.

Roadmap. Section 2 introduces streams and self-stabilization as defined in PADEC. Section 3 presents the composition. Section 4 details the squeezing toolbox and shows its application into the proof of correctness of the composition.

The composition and the stream toolboxes contain about 1500 lines of Coq specifications and 4800 lines of Coq proofs.[1] This represents about 25% of the whole PADEC library. We advocate the reader to visit the following webpage for a deeper understanding of our work.

http://www-verimag.imag.fr/~altisen/PADEC/

All documentation and source codes are available at this address.

2   Streams and Self-stabilization in the PADEC Library

PADEC is a Coq library designed to model and prove results on self-stabilizing algorithms. The framework makes an intensive use of (partial-)setoids, *i.e.*, types for which the equality is represented by a (partial-)equivalence relation. This choice is justified in [3] and has some consequences on the design of the framework. Nevertheless, we omit here the technical issues due to the use of such (partial-)setoids, since it is out of the scope of this paper.

We now present self-stabilizing algorithms as they are defined in distributed computing and the PADEC library. Beforehand, we introduce streams as they are used to model executions of self-stabilizing algorithms in PADEC.

2.1   Streams

We implement a stream as a potentially infinite sequence of at least one element. Each element belongs to some given type A. A stream is then defined as a value of the following type.

CoInductive Stream: Type := | O: A → Stream
                             | C: A → Stream → Stream.

Remark that such a stream cannot be empty since each constructor (O, C) enforces the existence of a first element. Moreover, it may be *finite or infinite* since the keyword **CoInductive** generates the greatest fixed point capturing potentially infinite constructions.[2] For instance, the finite stream of naturals 1 2 3 4 is given by s4 = C 1 (C 2 (C 3 (O 4))) and the infinite stream of naturals, made of an infinite number of 1, is defined by **CoFixpoint ones: Stream (A := nat) := C 1 ones**. Therefore, the above definition allows to construct both finite and infinite streams thanks to the two constructors. In contrast, streams from the standard Coq API [35] and those proposed by Bertot [8] are made of only one constructor, which enforces the stream to be necessarily infinite.

---

[1] As evaluated by the *ad hoc* tool coqwc.
[2] In contrast, the keyword **Inductive** generates the smallest fixed point and only captures finite constructions.

We define the function (H: Stream → A) which returns the first element of the stream, *e.g.*, (H s4) returns 1. For any function (f: A → B) and any type B, we note (f • H: Stream → B) the function defining the composition of H and f as follows: ((f • H) s) returns (f (H s)), for any stream s.

We now briefly introduce tools on streams that will be used in the sequel. The following predicates are usual temporal logic operators [15,33]. They are defined *w.r.t.* a given predicate P over streams. The first one checks that there is a suffix of the stream in which P is satisfied. The second one checks that P is satisfied in every suffix of the stream.

```
Inductive Eventually (P: Stream → Prop): Stream → Prop :=
| ev_now: ∀ s, P s → Eventually P s
| ev_later: ∀ a s, Eventually P s → Eventually P (C a s).

CoInductive Always (P: Stream → Prop): Stream → Prop :=
| al_one: ∀ a, P (O a) → Always P (O a)
| al_cons: ∀ a s, P (C a s) → Always P s → Always P (C a s).
```

Note the difference between the two definitions: Eventually is defined using the keyword **Inductive** since a proof of (Eventually P s), for some stream s and predicate P, should only contain a finite number of ev_later. In contrast, Always uses **CoInductive**: a proof of (Always P s) would potentially contain an infinite number of al_cons and so, should be lazily constructed. We defined many other properties and technical tools that ease the use of those predicates (see [2] for details), *e.g.*, we use Eventually to check that a stream is finite:

```
finite: Stream → Prop := Eventually P_finite.
```

where (P_finite s) holds if and only if the stream s is made of a single element a, *i.e.*, is equal to (O a).

2.2   Self-stabilization: Model and Semantics

Most of self-stabilizing algorithms are designed in the *atomic-state* model, a computational model introduced by Dijkstra [21], which abstracts away the communications between nodes of the network. The PADEC framework has been developed using this model (see [3]). However, we do not detail the model here, since this is not the heart of the contribution. Instead, we summarize features that are mandatory to present and understand our contributions.

A distributed algorithm is executed over a *network*, made of a *finite* number of *nodes* (we introduce the Coq type Node to represent nodes). Each node p is endowed with a *local state* (of type State) defined by the value of its local variables. Node p updates its local state by executing its local algorithm in *atomic moves*, where it first reads its own local state and that of its neighbors, and then only writes its own variables. Notice that some variables owned by p, usually system inputs, should never be written by its local algorithm. Such variables are declared *read-only*. A node is said to be *enabled* if its next move will actually modify its local state. Otherwise, the node is said to be *disabled*.

We call *environment* the global state of the network. In PADEC, environments are functions from `Node` to `State`: `Env := Node → State`, namely for an environment (`g: Env`) and a node (`n: Node`), (`g n`) is the local state of `n` in `g`. If no node is enabled in `g`, then `g` said to be *terminal*. This property is defined by the predicate `terminal: Env → **Prop**`. Each node can locally evaluate whether or not it is enabled. So, since the number of nodes is finite, the `terminal` property is *decidable*, *i.e.*, the evaluation of (`terminal g`) is computable:[3]

Lemma. `terminal_dec: ∀ g, { terminal g }+{ ¬terminal g }.`

Let `g` be the current environment. If `g` is not terminal, then a *step* of the distributed algorithm is performed as follows: every node `n` that is enabled in (`g n`) is candidate to be executed; some candidates (at least one) are nondeterministically *activated*, meaning that they atomically update their local state using their local algorithm, leading the system to a new environment `g'`. This nondeterminism actually materializes the asynchronism of the system.

Notice that two environments linked by a step are necessarily different. This point is fundamental in asynchronous deterministic algorithms: the system progress can only be observed when the environment changes. In PADEC, we use the relation `Step: Env → Env → **Prop**` to encode all possible steps.

A *maximal run* in the network is defined as a stream of environments, using type `Exec`: **Type** `:= Stream (A := Env)`, where every pair of consecutive environments in the stream is a step, and if the stream is finite then its last environment is necessarily terminal. This notion is captured by the predicate

`is_max_run (e: Exec): **Prop** := Always P_run e.`

where (`P_run e`) checks that the stream `e` matches one of the two following patterns. Either `e` is (`O g`) and the environment `g` is terminal, *i.e.*, (`terminal g`) holds; or `e` is (`C g e'`) (with `g` an environment and `e'` a stream) and there is a step from `g` to (`H e'`), *i.e.*, (`Step (H e) g'`) holds.

We model the nondeterminism of the system using an artifact called the *daemon*. In this paper, we focus on the so-called *weakly fair daemon* [24]: a maximal run is executed under the weakly fair daemon if and only if every node that is continuously enabled is eventually activated by the daemon. To encode the weakly fair daemon, we define the following predicate:

`weakly_fair (e: Exec): **Prop** := ∀ (n: Node),`
`   Always (fun e' => EN n e' → Eventually (AN n) e') e.`

Namely, all along a run `e`, whenever some node `n` is enabled (predicate (`EN n`)), it is eventually either activated or neutralized (predicate (`AN n`)), *i.e.*, either it is eventually chosen by the daemon to execute in a step, or it eventually becomes disabled, due to the move of some of its neighbors. Note that this definition involves both inductive and coinductive predicates.

---

[3] The notation `{ A }+{ B }` (so-called `sumbool` in Coq) means there exists an algorithm able to choose between Conditions `A` and `B`.

A self-stabilizing algorithm is designed to fulfill a given specification under some assumptions, often related to the system. In the literature, those assumptions are directly encoded in the configurations using constants whose values achieve some conditions. For example, an identified network is modeled using a constant variable, called identifier, for each process and assuming that every two distinct processes have different identifiers. Following the literature, we express those assumptions (predicate `Assume:` `Env` $\rightarrow$ **Prop**) on the read-only variables of the nodes. Such assumptions need only to be checked on the initial environment of a run. Indeed, they are then inherently satisfied all along the run since they only rely on read-only variables.

To sum up, we define an *execution* of the algorithm to be a stream of environments which is a maximal run satisfying the daemon constraints and where the read-only assumptions are satisfied in its first environment. Hence, executions are encoded by the following predicate.

```
is_exec (e: Exec): Prop :=
  (Assume • H) e ∧ is_max_run e ∧ weakly_fair e.
```

It is important to note that a self-stabilizing algorithm can be initiated from any environment where the read-only assumptions are satisfied. This, in particular, means that *every suffix of an execution is also an execution.*

The specification of an algorithm is given as a predicate $\mathcal{S}$: `Exec` $\rightarrow$ **Prop**. Then, an algorithm $\mathcal{A}$ is *self-stabilizing* (predicate `self_stabilization` $\mathcal{A}$: **Prop**) *w.r.t.* a specification $\mathcal{S}$ under the weakly fair daemon if there exists a set of environments called *legitimate* and detected using the predicate `LEG:` `Env` $\rightarrow$ **Prop**, such that for every execution e (implicitly e: `Exec` and `is_exec` e),

- if its initial environment is legitimate, then each of its environments is legitimate, *i.e.*, (`LEG` • `H`) e $\rightarrow$ `Always` (`LEG` • `H`) e *(Closure)*;
- it converges to a legitimate environment, *i.e.*, `Eventually` (`LEG` • `H`) e *(Convergence)*; and
- if it is initiated in a legitimate environment, then it satisfies the specification, *i.e.*, (`LEG` • `H`) e $\rightarrow$ $\mathcal{S}$ e *(Specification)*.

In this paper, we also consider the class of *silent* self-stabilizing algorithms. In the atomic-state model, an algorithm $\mathcal{A}$ is *silent* if all executions are finite: `silent` $\mathcal{A}$: **Prop** := $\forall$ (e: `Exec`), `is_exec` e $\rightarrow$ `finite` e. A silent algorithm is designed to converge to terminal environments satisfying some properties. So, the specification of such an algorithm is rather formulated as a predicate over environments $\mathcal{S}^g$: `Env` $\rightarrow$ **Prop**, henceforth called *environment specification*.

3   Composition

The hierarchical collateral composition has been introduced in [20] together with a simple sufficient condition to show its correctness. We now describe the operator, its modeling, and the certification of the sufficient condition in PADEC.

Beyond the higher confidence in the accuracy of the result, certification, by enforcing proofs to be more rigorous, leads to a deeper understanding of the result.

The goal of the hierarchical collateral composition operator is to mimic the sequential composition "$\mathcal{A}_1$; $\mathcal{A}_2$". $\mathcal{A}_1$ and $\mathcal{A}_2$ run concurrently modulo some priorities (see details below) and collaborate together using common variables. The goal of $\mathcal{A}_1$ is to self-stabilizingly output correct inputs to $\mathcal{A}_2$. $\mathcal{A}_2$ is self-stabilizing provided that its inputs, in particular those computed by $\mathcal{A}_1$, are correct. Hence, the actual convergence of $\mathcal{A}_2$ is ensured only after $\mathcal{A}_1$ has stabilized. For example, the clustering algorithm for general networks given in [18] is a hierarchical collateral composition $\mathcal{A}_1 \oplus \mathcal{A}_2$, where $\mathcal{A}_1$ is a spanning tree construction and $\mathcal{A}_2$ a clustering algorithm dedicated to tree topologies.

$\mathcal{A}_1$ should converge so that its output variables permanently fulfill the input assumptions of $\mathcal{A}_2$ to ensure that $\mathcal{A}_2$ stabilizes in nominal conditions. To that goal, we assume that $\mathcal{A}_1$ is silent, e.g., in [18], once the spanning tree construction has stabilized, all its variables, in particular those defining the tree, are constant.

For each node, the *local variables* of the composite algorithm $\mathcal{A}_1 \oplus \mathcal{A}_2$ are made of variables specific to $\mathcal{A}_1$ and $\mathcal{A}_2$ respectively, but also of variables common to $\mathcal{A}_1$ and $\mathcal{A}_2$. Those variables store, in particular, the output of $\mathcal{A}_1$ used as input by $\mathcal{A}_2$. They should be read-only in $\mathcal{A}_2$ since $\mathcal{A}_2$ should not prevent $\mathcal{A}_1$ from stabilizing by overwriting these variables.

In the previous collateral composition [27] of Gouda and Herman, the choice for an activated node to execute either $\mathcal{A}_1$ or $\mathcal{A}_2$, when both are enabled, was nondeterministic. In contrast, in the hierarchical collateral composition, the *composite algorithm* gives priority to $\mathcal{A}_1$ over $\mathcal{A}_2$ *locally at each node*. Let p be a node enabled *w.r.t.* $\mathcal{A}_1 \oplus \mathcal{A}_2$ in some environment and assume that p is activated by the daemon in the next step.

- If $\mathcal{A}_1$ is enabled at p (*n.b.*, $\mathcal{A}_2$ may be enabled at p too), then p makes a move of $\mathcal{A}_1$ only.
- Otherwise, p is disabled *w.r.t.* $\mathcal{A}_1$, but enabled *w.r.t.* $\mathcal{A}_2$, and so makes a move of $\mathcal{A}_2$ (only).

Hence, when p moves in $\mathcal{A}_1 \oplus \mathcal{A}_2$, it either executes $\mathcal{A}_1$ or $\mathcal{A}_2$, but not both. We should underline that this priority mechanism is only local: globally, a step of $\mathcal{A}_1 \oplus \mathcal{A}_2$ may contain moves of $\mathcal{A}_1$ only, moves of $\mathcal{A}_2$ only, but also a mix of them, yet executed at different nodes.

3.1   The Composite Algorithm in Coq

We model the composite algorithm $\mathcal{A}_1 \oplus \mathcal{A}_2$ in Coq as follows. We define the local states S3 of $\mathcal{A}_1 \oplus \mathcal{A}_2$ assuming that the local states of $\mathcal{A}_1$, noted S1, can be handled using the following getter and setter:

- `read1`: S3 $\rightarrow$ S1 is a projection from S3 to S1,
- `write1`: S1 $\rightarrow$ S3 $\rightarrow$ S3 modifies the S1-part of a composite state.

Functions read2 and write2 are defined similarly for the local states S2 of $\mathcal{A}_2$.[4] Those functions follow the properties given by the commutative diagram of Fig. 1. For example, to update the S1-part of the composite local state (x3: S3) with (x1: S1), we use write1(x1,x3): this produces a new S3 local state with S1-part x1, namely, read1(write1(x1,x3)) returns x1. Additionally, we encode the fact that any writing in the S2-part (by $\mathcal{A}_2$), that respects the read-only condition, actually does not modify the S1-part of an S3 state. Indeed, the common part between S1 and S2 is necessarily read-only for S2 (see x in Fig. 2).

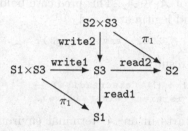

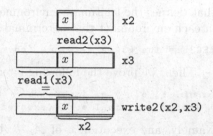

Fig. 1. Commutative diagram for read and write. π_1 gives access to the first element of the pair.

Fig. 2. write2 cannot modify S1-part. x is the common part between S1 and S2, read-only for S2.

We generalize the projections read1 and read2 to environments and streams. The projection envread1 to $\mathcal{A}_1$ of an environment g of $\mathcal{A}_1 \oplus \mathcal{A}_2$ is an environment for $\mathcal{A}_1$ defined as read1 • g. Namely, for a node n, the projection of (g n) on $\mathcal{A}_1$, is obtained by (read1(g n)). The projection on $\mathcal{A}_1$ of a stream s of $\mathcal{A}_1 \oplus \mathcal{A}_2$ is called execread1 and is obtained using a cofixed point that applies envread1 to every element of the stream (i.e., a map on a stream). In particular, ((H • execread1) s) and ((envread1 • H) s) represent one and the same environment. The projections envread2 and execread2 on $\mathcal{A}_2$ are defined similarly.

3.2 Correctness of the Composition

The composition operator is proven correct under the following hypotheses:

$\mathcal{H}_1$: The daemon is weakly fair.

$\mathcal{H}_2$: $\mathcal{A}_1$ is silent and self-stabilizing *w.r.t.* the environment specification $\mathcal{S}_1^g$: given the read-only assumption Assume1, each of its executions is finite and terminates in an environment satisfying $\mathcal{S}_1^q$.

$\mathcal{H}_3$: $\mathcal{A}_2$ is self-stabilizing *w.r.t.* specification $\mathcal{S}_2$: given the read-only assumption Assume2, each of its executions eventually reaches a legitimate environment (predicate LEG2) from which $\mathcal{S}_2$ is satisfied.

---

[4] S1, S2, S3 stand for type State dedicated to Algorithms $\mathcal{A}_1$, $\mathcal{A}_2$, $\mathcal{A}_1 \oplus \mathcal{A}_2$, respectively.

$\mathcal{H}_4$: The read-only assumption of $\mathcal{A}_1 \oplus \mathcal{A}_2$ is `Assume1` on $\mathcal{A}_1$-projections.
$\mathcal{H}_5$: $\mathcal{S}_1^g$ implies `Assume2`, *i.e.*, $\forall$ g, $\mathcal{S}_1^g$ (`envread1` g) $\rightarrow$ `Assume2` (`envread2` g).

Under those hypotheses, we have proven the theorem below for the specification
S := `fun e => Always` ($\mathcal{S}_1^g$ • H • `execread1`) e $\wedge$ ($\mathcal{S}_2$ • `execread2`) e.

Theorem. `Composition_Correctness: self_stabilization` $\mathcal{A}_1 \oplus \mathcal{A}_2$.

The above theorem states that $\mathcal{A}_1 \oplus \mathcal{A}_2$ eventually reaches an environment from which $\mathcal{S}_2$ holds and $\mathcal{S}_1^g$ is satisfied in all environments.

We now outline the proof of the theorem. We first have to exhibit a predicate that defines the legitimate environments `LEG3` of $\mathcal{A}_1 \oplus \mathcal{A}_2$. This predicate holds in each environment that is terminal for $\mathcal{A}_1$ and legitimate for $\mathcal{A}_2$:

`LEG3` := `fun g3 => terminal` (`envread1` g3) $\wedge$ `LEG2` (`envread2` g3).

Then, we prove the following intermediate result:

Lemma. `t1_e2:` $\forall$ e, `is_exec` e $\rightarrow$ (`terminal` • H) (`execread1` e) $\rightarrow$
    `Always` (`terminal` • H) (`execread1` e) $\wedge$ `is_exec` (`execread2` e).

Namely, any execution e of $\mathcal{A}_1 \oplus \mathcal{A}_2$ that starts in an $\mathcal{A}_1$-terminal environment remains in $\mathcal{A}_1$-terminal environments and is actually an execution for $\mathcal{A}_2$. First, from an environment which is terminal for $\mathcal{A}_1$, there is no way to update variables of $\mathcal{A}_1$. So, e remains in environments that are $\mathcal{A}_1$-terminal. This claim also implies that each step of e is actually a step of $\mathcal{A}_2$ and, consequently, (`execread2` e) is a maximal run of $\mathcal{A}_2$ satisfying the weakly fair condition. Finally, ((H • `execread2`) e) satisfies `Assume2`. Indeed, $\mathcal{A}_1$ being silent and self-stabilizing, this implies that if $\mathcal{A}_1$ starts in a terminal environment, then, this environment satisfies $\mathcal{S}_1^g$. Thus, we can use hypothesis $\mathcal{H}_5$ on the first environment of e. Hence, we can conclude that (`execread2` e) is an execution of $\mathcal{A}_2$.

In the rest of the explanation, we consider an arbitrary execution e of $\mathcal{A}_1 \oplus \mathcal{A}_2$.

Closure. To show the closure, we have to prove that if e starts in a legitimate environment of $\mathcal{A}_1 \oplus \mathcal{A}_2$ (*i.e.*, an environment satisfying `LEG3`), it always remains in such environments. This is straightforward using Lemma `t1_e2`. Indeed, first, e remains in environments that are $\mathcal{A}_1$-terminal. Second, as (`execread2` e) is an execution for $\mathcal{A}_2$, we can use the closure property of $\mathcal{A}_2$ on (`execread2` e) (since $\mathcal{A}_2$ is self-stabilizing) and prove that legitimate environments for $\mathcal{A}_2$ are maintained forever in (`execread2` e).

Specification. We have to prove that if e is initiated in `LEG3`, then (S e) holds. We use Lemma `t1_e2` again. First, every environment of e is $\mathcal{A}_1$-terminal, and so satisfies $\mathcal{S}_1^g$. Second, (`execread2` e) is an execution of $\mathcal{A}_2$ on which we can apply the specification property of $\mathcal{A}_2$ (since $\mathcal{A}_2$ is self-stabilizing), hence satisfies $\mathcal{S}_2$.

Convergence. We should prove that e eventually reaches an environment that is legitimate for $\mathcal{A}_1 \oplus \mathcal{A}_2$. This goal is split into three subgoals:

(1) `Eventually` (`terminal` • H) (`execread1` e)

i.e., e eventually reaches an environment which is terminal for $\mathcal{A}_1$. This part of the proof is postponed to Sect. 4. Claim (1) ensures that e contains a suffix σ that starts in a terminal environment for $\mathcal{A}_1$: we have ((terminal • H) (execread1 σ)). The second subgoal is then:

(2) Always (terminal • H) (execread1 σ)

i.e., σ remains $\mathcal{A}_1$-terminal. As any suffix of an execution is also an execution, so is σ. Hence, Claim (2) is immediate from Lemma t1_e2. The third subgoal is:

(3) Eventually (LEG2 • H) (execread2 σ)

After e has reached an environment that is terminal for $\mathcal{A}_1$, it eventually reaches an environment that is legitimate for $\mathcal{A}_2$. Indeed, its suffix σ eventually reaches an environment that is legitimate for $\mathcal{A}_2$: to prove this, we use the convergence of $\mathcal{A}_2$ (as $\mathcal{A}_2$ is self-stabilizing) since, by Lemma t1_e2, (execread2 σ) is an execution of $\mathcal{A}_2$. Now, as σ eventually reaches LEG2, so does e.

4   Squeezing Streams and Convergence of Composition

The main part of the proof consists in proving that any execution of the composite algorithm eventually reaches an environment which is terminal for $\mathcal{A}_1$ (Claim (1)). This requires to use the assumption that $\mathcal{A}_1$ is silent, *i.e.*, Hypothesis $\mathcal{H}_2$. To that goal, we consider an execution e of $\mathcal{A}_1 \oplus \mathcal{A}_2$ and we focus on its projection on $\mathcal{A}_1$, (execread1 e). Now, this latter stream is usually not an execution of $\mathcal{A}_1$ and $\mathcal{H}_2$ only applies to executions of $\mathcal{A}_1$. Actually, each step of e matches one of the two following cases: either at least one node executes $\mathcal{A}_1$ in the step, or all activated nodes only execute $\mathcal{A}_2$. In the former case, the projection of the step on $\mathcal{A}_1$ is a step of $\mathcal{A}_1$. In the latter case, the projection gives two identical environments of $\mathcal{A}_1$. Hence, (execread1 e) is made of steps of $\mathcal{A}_1$, separated by duplicates. So, to apply $\mathcal{H}_2$, it is mandatory to construct an execution of $\mathcal{A}_1$ by computing the *squeezing* of (execread1 e), *i.e.*, the stream obtained by removing all duplicates from (execread1 e).

In Subsect. 4.1, we describe how to compute the squeezing of a general stream. Again, it is a *filter* in the sense of Bertot [8] since it removes elements from the stream. Yet, its filtering predicate is particular, as it forbids any two consecutive elements to be equal. But, in contrast with Bertot [8], the squeezing applies to streams that can be finite or infinite and allows to remove an infinite suffix of duplicates. Therefore, we have an additional issue: the squeezing needs to decide at each step whether to continue or give up because a constant, potentially infinite, suffix has been reached.

The object resulting from squeezing – so-called *squeezed stream* – is complex since it is defined as an explicit construction. Consequently, dealing with it directly in proofs requires heavy Coq developments. To avoid such implementation details, we rather work on an abstraction stream relation, called *simulation*, which encompasses the useful properties of the squeezed stream.

4.1 Squeezing

We now explain how to build the squeezing of an arbitrary stream whose elements are of type A. Let s be such a stream. The squeezed version of s contains exactly the same elements as s, in the same order, yet without any duplicate.

For example, if s = 1 2 2 3 3 3 3 3 4 5 6 6 7 8 8 8 ... (s ends with an *infinite* suffix of 8), then the squeezing of s is the *finite* sequence s' = 1 2 3 4 5 6 7 8. Every element in s is still present in s', following the same increasing order, yet every duplicate has been removed from s, including the infinite sequence of 8. Note that a squeezing may not be finite, *e.g.*, if s is the infinite repetition of the pattern 1 2 3, then the squeezing of s is s itself.

We want to *build* the squeezed stream, *i.e.,* to define a function Squeeze which *computes* the squeezed version of an input stream s. This computation will be carried out by a coinductive function. To compute (Squeeze s), it is necessary to *test* whether all elements in the stream s are identical to (H s). If so, (Squeeze s) will be (O (H s)); otherwise it will be (C (H s) (Squeeze s*)), where s* is the maximal suffix of s starting with an element distinct from (H s). Now, a stream may be infinite, and so the aforementioned test is undecidable in general. Thus, we need extra information in order to make the decision and, since we will base the result of the squeezing algorithm on this decision, it has to be *constructive*. In Coq, constructive objects are in sort **Type** and carry computational content.[5] We assume (Skippable (H s) s) where:

```
Skippable (a: A) (s: Stream): Type :=
  { is_constant a s }+{ reach_diff a s }.
```

Any value of (Skippable (H s) s) carries either a proof of (is_constant (H s) s) or a proof of (reach_diff (H s) s).

For an element a and a stream s, (is_constant a s) means (Always (fun s => H s $\cong$ a) s),[6] *i.e.*, the stream s contains nothing but the element a, albeit finite or not. Then, (reach_diff a s) means that s begins with a finite number of a followed by some element different from a. To be able to compute Squeeze, (reach_diff a s) should also provide a way to compute the suffix s* of s where all the instances of a at the beginning of s have been removed. Actually, we implement (reach_diff a s) as (Acc (Rskip a) s). For an element a and two streams s1, s2, (Rskip a s1 s2) holds when either s1 and s2 are both reduced to the single element a or s2 is equal to (C a s1), *i.e.*, C a s1 $\cong$ s2 $\vee$ s1 $\cong$ O a $\wedge$ O a $\cong$ s2. The inductive proposition Acc is taken from the Coq.Init.Wf standard library which provides tools on well-founded inductions. Predicate (Acc (Rskip a) s) means that any descending chain from s, using relation (Rskip a), is finite. Using a well-founded induction on a value of (reach_diff a s), we are able to define a recursive function Skip with dependent arguments (a: A), (s: Stream), and (rd: reach_diff a s) that computes

---

[5] Conversely, objects in sort **Prop** are only proofs of logical statements.

[6] $\cong$ is a generic notation that represents equality; when it applies on streams, it implements pointwise equality.

the maximal suffix of s starting with an element distinct from a. Thus, whenever we obtain a proof of (reach_diff (H s) s), we can compute s* using Skip.

However, to be able to compute the corecursive call (Squeeze s*), we need to exhibit a value of (Skippable (H s*) s*). This means that we need an algorithm that may compute, repeatedly and lazily, along the stream, a value of (Skippable (H σ) σ), where σ is any suffix of s. This is performed by Always_, the counterpart in Type of Always. So, we obtain the following definition:

```
Squeezable (s: Stream): Type :=
  Always_ (fun s => Skippable (H s) s) s.
```

The construction of Squeeze can now be completed as a cofixed point with dependent arguments (s: Stream A) and (sq: Squeezable s) (*n.b.*, we omit parameter sq when it is clear from the context).

As a direct consequence of the definition, we can show that a squeezed stream contains no duplicate:

Lemma. Squeeze_Always_moves :
  ∀ (s: Stream) (sq: Squeezable s), Always moves (Squeeze s).

In the lemma, the predicate moves checks that a stream differs on its two first elements if they exist. The lemma is proven using a coinductive proof that follows the definition of Squeeze. It essentially relies on the fact that for every element a and stream s on which (Skip a s) can be evaluated (*i.e.*, which begins with a finite number of a), the first element of (Skip a s) is different from a.

4.2 Preserving Properties by Simulation

We now define the *simulation relation*. As usual, our simulation defines an abstract view, yet adapted to our context. Given two streams X and Y, (Y $\leq_{sim}$ X) means that Y is obtained from X by removing some of its duplicates, namely Y and X contains exactly the same elements, in the same order, yet each element is at most as duplicated in Y as in X. For instance, with s = 1 2 2 3 3 3 3 4 5 6 6 7 8 8... (ending with an infinite sequence of 8) and s' = 1 2 2 3 3 4 5 6 7 8..., we have (s' $\leq_{sim}$ s) since every value, from 1 to 8, appears in both sequences and the number of 1 (resp. 2, 3, 4, 5, 6, 7, 8) is smaller or equal in s'. The relation $\leq_{sim}$ is based on inductive and coinductive mechanisms, defined as follows:

```
CoInductive ≤_sim: Stream → Stream → Prop :=
| sim_constant: ∀ a s, is_constant a s → O a ≤_sim s
| sim_cons: ∀ a s1 s2 s3, s1 ≤_sim s2 → C_plus a s2 s3 →
                          C a s1 ≤_sim s3.
```

The first constructor sim_constant means that every stream made of one element a is smaller than any stream constantly made of a (albeit finite or infinite). The second constructor sim_cons means that given an element a and two streams s1 and s2 such that s1 is smaller than s2, if the stream s3 is obtained from s2 by adding a positive number of a (namely, (C_plus a s2 s3) holds), then (C a s1) is smaller than s3. The predicate C_plus is inductively defined and (C_plus a s1 (C a s2)) checks that either s1 and s2 are equal or (C_plus a s1 s2).

We can show that $\leq_{sim}$ is a *partial order*, and as squeezing means removing all duplicates of a stream, we can prove that for a given squeezable stream, its squeezing is minimal *w.r.t.* $\leq_{sim}$ (see [2] for details):

Lemma. Squeeze_is_min: $\forall$ (s: Stream) (sq: Squeezable s),
    Squeeze s $\leq_{sim}$ s $\wedge$ $\forall$ x, x $\leq_{sim}$ s $\rightarrow$ Squeeze s $\leq_{sim}$ x.

We show that some properties can be transferred between $\leq_{sim}$-related streams. Precisely, a property P is defined to be (decreasing) *monotonic* (resp. *comonotonic*) *w.r.t.* $\leq_{sim}$ as follows:

```
monotonic P    := ∀ x y, x ≤_sim y → P y → P x
comonotonic P  := ∀ x y, x ≤_sim y → P x → P y
```

The proof of Claim (1) requires to prove the *preservation* of the following properties. First, we prove a result related to the implication: for two predicates P and Q, such that P is comonotonic and Q is monotonic, we easily obtain that (fun s => P s $\rightarrow$ Q s) is monotonic. For some property P which is monotonic (resp. comonotonic), (Eventually P) is monotonic (resp. comonotonic): indeed if P is reached by a given stream y, then it is also reached by any stream x that contains less (resp. more) duplicates. Similarly, for some monotonic property P, (Always P) is monotonic. Some other *ad-hoc* properties are proven (co)monotonic, if necessary, using straightforward coinductions.

4.3 Proof of Claim (1)

The core of the proof is to use Squeeze on (execread1 e) and to show that the result is actually an execution of $\mathcal{A}_1$.

To allow the use of Squeeze (execread1 e), *we need to show that* (execread1 e) *is squeezable,* meaning that from any environment of (execread1 e), we can decide whether the remaining sequence of environments is constant. This proof uses the fact that e is weakly fair and that the predicate terminal is decidable. First, if initially e is terminal for $\mathcal{A}_1$, then it remains so forever, and (execread1 e) is a constant sequence made of the environment (H (execread1 e)) only. Second, we show that if initially, e is not terminal for $\mathcal{A}_1$, then necessarily, we have reach_diff (H (execread1 e)) (execread1 e) which means that (execread1 e) begins by a finite number of duplicates of (H (execread1 e)). Indeed, as (H e) is not terminal for $\mathcal{A}_1$, there exists a node which is enabled to execute its local algorithm $\mathcal{A}_1$ in e. It will remain continuously enabled until being activated or neutralized, meaning that the node or one of its neighbors has made a move of $\mathcal{A}_1$. This activation or neutralization eventually occurs due to the weakly fair assumption and the fact that $\mathcal{A}_1$ has priority over $\mathcal{A}_2$. Following this remark, the proof is done by induction on the weakly fair assumption. Third, whether or not e is initially terminal for $\mathcal{A}_1$ is decidable (Lemma `terminal_dec`). Hence, the proof that (`execread1 e`) is squeezable is performed coinductively and each step of the coinduction decides whether the current environment is terminal for $\mathcal{A}_1$.

So we can build `Se = Squeeze (execread1 e)` *and show it is an execution of* $\mathcal{A}_1$.

(a) `Se` *is initiated under* `Assume1` since a stream and its squeezing have the same initial environment.

(b) `Se` *is weakly fair.* We have `Se` $\leq_{sim}$ (`execread1 e`) by Lemma `Squeeze_is_min`. We show that (`execread1 e`) is weakly fair by induction and coinduction on the definition of `weakly_fair`. Now, we can prove that `weakly_fair` is monotonic directly using preservation properties. So, we conclude that `Se` is weakly fair.

(c) `Se` *is a maximal run.* We first prove the following intermediate claim:

(c1) $\forall$ `e1, Always moves e1` $\rightarrow$ `e1` $\leq_{sim}$ `execread1 e` $\rightarrow$
       `is_max_run e1`.

The proof is split into two subgoals: (`Always s_Step e1`) and (`Always s_terminal e1`). Let `s` be any stream. (`s_Step s`) means that when `s` is made of at least two elements (*i.e.*, `s` is equal to some (`C a ss`)), then (`Step (H ss) a`) holds. (`s_terminal s`) means that when `s` is made of a single element `a` (*i.e.*, `s` is equal to (`O a`))), then (`terminal a`) holds.

  Subgoal 1 follows from the fact that `Always (fun e => moves e` $\rightarrow$ `s_Step e)` is monotonic. This latter can be shown by a direct coinduction, which mainly relies on the fact that as `s_Step` applies on the first two elements of the stream and can hold only when they are different.

  For Subgoal 2, we use the assumption (`weakly_fair e`) to show the property

(c2) $\forall$ `g1 , is_constant g1 (execread1 e)` $\rightarrow$ `terminal g1` .

namely, if (`execread1 e`) is constantly made of an environment `g1`, then `g1` is terminal. Actually, we proceed by contradiction and prove that if `g1` is not terminal, then there exists a node `n` which is enabled in `g1`. Therefore, due to the weakly fair assumption, `n` will be eventually activated or neutralized in $\mathcal{A}_1 \oplus \mathcal{A}_2$, hence in $\mathcal{A}_1$, since $\mathcal{A}_1$ has priority over $\mathcal{A}_2$ in $\mathcal{A}_1 \oplus \mathcal{A}_2$. Then, by induction on (`Eventually (AN n) e`), we obtain that `e` cannot be constantly made of `g1`. Subgoal 2 is then obtained with a direct coinductive proof using Claim (c2).

  This concludes the proof of Claim (c1) which can be applied on `Se` since, again, (`Se` $\leq_{sim}$ `execread1 e`) and (`Always moves`) hold on `Se` (see Lemma `Squeeze_Always_moves`). Hence, `Se` is a maximal run. Actually, `e1` and `Se` represent one and the same stream, but working on `e1` has allowed to get rid of the (complex) construction of `Se = Squeeze (execread1 e)` in the proof.

As a conclusion, we deduce (by (a), (b), and (c)) that the squeezing `Se` of the stream (`execread1 e`) is an execution of $\mathcal{A}_1$ and use it on $\mathcal{H}_2$ ($\mathcal{A}_1$ is silent). Hence, `Se` is finite, *i.e.*, it eventually reaches a terminal environment. As `Eventually` is comonotonic, (`execread1 e`) eventually reaches a terminal environment too, hence Claim (1) holds. This concludes the proof of convergence.

5   Conclusion

The *composition theorem* proves that hierarchical collateral composition preserves self-stabilization when applied under convenient assumptions, in particular assuming weakly fair executions. It comes with a *toolbox for squeezing streams* that was mandatory to achieve the proof of the theorem. As an example, we instantiated the theorem with the two first layers of the algorithm proposed in [20]. The first layer builds a rooted spanning tree on an identified connected network; the second layer assumes such a tree exists and computes a k-dominating set of the network ($k \in \mathbb{N}$) using this tree. Both algorithms are self-stabilizing under a weakly fair daemon, and our result certifies that their composition is also self-stabilizing and so builds a k-dominating set of an arbitrary connected identified network.

Composition techniques, in particular the hierarchical collateral composition, are widely used in the self-stabilizing area [18,23,27] because adopting a modular approach is unavoidable to design and prove complex present-day algorithms. Certification of such techniques is a step beyond traditional handmade proofs that offers hugely more confidence in the correctness of the result; and also a step towards the certification of complex multi-layered algorithms.

References

1. Abel, A., Pientka, B., Thibodeau, D., Setzer, A.: Copatterns: programming infinite structures by observations. In: The 40th Annual ACM SIGPLAN-SIGACT Symposium on Principles of Programming Languages, POPL 2013, Rome, Italy, 23–25 January 2013 (2013)
2. Altisen, K., Corbineau, P., Devismes, S.: PADEC: A Framework for Certified Self-Stabilization. http://www-verimag.imag.fr/~altisen/PADEC/
3. Altisen, K., Corbineau, P., Devismes, S.: A framework for certified self-stabilization. Logical Methods Comput. Sci. (special issue of FORTE 2016) **13**(4) (2017)
4. Altisen, K., Devismes, S., Durand, A.: Concurrency in snap-stabilizing local resource allocation. J. Parallel Distrib. Comput. **102**, 42–56 (2017)
5. Auger, C., Bouzid, Z., Courtieu, P., Tixeuil, S., Urbain, X.: Certified impossibility results for byzantine-tolerant mobile robots. In: Higashino, T., Katayama, Y., Masuzawa, T., Potop-Butucaru, M., Yamashita, M. (eds.) SSS 2013. LNCS, vol. 8255, pp. 178–190. Springer, Cham (2013). https://doi.org/10.1007/978-3-319-03089-0_13
6. Beauquier, J., Gradinariu, M., Johnen, C.: Cross-over composition - enforcement of fairness under unfair adversary. In: Datta, A.K., Herman, T. (eds.) WSS 2001. LNCS, vol. 2194, pp. 19–34. Springer, Heidelberg (2001). https://doi.org/10.1007/3-540-45438-1_2
7. Bérard, B., Lafourcade, P., Millet, L., Potop-Butucaru, M., Thierry-Mieg, Y., Tixeuil, S.: Formal verification of mobile robot protocols. Distrib. Comput. **29**(6), 459–487 (2016). https://doi.org/10.1007/s00446-016-0271-1
8. Bertot, Y.: Filters on coinductive streams, an application to eratosthenes' sieve. In: Urzyczyn, P. (ed.) TLCA 2005. LNCS, vol. 3461, pp. 102–115. Springer, Heidelberg (2005). https://doi.org/10.1007/11417170_9

9. Bertot, Y., Castéran, P.: Interactive Theorem Proving and Program Development - Coq'Art: The Calculus of Inductive Constructions. Texts in Theoretical Computer Science. An EATCS Series. Springer, Heidelberg (2004). https://doi.org/10.1007/978-3-662-07964-5

10. Blin, L., Fraigniaud, P., Patt-Shamir, B.: On proof-labeling schemes versus silent self-stabilizing algorithms. In: Felber, P., Garg, V. (eds.) SSS 2014. LNCS, vol. 8756, pp. 18–32. Springer, Cham (2014). https://doi.org/10.1007/978-3-319-11764-5_2

11. Caron, E., Chuffart, F., Tedeschi, C.: When self-stabilization meets real platforms: an experimental study of a peer-to-peer service discovery system. Future Gener. Comput. Syst. **29**(6), 1533–1543 (2013)

12. Caron, E., Datta, A.K., Depardon, B., Larmore, L.L.: A self-stabilizing k-clustering algorithm for weighted graphs. J. Parallel Distrib. Comput. **70**(11), 1159–1173 (2010)

13. Castéran, P., Filou, V., Mosbah, M.: Certifying distributed algorithms by embedding local computation systems in the coq proof assistant. In: Symbolic Computation in Software Science (SCSS 2009) (2009)

14. Chen, M., Monin, J.F.: Formal verification of netlog protocols. In: Sixth International Symposium on Theoretical Aspects of Software Engineering, TASE 2012, Beijing, China, 4–6 July 2012 (2012)

15. Coupet-Grimal, S.: An axiomatization of linear temporal logic in the calculus of inductive constructions. J. Log. Comput. **13**(6), 801–813 (2003)

16. Courtieu, P.: Proving self-stabilization with a proof assistant. In: 16th International Parallel and Distributed Processing Symposium (IPDPS 2002), Fort Lauderdale, FL, USA, 15–19 April 2002, CD-ROM/Abstracts Proceedings (2002)

17. Courtieu, P., Rieg, L., Tixeuil, S., Urbain, X.: Certified universal gathering in $\mathbb{R}^2$ for oblivious mobile robots. In: Gavoille, C., Ilcinkas, D. (eds.) DISC 2016. LNCS, vol. 9888, pp. 187–200. Springer, Heidelberg (2016). https://doi.org/10.1007/978-3-662-53426-7_14

18. Datta, A.K., Devismes, S., Heurtefeux, K., Larmore, L.L., Rivierre, Y.: Competitive self-stabilizing k-clustering. Theor. Comput. Sci. **626**, 110–133 (2016)

19. Datta, A.K., Gurumurthy, S., Petit, F., Villain, V.: Self-stabilizing network orientation algorithms in arbitrary rooted networks. Stud. Inform. Univ. **1**(1), 1–22 (2001)

20. Datta, A.K., Larmore, L.L., Devismes, S., Heurtefeux, K., Rivierre, Y.: Self-stabilizing small k-dominating sets. IJNC **3**(1), 116–136 (2013)

21. Dijkstra, E.W.: Self-stabilizing systems in spite of distributed control. Commun. ACM **17**(11), 643–644 (1974)

22. Doan, H.T.T., Bonnet, F., Ogata, K.: Model checking of a mobile robots perpetual exploration algorithm. In: Liu, S., Duan, Z., Tian, C., Nagoya, F. (eds.) SOFL+MSVL 2016. LNCS, vol. 10189, pp. 201–219. Springer, Cham (2017). https://doi.org/10.1007/978-3-319-57708-1_12

23. Dolev, S.: Self-stabilization. MIT Press, Cambridge (2000)

24. Dubois, S., Tixeuil, S.: A Taxonomy of Daemons in Self-stabilization. CoRR abs/1110.0334 (2011) http://arxiv.org/abs/1110.0334

25. Fei, L., Yong, S., Hong, D., Yizhi, R.: Self stabilizing distributed transactional memory model and algorithms. J. Comput. Res. Dev. **51**(9), 2046 (2014)

26. Giménez, E.: An application of co-inductive types in Coq: verification of the alternating bit protocol. In: Berardi, S., Coppo, M. (eds.) TYPES 1995. LNCS, vol. 1158, pp. 135–152. Springer, Heidelberg (1996). https://doi.org/10.1007/3-540-61780-9_67

27. Gouda, M., Herman, T.: Adaptive programming. IEEE Trans. Softw. Eng. **17**, 911–921 (1991)
28. Küfner, P., Nestmann, U., Rickmann, C.: Formal verification of distributed algorithms. In: Baeten, J.C.M., Ball, T., de Boer, F.S. (eds.) TCS 2012. LNCS, vol. 7604, pp. 209–224. Springer, Heidelberg (2012). https://doi.org/10.1007/978-3-642-33475-7_15
29. Kulkarni, S.S., Rushby, J.M., Shankar, N.: A case-study in component-based mechanical verification of fault-tolerant programs. In: 1999 ICDCS Workshop on Self-stabilizing Systems, Austin, Texas, 5 June 1999, Proceedings (1999)
30. Lamport, L.: How to write a 21st century proof. J. Fixed Point Theory Appl. **11**(1), 43–63 (2012)
31. Leroy, X., Grall, H.: Coinductive big-step operational semantics. Inf. Comput. **207**(2), 284–304 (2009)
32. Paulson, L.C.: Mechanizing coinduction and corecursion in higher-order logic. J. Log. Comput. **7**(2), 175–204 (1997)
33. Pnueli, A.: The temporal logic of programs. In: 18th Annual Symposium on Foundations of Computer Science, Providence, Rhode Island, USA, 31 October–1 November 1977, pp. 46–57. IEEE Computer Society (1977)
34. Tel, G.: Introduction to Distributed Algorithms, 2nd edn. Cambridge University Press, Cambridge (2001)
35. The Coq Development Team: The Coq Proof Assistant Documentation, June 2012. http://coq.inria.fr/refman/

Parametric Updates in Parametric Timed Automata

Étienne André[1,2,3] , Didier Lime[4] , and Mathias Ramparison[1(✉)]

[1] Université Paris 13, LIPN, CNRS, UMR 7030, 93430 Villetaneuse, France
ramparison@lipn13.fr
[2] JFLI, CNRS, Tokyo, Japan
[3] National Institute of Informatics, Tokyo, Japan
[4] École Centrale de Nantes, LS2N, CNRS, UMR 6597, Nantes, France

Abstract. Verification of timed concurrent systems is hard, especially when the exact value of timing constants remains unknown. In this work, we propose a new subclass of Parametric Timed Automata (PTAs) enjoying a decidability result; we allow clocks to be compared to parameters in guards, as in classic PTAs, but also to be updated to parameters. If we update all clocks each time we compare a clock with a parameter and each time we update a clock to a parameter, we obtain a syntactic subclass for which we can decide the EF-emptiness problem ("is the set of parameter valuations for which some given location is reachable in the instantiated timed automaton empty?") and even perform the exact synthesis of the set of rational valuations such that a given location is reachable. To the best of our knowledge, this is the first non-trivial subclass of PTAs, actually even extended with parametric updates, for which this is possible.

1 Introduction

Timed automata (TAs) are a powerful formalism to model and verify timed concurrent systems, both expressive enough to model many interesting systems and enjoying several decidability properties. In particular, the reachability of a discrete state is PSPACE-complete [1]. In TAs, clocks can be compared with constants in guards, and can be updated to 0 along edges. This can model a system where processes synchronise (are reset) together periodically.

Timed automata may turn insufficient to verify systems where the timing constants themselves are subject to some uncertainty, or when they are simply not known at the early design stage. Parametric timed automata (PTAs) [2] address this drawback by allowing parameters (unknown constants) in the timing

This work is partially supported by the ANR national research program PACS (ANR-14-CE28-0002).
É. André—Partially supported by ERATO HASUO Metamathematics for Systems Design Project (No. JPMJER1603), JST.

J. A. Pérez and N. Yoshida (Eds.): FORTE 2019, LNCS 11535, pp. 39–56, 2019.
https://doi.org/10.1007/978-3-030-21759-4_3

constraints; this high expressive power comes at the cost of the undecidability of most interesting problems . In particular, the basic problem of EF-emptiness ("is the set of valuations for which a given location is reachable in the instantiated timed automaton empty?") is "robustly" undecidable: even for a single rational-valued [20] or integer-valued parameter [2,8], or when only strict constraints are used [15]. A well-known syntactic subclass of PTAs that enjoys limited decidability is L/U-PTAs [17], where the parameters set is partitioned into lower-bound and upper-bound parameters, *i.e.,* parameters that can only be compared to a clock as a lower-bound (resp. upper-bound). The EF-emptiness problem is decidable for L/U-PTAs [11,17] and for PTAs under several restrictions [13]; however, most other problems are undecidable (*e.g.,* [4,7,11,18,21]).

Contributions. We investigate parametric updates, which can model an unknown timing configuration in a system where processes need to synchronise together on common events, as in *e.g.,* programmable controller logic programs with concurrent tasks execution. We show that the EF-emptiness problem is decidable for PTAs augmented with parametric updates, with the additional condition that whenever a clock is compared to a parameter in a guard or updated to a parameter, all clocks must be updated (possibly to parameters)—this gives R-U2P-PTA. This result holds when the parameters are *bounded rationals in guards*, and possibly *unbounded rationals in updates*. Non-trivial decidable subclasses of PTAs are a rarity (to the best of our knowledge, only L/U-PTAs [17] and integer-points (IP-)PTAs [7]); this makes our positive result very welcome. In addition, not only the emptiness is decidable, but *exact synthesis* for bounded rational-valued parameters can be performed—which contrasts with L/U-PTAs and IP-PTAs as synthesis was shown intractable [7,18].

A full version of this paper with all detailed proofs is available at [6].

Related Work. Our construction is reminiscent of the parametric difference bound matrices (PDBMs) defined in [22, Sect. III.C] where the author revisit the result of the binary reachability relation over both locations and clock valuations in TAs; however, parameters of [22] are used to bound in time a run that reaches a given location, while we use parameters directly in guards and resets along the run, which make them active components of the run specifically for intersection with parametric guards, key point not tackled in [22].

Allowing parameters in clock updates is inspired by the updatable TA defined in [10] where clocks can be updated not only to 0 ("reset") but also to rational constants ("update"). In [5], we extended the result of [10] by allowing parametric updates (and no parameter elsewhere, *e.g.,* in guards): the EF-emptiness is undecidable even in the restricted setting of bounded rational-valued parameters, but becomes decidable when parameters are restricted to (unbounded) integers.

Synthesis is obviously harder than EF-emptiness: only three results have been proposed to synthesize the exact set of valuations for subclasses of PTAs, but they are all concerned with *integer*-valued parameters [5,11,18]. In contrast, we deal here with (bounded) rational-valued parameters—which makes this result the first of its kind. The idea of updating all clocks when compared to parameters comes from our class of *reset-PTAs* briefly mentioned in [7], but not thoroughly studied. Finally, updating clocks on each transition in which a parameter appears is reminiscent of initialized rectangular hybrid automata [16], which remains one of the few decidable subclasses of hybrid automata.

Section 2 recalls preliminaries. Section 3 presents R-U2P-PTA along with our decidability result. Section 4 gives a concrete application of our result.

2   Preliminaries

Throughout this paper, we assume a set $\mathbb{X} = \{x_1, \ldots, x_H\}$ of *clocks, i.e.*, real-valued variables evolving at the same rate. A clock valuation is $w : \mathbb{X} \to \mathbb{R}_+$. We write $\mathbf{0}$ for the clock valuation that assigns 0 to all clocks. Given $d \in \mathbb{R}_+$, $w + d$ (resp. $w - d$) denotes the valuation such that $(w + d)(x) = w(x) + d$ (resp. $(w - d)(x) = w(x) - d$ if $w(x) - d > 0$, 0 otherwise), for all $x \in \mathbb{X}$. We assume a set $\mathbb{P} = \{p_1, \ldots, p_M\}$ of *parameters, i.e.*, unknown constants. A parameter *valuation* v is a function $v : \mathbb{P} \to \mathbb{Q}_+$. We identify a valuation v with the point $(v(p_1), \ldots, v(p_M))$ of $\mathbb{Q}_+^M$. Given $d \in \mathbb{N}$, $v + d$ (resp. $v - d$) denotes the valuation such that $(v + d)(p) = v(p) + d$ (resp. $(v - d)(p) = v(p) - d$ if $v(p) - d > 0$, 0 otherwise), for all $p \in \mathbb{P}$.

In the following, we assume $\lhd \in \{<, \leq\}$ and $\bowtie \in \{<, \leq, \geq, >\}$.

A *parametric guard* g is a constraint over $\mathbb{X} \cup \mathbb{P}$ defined as the conjunction of inequalities of the form $x \bowtie z$, where x is a clock and z is either a parameter or a constant in $\mathbb{Z}$. A *non-parametric guard* is a parametric guard without parameters (*i.e.*, over $\mathbb{X}$).

Given a parameter valuation v, $v(g)$ denotes the constraint over $\mathbb{X}$ obtained by replacing in g each parameter p with $v(p)$. We extend this notation to an *expression*: a sum or difference of parameters and constants. Likewise, given a clock valuation w, $w(v(g))$ denotes the expression obtained by replacing in $v(g)$ each clock x with $w(x)$. A clock valuation w *satisfies* constraint $v(g)$ (denoted by $w \models v(g)$) if $w(v(g))$ evaluates to true. We say that v *satisfies* g, denoted by $v \models g$, if the set of clock valuations satisfying $v(g)$ is nonempty. We say that g is *satisfiable* if $\exists w, v$ s.t. $w \models v(g)$.

A *parametric update* is a partial function $u : \mathbb{X} \rightharpoonup \mathbb{N} \cup \mathbb{P}$ which assigns to some of the clocks an integer constant or a parameter. For v a parameter valuation, we define a partial function $v(u) : \mathbb{X} \rightharpoonup \mathbb{Q}_+$ as follows: for each clock $x \in \mathbb{X}$, $v(u)(x) = k \in \mathbb{N}$ if $u(x) = k$ and $v(u)(x) = v(p) \in \mathbb{Q}_+$ if $u(x) = p$ a parameter. A non-parametric update is $u_{np} : \mathbb{X} \rightharpoonup \mathbb{N}$. For a clock valuation w and a parameter valuation v, we denote by $[w]_{v(u)}$ the clock valuation obtained after applying $v(u)$.

Given a clock x and a clock valuation w, $\lfloor w(x) \rfloor$ denotes the integer part of $w(x)$ while $frac(w(x))$ denotes its fractional part. We define the same notation for parameter valuations.

We first define a new class of parametric timed automata and further define classic parametric timed automata and timed automata.

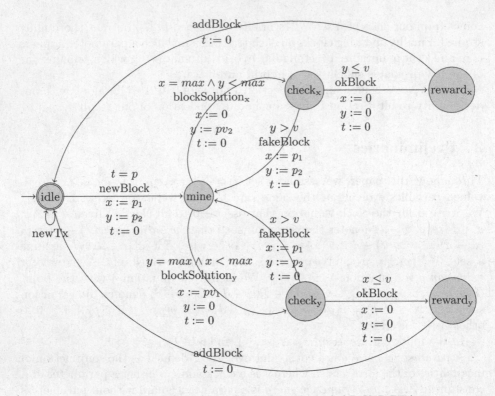

Fig. 1. A proof-of-work modeled with a bounded R-U2P-PTA.

Definition 1. *An update-to-parameter PTA (U2P-PTA) $\mathcal{A}$ is a tuple $\mathcal{A} = (\Sigma, L, l_0, \mathbb{X}, \mathbb{P}, \zeta)$, where: (i) Σ is a finite set of actions, (ii) L is a finite set of locations, (iii) $l_0 \in L$ is the initial location; (iv) $\mathbb{X}$ is a finite set of clocks, (v) $\mathbb{P}$ is a finite set of parameters, (vi) ζ is a finite set of edges $e = \langle l, g, a, u, l' \rangle$ where $l, l' \in L$ are the source and target locations, g is a parametric guard, $a \in \Sigma$ and $u : \mathbb{X} \rightharpoonup \mathbb{N} \cup \mathbb{P}$ is a parametric update function.*

An U2P-PTA is depicted in Fig. 1. Note that all clocks are updated whenever there is a comparison with a parameter (as in newBlock) or a clock is updated to a parameter (as in blockSolution$_x$). Given a parameter valuation v, we denote by $v(\mathcal{A})$ the structure where all occurrences of a parameter p_i have been replaced by $v(p_i)$. If $v(\mathcal{A})$ is such that all constants in guards and updates are integers, then $v(\mathcal{A})$ is a *updatable timed automaton* [10] but will be called *timed automaton* (TA) for the sake of simplicity in this paper.

A *bounded* U2P-PTA is a U2P-PTA with a bounded parameter domain that assigns to each parameter a minimum integer bound and a maximum integer bound. That is, each parameter p_i ranges in an interval $[a_i, b_i]$, with $a_i, b_i \in \mathbb{N}$. Hence, a bounded parameter domain is a hyperrectangle of dimension M.

A parametric timed automaton (PTA) [2] is a U2P-PTA where, for any edge $e = \langle l, g, a, u, l' \rangle \in \zeta$, $u : \mathbb{X} \rightharpoonup \{0\}$.

Definition 2 (Concrete semantics of a TA). *Given a U2P-PTA* $\mathcal{A} = (\Sigma, L, l_0, \mathbb{X}, \mathbb{P}, \zeta)$, *and a parameter valuation* v, *the concrete semantics of* $v(\mathcal{A})$ *is given by the timed transition system* $(S, s_0, \rightarrow)$, *with* $S = \{(l, w) \in L \times \mathbb{R}_+^H\}$, $s_0 = (l_0, \mathbf{0})$ *and* $\rightarrow$ *consists of the discrete and (continuous) delay transition relations:*

- *discrete transitions:* $(l, w) \overset{e}{\mapsto} (l', w')$, *if* $(l, w), (l', w') \in S$, *there exists* $e = \langle l, g, a, u, l' \rangle \in \zeta$, $w' = [w]_{v(u)}$, *and* $w \models v(g)$.
- *delay transitions:* $(l, w) \overset{d}{\mapsto} (l, w + d)$, *with* $d \in \mathbb{R}_+$.

Moreover we write $(l, w) \overset{e}{\longrightarrow} (l', w')$ for a combination of a delay and discrete transitions where $((l, w), e, (l', w')) \in \rightarrow$ if $\exists d, w'' : (l, w) \overset{d}{\mapsto} (l, w'') \overset{e}{\mapsto} (l', w')$.

Given a TA $v(\mathcal{A})$ with concrete semantics $(S, s_0, \rightarrow)$, we refer to the states of S as the *concrete states* of $v(\mathcal{A})$. A (concrete) *run* of $v(\mathcal{A})$ is a possibly infinite alternating sequence of concrete states of $v(\mathcal{A})$ and edges starting from s_0 of the form $s_0 \overset{e_0}{\longrightarrow} s_1 \overset{e_1}{\longrightarrow} \cdots \overset{e_{m-1}}{\longrightarrow} s_m \overset{e_m}{\longrightarrow} \cdots$, such that for all $i = 0, 1, \ldots, e_i \in \zeta$, and $(s_i, e_i, s_{i+1}) \in \rightarrow$.

Given a state $s = (l, w)$, we say that s is reachable (or that $v(\mathcal{A})$ reaches s) if s belongs to a run of $v(\mathcal{A})$. By extension, we say that l is reachable in $v(\mathcal{A})$, if there exists a state (l, w) that is reachable.

Throughout this paper, let K denote the largest constant in a given U2P-PTA, *i.e.*, the maximum of the largest constant compared to a clock in a guard and the largest upper bound of a parameter (if the U2P-PTA is bounded).

Let us recall the notion of clock region [1].

Definition 3 (clock region). *For two clock valuations* w *and* w', $\sim$ *is an equivalence relation defined by:* $w \sim w'$ *iff (i) for all clocks* x, *either* $\lfloor w(x) \rfloor = \lfloor w'(x) \rfloor$ *or* $w(x), w'(x) > K$; *(ii) for all clocks* x, y *with* $w(x), w(y) \leq K$, $frac(w(x)) \leq frac(w(y))$ *iff* $frac(w'(x)) \leq frac(w'(y))$; *(iii) for all clocks* x *with* $w(x) \leq K$, $frac(w(x)) = 0$ *iff* $frac(w'(x)) = 0$.
A clock region *is an equivalence class of* $\sim$.

Two clock valuations in the same clock region reach the same regions by time elapsing, satisfy the same guards and can take the same transitions [1].

In this paper, we address the *EF-emptiness* problem: **given a U2P-PTA** $\mathcal{A}$ **and a location** l, **is the set of parameter valuations** v **such that** l **is reachable in** $v(\mathcal{A})$ **empty?**

3   A Decidable Subclass of U2P-PTAs

We now impose that, whenever a guard or an update along an edge contains parameters, then all clocks must be updated (to constants or parameters). Our main contribution is to prove that this restriction makes EF-emptiness decidable.

Definition 4. *An* R-U2P-PTA *is a U2P-PTA where for any* $\langle l, g, a, u, l' \rangle \in \zeta$, u *is a total function whenever:*[1] *(i) g is a parametric guard, or (ii) $u(x) \in \mathbb{P}$ for some $x \in \mathbb{X}$.*

The main idea for proving decidability is the following: given an R-U2P-PTA $\mathcal{A}$ we will construct a finite region automaton that bisimulates $\mathcal{A}$, as in TA [1]. Our regions will contain both clocks and parameters, and will be a finite number. Since parameters are allowed in guards, we need to construct parameter regions and more restricted clock regions. We will define a form of Parametric Difference Bound Matrices (viz., p–PDBMs for precise PDBMs, inspired by [17]) in which, once valuated by a parameter valuation, two clock valuations have the same discrete behavior and satisfy the same non-parametric guards. A p–PDBM will define the *set of clocks and parameter valuations* that satisfies it, while once valuated by a parameter valuation, a valuated p–PDBM will define the *set of clock valuations* that satisfies it. A key point is that in our p–PDBMs the parametric constraints used in the matrix will be defined from a *finite* set of predefined expressions involving parameters and constants, and we will prove that this defines a finite number of p–PDBMs. Decidability will come from this fact. We define this set ($\mathcal{PLT}$ for parametric linear term) as follows: $\mathcal{PLT} = \{frac(p_i), 1 - frac(p_i), frac(p_i) - frac(p_j), frac(p_j) + 1 - frac(p_i), 1, 0, frac(p_i) - 1 - frac(p_j), -frac(p_i), frac(p_i) - 1\}$, for all $1 \leq i, j \leq M$. Given a parameter valuation v and $d \in \mathcal{PLT}$, we denote by $v(d)$ the term obtained by replacing in d each parameter p by $v(p)$. Let us now define an equivalence relation between parameter valuations v and v'.

Definition 5 (regions of parameters). *We write that $v \frown v'$ if (i) for all parameter p, $\lfloor v(p) \rfloor = \lfloor v'(p) \rfloor$; (ii) for all $d_1, d_2, d_3 \in \mathcal{PLT}$, $v(d_1) \leq v(d_2) + v(d_3)$ iff $v'(d_1) \leq v'(d_2) + v'(d_3)$;*

Parameter regions are defined as the equivalence classes of $\frown$. The definition is in a way similar to [1, Definition 4.3] but also involves comparisons of sums of elements of $\mathcal{PLT}$. In fact, we will need this kind of comparisons to define our p–PDBMs. Nonetheless we do not need more complicated comparisons as in R-U2P-PTA whenever a parametric guard or update is met the update is a total function: this preserves us from the parameter accumulation, *e.g.*, obtaining expressions of the form $5frac(p_i) - 1 - 3frac(p_j)$ (that may occur in usual PTAs).

In the following, our p–PDBMs will contain pairs of the form $D = (d, \lhd)$, where $d \in \mathcal{PLT}$. We therefore need to define comparisons on these pairs.

We define an associative and commutative operator $\oplus$ as $\lhd_1 \oplus \lhd_2 = <$ if $\lhd_1 \neq \lhd_2$, or $\lhd_1$ if $\lhd_1 = \lhd_2$. We define $D_1 + D_2 = (d_1 + d_2, \lhd_1 \oplus \lhd_2)$. Following the idea of parameter regions, we define the *validity* of a comparison between pairs

---

[1] In the following we only consider either non-parametric, or (necessarily total) fully parametric update functions. A total update function which is not fully parametric (*i.e.*, an update of some clocks to parameters and all others to constants) can be encoded as a total fully parametric update immediately followed by a (partial) non-parametric update function.

of the form $(d_i, \lessdot_i)$ within a given parameter region, *i.e.*, whether the comparison is *true* for all parameter valuations v in the parameter region R_p.

Definition 6 (validity of comparison). *Let R_p be a parameter region. Given any two linear terms d_1, d_2 over $\mathbb{P}$ (i.e., of the form $\sum_i \alpha_i p_i + d$ with $\alpha_i, d \in \mathbb{Z}$), the comparison $(d_1, \lessdot_1) \lessdot (d_2, \lessdot_2)$ is valid for R_p if:*

1. *$\lessdot = <$, and either (i) for all $v \in R_p$, $v(d_1) < v(d_2)$ evaluates to true, or (ii) for all $v \in R_p$, $v(d_1) \leq v(d_2)$ evaluates to true, $\lessdot_1 = <$ and $\lessdot_2 = \leq$;*
2. *$\lessdot = \leq$, and either (i) for all $v \in R_p$, $v(d_1) < v(d_2)$ evaluates to true, or (ii) for all $v \in R_p$, $v(d_1) \leq v(d_2)$ evaluates to true, and $\lessdot_1 = \lessdot_2$, or $\lessdot_1 = <$;*

Transitivity is immediate from the definition: if $D_1 \lessdot_1 D_2$ and $D_2 \lessdot_2 D_3$ are valid for R_p, $D_1(\lessdot_1 \oplus \lessdot_2) D_3$ is valid for R_p.

We can now define our data structure, namely p–PDBMs, inspired by the PDBMs of [17] themselves inspired by DBMs [14]. However, our p–PDBM compare differences of *fractional parts* of clocks, instead of clocks as in classical DBMs; therefore, our p–PDBMs are closer to clock regions than to DBMs and *fully contained* into clock regions of [1] A p–PDBM is a pair made of an integer vector (encoding the clocks integer part), and a matrix (encoding the parametric differences between any two clock fractional parts). Their interpretation also follows that of PDBMs and DBMs: for $i \neq 0$, the matrix cell $D_{i,0} = (d_{i,0}, \lessdot_{i0})$ is interpreted as the constraint $frac(x_i) \lessdot_{i0} d_{i,0}$, and $D_{0,i} = (d_{0,i}, \lessdot_{0i})$ as the constraint $-frac(x_i) \lessdot_{0i} d_{0,i}$. For $i \neq 0$ and $j \neq 0$, the matrix cell $D_{i,j} = (d_{i,j}, \lessdot_{ij})$ is interpreted as $frac(x_i) - frac(x_j) \lessdot_{ij} d_{i,j}$.

Definition 7 (p–PDBM). *Let R_p be a parameter region. A p–PDBM for R_p is a pair (E, D) with $E = (E_1, \cdots, E_H)$ a vector of H integers (or ∞ when it exceeds a possible upper-bound) which is the integer part of each clock, and D is an $(H + 1)^2$ matrix where each element $D_{i,j}$ is a pair $(d_{i,j}, \lessdot_{ij})$ for all $0 \leq i, j \leq H$, where $d_{i,j} \in \mathcal{PLT}$. Moreover, for all $0 \leq i \leq H$, $D_{i,i} = (0, \leq)$. In addition, for all i, j, k:*

1. *$(-1, <) \leq D_{0,i} \leq (0, \leq)$ and $(0, \leq) \leq D_{i,0} \leq (1, <)$ are valid for R_p,*
2. *For all $i \neq 0, j \neq 0$, either $(0, \leq) \leq D_{i,j} \leq (1, <)$ is valid for R_p and $(-1, <) \leq D_{j,i} \leq (0, \leq)$ is valid for R_p or $(0, \leq) \leq D_{j,i} \leq (1, <)$ is valid for R_p and $(-1, <) \leq D_{i,j} \leq (0, \leq)$ is valid for R_p.*
3. *$D_{i,j} \leq D_{i,k} + D_{k,j}$ is valid for R_p (canonical form).*
4. *If $d_{i,j} = -d_{j,i}$ and $d_{i,j} \neq \pm 1$ then $\lessdot_{ij} = \lessdot_{ji} = \leq$, else $\lessdot_{ij} = \lessdot_{ji} = <$,*

The use of *validity* ensures the consistency of the p–PDBM. We denote the set of all p–PDBMs that are *valid for R_p* by $p\text{-}\mathcal{PDBM}(R_p)$. Given a p–PDBM (E, D), it defines the subset of $\mathbb{R}^H \cup \mathbb{Q}^M$ satisfying the constraints $\bigwedge_{i,j \in [0,H]} frac(x_i) - frac(x_j) \lessdot_{i,j} d_{i,j} \wedge \bigwedge_{i \in [1,H]} \lfloor x_i \rfloor = E_i$.

Given a parameter valuation v, we denote by $(E, v(D))$ the *valuated p–PDBM*, *i.e.*, the set of clock valuations defined by:

$$\bigwedge_{i,j \in [0,H]} frac(x_i) - frac(x_j) \lessdot_{i,j} v(d_{i,j}) \wedge \bigwedge_{i \in [1,H]} \lfloor x_i \rfloor = E_i.$$

For a clock valuation w, we write $w \in (E, v(D))$ if it satisfies all constraints of $(E, v(D))$. Intuitively, our p–PDBMs are partitioned into three types.

(1) The *point* p–*PDBM* is a clock region defined by *only parameters* which contains only one clock valuation; it represents the unique clock valuation (for a given parameter valuation) obtained after a total parametric update in an U2P-PTA. Each clock is valuated to a parameter and each difference of clocks is valuated to a difference of parameters (it corresponds to constraints of the form $x = p$ and $x - y = p_i - p_j$).

Let v be a parameter valuation. We assume $\lfloor v(p_2) \rfloor = \lfloor v(p_1) \rfloor = k \in \mathbb{N}$ and $frac(v(p_1)) > frac(v(p_2))$. The p–PDBM obtained after an update $u(x) = v(p_2)$ and $u(y) = v(p_1)$ is represented using the following pair (where the indices $\mathbf{0}, \mathbf{x}, \mathbf{y}$ are shown for the sake of comprehension)

$$(E, D) = \left(\begin{pmatrix} k \\ k \end{pmatrix}, \begin{pmatrix} & \mathbf{0} & \mathbf{x} & \mathbf{y} \\ \mathbf{0} & (0, \leq) & (-frac(p_2), \leq) & (-frac(p_1), \leq) \\ \mathbf{x} & (frac(p_2), \leq) & (0, \leq) & (frac(p_2) - frac(p_1), \leq) \\ \mathbf{y} & (frac(p_1), \leq) & (frac(p_1) - frac(p_2), \leq) & (0, \leq) \end{pmatrix} \right)$$

Once valuated with v, it contains a unique clock valuation. We represent it as the black dot in Fig. 2.

(2) In contrast, a *border* p–*PDBM* is a clock region which can contain several clock valuations satisfying some possibly parametric constraints, or contain at least one clock valuation satisfying non-parametric constraints (as the corner-point region of [1]). In particular, the initial clock region $\{0^H\}$ and any clock region that is a single integer clock valuation is a p–PDBM. A *border* p–*PDBM* is characterized by at least one clock x

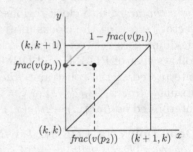

Fig. 2. Graphical representations of p–PDBMs and [1] regions (Color figure online)

s.t. $D_{x,0} = D_{0,x} = (0, \leq)$ and can be seen as a subregion of an open line segment or a corner point region of [1, Fig. 9 Example 4.4]. After an immediate update of x to k, the above p–PDBM (E, D) becomes

$$(E, D) = \left(\begin{pmatrix} k \\ k \end{pmatrix}, \begin{pmatrix} & \mathbf{0} & \mathbf{x} & \mathbf{y} \\ \mathbf{0} & (0, \leq) & (0, \leq) & (-frac(p_1), \leq) \\ \mathbf{x} & (0, \leq) & (0, \leq) & (-frac(p_1), \leq) \\ \mathbf{y} & (frac(p_1), \leq) & (frac(p_1), \leq) & (0, \leq) \end{pmatrix} \right)$$

We represent it once valuated with v as the blue dot in Fig. 2. The open line segment of [1, Fig. 9 example 4.4] can be represented as

$$\left(\begin{pmatrix} k \\ k \end{pmatrix}, \begin{pmatrix} & \mathbf{0} & \mathbf{x} & \mathbf{y} \\ \mathbf{0} & (0, \leq) & (0, \leq) & (0, <) \\ \mathbf{x} & (0, \leq) & (0, \leq) & (0, <) \\ \mathbf{y} & (1, <) & (1, <) & (0, \leq) \end{pmatrix} \right)$$

and is depicted as the vertical left black line in Fig. 2.

(3) A *center* p–*PDBM* is a clock region which can contain several clock valuations satisfying some possibly parametric constraints (as the open region of [1]). A *center* p–*PDBM* is characterized by at least one clock y s.t. $D_{y,0} =$

$(1, <)$ and for all x s.t. $D_{0,x} = (0, \lhd_{ox})$, then we have $\lhd_{ox} = \;<$ and can be seen as a subregion of an open region of [1, Fig. 9 Example 4.4]. After some time elapsing, and *before* any clock valuation reaches the next integer $k+1$—therefore the next *border* p–*PDBM*—, the above p–PDBM (E, D) becomes

$$(E, D) = \left(\begin{pmatrix} k \\ k \end{pmatrix}, \begin{pmatrix} & \mathbf{0} & \mathbf{x} & \mathbf{y} \\ \mathbf{0} & (0, \leq) & (0, <) & (-frac(p_1), <) \\ \mathbf{x} & (1 - frac(p_1), <) & (0, \leq) & (-frac(p_1), \leq) \\ \mathbf{y} & (1, <) & (frac(p_1), \leq) & (0, \leq) \end{pmatrix} \right)$$

We represent it once valuated with v as the red line in Fig. 2. The open region of [1, Fig. 9 Example 4.4] can be represented as

$$\left(\begin{pmatrix} k \\ k \end{pmatrix}, \begin{pmatrix} & \mathbf{0} & \mathbf{x} & \mathbf{y} \\ \mathbf{0} & (0, \leq) & (0, <) & (0, <) \\ \mathbf{x} & (1, <) & (0, \leq) & (0, <) \\ \mathbf{y} & (1, <) & (1, <) & (0, \leq) \end{pmatrix} \right)$$

and is depicted as the top left black triangle in Fig. 2.

Remark that sets of the form $\{ frac(w(x)) \mid 0 \leq frac(w(x)) \leq 1 \}$ are in contradiction with Definition 7 (4) and therefore cannot be part of a p–PDBM, as in the regions of [1]. Basically, only the first p–PDBM after a (necessarily total) parametric clock update will be a *point* p–*PDBM*; any following p–PDBM will be a *border* p–*PDBM* or a *center* p–*PDBM* until the next (total) parametric update.

The differentiation made in the previous paragraph between *border* p–*PDBM* and *center* p–*PDBM* is intended to give an intuition to the reader about the inclusion of p–PDBMs into [1] clock regions. Technical details are not relevant for a good understanding of this paper but are given in [6].

In the following Sect. 3.1, we are going to define operations on p–PDBMs (*i.e.*, update of clocks, time elapsing and guards satisfaction), and will show that the set of p–PDBMs is stable under these operations.

3.1 Operations on p–PDBMs

Non-parametric Update. To apply a non-parametric update on a p–PDBM, following classical algorithms for DBMs [9], we define an update operator.

Given a p–PDBM (E, D) and u_{np} a non-parametric update function that updates a clock x to $k \in \mathbb{N}$, $update((E, D), u_{np})$ defines a new p–PDBM by *(i)* updating E_x to k; *(ii)* setting the fractional part of x to 0: $D_{x,0} := D_{0,x} := (0, \leq)$; *(iii)* updating the new difference between fractional parts with all other clocks i, which is the range of values i can currently take: $D_{x,i} := D_{0,i}$ and $D_{i,x} := D_{i,0}$.

Intuitively, we update in (E, D) the lower and upper bounds of some clocks to $(0, \leq)$ and the difference between two clocks $D_{i,j}$ to $D_{0,j}$ if x_i is updated: that is, the new difference between two clocks if one has been updated is just the lower/upper bound of the one that is not updated. This allows us to conserve the canonical form as we only "moved" some cells in D that already verified the canonical form. Therefore $update((E, D), u_{np})$ is a p–PDBM.

The following lemma states that the update operator behaves as expected.

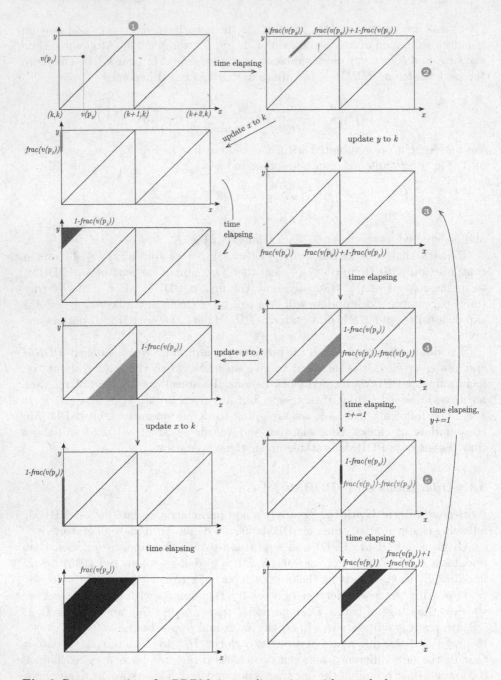

Fig. 3. Representation of p–PDBMs in two dimensions with two clocks x, y, two parameters p_1, p_2 and v s.t. $\lfloor v(p_1) \rfloor = \lfloor v(p_2) \rfloor$ and $frac(v(p_1)) > frac(v(p_2))$.

Lemma 1 (semantics of *update* on p-$\mathcal{PDBM}(R_p)$). *Let R_p be a parameter region and $(E, D) \in p$-$\mathcal{PDBM}(R_p)$. Let $v \in R_p$. Let u_{np} be a non-parametric update. For all clock valuations w, $w \in update((E, v(D)), u_{np})$ iff $w' \in (E, v(D))$ for some w' s.t. $w = [w']_{u_{np}}$.*

Proof idea. The technical part is ($\Rightarrow$). The idea is to prove that, given $w' \in update((E, v(D)), u_{np})$ there is a non-empty set of clock valuations w s.t. $w' = [w]_{u_{np}}$ that is precisely defined by the constraints in $(E, v(D))$.

Parametric Update. Given $(E, D) \in p$-$\mathcal{PDBM}(R_p)$ we write $\overline{update}((E, D), u)$ to denote the update of (E, D) by u, when u is a total parametric update function, *i.e.,* updating the set of clocks exclusively to parameters. We therefore obtain a *point* p-PDBM, containing the parametric set of constraints defining a unique clock valuation. The semantics is straightforward.

Time Elapsing. Given a parameter region R_p, recall that constraints satisfied by parameters are known, and we can order elements of $\mathcal{PLT}$. Thanks to this order, within a p-PDBM (E, D) the clocks with the (possibly parametric) largest fractional part *i.e.,* the clocks that have a larger fractional part than any other clock, can always be identified by their bounds in D. For a p-PDBM (E, D), we define the set of clocks with the largest fractional part (LFP) as $\mathsf{LFP}_{R_p}(D) = \{x \in [1, H] \mid 0 \le D_{x,i}$ is valid for R_p, for all $0 \le i \le H\}$. Clocks belonging to LFP are the first to reach the upper bound 1 by letting time elapse.

Note that several clocks may have the largest fractional parts (up to some syntactic replacements , in that case they satisfy the same constraints in (E, D)).

Let $(E, D) \in p$-$\mathcal{PDBM}(R_p)$ and $x \in \mathsf{LFP}_{R_p}(D)$. To formalize time elapsing until the largest fractional part $frac(x)$ reaches 1, we define a time elapsing operator that will decline in two variants depending on the input: *border* p-PDBM or *center/point* p-PDBM.

Given a *border* p-PDBM (E, D) with $E_x = k$, $TE((E, D))$ defines a new *center* p-PDBM by *(i)* setting $D_{x,0} := (1, <)$ as x is the first one that will reach $k + 1$; *(ii)* updating the upper bound of all other clocks i, which has increased: $D_{i,0} := D_{i,x} + (1, <)$; *(iii)* updating all lower bounds as they have to leave the *border*: $D_{0,i} := D_{0,i} + (0, <)$ (x included). This gives the range of possible clock valuations *before* $frac(x)$ reaches 1. Intuitively it represents the transformation from an open line segment or the corner-point region of [1] into an open region of [1].

The time elapsing operator also operates the transformation from an open region of [1] to the upper open line segment or the corner-point region of [1]. Given a *center/point* p-PDBM (E, D) where $E_x = k$, $TE((E, D))$ defines a new *border* p-PDBM by *(i)* setting $D_{x,0} := D_{0,x} - (0, \le)$ (Intuitively both became $(1, \le)$) and $E_x = k + 1$ (if $E_x \le K + 1$), as x is now in the upper *border*; *(ii)* updating the upper and lower bounds of all other clocks i: $D_{i,0} := D_{i,x} + (1, \le)$ and $D_{0,i} := D_{x,i} + (-1, \le)$; *(iii)* updating the new difference between fractional parts with all other clocks i, which is the range of values i can currently take (as in the update operator): $D_{x,i} := D_{0,i}$ and $D_{i,x} := D_{i,0}$.

Although we perform some additions such as $D_{j,i} + (1, <)$, we do not create new expressions that are not in $\mathcal{PLT}$. In fact, this addition is performed on a negative term (*e.g.*, $frac(p) - 1$), as x_i is a clock with the largest fractional part and adding 1 transforms it into another term of $\mathcal{PLT}$. The intuition is similar when performing additions such as $D_{i,j} + (-1, \leq)$: as x_i is a clock with the largest fractional part, $d_{i,j}$ is a positive term. The canonical form is also preserved by the last setting operations of the algorithm, as in the update operator. Therefore $TE((E, D))$ is a p–PDBM.

Proposition 1 (semantics of p–*PDBM* under *TE*). *Let R_p be a parameter region and $(E, D) \in$ p–$\mathcal{PDBM}(R_p)$. Let $v \in R_p$. There exists $w' \in TE((E, v(D)))$ iff there exist $w \in (E, v(D))$ and a delay δ s.t. $w' = w + \delta$.*

Proof idea. This proof is quite technical. Intuitively, we bound the difference of each upper bound $v(d_{i,0})$ and $w(x_i)$ and each lower bound $v(d_{0,i})$ and $w(x_i)$. This allows us to take a delay δ inside these bounds that allows us to reach the next p–PDBM.

Running example: Figure 3 represents graphically different p–PDBMs obtained after an update $u(x) = v(p_2)$ and $u(y) = v(p_1)$ (figure 1). Time elapsing before $y \in$ LFP reaches the next integer gives the *center* p–PDBM (figure 2)

$$(E, D) = \left(\begin{pmatrix} k \\ k \end{pmatrix}, \begin{pmatrix} & \mathbf{0} & \mathbf{x} & \mathbf{y} \\ \mathbf{0} & (0, \leq) & (-frac(p_2), <) & (-frac(p_1), <) \\ \mathbf{x} & (frac(p_2) + 1 - frac(p_1), <) & (0, \leq) & (-frac(p_1) + frac(p_2), \leq) \\ \mathbf{y} & (1, <) & (frac(p_1) - frac(p_2), \leq) & (0, \leq) \end{pmatrix} \right)$$

After an update of y to k prior to reaching $k + 1$, the *border* p–PDBM obtained is (figure 3)

$$(E, D) = \left(\begin{pmatrix} k \\ k \end{pmatrix}, \begin{pmatrix} & \mathbf{0} & \mathbf{x} & \mathbf{y} \\ \mathbf{0} & (0, \leq) & (-frac(p_2), <) & (0, \leq) \\ \mathbf{x} & (frac(p_2) + 1 - frac(p_1), <) & (0, \leq) & (frac(p_2) + 1 - frac(p_1), <) \\ \mathbf{y} & (0, \leq) & (-frac(p_2), <) & (0, \leq) \end{pmatrix} \right)$$

Time elapsing before $x \in$ LFP reaches the next integer gives the *center* p–PDBM (figure 4)

$$(E, D) = \left(\begin{pmatrix} k \\ k \end{pmatrix}, \begin{pmatrix} & \mathbf{0} & \mathbf{x} & \mathbf{y} \\ \mathbf{0} & (0, \leq) & (-frac(p_2), <) & (0, <) \\ \mathbf{x} & (1, <) & (0, \leq) & (frac(p_2) + 1 - frac(p_1), <) \\ \mathbf{y} & (1 - frac(p_2), <) & (-frac(p_2), <) & (0, \leq) \end{pmatrix} \right)$$

When $x \in$ LFP reaches $k + 1$, the *border* p–PDBM obtained is (figure 5)

$$(E, D) = \left(\begin{pmatrix} k + 1 \\ k \end{pmatrix}, \begin{pmatrix} & \mathbf{0} & \mathbf{x} & \mathbf{y} \\ \mathbf{0} & (0, \leq) & (0, \leq) & (-frac(p_1) + frac(p_2), <) \\ \mathbf{x} & (0, \leq) & (0, \leq) & (-frac(p_1) + frac(p_2), <) \\ \mathbf{y} & (1 - frac(p_2), <) & (1 - frac(p_2), <) & (0, \leq) \end{pmatrix} \right)$$

Non-parametric Guard. From [1, Sect. 4.2] we have that either every clock valuation of a clock region satisfies a guard, or none of them does. Note that a p–PDBM for R_p is contained into a clock region of [1, Section 4.2], therefore we have that if $w \in (E, v(D))$ satisfies a non-parametric guard g, then for all $w' \in (E, v(D))$ we also have w' satisfies g.

Let $v \in R_p$. We define $v \in guard_\forall(g, E, D)$ iff for all $w \in (E, v(D))$, $w \models g$. As any two $v, v' \in R_p$ satisfy the same constraints, it is straightforward that if $v \in guard_\forall(g, E, D)$, then for all $v' \in R_p$, $v' \in guard_\forall(g, E, D)$.

Parametric Guard. Using a projection on parameters does not create new constraints on parameters that are not already in a parameter region R_p. Indeed, a parametric guard g only adds new constraints of the form $x \bowtie p$ which gives again a comparison between elements of $\mathcal{PLT}$. Therefore, these new constraints already belong to $\mathcal{PLT}$ and we can decide whether the set of clock valuations satisfying this set of constraints is non-empty *i.e.*, given $v \in R_p$, $v(g)$ is satisfied by some clock valuation $w \in (E, v(D))$. This is a key point in the overall process of proving the decidability of our R-U2P-PTAs. Note that there will also be additional constraints involving clocks (with other clocks, constants or parameters), but they will not be relevant as we immediately update all clocks, therefore replacing these constraints with new constraints encoding the clock updates.

Let $v \in R_p$. We define $v \in p\text{-}guard_\exists(g, E, D)$ iff there is a $w \in (E, v(D))$ s.t. $w \models v(g)$.[2] Again, as any two $v, v' \in R_p$ satisfy the same constraints, it is straightforward that if $v \in p\text{-}guard_\exists(g, E, D)$, then for all $v' \in R_p$, $v' \in p\text{-}guard_\exists(g, E, D)$.

Now that we have defined useful operations on p–PDBMs, we are going, given a parameter region R_p, to construct a finite region automaton in which for any run, there is an equivalent concrete run in the R-U2P-PTA.

3.2   Parametric Region Automaton

Let $(E, D) \in p\text{-}\mathcal{PDBM}(R_p)$, we say $(E', D') \in \mathsf{Succ}((E, D)) \Leftrightarrow \exists\, i \geq 0$ s.t. $(E', v(D')) = TE^i((E, D))$. In other words, (E', D') is obtained after applying $TE((E, D))$ a finite number of times. $\mathsf{Succ}((E, D))$ is also called the *time successors* of (E, D).

In order to finitely simulate an R-U2P-PTA, we create a parametric region automaton.

Definition 8 (Parametric region automaton). *Let R_p be a parameter region. For an R-U2P-PTA $\mathcal{A} = (\Sigma, L, l_0, \mathbb{X}, \mathbb{P}, \zeta)$, given (E_0, D_0) the initial p–PDBM where all clocks are 0, the parametric region automaton $\mathcal{R}(\mathcal{A})$ over R_p is the tuple $(L', \Sigma, L'_0, \zeta')$ where: (i) $L' = L \times p\text{-}\mathcal{PDBM}(R_p)$ (ii)*

---

[2] Remark that here is why our construction works for EF-emptiness, but cannot be used for, *e.g.*, AF-emptiness ("is there a parameter valuation such that all runs reach a goal location l"): unlike $guard_\forall(g, E, D)$, not all clock valuations in a p–PDBM $(E, v(D))$ can satisfy a parametric guard if $v \in p\text{-}guard_\exists(g, E, D)$.

$L'_0 = (l_0, (E_0, D_0))$ (iii) $\zeta' = \{((l, (E, D)), e, (l', (E', D')) \in L' \times \zeta \times L' \mid$
either $\exists e = \langle l, g, a, u_{np}, l' \rangle \in \zeta$, g is a non-parametric guard, $\exists (E'', D'') \in$
$\mathsf{Succ}((E, D))$, $R_p \subseteq guard_\forall(g, (E'', D''))$ and $(E', D') = update(E'', D'', u_{np})$,
or $\exists e = \langle l, g, a, u, l' \rangle \in \zeta$, g is a parametric guard, $\exists (E'', D'') \in \mathsf{Succ}((E, D))$,
$R_p \subseteq p\text{-}guard_\exists(g, (E'', D''))$ and $(E', D') = \overline{update}(E'', D'', u).\}$

Let R_p be a parameter region, $\mathcal{A}$ be an R-U2P-PTA and $\mathcal{R}(\mathcal{A}) = (L', \Sigma, L'_0, \zeta')$.
A run in $\mathcal{R}(\mathcal{A})$ is an untimed sequence
$\sigma : (l_0, (E_0, D_0)) e_0 (l_1, (E_1, D_1)) e_1 \cdots (l_i, (E_i, D_i)) e_i (l_{i+1}, (E_{i+1}, D_{i+1})) e_{i+1} \cdots$
such that for all i we have $((l_i, (E_i, D_i)), e_i, (l_{i+1}, (E_{i+1}, D_{i+1}))) \in \zeta'$, which
we also write $(l_i, (E_i, D_i)) \xrightarrow{e_i} (l_{i+1}, (E_{i+1}, D_{i+1}))$ where e_i. Note that we label
our transitions with the edges of the R-U2P-PTA.

3.3 Decidability of EF-emptiness and Synthesis

Using our construction of the parametric region automaton $\mathcal{R}(\mathcal{A})$ for a given
R-U2P-PTA $\mathcal{A}$, we state the next proposition.

Proposition 2. *Let R_p be a parameter region. Let $\mathcal{A}$ be an R-U2P-PTA
and $\mathcal{R}(\mathcal{A})$ its parametric region automaton over R_p. There is a run σ :
$(l_0, (E_0, D_0)) \xrightarrow{e_0} (l_1, (E_1, D_1)) \xrightarrow{e_1} \cdots (l_{f-1}, (E_{f-1}, D_{f-1})) \xrightarrow{e_{f-1}} (l_f, (E_f, D_f))$
in $\mathcal{R}(\mathcal{A})$ iff for all $v \in R_p$ there is a run $\rho : (l_0, w_0) \xrightarrow{e_0} (l_1, w_1) \xrightarrow{e_1}$
$\cdots (l_{f-1}, w_{f-1}) \xrightarrow{e_{f-1}} (l_f, w_f)$ in $v(\mathcal{A})$ s.t. for all $0 \le i \le f$, $w_i \in (E_i, v(D_i))$.*

From Proposition 2, if there is a run reaching a goal location in an instantiated
R-U2P-PTA, then for another parameter valuation in the same parameter region
there is a run in the instantiated R-U2P-PTA with the same locations and
transitions (but possibly different delays), reaching the same location.

Theorem 1. *Let $\mathcal{A}$ be an R-U2P-PTA. Let R_p be a parameter region and $v \in
R_p$. If there is a run $\rho = (l_0, w_0) \xrightarrow{e_0} \cdots \xrightarrow{e_{i-1}} (l_i, w_i)$ in $v(\mathcal{A})$, then for all
$v' \in R_p$ there is a run $\rho' = (l_0, w'_0) \xrightarrow{e_0} \cdots \xrightarrow{e_{i-1}} (l_i, w'_i)$ in $v'(\mathcal{A})$ with for all i,
there is $(E_i, D_i) \in p\text{-}\mathcal{PDBM}(R_p)$ s.t. $w_i \in (E_i, v(D_i))$ and $w'_i \in (E_i, v'(D_i))$.*

Note that there is a finite number of p–PDBMs for each parameter region R_p.
Let $(E, D) \in p\text{-}\mathcal{PDBM}(R_p)$ and consider $\mathcal{PLT}$: D is an $(H+1)^2$ matrix made of
pairs $(d, \triangleleft)$ where $d \in \mathcal{PLT}$ and $\triangleleft \in \{\le, <\}$. Therefore the number of possible D
is bounded by $(2 \times (2 + 3 \times \binom{M}{2} + 4 \times M))^{(H+1)^2}$. Moreover the number of
possible values for E is unbounded, but only a finite subset of all values needs
to be explored, *i.e.*, those smaller than $K + 1$: indeed, following classical works
on timed automata [1,10], (integer) values exceeding the largest constant used
in the guards or the parameter bounds are equivalent.

To test EF-emptiness given a bounded R-U2P-PTA $\mathcal{A}$ and a goal location l,
we first enumerate all parameter regions (which are in finite number), and apply

for each R_p the following process: we pick $v \in R_p$ (*e.g.*, using a linear programming algorithm [19]). Then, we consider $v(\mathcal{A})$ which is an updatable timed automaton and test the reachability of l in $v(\mathcal{A})$ [10]. Then EF-emptiness is false if and only if there is v and a run in $v(\mathcal{A})$ reaching l.

Theorem 2. *The EF-emptiness problem is PSPACE-complete for bounded R-U2P-PTAs.*

Given a goal location l and a bounded R-U2P-PTA $\mathcal{A}$, we can exactly synthesize the parameter valuations v s.t. there is a run in $v(\mathcal{A})$ reaching l by enumerating each parameter region (of which there is a finite number) and test if l is reachable for one of its parameter valuations. The result of the synthesis is the union of the parameter regions for which one valuation (and, from our results, all valuations in that region) indeed reaches the goal location in the instantiated TA.

Corollary 1. *Given a bounded R-U2P-PTA $\mathcal{A}$ and a goal location l we can effectively compute the set of parameter valuations v s.t. there is a run in $v(\mathcal{A})$ reaching l.*

Remark 1. By bounding parameter valuations in guards but not those used in updates, we still have a finite number of parameter regions. Indeed, an integer vector E with components E_x greater than $\lfloor K \rfloor + 1$ is equivalent to an integer vector E' with $E'_x = E_x$ if $E_x < \lfloor K \rfloor + 1$ and $E'_x = \lfloor K \rfloor + 1$ if $E_x \geq \lfloor K \rfloor + 1$. Moreover for all p, we have to replace each parameter valuation v used in an update by $v(p) = v'(p)$ if $v(p) \leq K$ and $v'(p) = K + 1$ if $v(p) > K$.

4   Case Study

We implemented EFsynth for R-U2P-PTAs in IMITATOR, a parametric model checker for (extensions of) PTAs [3].

Our class is the first for which synthesis is possible over bounded rational parameters. We believe our formalism is useful to model several categories of case studies, notably distributed systems with a periodic (global) behavior for which the period is unknown: this can be encoded using a parametric guard while resetting all clocks—possibly to other parameters.

Consider the R-U2P-PTA in Fig. 1 with six locations, three clocks compared to parameters (x, y, t), one constant (max) and six parameters $(p, p_1, p_2, v, pv_1, pv_2)$.

We consider the case of a network of peers exchanging transactions grouped by blocks, *e.g.*, a blockchain, using the Proof-of-Work as a mean to validate new blocks to add. In this simplified example, we consider a set of two peers (represented by x, y) which have different computation power (represented by p_1, p_2). Peers write new transactions on the current block (newTx). If it is full ($t = p$), both peers try to add a new block (newBlock) to write the transaction on it. We update x to p_1, y to p_2, and t to 0 as the peers have a different computation power, and they start "mining" the block (find a solution to a computation problem). Either x or y will eventually offer a solution to the problem (blockSolution$_x$ if $x = max$ or blockSolution$_y$ if $y = max$). If y offers a solution, x will check whether the solution is correct: x is updated to pv_1 to represent its rapidity to verify an offer. x can refuse the offer if the verification is too long (fakeBlock if $x > v$) therefore the mining step restarts. x can approve the offer (okBlock if $x \leq v$), y is rewarded and the block is added to the blockchain (addBlock).

We are interested in a malicious peer x that wants to avoid y to be rewarded for every new block. Therefore x asks: *"what are the possible computation power configurations and verification rapidity so that y is eventually rewarded"* (EF(reward$_y$)-synthesis), considered as a bug state in the automaton.

We run this R-U2P-PTA using IMITATOR [3]. We set $max = 30$ units of time and also the upper bound of p and $1 \geq v > 0$ unit of time. IMITATOR computes a disjunction of constraints so that reward$_y$ is unreachable: we keep two relevant ones; *(i)* $p_1 \geq p_2$: x has strictly more computation power than y in which case x always offers a block solution, or has the same computation power than y in which case the systems blocks. x should invest heavily into hardware to keep its computation power high; *(ii)* $pv_1 > v$: the malicious peer x is always faster to verify the solution offered by y and refuses it. The blockchain is probably compromised.

Using a parameter valuation respecting one of the previous constraints guarantees that y is never rewarded.

5   Conclusion and Perspectives

Our class of bounded R-U2P-PTAs is one of the few subclasses of PTAs (actually even extended with parametric updates) to enjoy decidability of EF-emptiness. In addition, R-U2P-PTAs is the first "subclass" of PTAs to allow exact synthesis of bounded *rational*-valued parameters.

Beyond reachability emptiness, we aim at studying unavoidability-emptiness and language preservation emptiness, as well as their synthesis.

Finally, we would like to investigate whether our parametric updates can be applied to decidable hybrid extensions of TAs [12, 16].

Acknowledgements. We would like to thank anonymous reviewers for constructive remarks.

References

1. Alur, R., Dill, D.L.: A theory of timed automata. Theor. Comput. Sci. **126**(2), 183–235 (1994). https://doi.org/10.1016/0304-3975(94)90010-8
2. Alur, R., Henzinger, T.A., Vardi, M.Y.: Parametric real-time reasoning. In: STOC, pp. 592–601. ACM (1993).https://doi.org/10.1145/167088.167242

3. André, É., Fribourg, L., Kühne, U., Soulat, R.: IMITATOR 2.5: a tool for analyzing robustness in scheduling problems. In: Giannakopoulou, D., Méry, D. (eds.) FM 2012. LNCS, vol. 7436, pp. 33–36. Springer, Heidelberg (2012). https://doi.org/10.1007/978-3-642-32759-9_6, http://www.lsv.fr/Publis/PAPERS/PDF/AFKS-fm12.pdf

4. André, É., Lime, D.: Liveness in L/U-parametric timed automata. In: ACSD, pp. 9–18. IEEE (2017). https://doi.org/10.1109/ACSD.2017.19

5. André, É., Lime, D., Ramparison, M.: Timed automata with parametric updates. In: Juhás, G., Chatain, T., Grosu, R. (eds.) ACSD, pp. 21–29. IEEE (2018, to appear). https://doi.org/10.1109/ACSD.2018.000-2

6. André, É., Lime, D., Ramparison, M.: Parametric updates in parametric timed automata (full version) (2019). https://lipn.univ-paris13.fr/~ramparison/articles/ResetPTAfull.pdf

7. André, É., Lime, D., Roux, O.H.: Decision problems for parametric timed automata. In: Ogata, K., Lawford, M., Liu, S. (eds.) ICFEM 2016. LNCS, vol. 10009, pp. 400–416. Springer, Cham (2016). https://doi.org/10.1007/978-3-319-47846-3_25

8. Beneš, N., Bezděk, P., Larsen, K.G., Srba, J.: Language emptiness of continuous-time parametric timed automata. In: Halldórsson, M.M., Iwama, K., Kobayashi, N., Speckmann, B. (eds.) ICALP 2015. LNCS, vol. 9135, pp. 69–81. Springer, Heidelberg (2015). https://doi.org/10.1007/978-3-662-47666-6_6

9. Bengtsson, J., Yi, W.: Timed automata: semantics, algorithms and tools. In: Desel, J., Reisig, W., Rozenberg, G. (eds.) ACPN 2003. LNCS, vol. 3098, pp. 87–124. Springer, Heidelberg (2004). https://doi.org/10.1007/978-3-540-27755-2_3

10. Bouyer, P., Dufourd, C., Fleury, E., Petit, A.: Updatable timed automata. Theor. Comput. Sci. **321**(2–3), 291–345 (2004). https://doi.org/10.1016/j.tcs.2004.04.003

11. Bozzelli, L., La Torre, S.: Decision problems for lower/upper bound parametric timed automata. Formal Methods Syst. Des. **35**(2), 121–151 (2009). https://doi.org/10.1007/s10703-009-0074-0

12. Brihaye, T., Doyen, L., Geeraerts, G., Ouaknine, J., Raskin, J.-F., Worrell, J.: Time-bounded reachability for monotonic hybrid automata: complexity and fixed points. In: Van Hung, D., Ogawa, M. (eds.) ATVA 2013. LNCS, vol. 8172, pp. 55–70. Springer, Cham (2013). https://doi.org/10.1007/978-3-319-02444-8_6

13. Bundala, D., Ouaknine, J.: Advances in parametric real-time reasoning. In: Csuhaj-Varjú, E., Dietzfelbinger, M., Ésik, Z. (eds.) MFCS 2014. LNCS, vol. 8634, pp. 123–134. Springer, Heidelberg (2014). https://doi.org/10.1007/978-3-662-44522-8_11

14. Dill, D.L.: Timing assumptions and verification of finite-state concurrent systems. In: Sifakis, J. (ed.) CAV 1989. LNCS, vol. 407, pp. 197–212. Springer, Heidelberg (1990). https://doi.org/10.1007/3-540-52148-8_17

15. Doyen, L.: Robust parametric reachability for timed automata. Inf. Process. Lett. **102**(5), 208–213 (2007). https://doi.org/10.1016/j.ipl.2006.11.018

16. Henzinger, T.A., Kopke, P.W., Puri, A., Varaiya, P.: What's decidable about hybrid automata? J. Comput. Syst. Sci. **57**(1), 94–124 (1998). https://doi.org/10.1006/jcss.1998.1581

17. Hune, T., Romijn, J., Stoelinga, M., Vaandrager, F.W.: Linear parametric model checking of timed automata. J. Logic Algebraic Program. **52–53**, 183–220 (2002). https://doi.org/10.1016/S1567-8326(02)00037-1

18. Jovanović, A., Lime, D., Roux, O.H.: Integer parameter synthesis for timed automata. IEEE Trans. Softw. Eng. **41**(5), 445–461 (2015). https://doi.org/10.1109/TSE.2014.2357445

19. Karmarkar, N.: A new polynomial-time algorithm for linear programming. Combinatorica **4**(4), 373–396 (1984). https://doi.org/10.1007/BF02579150
20. Miller, J.S.: Decidability and complexity results for timed automata and semi-linear hybrid automata. In: Lynch, N., Krogh, B.H. (eds.) HSCC 2000. LNCS, vol. 1790, pp. 296–310. Springer, Heidelberg (2000). https://doi.org/10.1007/3-540-46430-1_26
21. Quaas, K.: MTL-model checking of one-clock parametric timed automata is undecidable. In: André, É., Frehse, G. (eds.) SynCoP. EPTCS, vol. 145, pp. 5–17 (2014). https://doi.org/10.4204/EPTCS.145.3
22. Quaas, K., Shirmohammadi, M., Worrell, J.: Revisiting reachability in timed automata. In: LICS, pp. 1–12. IEEE Computer Society (2017). https://doi.org/10.1109/LICS.2017.8005098

Parametric Statistical Model Checking
of UAV Flight Plan

Ran Bao[1,2], Christian Attiogbe[2] , Benoît Delahaye[2(✉)] , Paulin Fournier[2],
and Didier Lime[3]

[1] PIXIEL GROUP, Nantes, France
https://www.pixiel-group.com/
[2] Université de Nantes - LS2N UMR CNRS 6004, Nantes, France
benoit.delahaye@univ-nantes.fr
[3] Centrale Nantes - LS2N UMR CNRS 6004, Nantes, France

Abstract. Unmanned Aerial Vehicles (UAV) are now widespread in our
society and are often used in a context where they can put people at risk.
Studying their reliability, in particular in the context of flight above a
crowd, thus becomes a necessity. In this paper, we study the modeling
and analysis of UAV in the context of their flight plan. To this purpose,
we build a parametric probabilistic model of the UAV and use it, as well
as a given flight plan, in order to model its trajectory. This model takes
into account parameters such as potential filter or sensor (like GPS) failure as well as wind force and direction. Because of the nature and complexity of the successive obtained models, their exact verification using
tools such as PRISM or PARAM is impossible. We therefore develop a
new approximation method, called Parametric Statistical Model Checking, in order to compute failure probabilities. This method has been
implemented in a prototype tool, which we use to resolve complex issues
in a practical case study.

Keywords: UAV · Formal model · Markov chain ·
Parametric statistical model checking

1 Introduction

Unmanned Aerial Vehicles (UAV) are more and more present in our lives through
entertainment or industrial activities. They can be dangerous for their environment, for instance in case of a failure when an UAV (aka a drone) is flying above
a crowd. Unfortunately until today, there does not exist any kind of UAV reg-
ulation around the world. Only some recommendations are used; for instance
in order to avoid accidents in case of malfunctioning, a drone should never fly
above a crowd.

In this context, we are working with PIXIEL group to build a reliable UAV
control system. PIXIEL group is a company expert in safety drones and public

Supported by PIXIEL and Association Nationale Recherche Technologie (ANRT).

© IFIP International Federation for Information Processing 2019
Published by Springer Nature Switzerland AG 2019
J. A. Pérez and N. Yoshida (Eds.): FORTE 2019, LNCS 11535, pp. 57–74, 2019.
https://doi.org/10.1007/978-3-030-21759-4_4

performances including UAVs. For example, PIXIEL is in particular known for developing a public performance in the French entertainment park called "Puy du Fou" that includes both human actors and drones. The company is strongly attached to the safety of the public. Therefore, ensuring that its UAV systems are secure for humans during the performances is a priority. As for the current practices, the performances including UAVs are only allowed to occur when the weather is sunny and when the area above which the UAVs fly is unauthorized for actors and public. However, there is no certification proving that the UAVs always follow their intended flight plan.

The management of performances indeed requires to pay close attention to the drone trajectory computation as well as to the accuracy of the measurements concerning its immediate position in space and its movements. However, a rigorous study is necessary to ensure reliability of the drone control system, for instance by decreasing the risks of failure using the appropriate tuning of the drone flying parameters which impact the computation of its trajectory. Accordingly, the questions are *how to prove that the UAV failure probability is low and which parameters have to be taken into account to ensure human safety during performances including UAVs.*

High-quality aircrafts such as Hexarotors can easily avoid the majority of minor failures related to hardware because they can fly with only five motors and the probability of concurrent failure of more than two motors is in general negligible. In the same way, in case of battery failure, the UAV is able to land down on a specified area without any safety issue for the environment as long as it is situated in a safe zone where humans are not endangered. However, software failure may be a lot more problematic and complex to study. In this case, the UAV behavior might become unpredictable. One critical issue in this context is the potential inaccuracy of position estimation in drone systems, either as a result of inaccurate sensor measurements or of misinterpretation of data coming from those sensors. Besides aircraft system failure consideration, there is also a far more critical aspect to take into account: the weather environment. Therefore, a general approach to improve UAV safety is to study the impact of inaccuracy in position measurements on the resulting flight path compared to a given, fixed, flight plan while taking into account weather conditions.

There are many works dedicated to the UAV domain. In [20] Koppány Máthé and Lucian Buşoniu basically explain the functioning of a drone. UAV movement recognition is studied in [10]. Automatic landing on target is described in [17] and monitoring and conservation are dealt with in [11]. Some works also try to detect breakdowns and malfunctions that can impact drones. We can mention *inter alia*, the detection of communication errors in a multi-drone framework studied in [13] or the development of a basic diagnosis model for solving system issues in [9]. Our work is closer to this second category of topics. However, to the best of our knowledge, there are no existing works on the parametric study of the impact of component inaccuracy on UAV trajectory. In [5,24] the authors study through the *secure estimation problems* how to estimate the true states of an UAV system when the measurements from sensors are corrupted, for instance by attackers. In their work, these authors reformulate the estimation problem into the error correction problem and then they use the successively observed measurement anomalies to reconstruct the correct states of the system. While the used techniques are completely different, the objectives of avoiding bad states is similar to ours, in avoiding the states reaching bad security zones.

The purpose of our work is therefore to provide means to study the reliability of UAVs in the context of a given flight plan. In order to do that, we have to build a formal (mathematical) model which will allow us (1) to analyze the drone system and detect the most important parameters, and (2) to tune those parameters in order to reduce the system failure probability. To this intent, we thoroughly study the UAV system, formalize it and analyze it with using parametric probabilistic methods. Among the components of a drone system, we particularly focus on the *Flight Control System* (FCS), which is responsible for computing estimations of the UAV position during its flight in order to adapt its trajectory to a given predefined flight plan. We therefore build a formal model of the flight controler in terms of parametric probabilistic models that takes into account the potential inaccuracy of the position estimation. Since UAVs are particularly sensitive to the weather environment (and in particular to wind conditions), we also enhance our model in order to take into account potential wind perturbations. Since wind force can drastically vary from one point of a given flight plan to another, we also use parameters to encode the wind force and allow our model to adapt to particular weather conditions.

The contributions of this paper are:

- a method to build a parametric model of UAV systems; the parameters can then be finely tuned until reaching values that ensure defined safety thresholds;
- a parametric statistical model checking technique; this enables us to formally analyze the parametric models build for the drones. Indeed because of the complexity of the built models, tools such as PRISM [15,16] and PARAM [12] were limited for their analysis.
- an illustration of the use of our method on a complex industrial case study.

The paper is organized as follows. In Sect. 2 we provide the essential background to understand UAV functioning and then we build a formal model that support their behaviours. Section 3 is an introduction to parametric Markov chains and Statistical Model Checking. Implementations of the models and experimentations are presented in Sect. 4; finally Sect. 5 draws conclusions and further work.

2   Building a Formal Model of UAV

In this section, we present our method to build the UAV model. Recall that we are interested in studying UAV safety, i.e. studying the probability that a UAV encounters dangerous situations. These situations are of two kinds: either the UAV can stop flying and fall, or it can enter a "forbidden" zone were it endangers humans. As explained earlier, professional UAV can handle the falling risk through material redundancy. Moreover, as long as a UAV stays in a "safe" zone, it will not endanger human even in case of falling. The aim of our model is therefore to evaluate the probability for a UAV to enter a "forbidden" zone.

We start by explaining how the zones are computed with respect to the given flight plan. We then show how the UAV software can be decomposed into components and focus on the most important ones. Finally, we detail how the formal (mathematical) models for the important components are built and present the resulting global model.

2.1   Safety Zones

In the context of software, considerations in airborne systems and equipment certification (named DO-178C) defined five levels of safety zones, the most secure being Zone 1 and the most dangerous being Zone 5. These zones are characterized by their distance from the intended flight plan, as shown in Fig. 1.

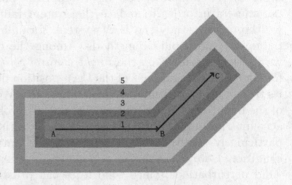

Fig. 1. Safety zones

The size of each safety zone is not definitely fixed; it can be defined for a specific requirement or for a given application. In practice the safety zones are specifically defined for a flight environment and for a given flight plan. The main principle is that no human should be present in Zones 1 to 3, while a few people can be present in Zone 4 and most people can be present in Zone 5. As a consequence, the probability that the UAV endangers humans is directly proportional to the probability that it enters Zones 4 or 5. In the following of the paper, our target will therefore be to compute this probability.

2.2   Drone Components

We now move to the decomposition of the UAV hardware and UAV software into components and introduce the most important component in the UAV system: the flight controller (FC). The FC is responsible for collecting data from various sensors, using this data to compute the precise *position* and *attitude* of the drone and adjust the attitude in order to follow the given flight plan to the best of its ability.

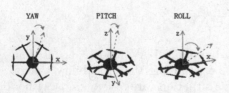

Fig. 2. Attitude coordinates

Notice the difference between position and attitude: while the position of the UAV is defined by 3-dimensional coordinates x, y and z, its attitude is the collection of *yaw*, *pitch* and *roll* measurements for the UAV compared to the vertical (see Fig. 2). The attitude allows to control the movement

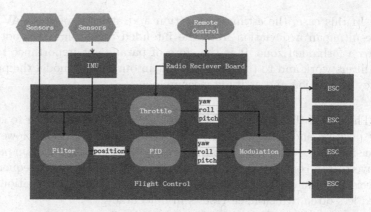

Fig. 3. Flight control overview

of the UAV: by controlling the speed of each motor, one can control which motor will be the highest, and hence control the direction the UAV will fly to.

Flight Controller. As explained above, the FC is the central component in any UAV as it is responsible for collecting data from sensors and translating them to the UAV attitude. An overview of the FC of an UAV is given in Fig. 3. Remark that the FC can be linked to components responsible for communicating with a remote control. While these components are necessary in order to allow a pilot to take over when the automatic flight mode of the UAV fails, we will consider in the following that this is not the case and that the UAV we study are always in automatic flight mode.

As one can see from Fig. 3, the intuitive behavior of the FC is as follows. The filter uses sensors measurements in order to compute the current drone position and attitude. Since the data can be noisy and inaccurate, the filter uses complex algorithms in order to clean the noises in the measurements and compute a realistic position and attitude. Remark that in some cases, the filter can itself introduce inaccuracy in the computed position and attitude, which can be problematic. Once the estimated current position and attitude are computed, the Proportional Integral Derivative (PID) uses this information to compute the local trajectory that the drone has to follow in order to be as close as possible to its intended flight plan. This local trajectory is then transformed into a new value for the attitude of the drone. Finally, Modulation transforms this attitude into signal to the Electronic Speed Controller (ESC) which is responsible for controlling each motor's speed.

Recall that we are interested in computing the probability that a UAV enters a forbidden zone while following its flight plan. By construction, as long as the position and attitude measurements are perfect, there is no reason why the UAV should deviate from its intended trajectory, and therefore the probability that it enters a forbidden zone is null. However, as explained above, the data gathered from sensors can be noisy and inaccuracy can sometimes be introduced through filtering. In this case, the estimated position and attitude of the UAV can be faulty, resulting in a deviation from the intended flight plan and potentially leading to a forbidden zone. It is therefore of paramount importance to study how the filters work and to take into account in our formal model the potential inaccuracy of position and attitude measurement.

Filter. The role of the filter is to use sensors measurements in order to compute the UAV position and attitude with the highest possible precision. However, the high precision comes with a cost in terms of complexity: in order to gain precision, filters have to run complex algorithms which takes time. As a consequence, the most precise filters are also the slowest, which implies that the position can be estimated less often, which itself results in inaccuracy.

There exists a large amount of filters in UAV industry, among which one can find Extended Kalman Filter (EKF) [22], Explicit Complement Filter [8], Gradient Descent [19], Conjugate Gradient, and a more accurate but slower filter: Unscented Kalman Filter (UKF) [6], etc. Usually, researchers use EKF as a fundamental to compare to other kinds of filters and explain precision and speed differences. All filters improve their accuracy during the flight through training, in particular by recording recurrent noises and correcting them. However, this training is only valid through a single flight and is lost as soon as the UAV lands.

Since the accuracy of the estimated position and attitude is of paramount importance for computing the probability of entering a forbidden zone, and since the choice of filter has a direct impact on this measurement, we chose to implement this accuracy as a *parameter* of our model. This will be explained in more details in Sect. 2.4.

2.3   Formal Model of the UAV in Its Environment

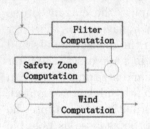

Fig. 4. A flow diagram of the formalization steps

We use a flow diagram to present our global approach for formalizing the UAV functioning (See Fig. 4). After a step where the filter computation reflects the precision of position and attitude estimation, we consider the computations of the probabilities to reach the given safety zones in the next time-step; accordingly, the idea is to adapt the next attitude according to the original flight plan in order to be more secure. The last step allows to incorporate wind perturbations and compute the next UAV position.

As explained above, the filter is one of the most crucial components and its ability to estimate the UAV position precisely has a huge impact on the probability of reaching a forbidden zone. For this reason, we choose to represent the accuracy of the estimated position of the UAV (therefore including both sensor measurements and filter correction) as a parameter of our model. In the following, we show how the next position of the UAV is computed according to the current estimated position, and how errors in the estimation can lead to the drone entering forbidden zones.

Computation of the Next Position. We now explain how the next position is computed according to the estimated current position. In particular, we show that inaccuracy in the estimation can lead the UAV to entering a forbidden zone.

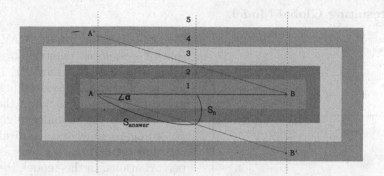

Fig. 5. Issue on drone location and misleading positions

For the sake of simplicity, we assume here that the UAV moves in 2 dimensions only and that inaccuracy only occurs on one of them. Figure 5 illustrates the situation. Assume that the intended flight plan consists in going from point A to point B. Assume also that the current position of the UAV is exactly on A but that the estimated position (taking into account sensors and filter inaccuracy) is on A'. As a consequence, the PID will try to correct the current deviation by changing the angle of the UAV in order to lead it back to B. However, since the UAV is really on A, the correction will instead lead the UAV to a position B', in the forbidden zone. Fortunately, the position estimation takes place several times between A and B, according to the filter frequency f. Therefore, a new position will be estimated before reaching B', hopefully with a better accuracy, which will allow the PID to again correct the trajectory. We should also take into account that the speed of the UAV is also computed according to the flight plan, which precises the remaining time and distance before the next checkpoint. We now show how we can compute the safety zone where the UAV ends before the position is estimated again. In Fig. 5, this zone is represented by the distance S_n.

Let S_{answer} be the distance that the UAV covers before a new estimation of the position. Let V be the velocity of the UAV, which is computed by the PID in order to reach B on time, i.e. in precisely T time units. We therefore have $V = A'B/T$, and $S_{answer} = V/f = (A'B)/(T * f)$. Finally, $AA'/A'B = S_n/S_{answer}$, and therefore

$$S_n = \frac{AA'}{T * f}.$$

Remark that the resulting deviation is directly proportional to AA'/f, hence the necessity to take into account the trade-off between accuracy and filter speed in order to optimize the probability of never entering any dangerous zone.

Taking into account wind perturbations follows a similar computation than the one presented above. This allows us to incorporate wind parameters as well in our model.

2.4   Resulting Global Model

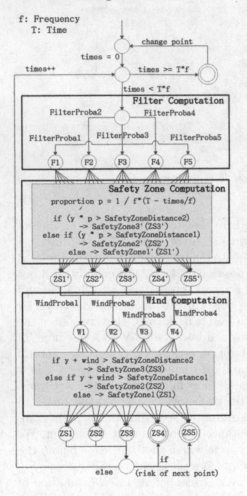

Fig. 6. Global behaviour of the FCS

The global model of the UAV flight control system is depicted in Fig. 6. The purpose of this model is to represent the computations taking place in the FCS in order to adapt the UAV trajectory to the intended flight plan according to inaccurate position and attitude estimations as well as wind perturbations. In this model, the exact position of the UAV is encoded using 3-d coordinates. These coordinates are then compared to the intended flight plan in order to decide to which safety zone they belong. As soon as the UAV reaches one of the forbidden zones (4 or 5), the computation stops.

The model uses several probabilistic parameters. Parameters FilterProba1, FilterProba2, FilterProba3, FilterProba4 and FilterProba5 represent the accuracy of the position and attitude estimation by both the filter and the sensors. The resulting probabilistic choice depicted in the box labelled **Filter Computation** therefore dictates the distance between the exact and estimated position of the UAV. This choice is followed by a computation in the box labelled **Safety Zone Computation** that computes the exact coordinates of the next position of the drone and allows to decide the safety zone to which this position belongs. When the wind is not taken into account, the result of this computation is enough to decide whether the model should pursue its execution. When the wind is taken into account, another step follows, depicted in the box labelled **Wind Computation**, where other probabilistic parameters are used in order to decide the wind strength (we assume that the direction is constant) and a new position taking into account these perturbations is computed. Finally, the zone to which this last position belongs is computed and, depending on whether this zone is safe, the model goes on to another position estimation.

Remark that the filter frequency and the position and distance of checkpoints in the flight plan are given as inputs to the model. The position of checkpoints in the flight plan allows to compute the required UAV speed, while the frequency of the filter allows to fix the number of position estimations that will happen in a given flight plan (i.e. the number of loops the model goes through, at most).

3   Parametric Statistical Model Checking

As explained above, we have developed a parametric probabilistic model in order to represent the behaviour of our UAV according to a given flight plan. We now introduce the necessary theory to formally compute the probabilies of a given UAV entering a forbidden zone in the context of its flight plan. We start by recalling a classical verification technique called Statistical Model Checking (SMC), then introduce the modeling formalism we use: parametric Markov Chains (pMCs) and finally show how SMC can be adapted to this formalism.

3.1   Standard Statistical Model Checking

Recall that a Markov Chain (MC) is a purely probabilistic model $\mathcal{M} = (S, s_0, P)$, where S is a set of states, $s_0 \in S$ is the initial state, and $P : S \times S \rightarrow [0, 1]$ is a probabilistic transition function that, given a pair of states (s_1, s_2), yields the probability of moving from s_1 to s_2.

Given a MC $\mathcal{M}$, one can define a probability measure on the infinite executions of $\mathcal{M}$ using a standard construction based on the σ-algebra of cylinders.

A run of a MC is a sequence of states $s_0, s_1 \ldots$ such that for all i, $P(s_i, s_{i+1}) > 0$. Given a finite run $\rho = s_0 s_1 \ldots s_l$, its length, written $|\rho|$ represents the number of transitions it goes through (including repetitions). Here $|\rho| = l$. We write $\Gamma_{\mathcal{M}}(l)$ (or simply $\Gamma(l)$ when $\mathcal{M}$ is clear from the context) for the set of all finite runs of length l, and $\Gamma_{\mathcal{M}}$ for all finite runs i.e. $\Gamma_{\mathcal{M}} = \cup_{l \in \mathbb{N}} \Gamma_{\mathcal{M}}(l)$. As usual we define the probability measure, written $\mathbb{P}_{\mathcal{M}}$ on runs based on the sigma-algebra of cylinders (see e.g. [2]). This gives us that for any finite run $\rho = s_0 s_1 \ldots s_n$, $\mathbb{P}_{\mathcal{M}}(\rho) = \prod_{i=1}^{n} P(s_{i-1}, s_i)$. In the rest of the section, we only consider *finite* runs. Given a reward function $r : \Gamma(l) \rightarrow \mathbb{R}$, we write $\mathbb{E}_{\mathcal{M}}^l(r)$ for the expected value of r on the runs of length l of a given MC $\mathcal{M}$.

Statistical Model Checking [23] is an approximation technique that allows to compute an estimation of the probability that a purely probabilistic systems satisfies a given property[1]. In particular, the Monte Carlo technique uses samples of the runs of length l, $\Gamma(l)$, of a given Markov chain $\mathcal{M}$ in order to estimate the probability that $\mathcal{M}$ satisfies a given bounded linear property. It can also be used

---

[1] Particular SMC techniques also allow to estimate the satisfaction of qualitative properties [18].

for approximating the expected value of a given reward function r on the runs $\Gamma(l)$ of $\mathcal{M}$. In order to provide some intuition, we briefly recall how standard Monte Carlo analysis works in the context of statistical model checking of MC. In this context, a set of n samples of the runs of the MC. These runs are generated at random using the probability distribution define through the Markov chain. Each of these samples is evaluated, yielding a reward value according to the reward function r. According to the law of large numbers (see e.g. [21]), the mean value of the samples provides a good estimator for the expected value of the reward function r on the runs of the given MC. Moreover, the central limit theorem provides a confidence interval that only depends on the number of samples (provided this number is large enough).

3.2 Parametric Markov Chains (pMC)

Markov Chains are inadequate in the context of drone flight plan analysis. Indeed, the models we develop in this context are subject to uncertainties that we model using parameters, such as precision of the position and attitude estimations and wind strength. The resulting models are therefore not purely probabilistic since they contain parameters. As a consequence, we need to use a more expressive type of model that allows to take into account probabilistic parameters, such as Parametric Markov Chains (see e.g. [1]).

A pMC is a tuple $\mathcal{M} = (S, s_0, P, \mathbb{X})$ such that S is a finite set of states, $s_0 \in S$ is the initial state, $\mathbb{X}$ is a finite set of parameters, and $P : S \times S \rightarrow Poly(\mathbb{X})$ is a parametric transition probability function, expressed as a polynomial on $\mathbb{X}$. A parameter valuation is a function $v : \mathbb{X} \rightarrow [0, 1]$ that assigns values to parameters. A parameter valuation v is valid w.r.t. a given pMC $\mathcal{M}$ if, when replacing parameters with their assigned values, the resulting object is a MC (i.e. the outgoing probabilities of all states sum up to 1). If v is a valid parameter valuation with respect to $\mathcal{M}$, the resulting Markov chain is written $\mathcal{M}^{\sqsubseteq}$.

Given a pMC $\mathcal{M}$, a run ρ of $\mathcal{M}$ is a sequence of states $s_0 s_1 \ldots$ such that for all $i \geq 0$, $P(s_i, s_{i+1}) \neq 0$ (i.e. the probability is either a strictly positive real constant or a function of the parameters). As for MCs, we write $\Gamma_{\mathcal{M}}(l)$ for the set of all finite runs of length l and $\Gamma_{\mathcal{M}}$ for the set of all finite runs.

Observe that for any valid parameter valuation v, $\Gamma_{\mathcal{M}^v}(l) \subseteq \Gamma_{\mathcal{M}}(l)$ since v may assign 0 to some transition probabilities.

3.3 Parametric SMC

As it is, standard SMC cannot be used in the context of pMC because of their parametric nature. Indeed, we cannot produce samples according to the parametric transition probabilities. Luckily, the underlying theory used in SMC can be extended in order to take into account parameters. The method we propose in the following is in line with a technique called *importance sampling* (see [21] for a description). The purpose of this technique is to sample a stochastic system using a chosen probability distribution (which is not the original distribution present in this system) and "compensate" the results using a *likelihood ratio* in order to estimate a measure according to the original distribution. In the context of SMC, importance sampling has mainly been used in order to estimate the probability of rare events [3] and/or to reduce the number of required samples in order to obtain a given level of guarantee [14]. It has also been used in the context of parametric continuous-time Markov chains in order to estimate the value of a given objective function on the whole parameter space while using a reduced number of samples [4]. However, to the best of our knowledge, importance sampling has never been used in order to produce symbolic functions of the parameters as we do here.

The intuition of the method we propose here is to fix the transition probabilities to an arbitrary function f, which we call *normalization function*, and to use these transition probabilities in order to produce samples of the pMC $\mathcal{M}$. However, instead of evaluating the obtained runs by directly using the desired reward function r, we define a new (parametric) reward function r' that takes into account the parametric transition probabilities. We show that, under any parameter valuation v, the evaluation of the mean value of r' on the set of samples is a good estimator for the expected value of the reward r on $\mathcal{M}^v$. The central limit theorem (see e.g. [21]) also allows to produce parametric confidence intervals, but we do not go into details here (see [7] for more details on this topic).

Remark. The choice of the normalization function is crucial. In particular, the results presented below require that the graph structure of the MC obtained with this normalization function is identical to the graph structure of the MC obtained using the chosen parameter valuation. This is discussed in more details in [7]. In the following, we only consider parameter valuations that assign non-zero probability to parameterized transitions. Since we use the uniform normalization function, the graph structures of the obtained MCs are indeed identical, which ensures that the results presented below hold as expected.

Let $Pa : \Gamma_{\mathcal{M}} \to Poly(\mathbb{X})$ be a parametric reward function. For any valid valuation v and any run $\rho \in \Gamma_{\mathcal{M}^v}$ we have $\mathbb{P}_{\mathcal{M}^v}(\rho) = Pa(\rho)(v)$.

Given any valid normalization function f and any run $\rho \in \Gamma_{\mathcal{M}}$, let parametric reward function r' be $r'(\rho) = \frac{Pa(\rho)}{\mathbb{P}_{\mathcal{M}^f}(\rho)} r(\rho)$.

We now prove that the expected values are equal. Let $\rho \in \Gamma_{\mathcal{M}^f}(l)$ be a random sample of $\mathcal{M}^f$ and let Y be the random variable defined as follows $Y = r'(\rho)$. The following computation shows that, under any valid parameter valuation v such that $\mathcal{M}^f$ and $\mathcal{M}^v$ have the same structure, we have $\mathbb{E}(Y)(v) = \mathbb{E}^l_{\mathcal{M}^v}(r)$.

$$\mathbb{E}(Y)(v) = \left(\sum_{\rho \in \Gamma_{\mathcal{M}^f}(l)} \mathbb{P}_{\mathcal{M}^f}(\rho) y(\rho) \right)(v)$$

$$= \left(\sum_{\rho \in \Gamma_{\mathcal{M}^f}(l)} \mathbb{P}_{\mathcal{M}^f}(\rho) \frac{Pa(\rho)}{\mathbb{P}_{\mathcal{M}^f}(\rho)} r(\rho) \right)(v)$$

$$= \sum_{\rho \in \Gamma_{\mathcal{M}^f}(l)} Pa(\rho)(v) r(\rho)$$

$$= \sum_{\rho \in \Gamma_{\mathcal{M}^f}(l)} \mathbb{P}_{\mathcal{M}^f}(\rho) r(\rho)$$

$$= \sum_{\rho \in \Gamma_{\mathcal{M}^v}(l)} \mathbb{P}_{\mathcal{M}^f}(\rho) r(\rho)$$

$$= \mathbb{E}^l_{\mathcal{M}^v}(r)$$

Our adaptation of the Monte Carlo technique for pMC is thus to estimate the expected value of Y in order to obtain a good estimator for the expectation of r. Let $\rho_1, \ldots, \rho_n$ be a set of n runs of length l of $\mathcal{M}^f$. Let Y_i be the random variable with values in $Poly(\mathbb{X})$ such that $Y_i = r'(\rho_i)$. Notice that the Y_i are independent copies of the random variable Y. Y_i are therefore independent and identically distributed. Let γ be the parametric function giving their mean value. By the results above, for all valid parameter valuation v such that $\mathcal{M}^v$ and $\mathcal{M}^f$ have the same structure, $\mathbb{E}^l_{\mathcal{M}^v}(r) = \mathbb{E}(Y)(v) = \mathbb{E}(\sum_{i=1}^n Y_i/n)(v) = \gamma(v)$. Our parametric approximation of the expected value is therefore:

$$\widehat{\gamma} = \sum_{i=1}^n Y_i/n.$$

In the sequel we will this use Parametric Statistical Model Checking (PSMC) to check the formal model we will implement for the UAV.

4   Implementation, Experimentations and Results

While our complete formal model has been introduced in Sect. 2 in the form of an automata, we now explain how we successively implemented and improved the model by considering different formalisms and model checking tools. At each step, we show the limitations of the related model which leads to the next step of the implementation. The different steps of the model implementations are depicted in Fig. 7.

To start, a first partial version of the formal model of Sect. 2.3 was implemented as a PRISM model using the PRISM tool [16], without parameters.

This first version, as depicted in Fig. 7a, corresponds to a very simple UAV flight plan, going in a straight line from point A to point B in T time units. In this context, the intermediate positions are estimated $T * f$ times, where f is the frequency of the filter. The sizes used for the five security zones are respectively 20 m, 40 m, 60 m, 80 m and 100 m.

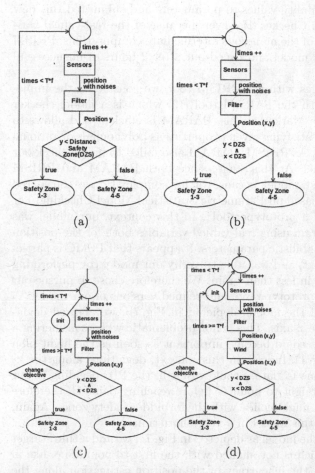

(a)   (b)

(c)   (d)

Fig. 7. Incremental development of the SMC model

As explained in Sect. 2, the filter removes the noise corrupting data coming from sensors. In this first version, we only consider potential deviations along the y-axis. At each computation step, the inaccurate position given by the filter is computed using the accuracy of the filter and sensors (as a single real-valued variable), and compared to the intended position as given by the flight plan. The safety zone is deduced from the distance between the estimated position and the intended position. If the UAV enters Zones 4 or 5, the computation stops.

In this first model, the accuracy of the filter is probabilistic but not parametric, i.e. probability values have been encoded directly in the model. These values are the results of a set of experiments performed by using a flight controller plugged on a production line with a predefined path with a loop. We launched several runs of the device on the production line path and measured the outputs of the EKF filter. These measures then allowed us to compute the estimated position, which can then be compared to the exact position on the production line. We consequently obtained probabilities for the accuracy of the position estimation using an EKF filter and sensors coming from an industrial UAV. However, the major drawback of these experimentations is that they did not reflect a realistic UAV environment. In particular, since the experiment was conducted indoor using a fixed production line, the precision of some of the sensors (GPS for instance) is not representative of the precision one could obtain in a realistic flight environment. Although we were able to verify this model using PRISM, the results are not representative and can only be considered as a proof-of-concept. Since our aim is to study the same problem for different accuracy probabilities, we changed the exact probability values to parameters and submitted this new model to the PRISM Model Checker. However, because of the real-valued variables used in the model and of the numerous intermediate computations, PRISM was not able to handle this model and timed-out after 2 hours of unsuccessful computations.

Facing these shortcomings with the PRISM tool, we considered the implementation of our model with the PARAM tool [12] which is a model checker for parametric discrete-time Markov chains. PARAM is efficient and allows to compute the probability of satisfying given properties as polynomials or rational functions of the parameters. As PRISM, PARAM also failed to model check our current version of the model. At this stage, since both PARAM and PRISM failed to verify our simplest model because of its complexity, we considered using a different approach based on Parametric Statistical Model Checking. For this purpose, we developed a prototype tool[2]. In this context, our model was expressed as a python program using real-valued variables both for the position of the UAV and for the probabilistic parameters. It appears that PSMC is particularly efficient in this context, and was able to verify our model (by performing more than 20k simulations) in less than 1 min. We therefore chose to pursue our experimentation using this prototype tool and refined versions of our model.

In the second version of the model, depicted in Fig. 7b, we allowed deviations to also occur along the x-axis. This is not problematic when considering a straight line flight plan, but could become important as soon as the flight plan is curved (as the one in Fig. 1). Indeed, in this context, deviations along the x-axis (for example if the drone is "late") could result in the PID deciding to cut the trajectory, i.e. going straight to point C before reaching point B, therefore promoting a trajectory that might colide with the forbidden safety zones. Again, our tool managed to verify this model in a very short time.

For the third version of the model as depicted in Fig. 7c, we add a third target point to the flight plan, which is not aligned with the first to points, i.e. like in Fig. 1. In this third version, the inacurracy of the position estimation along the x-axis also allows the UAV to be "late" and decide to cut the flight plan as explained above.

Finally, the last version, as depicted in Fig. 7d, takes into account wind perturbations. We assumed here that the wind direction was constant but that the wind force was again parametric. This will allow us to study the right trade-off between filter capacity and frequency *depending on the weather conditions*. This last version is the most complex we studied, and therefore took more time to verify than the previous ones. With our prototype tool, it took 190 s to perform the verification using 10k simulations in this context while the same amount of simulations only took 28 s for the previous model (without wind parameters).[3]

---

[2] available at https://github.com/paulinfournier/MCpMC.

[3] We do not share the exact models used in our prototype tool for confidentiality reasons, but the models used in PRISM and PARAM can be found here: https://github.com/br4444/modelPrism/tree/master.

The outputs of our prototype tool are multivariate polynomials on the parameters of our model. Given the number of parameters, the size of the model and the length of the considered simulations, these polynomials are quite complex and therefore difficult to report in this paper. As an example, below is the output polynomial representing the probability that a UAV enters Zones 4 or 5 using our last version of the model:

$$0.43 * ProbaFilter_3 * ProbaWind_1 + 0.16 * ProbaFilter_3 * ProbaWind_2$$
$$+ 0.17 * ProbaFilter_3 * ProbaWind_3 + 0.28 * ProbaFilter_3 * ProbaWind_4$$
$$+ 0.85 * ProbaFilter_4 * ProbaWind_1 + \ldots$$

Instead of showing the resulting polynomials, we will only present the evaluation of these polynomials using realistic values for the parameters. We defined two scenarios (Scenario 1, Scenario 2) with one set of values of parameters for each scenario. For these two scenarios, ProbaF0 (resp F1, F2, F3, F4) models the probability that the estimated position is from 0 to 2 m (resp. 2–4 m, 4–6 m, 6–8 m, 8–10 m) from the real position. In the first (resp. second) scenario, we have set these values to 0.15/0.3/0.4/0.1/0.05 (resp. 0.1/0.25/0.35/0.2/0.1). According to experiments done at PIXIEL, the first scenario is more realistic than the second one. Similarly, the wind parameters correspond to the probability of having a wind force of 0–20 km/h, 20–30 km/h, 30–50 km/h and 50–70 km/h respectively and have been set to 0.55/0.43/0.01/0.01 (which corresponds to typical weather conditions in Nantes, France) for the numerical evaluation. In both scenarios, Zone 4 (resp. 5) is situated 8 m (resp. 50 m) from the flight plan.

In Table 1, we gather the results for running the simulation for the two considered scenarios; the simulation with PSMC is performed with 10k, 20k and 50k samples. Each time, a polynomial is computed and then evaluated using the parameter values given above. In order to illustrate the stability of our results despite their statistical nature, each complete scenario was performed two times (labelled V1 and V2 in the table). The value reported in the table represents the probability of the UAV eventually reaching Zones 4 or 5 during its flight. Experiments were performed using the formal models presented in Fig. 7c (without wind) and Fig. 7d (including wind perturbations) on a flight plan resembling the one shown in Fig. 1, with a total flight duration of 5 s and a filter frequency of 1 Hz. We considered two versions of the model from Fig. 7d: 7d(np) where wind strength is directly input as a constant probability in the model (resulting in a polynomial where the only variables represent the precision of position estimation), and Fig. 7d(p) where wind strength is input as parameter variables in the model (allowing to evaluate/optimize the resulting polynomial according to any wind strength). Remark that the results in the first case are more precise because there are less variables in the polynomial, and obtained in a more efficient manner. Depending on whether we are interested in specific or generic information concerning the weather environment, we can chose to use the first of the second version. Remark that the probabilities of entering the forbidden zones are quite high. This is not surprising as Zone 4 is situated 8 m from the intended trajectory and the precision of position estimation can be up to 10 m.

Table 1. Results of the experiments

	Model	10k		20k		50k	
		V1	V2	V1	V2	V1	V2
Running time	Fig. 7c	28 s		51–54 s		142–143 s	
Scenario 1	Fig. 7c	4.99%	5.09%	4.74%	5.10%	4.91%	4.98%
Scenario 2	Fig. 7c	10.38%	10.04%	9.82%	10.05%	9.95%	9.81%
Running time	Fig. 7d(np)	28 s		53–54 s		149–155 s	
Scenario 1	Fig. 7d(np)	5.43%	5.31%	5.61%	5.21%	5.59%	5.47%
Scenario 2	Fig. 7d(np)	10.8%	10.9%	10.8%	10.8%	10.9%	10.7%
Running time	Fig. 7d(p)	185–190 s		311–314 s		612–621 s	
Scenario 1	Fig. 7d(p)	4.95%	5.97%	5.28%	6.62%	4.16%	5.61%
Scenario 2	Fig. 7d(p)	9.55%	9.87%	10.3%	11.3%	9.57%	10.7%

These values have been made deliberately high for the purpose of this study but can be chosen more realistically when verifying the real model.

5 Conclusion and Future Work

In this paper, we have presented a formal model to study the safety of a UAV in automatic flight following a predefined flight plan. This formal model consists in a parametric Markov Chain and takes that takes into account the precision of position and attitude estimation using sensors and filters as well as potential wind perturbations. We have also proposed a new verification technique for parametric probabilistic model: parametric Statistical Model Checking. This new technique has been implemented in a prototype tool. While state of the art tools such as PRISM and PARAM have timed out on the verification of the simplest version of our formal model, our prototype tool has been able to successfully verify the most complex version in less than 12 min.

In the future, we plan to keep enhancing our model in order to include filter frequency to be used as a parameter in the model. Using these parameters will allow us to obtain the parametric probability to enter dangerous zones depending on both the filter frequency and the precision probabilities. Studying/optimizing this parametric probability will allow PIXIEL to work on the trade-off between frequency and precision in order to choose their components wisely depending on their intended flight plan.

References

1. Alur, R., Henzinger, T.A., Vardi, M.Y.: Parametric real-time reasoning. In: Proceedings of the Twenty-Fifth Annual ACM Symposium on Theory of Computing, 16–18 May 1993, San Diego, CA, USA. pp. 592–601 (1993). https://doi.org/10.1145/167088.167242
2. Baier, C., Katoen, J.: Principles of Model Checking. MIT Press, Cambridge (2008)
3. Barbot, B., Haddad, S., Picaronny, C.: Coupling and importance sampling for statistical model checking. In: Flanagan, C., König, B. (eds.) TACAS 2012. LNCS, vol. 7214, pp. 331–346. Springer, Heidelberg (2012). https://doi.org/10.1007/978-3-642-28756-5_23
4. Bortolussi, L., Milios, D., Sanguinetti, G.: Smoothed model checking for uncertain Continuous-Time Markov Chains. Inf. Comput. **247**, 235–253 (2016)
5. Chang, Y.H., Hu, Q., Tomlin, C.J.: Secure estimation based Kalman Filter forcyber-physical systems against sensor attacks. Automatica **95**, 399–412 (2018). https://doi.org/10.1016/j.automatica.2018.06.010
6. de Marina, H.G., Pereda, F.J., Giron-Sierra, J.M., Espinosa, F.: UAV attitude estimation using unscented Kalman Filter and TRIAD. IEEE Trans. Ind. Electron. **59**(11), 4465–4474 (2012). https://doi.org/10.1109/TIE.2011.2163913
7. Delahaye, B., Fournier, P., Lime, D.: Statistical model checking for parameterized models, February 2019. https://hal.archives-ouvertes.fr/hal-02021064, working paper or preprint
8. Euston, M., Coote, P., Mahony, R., Kim, J., Hamel, T.: A complementary filter for attitude estimation of a fixed-wing UAV. In: 2008 IEEE/RSJ International Conference on Intelligent Robots and Systems, pp. 340–345, September 2008. https://doi.org/10.1109/IROS.2008.4650766
9. Freddi, A., Longhi, S., Monteriù, A.: A model-based fault diagnosis system for unmanned aerial vehicles. IFAC Proc. **42**(8), 71–76 (2009). https://doi.org/10.3182/20090630-4-ES-2003.00012, http://www.sciencedirect.com/science/article/pii/S147466701635755X. 7th IFAC Symposium on Fault Detection, Supervision and Safety of Technical Processes
10. Gąsior, P., Bondyra, A., Gardecki, S.: Development of vertical movement controller for multirotor UAVs. In: Szewczyk, R., Zieliński, C., Kaliczyńska, M. (eds.) ICA 2017. AISC, vol. 550, pp. 339–348. Springer, Cham (2017). https://doi.org/10.1007/978-3-319-54042-9_31
11. Gonzalez, L.F., Montes, G.A., Puig, E., Johnson, S., Mengersen, K.L., Gaston,K.J.: Unmanned aerial vehicles (UAVs) and artificial intelligencerevolutionizing wildlife monitoring and conservation. Sensors **16**(1), 97 (2016). https://doi.org/10.3390/s16010097
12. Hahn, E.M., Hermanns, H., Wachter, B., Zhang, L.: PARAM: a model checker for parametric Markov models. In: Touili, T., Cook, B., Jackson, P. (eds.) Computer Aided Verification, pp. 660–664. Springer, Berlin Heidelberg, Berlin, Heidelberg (2010). https://doi.org/10.1007/978-3-642-14295-6_56
13. Heredia, G., Caballero, F., Maza, I., Merino, L., Viguria, A., Ollero, A.: Multi-unmanned aerial vehicle (UAV) cooperative fault detection employing differential global positioning (DGPS), inertial and vision sensors. Sensors **9**(9), 7566–7579 (2009). https://doi.org/10.3390/s90907566
14. Jegourel, C., Legay, A., Sedwards, S.: Cross-entropy optimisation of importance sampling parameters for statistical model checking. In: Madhusudan, P., Seshia, S.A. (eds.) CAV 2012. LNCS, vol. 7358, pp. 327–342. Springer, Heidelberg (2012). https://doi.org/10.1007/978-3-642-31424-7_26

15. Kwiatkowska, M., Norman, G., Parker, D.: PRISM: probabilistic model checking for performance and reliability analysis. ACM SIGMETRICS Perform. Eval. Rev. **36**(4), 40–45 (2009)

16. Kwiatkowska, M., Norman, G., Parker, D.: PRISM 4.0: verification of probabilistic real-time systems. In: Gopalakrishnan, G., Qadeer, S. (eds.) CAV 2011. LNCS, vol. 6806, pp. 585–591. Springer, Heidelberg (2011). https://doi.org/10.1007/978-3-642-22110-1_47

17. Kyristsis, S., et al.: Towards autonomous modular UAV missions: the detection, geo-location and landing paradigm. Sensors**16**(11), 1844 (2016). https://doi.org/10.3390/s16111844

18. Legay, A., Delahaye, B., Bensalem, S.: Statistical model checking: an overview. In: Barringer, H., et al. (eds.) RV 2010. LNCS, vol. 6418, pp. 122–135. Springer, Heidelberg (2010). https://doi.org/10.1007/978-3-642-16612-9_11

19. Madgwick, S.O.H.: An efficient orientation filter for inertial and inertial/magnetic sensor arrays (2010)

20. Máthé, K., Busoniu, L.: Vision and control for UAVs: a survey of general methods and of inexpensive platforms for infrastructure inspection. Sensors **15**(7), 14887–14916 (2015). https://doi.org/10.3390/s150714887

21. Rubinstein, R.Y., Kroese, D.P.: Simulation and the Monte Carlo Method, vol. 10. Wiley, Hoboken (2016)

22. Sabatelli, S., Galgani, M., Fanucci, L., Rocchi, A.: A double-stage Kalman filter for orientation tracking with an integrated processor in 9-DIMU. IEEE Trans. Instrum. Meas. **62**(3), 590–598 (2013). https://doi.org/10.1109/TIM.2012.2218692

23. Sen, K., Viswanathan, M., Agha, G.: On statistical model checking of stochastic systems. In: Etessami, K., Rajamani, S.K. (eds.) CAV 2005. LNCS, vol. 3576, pp. 266–280. Springer, Heidelberg (2005). https://doi.org/10.1007/11513988_26

24. Zhou, Z., Ding, J., Huang, H., Takei, R., Tomlin, C.: Efficient path planning algorithms in reach-avoid problems. Automatica **89**, 28–36 (2018). https://doi.org/10.1016/j.automatica.2017.11.035

Only Connect, Securely

Chandrika Bhardwaj$^{(\boxtimes)}$ and Sanjiva Prasad

Indian Institute of Technology Delhi, New Delhi, India
{chandrika,sanjiva}@cse.iitd.ac.in

Abstract. The *lattice model* proposed by Denning in her seminal work provided secure information flow analyses with an intuitive and uniform mathematical foundation. Different organisations, however, may employ quite different security lattices. In this paper, we propose a connection framework that permits different organisations to exchange information while maintaining both security of information flow as well as their autonomy in formulating and maintaining security policies. Our prescriptive framework is based on the rigorous mathematical framework of *Lagois connections* given by Melton, together with a simple operational model for transferring object data between domains. The merit of this formulation is that it is simple, minimal, adaptable and intuitive, and provides a formal framework for establishing secure information flow across autonomous interacting organisations. We show that our framework is semantically sound, by proving that the connections proposed preserve standard correctness notions such as non-interference.

Keywords: Security class lattice · Information Flow ·
Lagois connection · Atomic operations · Non-interference

1 Introduction

Denning's seminal work [7] proposed *complete lattices*[1] as the appropriate mathematical framework for questions regarding *secure information flow* (SIF), *i.e.*, only authorised flows of information are possible. An information flow model (IFM) is characterised as $\langle N, P, SC, \sqcup, \sqsubseteq \rangle$ where: *Storage objects* in N are assigned *security classes* drawn from a (finite) complete lattice SC. P is a set of processes (also assigned security classes as clearances). The partial ordering $\sqsubseteq$ represents *permitted flows* between classes; reflexivity and transitivity capture intuitive aspects of information flow; antisymmetry helps avoid redundancies in the framework, and the join operation $\sqcup$ succinctly captures the combination of information belonging to different security classes in arithmetic, logical

---

[1] Denning showed that the proposed structures, namely complete join semi-lattices with a least element, are in fact complete lattices.

Supported by Indo-Japanese project *Security in the IoT Space*, DST, Govt of India.

J. A. Pérez and N. Yoshida (Eds.): FORTE 2019, LNCS 11535, pp. 75–92, 2019.
https://doi.org/10.1007/978-3-030-21759-4_5

and computational operations. This lattice model provides an abstract uniform framework that identifies the commonalities of the variety of analyses for different applications – *e.g.*, confidentiality and trust – whether at the *language* level or at a *system* level. In the ensuing decades, the vast body of secure information flow analyses has been built on these mathematical foundations, with the development of a plethora of static and dynamic analysis techniques for programming languages [13,15,17,19–21], operating systems [2,8,12,20,25], databases [22], and hardware architectures [9,27], etc.

The soundness of this lattice model was expressed in terms of semantic notions of system behaviour, for instance, as properties like non-interference [10] by Volpano *et al.* [23] and others. Alternative semantic notions of security such as safety properties have been proposed as well, *e.g.*, [1], but for brevity we will not explore these further.

The objective of this paper is to propose a simple way in which large-scale distributed secure systems can be built by connecting component systems in a secure and modular manner. Our work begins with the observation that large information systems are not monolithic: Different organisations define their own information flow policies independently, and subsequently collaborate or federate with one another to exchange information. In general, the security classes and the lattices of any two organisations may be quite different—*there is no single universal security class lattice*. Moreover, *modularity* and *autonomy* are important requirements since each organisation would naturally wish to retain control over its own security policies and the ability to redefine them. Therefore, fusing different lattices by taking their union is an unsatisfactory approach, more so since the security properties of application programs would have to be re-established in this possibly enormous lattice.

When sharing information, most organisations limit the cross-domain communications to a limited set of security classes (which we call *transfer* classes). In order to ensure that shared data are not improperly divulged, two organisations usually negotiate agreements or memorandums of understanding (MoUs), promising that they will respect the security policies of the other organisation. We argue that a good notion of secure connection should require reasoning only about those flows from just the transfer classes mentioned in a MoU. Usually, cross-domain communication involves downgrading the security class of privileged information to public information using primitives such as encryption, and then upgrading the information to a suitable security class in the other domain. Such approaches, however, do not gel well with correctness notions such as non-interference. Indeed the question of how to translate information between security classes of different lattices is interesting [6].

Contributions of This Paper. In this paper, we propose a simple framework and sufficient conditions under which secure flow guarantees can be enforced without exposing the complexities and details of the component information flow models. The framework consists of (1) a way to connect security classes of one organisation to those in another while satisfying intuitive requirements; (2) a simple language that extends the operations within an organisation with primitives for transferring data between organisations; and (3) a type system and operational model for these constructs, which we use to establish that the framework conserves security.

In Sect. 2, we first identify, using intuitive examples, violations in secure flow that may arise when two secure systems are permitted to exchange information in both directions. Based on these lacunae, we formulate *security* and *precision* requirements for secure bidirectional flow. We then propose a framework that guarantees the absence of such policy violations, without impinging on the autonomy of the individual systems, without the need for re-verifying the security of the application procedures in either of the domains, and confining the analysis to only the transfer classes involved in potential exchange of data. Our approach is based on *monotone functions* and an elegant theory of *connections* [16] between the security lattices. Theorem 1 shows that *Lagois connections* between the security lattices satisfy the security and precision requirements.

We present in Sect. 3 a minimal operational language consisting of a small set of *atomic primitives* for effecting the transfer of data between domains. The framework is simple and can be adapted for establishing secure connections between distributed systems at any level of abstraction (language, system, database, ...). We assume each domain uses *atomic transactional operations* for object manipulation and intra-domain computation. The primitives of our model include reliable communication between two systems, transferring object data in designated *output* variables of one domain to designated *input* variables of a specified security class in the other domain. We also assume a generic set of operations in each domain for copying data from input variables to domain objects, and from domain objects to output variables. To avoid interference between inter-domain communication and the computations within the domains, we assume that the sets of designated input and output variables are all mutually exclusive of one another, and also with the program/system variables used in the computations within each domain. Thus by design we avoid the usual suspects that cause interference and insecure transfer of data. The operational description of the language consists of the primitives together with their execution rules (Sect. 3.1).

The correctness of our framework is demonstrated by expressing soundness (with respect to the operational semantics) of a type system (Sect. 3.2), stated in terms of the security lattices and their connecting functions. In particular, Theorem 7 shows the standard semantic property of *non-interference* in *both domains* holds of all operational behaviours. We adapt and *extend* the approach taken by Volpano et al. [23] to encompass systems coupled using the Lagois connection conditions, and (assuming atomicity of the data transfer operations) show that *security is conserved*. Since our language is a minimal imperative model with atomic transactions, reads and writes as the basic elements, we are able to work with a simplified version of the type system of Volpano et al.. In particular, our language does not include conditional constructs in the transfer of data between domains, and assumes all conditional computation is absorbed within atomic intradomain transactions. Thus, we do not have to concern ourselves with issues of implicit flows that arise due to branching structures (*e.g.*, conditionals

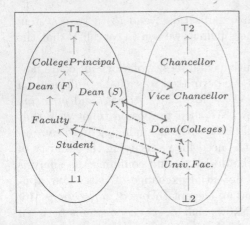

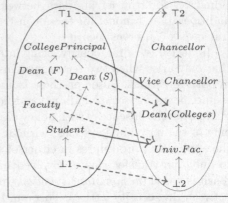

Fig. 1. Solid green arrows represent permitted flows according to the information exchange arrangement between a college and a university. Red dash-dotted arrows highlight a *new* flow that is a security violation. (Color figure online)

Fig. 2. Unidirectional flow: If the solid blue arrows denote identified flows connecting important classes, then the dashed green arrows are constrained by monotonicity to lie between them. (Color figure online)

and loops in programming language level security, pipeline mispredictions at the architectural level, etc.) While non-interference is the property addressed in this paper, we believe that our formulation is general enough to be applicable to other behavioural notions of secure information flow as a safety property [1].

In Sect. 4, we briefly review some related work. We conclude in Sect. 5 with a discussion on our approach and directions for future work.

2   Lagois Connections and All that

Motivating Examples. Consider a university system in which students study in semi-autonomously administered colleges (one such is C) that are affiliated to a university (U). The university also has "university professors" with whom students can take classes. We assume each institution has established the security of its information flow mechanisms and policies.

We first observe that formulating an agreement *between* the institutions which respects the flow policies within each institution is not entirely trivial. Consider an arrangement where the College *Faculty* and *University Faculty* can share information (say, course material and examinations), and the *Dean of Colleges* in the University can exchange information (*e.g.*, students' official grade-sheets) with the college's *Dean of Students*. Even such an apparently reasonable arrangement suffers from insecurities, as illustrated in Fig. 1 by the flow depicted using dashed red arrows, where information can flow from the college's *Faculty* to the college's *Dean of Students*. (Moral: internal structure of the lattices matters.)

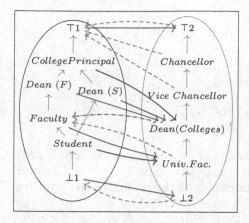 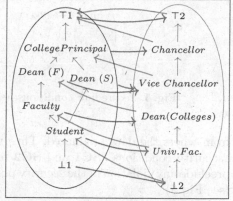

Fig. 3. The solid blue/green and dashed brown/red arrows respectively define monotone functions in each direction. However, the dash-dotted red arrow highlights a flow that is a security violation. (Color figure online)

Fig. 4. The arrows define a secure and precise connection. However, the security classification escalates quickly in a few round-trips when information can flow in both directions.

As long as information flows *unidirectionally* from colleges to the University, *monotone functions* from the security classes of the college lattice C to those in the university security lattice U *suffice* to ensure secure information flow. A function $\alpha : C \to U$ is called *monotone* if whenever $sc_1 \sqsubseteq sc_2$ in C then $\alpha(sc_1) \sqsubseteq' \alpha(sc_2)$ in U.[2] Monotonicity also constrains possible flows between classes of the two domains, once certain important flows between certain classes have been identified (see Fig. 2). Moreover, since monotone functions are closed under composition, one can chain them to create secure *unidirectional* information flow connections through a series of administrative domains. Monotonicity is a basic principle adopted for information flow analyses, *e.g.* [13].

However, when there is "blowback" of information, mere monotonicity is *inadequate* for ensuring SIF. Consider the bidirectional flow situation in Fig. 3, where data return to the original domain. Monotonicity of both functions $\alpha : C \to U$ and $\gamma : U \to C$ does *not* suffice for security because the composition $\gamma \circ \alpha$ may *not* be non-decreasing. In Fig. 3, both α and γ are monotone but their composition can lead to information leaking from a higher class, *e.g.*, *College Principal*, to a lower class, *e.g.*, *Faculty* within C—an outright violation of the college's security policy. Similarly, composition $\alpha \circ \gamma$ may lead to violation of the University's security policy.

Requirements. We want to ensure that any "round-trip" flow of information, *e.g.*, from a domain L to M and back to L, is a permitted flow in the lattice L,

---

[2] Note that it is not necessary for the function α to be total or surjective.

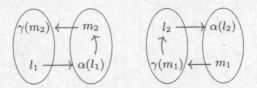

Fig. 5. Secure flow conditions: (**sc1**) $l_1 \sqsubseteq \gamma(m_2)$ (**sc2**) $m_1 \sqsubseteq' \alpha(l_2)$.

from where the data originated. Thus we require the following (tersely stated) "security conditions" **SC1** and **SC2** on $\alpha : L \to M$ and $\gamma : M \to L$, which preclude any violation of the security policies of both the administrative domains (see Fig. 5):

$$\textbf{SC1}\ \ \lambda l.l \sqsubseteq \gamma \circ \alpha \qquad\qquad \textbf{SC2}\ \ \lambda m.m \sqsubseteq \alpha \circ \gamma$$

In other words, the data can flow only in accordance with the flows permitted by the ordering relations of the two lattices.

We also desire *precision*, based on a principle of least privilege escalation—if data are exchanged between the two domains without any computation done on them, then the security level should not be needlessly raised. Precision is important for meaningful and useful analyses; otherwise data would be escalated to security classes which permit very restricted access.

$$\textbf{PC1}\ \ \alpha(l_1) = \bigsqcup \{m_1 \mid \gamma(m_1) = l_1\},\ \ \forall l_1 \in \gamma[M]$$
$$\textbf{PC2}\ \ \gamma(m_1) = \bigsqcup \{l_1 \mid \alpha(l_1) = m_1\},\ \ \forall m_1 \in \alpha[L]$$

Further, if the data were to go back and forth between two domains more than once, the security classes to which data belong should not become increasingly restrictive after consecutive bidirectional data sharing (See Fig. 4, which shows monotone functions that keep climbing up to the top). This convergence requirement may be stated informally as conditions **CC1** and **CC2**, requiring *fixed points* for the compositions $\gamma \circ \alpha$ and $\alpha \circ \gamma$. Since security lattices are finite, **CC1** and **CC2** necessarily hold – such fixed points exist, though perhaps only at the topmost elements of the lattice. We would therefore desire a stronger requirement, where fixed points are reached as low in the orderings as possible.

Galois Connections Aren't the Answer. Any discussion on a pair of partial orders linked by a pair of monotone functions suggests the notion of a Galois connection, an elegant and ubiquitous mathematical structure that finds use in computing, particularly in static analyses. However, Galois connections are not the appropriate structure for bidirectional informational flow control.

Let L and M be two complete security class lattices, and $\alpha : L \to M$ and $\gamma : M \to L$ be two monotone functions such that (L, α, γ, M) forms a Galois connection. Recall that a Galois connection satisfies the condition

$$\textbf{GC1}\ \ \forall l_1 \in L, m_1 \in M, \quad \alpha(l_1) \sqsubseteq' m_1 \iff l_1 \sqsubseteq \gamma(m_1)$$

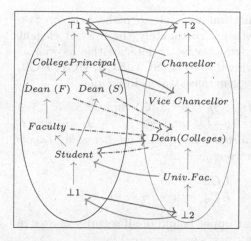 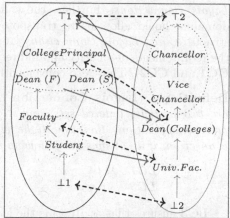

Fig. 6. The arrows between the domains define a Galois Connection. However, the red dash-dotted arrows highlight flow security violations when information can flow in both directions. (Color figure online)

Fig. 7. A useful increasing Lagois connection for sharing data. Dashed black arrows define permissible flows between buds.

So in a Galois connection we have $\alpha(\gamma(m_1)) \sqsubseteq' m_1 \iff \gamma(m_1) \sqsubseteq \gamma(m_1)$. Since $\gamma(m_1) \sqsubseteq \gamma(m_1)$ holds trivially, we get $\alpha(\gamma(m_1)) \sqsubseteq' m_1$. If $\alpha(\gamma(m_1)) \neq' m_1$ then $\alpha(\gamma(m_1)) \sqsubset' m_1$ (strictly), which would violate secure flow requirement **SC2**. Figure 6 illustrates such a situation.

Why Not Galois Insertions? Now suppose L and M are two complete security class lattices, and $\alpha : L \to M$ and $\gamma : M \to L$ be two monotone functions such that (L, α, γ, M) forms a *Galois insertion*, *i.e.*, a Galois connection where α is surjective:

$$\textbf{GI} \quad \lambda l.l \sqsubseteq \gamma \circ \alpha \quad \text{and} \quad \lambda m'.m' = \alpha \circ \gamma$$

Then the flow of information permitted by α and γ is guaranteed to be secure. However, Galois insertions mandate conditions on the definitions of functions α and γ that are much too strong, *i.e.*,

- $\gamma : M \to L$ is *injective*, *i.e.*, $\forall m_1, m_2 \in M : \gamma(m_1) = \gamma(m_2) \implies m_1 = m_2$
- $\alpha : L \to M$ is *surjective*, *i.e.*, $\forall m_1 \in M, \exists l_1 \in L : \alpha(l_1) = m_1$.

Typically data are shared only from a few security classes of any organisation. Organisations rarely make public their entire security class structure and permitted flow policies. Organisations also typically do not want any external influences on some subsets of its security classes. Thus, if not all elements of M are transfer classes, it may be impossible to define a Galois insertion (L, α, γ, M) because we cannot force α to be surjective.

Lagois Connections. Further, the connection we seek to make between two domains should allow us to transpose them. Fortunately there is an elegant structure, *i.e.*, *Lagois Connections* [16], which exactly satisfies this as well as the requirements of security and bidirectional sharing (**SC1, SC2, PC1, PC2, CC1** and **CC2**). They also conveniently generalise Galois insertions.

Definition 1 (Lagois Connection [16]**).** *If $L = (L, \sqsubseteq)$ and $M = (M, \sqsubseteq')$ are two partially ordered sets, and $\alpha : L \to M$ and $\gamma : M \to L$ are order-preserving functions, then we call the quadruple (L, α, γ, M) an increasing Lagois connection, if it satisfies the following properties:*

LC1	$\lambda l. l \sqsubseteq \gamma \circ \alpha$	*LC2*	$\lambda m'. m' \sqsubseteq' \alpha \circ \gamma$
LC3	$\alpha \circ \gamma \circ \alpha = \alpha$	*LC4*	$\gamma \circ \alpha \circ \gamma = \gamma$

LC3 ensures that $\gamma(\alpha(c_1))$ is the least upper bound of all security classes in C that are mapped to the same security class, say $u_1 = \alpha(c_1)$ in U.

The main result of this section is that if the negotiated monotone functions α and γ form a Lagois connection between the security lattices L and M, then information flows permitted are secure and precise.

Theorem 1. *Let L and M be two complete security class lattices, $\alpha : L \to M$ and $\gamma : M \to L$ be two monotone functions. Then the flow of information permitted by α, γ satisfies conditions **SC1, SC2, PC1, PC2, CC1** and **CC2** if (L, α, γ, M) is an increasing Lagois connection.*

Proof. Condition **SC1** holds because if $\alpha(l_1) \sqsubseteq' m_2$, by monotonicity of γ, $\gamma(\alpha(l_1)) \sqsubseteq \gamma(m_2)$. But by **LC1**, $l_1 \sqsubseteq \gamma(\alpha(l_1))$. So $l_1 \sqsubseteq \gamma(m_2)$. (A symmetric argument holds for **SC2**.) Conditions **PC1** and **PC2** are shown in Proposition 3.7 of [16]. Conditions **CC1** and **CC2** hold since the compositions $\gamma \circ \alpha$ and $\alpha \circ \gamma$ are *closure* operators, *i.e.*, idempotent, extensive, order-preserving endo-functions on L and M.

In fact, Lagois connections (e.g. Fig. 7) ensure that information in a security class in the original domain remains accessible even after doing a round-trip from the other domain (Proposition 3.8 in [16]):

$$\gamma(\alpha(l)) = \sqcap\{l^* \in \gamma[M] \mid l \sqsubseteq l^*\}, \tag{1}$$

$$\alpha(\gamma(m)) = \sqcap\{m^* \in \alpha[L] \mid m \sqsubseteq' m^*\}. \tag{2}$$

Properties of Lagois Connections. We list some properties of Lagois connections that assist in the construction of a secure connection, and in identifying those security classes that play an important role in the connection. Proposition 2 says that the two functions γ and α uniquely determine each other.

Proposition 2 (Proposition 3.9 in [16])**.** *If (L, α, γ, M) is a Lagois connection, then the functions α and γ uniquely determine each other; in fact*

$$\gamma(m) = \bigsqcup \alpha^{-1}\left[\sqcap\{m^* \in \alpha[L] \mid m \sqsubseteq' m^*\}\right] \tag{3}$$

$$\alpha(l) \;=\; \bigsqcup \, \gamma^{-1}[\, \sqcap\{\; l^* \in \gamma \,[\, M\,] \mid l \sqsubseteq l^*\}\,]\,] \tag{4}$$

Proposition 3 shows the existence of dominating members in their pre-images, which act as equivalence-class representatives of the equivalence relations $\sim_M$ and $\sim_L$ induced by the functions γ and α.

Proposition 3 (Proposition 3.7 in [16]). *Let (L, α, γ, M) be a Lagois connection and let $m \in \alpha[L]$ and $l \in \gamma[M]$. Then $\alpha^{-1}(m)$ has a largest member, which is $\gamma(m)$, and $\gamma^{-1}(l)$ has a largest member, which is $\alpha(l)$.*

That is, for all $m \in \alpha[L]$ and $l \in \gamma[M]$, $\gamma(m)$ and $\alpha(l)$ exist. Also, the images $\gamma[M]$ and $\alpha[L]$ are isomorphic lattices. $L^* = \gamma[\alpha[L]] = \gamma[M]$ and $M^* = \alpha[\gamma[M]] = \alpha[L]$ define a system of representatives for $\sim_L$ and $\sim_M$. Element $m^* = \alpha(\gamma(m'))$ in M^*, called a *budpoint*, acts as the representative of the equivalence class $[m']$ in the following sense:

$$if\ m \in M\ and\ m^* \in M^*\ with\ m \sim_M m^*\ then\ m \sqsubseteq' m^* \tag{5}$$

Symmetrically, $L^* = \gamma[\alpha[L]] = \gamma[M]$ defines a system of representatives for $\sim_L$. These budpoints play a significant role in delineating the connection between the transfer classes in the two lattices.

Further, Proposition 4 shows that these budpoints are closed under meets. This property enables us to confine our analysis to just these classes when reasoning about bidirectional flows.

Proposition 4 (Proposition 3.11 in [16]). *If (L, α, γ, M) is a Lagois connection and $A \subseteq \gamma[M]$, then*

1. *the meet of A in $\gamma[M]$ exists if and only if the meet of A in L exists, and whenever either exists, they are equal.*
2. *the join $\hat{a}$ of A in $\gamma[M]$ exists if the join $\check{a}$ of A in L exists, and in this case $\hat{a} = \gamma(\alpha(\check{a}))$*

3 An Operational Model

3.1 Computational Model

Let us consider two different organisations L and M that want to share data with each other. We start with the assumptions that the two domains comprise storage objects Z and Z' respectively, which are manipulated using their own sets of *atomic* transactional operations, ranged over by t and t' respectively. We further assume that these transactions within each domain are internally secure with respect to their flow models, and have no insecure or interfering interactions with the environment. Thus, we are agnostic to the level of abstraction of the systems we aim to connect securely, and since our approach treats the application domains as "black boxes", it is readily adaptable to any level of discourse (language, system, OS, database) found in the security literature.

We extend these operations with a minimal set of operations to transfer data between the two domains. To avoid any concurrency effects, interference or race conditions arising from inter-domain transfer, we augment the storage objects of both domains with a fresh set of *export* and *import* variables into/from which the data of the domain objects can be copied *atomically*. We designate these sets X, X' as the respective *export* variables, and Y, Y' as the respective *import* variables, with the corresponding variable instances written as x_i, x_i' and y_i, y_i'. These export and import variables form mutually disjoint sets, and are distinct from any extant domain objects manipulated by the applications within a domain. These variables are used exclusively for transfer, and are manipulated atomically. We let w_i range over all variables in $N = Z \cup X \cup Y$ (respectively w_i' over $N' = Z' \cup X' \cup Y'$). Domain objects are copied *to export* variables and *from import* variables by special operations $rd(z, y)$ and $wr(x, z)$ (and $rd'(z', y')$ and $wr'(x', z')$ in the other domain). We assume *atomic transfer* operations (*trusted by both domains*) T_{RL}, T_{LR} that copy data from the export variables of one domain to the import variables of the other domain as the only mechanism for inter-domain flow of data. Let "phrase" p denote a command in either domain or a transfer operation, and let s be any (empty or non-empty) sequence of phrases.

(command) $c ::= t \mid rd(z, y) \mid wr(x, z)$ $c' ::= t' \mid rd'(z', y') \mid wr'(x', z')$

(phrase) $p ::= T_{RL}(x', y) \mid T_{LR}(x, y') \mid c \mid c'$ (seq) $s ::= \epsilon \mid s_1; p$

$$\text{T} \quad \frac{\mu \vdash t \Rightarrow \nu}{\langle \mu, \mu' \rangle \vdash t \Rightarrow \langle \nu, \mu' \rangle} \qquad \text{T'} \quad \frac{\mu' \vdash t' \Rightarrow \nu'}{\langle \mu, \mu' \rangle \vdash t' \Rightarrow \langle \mu, \nu' \rangle}$$

$$\text{WR} \quad \frac{}{\langle \mu, \mu' \rangle \vdash wr(x, z) \Rightarrow \langle \mu[x := \mu(z)], \mu' \rangle}$$

$$\text{WR'} \quad \frac{}{\langle \mu, \mu' \rangle \vdash wr'(x', z') \Rightarrow \langle \mu, \mu'[x' := \mu'(z')] \rangle}$$

$$\text{RD} \quad \frac{}{\langle \mu, \mu' \rangle \vdash rd(z, y) \Rightarrow \langle \mu[z := \mu(y)], \mu' \rangle}$$

$$\text{RD'} \quad \frac{}{\langle \mu, \mu' \rangle \vdash rd'(z', y') \Rightarrow \langle \mu, \mu'[z' := \mu'(y')] \rangle}$$

$$\text{TRL} \quad \frac{}{\langle \mu, \mu' \rangle \vdash T_{RL}(y, x') \Rightarrow \langle \mu[y := \mu'(x')], \mu' \rangle}$$

$$\text{TLR} \quad \frac{}{\langle \mu, \mu' \rangle \vdash T_{LR}(y', x) \Rightarrow \langle \mu, \mu'[y' := \mu(x)] \rangle}$$

$$\text{SEQ0} \quad \frac{}{\langle \mu, \mu' \rangle \vdash \epsilon \Rightarrow^* \langle \mu, \mu' \rangle}$$

$$\text{SEQS} \quad \frac{\langle \mu, \mu' \rangle \vdash s_1 \Rightarrow^* \langle \mu_1, \mu_1' \rangle, \quad \langle \mu_1, \mu_1' \rangle \vdash p \Rightarrow \langle \mu_2, \mu_2' \rangle}{\langle \mu, \mu' \rangle \vdash s_1; p \Rightarrow^* \langle \mu_2, \mu_2' \rangle}$$

Fig. 8. Execution rules

A *store* (typically μ, ν, μ', ν') is a finite-domain function from variables to a set of values (not further specified). We write, *e.g.*, $\mu(w)$ for the contents of the store μ at variable w, and $\mu[w := \mu'(w')]$ for the store that is the same as μ everywhere except at variable w, where it now takes value $\mu'(w')$.

The rules specifying execution of commands are given in Fig. 8. Assuming the specification of intradomain transactions (t, t') of the form $\mu \vdash t \implies \nu$ and $\mu' \vdash t' \implies \nu'$, our rules allow us to specify judgments of the form $\langle \mu, \mu' \rangle \vdash p \implies \langle \nu, \nu' \rangle$ for phrases, and the reflexive-transitive closure for sequences of phrases. Note that phrase execution occurs *atomically*, and the intra-domain transactions, as well as copying to and from the export/import variables affect the store in only one domain, whereas the *atomic transfer* is only between export variables of one domain and the import variables of the other.

3.2 Typing Rules

Let the two domains have the respective different IFMs:

$$FM_L = \langle N, P, SC, \sqcup, \sqsubseteq \rangle \qquad FM_M = \langle N', P', SC', \sqcup, \sqsubseteq' \rangle,$$

such that the flow policies in both are defined over different sets of security classes SC and SC'.[3]

The (security) types of the core language are as follows. Metavariables l and m' range over the sets of security classes, SC and SC' respectively, which are partially ordered by $\sqsubseteq$ and $\sqsubseteq'$. A type assignment λ is a finite-domain function from variables N to SC (respectively, λ' from N' to SC'). The important restriction we place on λ and λ' is that they map export and import variables X, X, Y', Y only to points in the security lattices SC and SC' respectively which are in the domains of γ and α, *i.e.*, these points participate in the Lagois connection. Intuitively, a variable w mapped to security class l can store information of security class l or lower. The type system works with respect to a given type assignment. Given a security level, *e.g.*, l, the typing rules track for each command *within that domain* whether all written-to variables in that domain are of security classes "above" l, and additionally for transactions within a domain, they ensure "simple security", *i.e.*, that all variables which may have been read belong to security classes "below" l. We assume for the transactions within a domain, *e.g.*, L, we have a type system that will give us judgments of the form $\lambda \vdash c : l$. The novelty of our approach is to extend this framework to work over two connected domains, *i.e.*, given implicit security levels of the contexts in the respective domains. Cross-domain transfers will require pairing such judgments, and thus our type system will have judgments of the form

$$\langle \lambda, \lambda' \rangle \vdash p : \langle l, m' \rangle$$

We introduce a set of typing rules for the core language, given in Fig. 9. In many of the rules, the type for one of the domains is not constrained by the rule, and so any suitable type may be chosen as determined by the context, *e.g.*, m' in the rules TT, TRD, TWR and TT_{RL}, and both l and m' in COM0.

---

[3] Without loss of generality, we assume that $SC \cap SC' = \emptyset$, since we can suitably rename security classes.

$$\text{TT} \quad \frac{}{\langle \lambda, \lambda' \rangle \vdash t : \langle l, m' \rangle} \text{ if for all } z \text{ assigned in } t, \, l \sqsubseteq \lambda(z)$$
$$\& \text{ for all } z_1 \text{ read in } t, \, \lambda(z_1) \sqsubseteq l$$

$$\text{TT'} \quad \frac{}{\langle \lambda, \lambda' \rangle \vdash t' : \langle l, m' \rangle} \text{ if for all } z' \text{ assigned in } t', \, m' \sqsubseteq' \lambda'(z')$$
$$\& \text{ for all } z'_1 \text{ read in } t', \, \lambda'(z'_1) \sqsubseteq' m'$$

$$\text{TRD} \quad \frac{\lambda(y) \sqsubseteq \lambda(z)}{\langle \lambda, \lambda' \rangle \vdash rd(z, y) : \langle \lambda(z), m' \rangle}$$

$$\text{TRD'} \quad \frac{\lambda'(y') \sqsubseteq' \lambda'(z')}{\langle \lambda, \lambda' \rangle \vdash rd'(z', y') : \langle l, \lambda'(z') \rangle}$$

$$\text{TWR} \quad \frac{\lambda(z) \sqsubseteq \lambda(x)}{\langle \lambda, \lambda' \rangle \vdash wr(x, z) : \langle \lambda(x), m' \rangle}$$

$$\text{TWR'} \quad \frac{\lambda'(z') \sqsubseteq' \lambda'(x')}{\langle \lambda, \lambda' \rangle \vdash wr'(x', z') : \langle l, \lambda'(x') \rangle}$$

$$\text{TT}_{RL} \quad \frac{\gamma(\lambda'(x')) \sqsubseteq \lambda(y)}{\langle \lambda, \lambda' \rangle \vdash T_{RL}(y, x') : \langle \lambda(y), \lambda'(x') \rangle}$$

$$\text{TT}_{LR'} \quad \frac{\alpha(\lambda(x)) \sqsubseteq' \lambda'(y')}{\langle \lambda, \lambda' \rangle \vdash T_{LR}(y', x) : \langle \lambda(x), \lambda'(y') \rangle}$$

$$\text{COM0} \quad \frac{}{\langle \lambda, \lambda' \rangle \vdash \epsilon : \langle l, m' \rangle}$$

$$\text{COMS} \quad \frac{\langle \lambda, \lambda' \rangle \vdash p : \langle l_1, m'_1 \rangle \quad \langle \lambda, \lambda' \rangle \vdash s : \langle l, m' \rangle}{\langle \lambda, \lambda' \rangle \vdash s; p : \langle l_1 \sqcap l, m'_1 \sqcap m' \rangle}$$

Fig. 9. Typing rules

For transactions *e.g.*, t entirely within domain L, the typing rule TT constrains the type in the left domain to be at a level l that dominates all variables read in t, and which is dominated by all variables written to in t, but places no constraints on the type m' in the other domain M. In the rule TRD, since a value in import variable y is copied to the variable z, we have $\lambda(y) \sqsubseteq \lambda(z)$, and the type in the domain L is $\lambda(z)$ with no constraint on the type m' in the other domain. Conversely, in the rule TWR, since a value in variable z is copied to the export variable x, we have $\lambda(z) \sqsubseteq \lambda(x)$, and the type in the domain L is $\lambda(x)$ with no constraint on the type m' in the other domain. In the rule TT_{RL}, since the contents of a variable x' in domain M are copied into a variable y in domain L, we require $\gamma(\lambda'(x')) \sqsubseteq \lambda(y)$, and constrain the type in domain L to $\lambda(y)$. The constraint in the other domain is unimportant (but for the sake of convenience, we peg it at $\lambda'(x')$). Finally, for the types of sequences of phrases, we take the meets of the collected types in each domain respectively, so that we can guarantee that no variable of type lower than these meets has been written into during the sequence. Note that Proposition 4 ensures that these types have the desired properties for participating in the Lagois connection.

3.3   Soundness

We now establish soundness of our scheme by showing a non-interference theorem with respect to operational semantics and the type system built on the security lattices. This theorem may be viewed as a conservative adaptation (to a minimal secure data transfer framework in a Lagois-connected pair of domains) of the main result of Volpano et al. [23].

We assume that underlying base transactional languages in each of the domains have the following simple property (stated for L, but an analogous property is assumed for M). Within each transaction t, for each assignment of an expression e to any variable z, the following holds: If μ, ν are two stores such that for all $w \in vars(e)$, we have $\mu(w) = \nu(w)$, then after executing the assignment, we will get $\mu(z) = \nu(z)$. That is, if two stores are equal for all variables appearing in the expression e, then the value assigned to the variable z will be the same. This assumption plays the rôle of "Simple Security" of expressions in [23] in the proof of the main theorem. The type system plays the rôle of "Confinement". We start with two obvious lemmas about the operational semantics, namely preservation of domains, and a "frame" lemma:

Lemma 5 *(Domain preservation).* If $\langle \mu, \mu' \rangle \vdash s \Rightarrow^* \langle \mu_1, \mu_1' \rangle$, then $dom(\mu) = dom(\mu_1)$, and $dom(\mu') = dom(\mu_1')$.

Proof. By induction on the length of the derivation of $\langle \mu, \mu' \rangle \vdash s \Rightarrow^* \langle \mu_1, \mu_1' \rangle$.

Lemma 6 *(Frame).* If $\langle \mu, \mu' \rangle \vdash s \Rightarrow^* \langle \mu_1, \mu_1' \rangle$, $w \in dom(\mu) \cup dom(\mu')$, and w is not assigned to in s, then $\mu(w) = \mu_1(w)$ and $\mu'(w) = \mu_1'(w)$.

Proof. By induction on the length of the derivation of $\langle \mu, \mu' \rangle \vdash s \Rightarrow^* \langle \mu_1, \mu_1' \rangle$.

The main result of the paper assumes an "adversary" that operates at a security level l in domain L and at security level m' in domain M. Note however, that these two levels are interconnected by the monotone functions $\alpha : L \to M$ and $\gamma : M \to L$, since these levels are connected by the ability of information at one level in one domain to flow to the other level in the other domain. The following theorem says that if (a) a sequence of phrases is well-typed, and (b, c) we start its execution in two store configurations that are (e) indistinguishable with respect to all objects having security class below l and m' in the respective domains, then the corresponding resulting stores after execution continue to remain indistinguishable on all variables with security classes below these adversarial levels.

Theorem 7 (Type Soundness). *Suppose l, m' are the "adversarial" type levels in the respective domains, which satisfy the condition $l = \gamma(m')$ and $m' = \alpha(l)$. Let*

(a) $\langle \lambda, \lambda' \rangle \vdash s : \langle l_0, m_0' \rangle$;   (s has security type $\langle l_0, m_0' \rangle$)
(b) $\langle \mu, \mu' \rangle \vdash s \Rightarrow^* \langle \mu_f, \mu_f' \rangle$;   (execution of s starting from $\langle \mu, \mu' \rangle$)
(c) $\langle \nu, \nu' \rangle \vdash s \Rightarrow^* \langle \nu_f, \nu_f' \rangle$;   (execution of s starting from $\langle \nu, \nu' \rangle$)

(d) $dom(\mu) = dom(\nu) = dom(\lambda)$ and $dom(\mu') = dom(\nu') = dom(\lambda')$;

(e) $\mu(w) = \nu(w)$ for all w such that $\lambda(w) \sqsubseteq l$, and $\mu'(w') = \nu'(w')$ for all w' such that $\lambda'(w') \sqsubseteq' m'$.

Then $\mu_f(w) = \nu_f(w)$ for all w such that $\lambda(w) \sqsubseteq l$, and $\mu'_f(w') = \nu'_f(w')$ for all w' such that $\lambda'(w') \sqsubseteq' m'$.

Proof. By induction on the length of sequence s. The base case is vacuously true. We now consider a sequence $s_1; p$. $\langle \mu, \mu' \rangle \vdash s_1 \Rightarrow^* \langle \mu_1, \mu'_1 \rangle$ and $\langle \mu_1, \mu'_1 \rangle \vdash p \Rightarrow \langle \mu_f, \mu'_f \rangle$ and $\langle \nu, \nu' \rangle \vdash s_1 \Rightarrow^* \langle \nu_1, \nu'_1 \rangle$ and $\langle \nu_1, \nu'_1 \rangle \vdash p \Rightarrow \langle \nu_f, \nu'_f \rangle$ By induction hypothesis applied to s_1, we have $\mu_1(w) = \nu_1(w)$ for all w such that $\lambda(w) \sqsubseteq l$, and $\mu'_1(w') = \nu'_1(w')$ for all w' such that $\lambda'(w') \sqsubseteq' m'$.

Let $\langle \lambda, \lambda' \rangle \vdash s_1 : \langle l_s, m'_s \rangle$, and $\langle \lambda, \lambda' \rangle \vdash p : \langle l_p, m'_p \rangle$. We examine four cases for p (the remaining cases are symmetrical).

Case p is t: Consider any w such that $\lambda(w) \sqsubseteq l$. If $w \in X \cup Y$ (*i.e.*, it doesn't appear in t), or if $w \in Z$ but is not assigned to in t, then by Lemma 6 and the induction hypothesis, $\mu_f(w) = \mu_1(w) = \nu_1(w) = \nu_f(w)$.

Now suppose z is assigned to in t. From the condition $\langle \lambda, \lambda' \rangle \vdash p : \langle l_p, m'_p \rangle$, we know that for all z_1 assigned in t, $l_p \sqsubseteq \lambda(z_1)$ and for all z_1 read in t, $\lambda(z_1) \sqsubseteq l_p$. Now if $l \sqsubseteq l_p$, then since in t no variables z_2 such that $\lambda(z_2) \sqsubseteq l$ are assigned to. Therefore by Lemma 6, $\mu_f(w) = \mu_1(w) = \nu_1(w) = \nu_f(w)$, for all w such that $\lambda(w) \sqsubseteq l$.

If $l_p \sqsubseteq l$, then for all z_1 read in t, $\lambda(z_1) \sqsubseteq l_p$. Therefore, by assumption on transaction t, if any variable z is assigned an expression e, since μ_1, ν_1 are two stores such that for all $z_1 \in Z_e = vars(e)$, $\mu_1(z_1) = \nu_1(z_1)$, the value of e will be the same. By this simple security argument, after the transaction t, we have $\mu_f(z) = \nu_f(z)$. Since the transaction happened entirely and atomically in domain L, we do not have to worry ourselves with changes in the other domain M, and do not need to concern ourselves with the adversarial level m'.

Case p is $rd(z, y)$: Thus $\langle \lambda, \lambda' \rangle \vdash rd(z, y) : \langle \lambda(z), m' \rangle$, which means $\lambda(y) \sqsubseteq \lambda(z)$. If $l \sqsubseteq \lambda(z)$, there is nothing to prove (Lemma 6, again). If $\lambda(z) \sqsubseteq l$, then since by I.H., $\mu_1(y) = \nu_1(y)$, we have $\mu_f(z) = \mu_1[z := \mu_1(y)](z) = \nu_1[z := \nu_1(y)](z) = \nu_f(z)$.

Case p is $wr(x, z)$: Thus $\langle \lambda, \lambda' \rangle \vdash wr(x, z) : \langle \lambda(x), m' \rangle$, which means $\lambda(z) \sqsubseteq \lambda(x)$. If $l \sqsubseteq \lambda(x)$, there is nothing to prove (Lemma 6, again). If $\lambda(x) \sqsubseteq l$, then since by I.H., $\mu_1(z) = \nu_1(z)$, we have $\mu_f(x) = \mu_1[x := \mu_1(z)](x) = \nu_1[x := \nu_1(z)](x) = \nu_f(x)$.

Case p is $T_{RL}(y, x')$: So $\langle \lambda, \lambda' \rangle \vdash T_{RL}(y, x') : \langle \lambda(y), \lambda'(x') \rangle$, and $\gamma(\lambda'(x')) \sqsubseteq \lambda(y)$. If $l \sqsubseteq \lambda(y)$, there is nothing to prove (Lemma 6, again). If $\lambda(y) \sqsubseteq l$, then by transitivity, $\gamma(\lambda'(x')) \sqsubseteq l$. By monotonicity of α: $\alpha(\gamma(\lambda'(x'))) \sqsubseteq' \alpha(l) = m'$ (By our assumption on l and m'). But by **LC2**, $\lambda'(x') \sqsubseteq' \alpha(\gamma(\lambda'(x')))$. So by transitivity, $\lambda'(x') \sqsubseteq' m'$. Now, by I.H., since $\mu'_1(x') = \nu'_1(x')$, we have $\mu_f(y) = \mu_1[y := \mu'_1(x')](y) = \nu_1[y := \nu'_1(x')](y) = \nu_f(y)$.

4   Related Work

The notion of Lagois connections [16] has surprisingly not been employed much in computer science. The only cited use of this idea seems to be the work of Huth [11] in establishing the correctness of programming language implementations. To our knowledge, our work is the only one to propose their use in secure information flow control.

Abstract Interpretation and type systems [5] have been used in secure flow analyses, *e.g.*, [3,4] and [24], where security types are defined using Galois connections employing, for instance, a standard collecting semantics. Their use of two domains, concrete and abstract, with a Galois connection between them, for performing static analyses *within a single domain* should not be confused with our idea of secure connections between independently-defined security lattices of two organisations.

There has been substantial work on SIF in a distributed setting at the systems level. DStar [26] for example, uses sets of opaque identifiers to define security classes. The DStar framework extends a *particular* Decentralized Information Flow Control (DIFC) model [12,25] for operating systems to a distributed network. The only partial order that is considered in DStar's security lattice is subset inclusion. So it is not clear if DStar can work on general IFC mechanisms such as FlowCaml [19], which can use any partial ordering. Nor can it express the labels of JiF [17] or Fabric [13] completely. DStar allows bidirectional communication between processes R and S only if $L_R \sqsubseteq_{O_R} L_S$ and $L_S \sqsubseteq_{O_S} L_R$, *i.e.*, if there is an order-isomorphism between the labels. Our motivating examples indicate such a requirement is far too restrictive for most practical arrangements for data sharing between organisations.

Fabric [13,14] adds *trust relationships* directly derived from a principal hierarchy to support federated systems with mutually distrustful nodes and allows dynamic delegation of authority.

Most of the previous DIFC mechanisms [2,8,12,17,20,25] including Fabric are susceptible to the vulnerabilities illustrated in our motivating examples, which we will mention in the concluding discussion.

5   Conclusions and Future Work

Our work is similar in spirit to Denning's motivation for proposing lattices, namely to identify a simple and mathematically elegant structure in which to frame the construction of scalable secure information flow in a modular manner that preserved the autonomy of the individual organisations. From the basic requirements, we identified the elegant theory of Lagois connections as an appropriate structure. Lagois connections provide us a way to connect the security lattices of two (secure) systems in a manner that does not expose their entire internal structure and allows us to reason only in terms of the interfaced security classes. We believe that this framework is also applicable in more intricate information flow control formulations such as decentralised IFC [18] and models with declassification, as well as formulations with data-dependent security classes [15]. We intend to explore these aspects in the future.

In this paper, we also proposed a minimal operational model for the transfer of data between the two domains. This formulation is spare enough to be adaptable at various levels of abstraction (programming language, systems, databases), and is intended to illustrate that the Lagois connection framework can *conserve* security, using non-interference as the semantic notion of soundness. The choice of non-interference and the use of a type system in the manner of Volpano *et al.* [23] was to illustrate in familiar terms how those techniques (removed from a particular language formulation) could be readily adapted to work in the context of secure connections between lattices. In this exercise, we made suitable assumptions of atomicity and the use of fresh variables for communication, so as to avoid usual sources of interference. By assuming that the basic intra-domain transactions are atomic and by not permitting conditional transfer of information across domains in the language, we have avoided dealing with issues related to implicit flows. We believe that the Lagois connection framework for secure flows between systems is readily adaptable for notions of semantic correctness other than non-interference, though that is an exercise for the future.

In the future we intend to explore how the theory of Lagois connections constitutes a robust framework that can support the discovery, decomposition, update and maintenance of secure MoUs for exchanging information. In this paper, we concerned ourselves only with two domains and bidirectional information exchange. Compositionality of Lagois connections allows these results to extend to chaining connections across several domains. In the future, we also intend to explore how one may secure more complicated information exchange arrangements than merely chains of bidirectional flow.

We close this discussion with a reminder of why it is important to have a framework in which secure flows should be treated in a modular and autonomous manner. Consider Myer's DIFC model described in [18], where a principal can delegate to others the capacity to act on its behalf. We believe that this notion does not scale well to large, networked systems since a principal may repose different levels of trust in the various hosts in the network. For this reason, we believe that frameworks such as Fabric [13,14] may provide more power than mandated by a principle of least privilege. In general, since a principal rarely vests unqualified trust in another in all contexts and situations, one should confine the influence of the principals possessing delegated authority to only specific domains. A mathematical framework that can deal with localising trust and delegation of authority in different domains and controlling the manner in which information flow can be secured deserves a deeper study. We believe that algebraic theories such as Lagois connections can provide the necessary structure for articulating these concepts.

Acknowledgments. The second author thanks Deepak Garg for insightful discussions on secure information flow. Part of the title is stolen from E.M. Forster.

References

1. Boudol, G.: Secure information flow as a safety property. In: Degano, P., Guttman, J., Martinelli, F. (eds.) FAST 2008. LNCS, vol. 5491, pp. 20–34. Springer, Heidelberg (2009). https://doi.org/10.1007/978-3-642-01465-9_2
2. Cheng, W., et al.: Abstractions for usable information flow control in Aeolus. In: 2012 USENIX Annual Technical Conference, Boston, MA, USA, 13–15 June 2012, pp. 139–151 (2012)
3. Cortesi, A., Ferrara, P., Halder, R., Zanioli, M.: Combining symbolic and numerical domains for information leakage analysis. Trans. Comput. Sci. **31**, 98–135 (2018)
4. Cortesi, A., Ferrara, P., Pistoia, M., Tripp, O.: Datacentric semantics for verification of privacy policy compliance by mobile applications. In: D'Souza, D., Lal, A., Larsen, K.G. (eds.) VMCAI 2015. LNCS, vol. 8931, pp. 61–79. Springer, Heidelberg (2015). https://doi.org/10.1007/978-3-662-46081-8_4
5. Cousot, P.: Types as Abstract Interpretations. In: Conference Record of POPL 1997: The 24th ACM SIGPLAN-SIGACT Symposium on Principles of Programming Languages, Papers Presented at the Symposium, Paris, France, 15–17 January 1997, pp. 316–331 (1997)
6. Deng, S., Gümüsoglu, D., Xiong, W., Gener, Y.S., Demir, O., Szefer, J.: SecChisel: language and tool for practical and scalable security verification of security-aware hardware architectures. IACR Cryptology ePrint Archive 2017/193 (2017). http://eprint.iacr.org/2017/193
7. Denning, D.E.: A lattice model of secure information flow. Commun. ACM **19**(5), 236–243 (1976)
8. Efstathopoulos, P., et al.: Labels and event processes in the Asbestos operating system. In: Proceedings of the 20th ACM Symposium on Operating Systems Principles 2005, SOSP 2005, Brighton, UK, 23–26 October 2005, pp. 17–30 (2005)
9. Ferraiuolo, A., Zhao, M., Myers, A.C., Suh, G.E.: Hyperflow: a processor architecture for nonmalleable, timing-safe information flow security. In: Proceedings of the 2018 ACM SIGSAC Conference on Computer and Communications Security, CCS 2018, Toronto, ON, Canada, 15–19 October 2018, pp. 1583–1600 (2018)
10. Goguen, J.A., Meseguer, J.: Security policies and security models. In: 1982 IEEE Symposium on Security and Privacy, Oakland, CA, USA, 26–28 April 1982, pp. 11–20 (1982)
11. Huth, M.: On the equivalence of state-transition systems. In: Burn, G., Gay, S., Ryan, M. (eds.) Theory and Formal Methods 1993. Workshops in Computing, pp. 171–182. Springer, London (1993). https://doi.org/10.1007/978-1-4471-3503-6_13
12. Krohn, M.N., et al.: Information flow control for standard OS abstractions. In: Proceedings of the 21st ACM Symposium on Operating Systems Principles 2007, SOSP 2007, Stevenson, Washington, USA, 14–17 October 2007, pp. 321–334 (2007)
13. Liu, J., Arden, O., George, M.D., Myers, A.C.: Fabric: building open distributed systems securely by construction. J. Comput. Secur. **25**(4–5), 367–426 (2017)
14. Liu, J., George, M.D., Vikram, K., Qi, X., Waye, L., Myers, A.C.: Fabric: a platform for secure distributed computation and storage. In: Proceedings of the 22nd ACM Symposium on Operating Systems Principles 2009, SOSP 2009, Big Sky, Montana, USA, 11–14 October 2009, pp. 321–334 (2009)
15. Lourenço, L., Caires, L.: Dependent information flow types. In: Proceedings of the 42nd Annual ACM SIGPLAN-SIGACT Symposium on Principles of Programming Languages, POPL 2015, Mumbai, India, 15–17 January 2015, pp. 317–328 (2015)

16. Melton, A., Schröder, B.S.W., Strecker, G.E.: Lagois connections - a counterpart to Galois connections. Theor. Comput. Sci. **136**(1), 79–107 (1994)
17. Myers, A.C.: JFlow: practical mostly-static information flow control. In: Proceedings of the 26th ACM SIGPLAN-SIGACT Symposium on Principles of Programming Languages, POPL 1999, San Antonio, TX, USA, 20–22 January 1999, pp. 228–241 (1999)
18. Myers, A.C.: Mostly-static decentralized information flow control. Ph.D. thesis, Massachusetts Institute of Technology, Cambridge, MA, USA (1999). http://hdl.handle.net/1721.1/16717
19. Pottier, F., Simonet, V.: Information flow inference for ML. ACM Trans. Program. Lang. Syst. **25**(1), 117–158 (2003)
20. Roy, I., Porter, D.E., Bond, M.D., McKinley, K.S., Witchel, E.: Laminar: practical fine-grained decentralized information flow control. In: Proceedings of the 2009 ACM SIGPLAN Conference on Programming Language Design and Implementation, PLDI 2009, Dublin, Ireland, 15–21 June 2009, pp. 63–74 (2009)
21. Sabelfeld, A., Myers, A.C.: Language-based information-flow security. IEEE J. Sel. Areas Commun. **21**(1), 5–19 (2003)
22. Schultz, D.A., Liskov, B.: IFDB: decentralized information flow control for databases. In: Eighth Eurosys Conference 2013, EuroSys 2013, Prague, Czech Republic, 14–17 April 2013, pp. 43–56 (2013)
23. Volpano, D.M., Irvine, C.E., Smith, G.: A sound type system for secure flow analysis. J. Comput. Secur. **4**(2/3), 167–188 (1996)
24. Zanotti, M.: Security typings by abstract interpretation. In: Hermenegildo, M.V., Puebla, G. (eds.) SAS 2002. LNCS, vol. 2477, pp. 360–375. Springer, Heidelberg (2002). https://doi.org/10.1007/3-540-45789-5_26
25. Zeldovich, N., Boyd-Wickizer, S., Kohler, E., Mazières, D.: Making information flow explicit in histar. In: 7th Symposium on Operating Systems Design and Implementation (OSDI 2006), Seattle, WA, USA, 6–8 November, pp. 263–278 (2006)
26. Zeldovich, N., Boyd-Wickizer, S., Mazières, D.: Securing distributed systems with information flow control. In: Proceedings of 5th USENIX Symposium on Networked Systems Design & Implementation, NSDI 2008, San Francisco, CA, USA, 16–18 April 2008, pp. 293–308 (2008)
27. Zhang, D., Wang, Y., Suh, G.E., Myers, A.C.: A hardware design language for timing-sensitive information-flow security. In: Proceedings of the Twentieth International Conference on Architectural Support for Programming Languages and Operating Systems, ASPLOS 2015, Istanbul, Turkey, 14–18 March 2015, pp. 503–516 (2015)

Output-Sensitive Information Flow Analysis

Cristian Ene(✉), Laurent Mounier, and Marie-Laure Potet

Univ. Grenoble Alpes, CNRS, Grenoble INP, VERIMAG, 38000 Grenoble, France
{Cristian.Ene,Laurent.Mounier,Marie-laure.Potet}@univ-grenoble-alpes.fr

Abstract. *Constant-time* programming is a countermeasure to prevent cache based attacks where programs should not perform memory accesses that depend on secrets. In some cases this policy can be safely relaxed if one can prove that the program does not leak more information than the public outputs of the computation.

We propose a novel approach for verifying constant-time programming based on a new information flow property, called *output-sensitive non-interference*. Noninterference states that a public observer cannot learn anything about the private data. Since real systems need to intentionally declassify some information, this property is too strong in practice. In order to take into account public outputs we proceed as follows: instead of using complex explicit declassification policies, we partition variables in three sets: input, output and leakage variables. Then, we propose a typing system to statically check that leakage variables do not leak *more information about the secret inputs than the public normal output*. The novelty of our approach is that we track the dependence of leakage variables with respect not only to the initial values of input variables (as in classical approaches for noninterference), but taking also into account the final values of output variables. We adapted this approach to LLVM IR and we developed a prototype to verify LLVM implementations.

Keywords: Information flow · Output-sensitive non-interference · Type system

1 Introduction

An important task of cryptographic research is to verify cryptographic implementations for security flaws, in particular to avoid so-called timing attacks. Such attacks consist in measuring the execution time of an implementation on its execution platform. For instance, Brumley and Bonch [12] showed that it was possible to mount remote timing attacks by against OpenSSL's implementation of the RSA decryption operation and to recover the key. Albrecht and Paterson

This work is supported by the French National Research Agency in the framework of the "Investissements d' avenir" program (ANR-15-IDEX-02).

© IFIP International Federation for Information Processing 2019
Published by Springer Nature Switzerland AG 2019
J. A. Pérez and N. Yoshida (Eds.): FORTE 2019, LNCS 11535, pp. 93–110, 2019.
https://doi.org/10.1007/978-3-030-21759-4_6

[3] showed that the two levels of protection offered against the Lucky 13 attack from [2] in the first release of the new implementation of TLS were imperfect. A related class of attacks are *cache-based attacks* in which a malicious party is able to obtain memory-access addressses of the target program which may depend on secret data through observing cache accesses. Such attacks allow to recover the complete AES keys [17].

A possible countermeasure is to follow a very strict programming discipline called **constant-time programming**. Its principle is to avoid branchings controlled by secret data and memory load/store operations indexed by secret data. Recent secure C libraries such as NaCl [10] or mbedTLS[1] follow this programming discipline. Until recently, there was no rigorous proof that constant-time algorithms are protected to cache-based attacks. Moreover, many cryptographic implementations such as PolarSSL AES, DES, and RC4 make array accesses that depend on secret keys and are not constant time. Recent works [4,6,11] fill this gap and develop the first formal analyzes that allow to verify if programs are correct with respect to the constant-time paradigm.

An interesting extension was brought by Almeida et al. [4] who enriched the constant-time paradigm *"distinguishing not only between public and private input values, but also between private and publicly observable output values"*. This distinction raises interesting technical and theoretical challenges. Indeed, constant-time implementations in cryptographic libraries like OpenSSL include optimizations for which paths and addresses can depend not only on public input values, but also on publicly observable output values. Hence, considering only input values as non-secret information would thus incorrectly characterize those implementations as non-constant-time. [4] also develops a verification technique based on *symbolic execution*. However, the soundness of their approach depends in practice on the soundness of the underlying symbolic execution engine, which is very difficult to guarantee for real-world programs with loops. Moreover, their product construction can be very expensive in the worst case.

In this paper we deal with *statically checking programs* for **output-sensitive constant-time** correctness: programs can still do branchings or memory accesses controlled by secret data if the information that is leaked is subsumed by the normal output of the program. To give more intuition about the property that we want to deal with, let us consider the following example, where *ct_eq* is a constant time function that allows to compare the arguments:

```
good = 1;
for (i=0; i<B_Size; i++){good = good & ct_eq(secret[i],in_p[i]);}
if (!good) { for(i=0; i<B_Size; i++) secret[i] = 0; }
return good;
```

Let suppose that the array variable *secret* is secret, and all the other variables are public. Intuitively this a sort of one-time check password verifying that *in_p* = *secret* and otherwise overwrites the array *secret* with zero. Obviously, this function is not constant-time as the variable *good* depends on *secret*, and

---

[1] mbed TLS (formerly known as PolarSSL). https://tls.mbed.org/.

hence branching on *good* violates the principles of constant-time programming. It is easy to transform this program into an equivalent one which is constant time. For example one could replace

```
if (!good) { for(i=0; i<B_Size; i++) secret[i] = 0; }
```

by

```
for (i=0; i<B_Size; i++) {secret[i] = secret[i] & ct_eq(good,1);}
```

But branching on *good* is a benign optimization, since anyway, the value of *good* is the normal output of the program. Hence, even if the function is not constant-time, it should be considered **output-sensitive constant time** with respect to its specification. Such optimization opportunities arise whenever the interface of the target application specifies what are the publicly observable outputs, and this information is sufficient to classify the extra leakage as benign [4].

The objective of this work is to propose a *static method* to check if a program is *output-sensitive constant time secure*. We emphasize that our goal is **not** to verify that the legal output leaks "too much", but rather to ensure that the unintended (side-channel) output does not leak **more than** this legal output.

First, we propose a novel approach for verifying constant-time security based on a new information flow property, called *output-sensitive noninterference*. Information-flow security prevents confidential information to be leaked to public channels. Noninterference states that a public observer cannot learn anything about the private data. Since real systems need to intentionally declassify some information, this property is too strong. An alternative is *relaxed noninterference* which allows to specify explicit *downgrading policies*. In order to take into account public outputs while staying independent of how programs intentionally declassify information, we develop an alternative solution: instead of using complex explicit policies for functions, we partition variables in three sets: input, output and *leakage variables*. Hence we distinguish between the legal public output and the information that can leak through side-channels, expressed by adding fresh additional leakage variables. Then we propose a typing system that can statically check that leakage variables do not leak more secret information than the public normal output. The novelty of our approach is that we track the dependence of leakage variables with respect to both the *initial value of input variables* (as classically the case for noninterference) and *final values of output variables*. Then, we show how to verify that a program written in a high-level language is output-sensitive constant time secure by using this typing system.

Since timed and cache-based attacks target the executions of programs, it is important to carry out this verification in a language close to the machine-executed assembly code. Hence, we adapt our approach to a generic unstructured assembly language inspired from LLVM and we show how we can verify programs coded in LLVM. Finally, we developed a prototype tool implementing our type system and we show how it can be used to verify LLVM implementations.

To summarize, this work makes the following contributions described above:
- in Sect. 2 we reformulate output-sensitive constant-time as a new interesting

$$(x := e, \sigma) \longrightarrow \sigma[x \mapsto \sigma(e)] \qquad \qquad (\text{skip}, \sigma) \longrightarrow \sigma$$

$$\frac{(c_1, \sigma) \longrightarrow \sigma'}{(c_1; c_2, \sigma) \longrightarrow (c_2, \sigma')} \qquad \qquad \frac{(c_1, \sigma) \longrightarrow (c'_1, \sigma')}{(c_1; c_2, \sigma) \longrightarrow (c'_1; c_2, \sigma')}$$

$$\frac{\sigma(e) = 1 \;?\; i = 1: \; i = 2}{(\text{If } e \text{ then } c_1 \text{ else } c_2 \text{ fi} , \sigma) \longrightarrow (c_i, \sigma)} \qquad \qquad \frac{\sigma(e) \neq 1}{(\text{While } e \text{ Do } c \text{ oD} , \sigma) \longrightarrow \sigma}$$

$$\frac{\sigma(e) = 1}{(\text{While } e \text{ Do } c \text{ oD} , \sigma) \longrightarrow (c; \text{While } e \text{ Do } c \text{ oD} , \sigma)}$$

Fig. 1. Operational semantics of the While language

noninterference property and we provide a sound type system that guarantees that well-typed programs are output-sensitive noninterferent;

- in Sect. 3 we show that this general approach can be used to verify that programs written in a high-level language are output-sensitive constant time;

- in Sect. 4 we adapt our approach to the LLVM-IR language and we develop a prototype tool that can be used to verify LLVM implementations.

An extended version of this paper, including all proofs and complete type systems is available on-line[2].

2 Output-Sensitive Non-interference

2.1 The While Language and Output-Sensitive Noninterference

In order to reason about the security of the code, we first develop our framework in *While*, a simple high-level structured programming language. In Sect. 3 we shall enrich this simple language with arrays and in Sect. 4 we adapt our approach to a generic unstructured assembly language. The syntax of While programs is listed below:

$$c ::= x := e \mid \text{skip} \mid c_1; c_2 \mid \text{If } e \text{ then } c_1 \text{ else } c_2 \text{ fi} \mid \text{While } e \text{ Do } c \text{ oD}$$

Meta-variables x, e and c range over the sets of program variables Var, expressions and programs, respectively. We leave the syntax of expressions unspecified, but we assume they are deterministic and side-effect free. The semantics is shown in Fig. 1. The reflexive and transitive closure of $\longrightarrow$ is denoted by $\Longrightarrow$. A state σ maps variables to values, and we write $\sigma(e)$ to denote the value of expression e in state σ. A configuration (c, σ) is a program c to be executed along with the current state σ. Intuitively, if we want to model the security of some program c with respect to side-channel attacks, we can assume that there are three special

---

[2] https://www-verimag.imag.fr/~Cristian.Ene/OSNI/main.pdf.

subsets of variables: X_I the public input variables, X_O the public output variables and X_L the variables that leak information to some malicious adversary. Then, output sensitive noninterference asks that every two complete executions starting with X_I-equivalent states and ending with X_O-equivalent final states must be indistinguishable with respect to the leakage variables X_L.

Definition 1. *(adapted from [4]) Let $X_I, X_O, X_L \subseteq Var$ be three sets of variables, intended to represent the input, the output and the leakage of a program. A program c is (X_I, X_O, X_L)-secure when all its executions starting with X_I-equivalent stores and leading to X_O-equivalent final stores, give X_L-equivalent final stores. Formally, for all $\sigma, \sigma', \rho, \rho'$, if $\langle c, \sigma \rangle \Longrightarrow \sigma'$ and $\langle c, \rho \rangle \Longrightarrow \rho'$ and $\sigma =_{X_I} \rho$ and $\sigma' =_{X_O} \rho'$, then $\sigma' =_{X_L} \rho'$.*

2.2   Typing Rules

This section introduces a type-based information flow analysis that allows to check whether a While program is output-sensitive noninterferent, i.e. the program does not leak more information about the secret inputs than the public normal output.

As usual, we consider a flow lattice of security levels $\mathcal{L}$. An element x of $\mathcal{L}$ is an atom if $x \neq \bot$ and there exists no element $y \in \mathcal{L}$ such that $\bot \sqsubset y \sqsubset x$. A lattice is called *atomistic* if every element is the join of atoms below it.

Assumption 2.21. *Let $(\mathcal{L}, \sqcap, \sqcup, \bot, \top)$ be an atomistic continuous bounded lattice. As usual, we denote $t_1 \sqsubseteq t_2$ iff $t_2 = t_1 \sqcup t_2$. We assume that there exists a distinguished subset $\mathcal{T}_O \subseteq \mathcal{L}$ of atoms.*

Hence, from the above assumption, for any $\tau_o \in \mathcal{T}_O$ and for any $t_1, t_2 \in \mathcal{L}$:

1. $\tau_o \sqsubseteq t_1 \sqcup t_2$ implies $\tau_o \sqsubseteq t_1$ or $\tau_o \sqsubseteq t_2$,
2. $\tau_o \sqsubseteq t_1$ implies that there exists $t \in \mathcal{L}$ such that $t_1 = t \sqcup \tau_o$ and $\tau_o \not\sqsubseteq t$.

A type environment $\Gamma : Var \mapsto \mathcal{L}$ describes the security levels of variables and the dependency with respect to the current values of variables in X_O. In order to catch dependencies with respect to current values of output variables, we associate to each output variable $o \in X_O$ a fixed and unique symbolic type $\alpha(o) \in \mathcal{T}_O$. For example if some variable $x \in Var$ has the type $\Gamma(x) = Low \sqcup \alpha(o)$, it means that the value of x depends only on public input and the current value of the output variable $o \in X_O$.

Hence, we assume that there is a fixed injective mapping $\alpha : X_0 \mapsto \mathcal{T}_0$ such that $\bigwedge_{o_1, o_2 \in X_O} (o_1 \neq o_2 \Rightarrow \alpha(o_1) \neq \alpha(o_2)) \wedge \bigwedge_{v \in X_O} (\alpha(o) \in \mathcal{T}_O)$. We extend mappings Γ and α to sets of variables in the usual way: given $A \subseteq Var$ and $B \subseteq X_O$ we note $\Gamma(A) \overset{def}{=} \bigsqcup_{x \in A} \Gamma(x)$, $\alpha(B) \overset{def}{=} \bigsqcup_{x \in B} \alpha(x)$.

Our type system aims to satisfy the following output sensitive non-interference condition: if the *final* values of output variables in X_O remain the same, only changes to *initial* inputs with types $\sqsubseteq t$ should be visible to *leakage* outputs with type $\sqsubseteq t \sqcup \alpha(X_O)$. More precisely, given a derivation $\vdash_\alpha \Gamma\{c\}\Gamma'$, the final value of a variable x with final type $\Gamma'(x) = t \sqcup \alpha(A)$ for some $t \in \mathcal{L}$ and $A \subseteq X_O$, should depend at most on the initial values of those variables y with initial types $\Gamma(y) \sqsubseteq t$ and on the final values of variables in A. We call "real dependencies" the dependencies with respect to initial values of variables and "symbolic dependencies" the dependencies with respect to the current values of output variables. Following [19] we formalize the non-interference condition satisfied by the typing system using reflexive and symmetric relations.

We write $=_{A_0}$ for relation which relates mappings which are equal on all values in A_0 i.e. for two mappings $f_1, f_2 : A \mapsto B$ and $A_0 \subseteq A$, $f_1 =_{A_0} f_2$ iff $\forall a \in A_0, f_1(a) = f_2(a)$. For any mappings $f_1 : A_1 \mapsto B$ and $f_2 : A_2 \mapsto B$, we write $f_1[f_2]$ the operation which updates f_1 according to f_2, namely $(f_1[f_2])(x) =$ if $x \in A_2$ then $f_2(x)$ else $f_1(x)$. Given $\Gamma : Var \mapsto \mathcal{L}$, $X \subseteq Var$ and $t \in \mathcal{L}$, we write $=_{\Gamma,X,t}$ for the reflexive and symmetric relation which relates states that are equal on all variables having type $v \sqsubseteq t$ in environment Γ, provided that they are equal on all variables in X: $\sigma =_{\Gamma,X,t} \sigma'$ iff $\sigma =_X \sigma' \Rightarrow (\forall x, (\Gamma(x) \sqsubseteq t \Rightarrow \sigma(x) = \sigma'(x)))$. When $X = \emptyset$, we omit it, hence we write $=_{\Gamma,t}$ instead of $=_{\Gamma,\emptyset,t}$.

Definition 2. [20] *Let $\mathcal{R}$ and $\mathcal{S}$ be reflexive and symmetric relations on states. We say that program c maps $\mathcal{R}$ into $\mathcal{S}$, written $c : \mathcal{R} \Longrightarrow \mathcal{S}$, iff $\forall \sigma, \rho$, if $\langle c, \sigma \rangle \Longrightarrow \sigma'$ and $\langle c, \rho \rangle \Longrightarrow \rho'$ then $\sigma \mathcal{R} \rho \Rightarrow \sigma' \mathcal{S} \rho'$.*

The type system we propose enjoys the following useful property:
if $\vdash_\alpha \Gamma\{c\}\Gamma'$ then $c : =_{\Gamma,\Gamma(X_I)} \Longrightarrow =_{\Gamma',X_O,\alpha(X_O) \sqcup \Gamma(X_I)}$

This property is an immediate consequence of Theorem 2.

Hence, in order to prove that the above program c is output sensitive non-interferent according to Definition 1, it is enough to check that for all $x_l \in X_L$, $\Gamma'(x_l) \sqsubseteq \alpha(X_O) \sqcup \Gamma(X_I)$. Two executions of the program c starting from initial states that coincide on input variables X_I, and ending in final states that coincide on output variables X_O, will coincide also on the leaking variables X_L.

We now formally introduce our typing system. Due to assignments, values and types of variables change dynamically. For example let us assume that at some point during the execution, the value of x depends on the initial value of some variable y and the current value of some output variable o (which itself depends on the initial value of some variable h), formally captured by an environment Γ where $\Gamma(o) = \Gamma_0(h)$ and $\Gamma(x) = \Gamma_0(y) \sqcup \alpha(o)$, where Γ_0 represents the initial environment. If the next to be executed instruction is some assignment to o, then the current value of o will change, so we have to mirror this in the new type of x: even if the value of x does not change, its new type will be $\Gamma'(x) = \Gamma_0(y) \sqcup \Gamma_0(h)$ (assuming that $\alpha(o) \not\sqsubseteq \Gamma_0(y)$). Hence $\Gamma'(x)$ is obtained by replacing in $\Gamma(x)$ the symbolic dependency $\alpha(o)$ with the real dependency $\Gamma(o)$.

$$\text{As1} \; \frac{x \notin X_O}{p \vdash_\alpha \Gamma\{x := e\}\Gamma[x \mapsto p \sqcup \Gamma[\alpha](fv(e))]} \qquad \text{As2} \; \frac{x \in X_O \setminus fv(e) \qquad \Gamma_1 = \Gamma \lhd_\alpha x}{p \vdash_\alpha \Gamma\{x := e\}\Gamma_1[x \mapsto p \sqcup \Gamma_1[\alpha](fv(e))]}$$

$$\text{Skip} \; \frac{}{p \vdash_\alpha \Gamma\{skip\}\Gamma} \qquad \text{As3} \; \frac{x \in X_O \cap fv(e) \qquad \Gamma_1 = \Gamma \lhd_\alpha x}{p \vdash_\alpha \Gamma\{x := e\}\Gamma_1[x \mapsto p \sqcup \Gamma(x) \sqcup \Gamma_1[\alpha](fv(e) \setminus x)]}$$

$$\text{Seq} \; \frac{p \vdash_\alpha \Gamma\{c_1\}\Gamma_1 \qquad p \vdash_\alpha \Gamma_1\{c_2\}\Gamma_2}{p \vdash_\alpha \Gamma\{c_1;c_2\}\Gamma_2} \qquad \text{Sub} \; \frac{p_0 \sqsubseteq p_1 \quad \Gamma \sqsubseteq \Gamma' \quad p_1 \vdash_\alpha \Gamma'\{c\}\Gamma_1' \quad \Gamma_1' \sqsubseteq \Gamma_1}{p_0 \vdash_\alpha \Gamma\{c\}\Gamma_1}$$

$$\text{If} \; \frac{\begin{array}{c} p' = (\Gamma[\alpha](fv(e)), \Gamma) \lhd_\alpha (\mathbf{aff}^O(c_1) \cup \mathbf{aff}^O(c_2)) \\ p \sqcup p' \vdash_\alpha \Gamma\{c_i\}\Gamma_i \qquad \Gamma' = \Gamma_1 \lhd_\alpha \mathbf{aff}^O(c_2) \sqcup \Gamma_2 \lhd_\alpha \mathbf{aff}^O(c_1) \end{array}}{p \vdash_\alpha \Gamma\{\text{If } e \text{ then } c_1 \text{ else } c_2 \text{ fi }\}\Gamma'}$$

$$\text{Wh} \; \frac{\begin{array}{c} p_e = (\Gamma[\alpha](fv(e)), \Gamma) \lhd_\alpha \mathbf{aff}^O(c) \\ p \sqcup p_e \vdash_\alpha \Gamma\{c\}\Gamma' \qquad \Gamma' \sqcup (\Gamma \lhd_\alpha \mathbf{aff}^O(c)) \sqsubseteq \Gamma \end{array}}{p \vdash_\alpha \Gamma\{\text{While } e \text{ Do } c \text{ oD }\}\Gamma}$$

Fig. 2. Flow-sensitive typing rules for commands with output

Definition 3. *If $t^0 \in \mathcal{T}_O$ is an atom and $t',t \in \mathcal{L}$ are arbitrary types, then we denote by $t[t'/t^0]$ the type obtained by replacing (if any) the occurrence of t^0 by t' in the decomposition in atoms of t. Now we extend this definition to environments: let $x \in X_O$ and $p \in \mathcal{L}$. Then $\Gamma_1 \stackrel{def}{=} \Gamma \lhd_\alpha x$ represents the environment where the symbolic dependency on the last value of x of all variables is replaced by the real type of x: $\Gamma_1(y) \stackrel{def}{=} (\Gamma(y))[\Gamma(x)/\alpha(x)]$. Similarly, $(p, \Gamma) \lhd_\alpha x \stackrel{def}{=} p[\Gamma(x)/\alpha(x)]$.*

We want now to extend the above definition from a single output variable x to subsets $X \subseteq X_O$. Our typing system will ensure that each generated environment Γ will not contain circular symbolic dependencies between output variables, i.e., there are no output variable $o_1, o_2 \in X_O$ such that $\alpha(o_1) \sqsubseteq \Gamma(o_2)$ and $\alpha(o_2) \sqsubseteq \Gamma(o_1)$. We can associate a graph $\mathcal{G}(\Gamma) = (X_O, E)$ to an environment Γ, such that $(o_1, o_2) \in E$ iff $\alpha(o_1) \sqsubseteq \Gamma(o_2)$. We say that Γ is **well formed**, denoted $\mathcal{AC}(\Gamma)$, if $\mathcal{G}(\Gamma)$ is an acyclic graph. For acyclic graphs $\mathcal{G}(\Gamma)$ we extend Definition 3 to subsets $X \subseteq X_O$, by first fixing an ordering $X = \{x_1, x_2, \dots x_n\}$ of variables in V compatible with the graph (i.e. $j \leq k$ implies that there is no path from x_k to x_j), and then $(p, \Gamma) \lhd_\alpha X \stackrel{def}{=} (((p, \Gamma) \lhd_\alpha x_1) \lhd_\alpha x_2) \dots \lhd_\alpha x_n$.

Let $\mathbf{aff}(c)$ be the set of assigned variables in a program c and let us denote $\mathbf{aff}^I(c) \stackrel{def}{=} \mathbf{aff}(c) \cap (Var \setminus X_O)$ and $\mathbf{aff}^O(c) \stackrel{def}{=} \mathbf{aff}(c) \cap X_O$. We define the ordering over environments: $\Gamma_1 \sqsubseteq \Gamma_2 \stackrel{def}{=} \bigwedge_{x \in Var} \Gamma_1(x) \sqsubseteq \Gamma_2(x)$. For a command c, judgements have the form $p \vdash_\alpha \Gamma\{c\}\Gamma'$ where $p \in \mathcal{L}$ and Γ and Γ' are type environments well-formed. The inference rules are shown in Fig. 2. The idea is that if Γ describes the security levels of variables which hold before execution of

(1) $o_1 := x + 1$

(2) $y := o_1 + z$

(3) $o_1 := u$

(4) $z := o_1 + o_3$

(5) If $(o_2 = o_3 + x)$
(6) then $o_1 := o_2$

(7) else $o_2 := o_1$

(8) fi

$$p = \bot, \quad \Gamma_0 = [y \to Y, z \to Z, o_1 \to O_1, o_2 \to O_2]$$

$$\Gamma_1 = [y \to Y, z \to Z, \mathbf{o_1 \to X}, o_2 \to O_2]$$

$$\Gamma_2 = [\mathbf{y \to \overline{O_1} \sqcup Z}, z \to Z, o_1 \to X, o_2 \to O_2]$$

$$\Gamma_3 = [\mathbf{y \to X \sqcup Z}, z \to Z, \mathbf{o_1 \to U}, o_2 \to O_2]$$

$$\Gamma_4 = [y \to X \sqcup Z, \mathbf{z \to \overline{O_1} \sqcup \overline{O_3}}, o_1 \to U, o_2 \to O_2]$$

$$\mathbf{p = \overline{O_3} \sqcup O_2 \sqcup X}$$

$$\Gamma_6 = [y \to X \sqcup Z, \mathbf{z \to U \sqcup \overline{O_3}}, \mathbf{o_1 \to \overline{O_3} \sqcup O_2 \sqcup X \sqcup \overline{O_2}}, o_2 \to O_2]$$

$$\Gamma_7 = [y \to X \sqcup Z, z \to \overline{O_1} \sqcup \overline{O_3}, o_1 \to U, o_2 \to \mathbf{\overline{O_3} \sqcup O_2 \sqcup X \sqcup \overline{O_1}}]$$

$$\Gamma_8 = (\Gamma_6 \triangleleft_\alpha o_2) \sqcup (\Gamma_7 \triangleleft_\alpha o_1) = [y \to X \sqcup Z, \mathbf{z \to U \sqcup \overline{O_3}},$$
$$o_1 \to \mathbf{\overline{O_3} \sqcup O_2 \sqcup X \sqcup U}, o_2 \to \mathbf{\overline{O_3} \sqcup O_2 \sqcup X \sqcup U}]$$

Fig. 3. Example of application for our typing system

c, then Γ' will describe the security levels of those variables after execution of c. The type p represents the usual program counter level and serves to eliminate indirect information flows; the derivation rules ensure that all variables that can be changed by c will end up (in Γ') with types greater than or equal to p. As usual, whenever $p = \bot$ we drop it and write $\vdash_\alpha \Gamma\{c\}\Gamma'$ instead of $\bot \vdash_\alpha \Gamma\{c\}\Gamma'$. Throughout this paper the type of an expression e is defined simply by taking the lub of the types of its free variables $\Gamma[\alpha](fv(e))$, for example the type of $x+y+o$ where o is the only output variable is $\Gamma(x) \sqcup \Gamma(y) \sqcup \alpha(o)$. This is consistent with the typings used in many systems, though more sophisticated typing rules for expressions would be possible in principle. Notice that considering the type of an expression to be $\Gamma[\alpha](fv(e))$ instead of $\Gamma(fv(e))$ allows to capture the dependencies with respect to the current values of output variables. In order to give some intuition about the rules, we present a simple example in Fig. 3.

Example 1. Let $\{x, y, z, u\} \subseteq Var \setminus X_O$ and $\{o_1, o_2, o_3\} \subseteq X_O$ be some variables, and let us assume that $\forall i \in \{1, 2, 3\}$, $\alpha(o_i) = O_i$. We assume that the initial environment is $\Gamma_0 = [x \to X, y \to Y, z \to Z, u \to U, o_1 \to O_1, o_2 \to O_2, o_3 \to O_3]$. Since the types of variables x, u and o_3 do not change, we omit them in the following. We highlighted the changes with respect to the previous environment. After the first assignment, the type of o_1 becomes X, meaning that the current value of o_1 depends on the initial value of x. After the assignment $y := o_1 + z$, the type of y becomes $\overline{O_1} \sqcup Z$, meaning that the current value of y depends on the initial value of z and the current value of o_1. After the assignment $o_1 = u$, the type of y becomes $X \sqcup Z$ as o_1 changed and we have to mirror this in the dependencies of y, and the type of o_1 becomes X. When we enter in the If, the program counter level changes to $p = \overline{O_3} \sqcup O_2 \sqcup X$ as the expression $o_2 = o_3 + x$

depends on the values of variables o_2, o_3, x, but o_2 and o_3 are output variables and o_2 will be assigned by the If command, hence we replace the "symbolic" dependency $\alpha(o_2) = \overline{O_2}$ by its "real" dependency $\Gamma(o_2) = O_2$. At the end of the If command, we do the join of the two environments obtained after the both branches, but in order to prevent cycles, we first replace the "symbolic" dependencies by the corresponding "real" dependencies for each output variable that is assigned by the other branch.

As already stated above, our type system aims to capture the following non-interference condition: given a derivation $p \vdash_\alpha \Gamma\{c\}\Gamma'$, the final value of a variable x with final type $t \sqcup \alpha(X_O)$, should depend at most on the initial values of those variables y with initial types $\Gamma(y) \sqsubseteq t$ and on the final values of variables in X_O. Or otherwise said, executing a program c on two initial states σ and ρ such that $\sigma(y) = \rho(y)$ for all y with $\Gamma(y) \sqsubseteq t$ which ends with two final states σ' and ρ' such that $\sigma'(o) = \rho'(o)$ for all $o \in X_O$ will satisfy $\sigma'(x) = \rho'(x)$ for all x with $\Gamma'(x) \sqsubseteq t \sqcup \alpha(X_O)$. In order to prove the soundness of the typing system, we need a stronger invariant denoted $\mathcal{I}(t, \Gamma)$: intuitively, $(\sigma, \rho) \in \mathcal{I}(t, \Gamma)$ means that for each variable x and $A \subseteq X_O$, if $\sigma =_A \rho$ and $\Gamma(x) \sqsubseteq t \sqcup \alpha(A)$, then $\sigma(x) = \rho(x)$. Formally, given $t \in \mathcal{L}$ and $\Gamma : Var \mapsto \mathcal{L}$, we define $\mathcal{I}(t, \Gamma) \overset{def}{=} \bigcap_{A \subseteq X_O} =_{\Gamma, A, \alpha(A) \sqcup t}$.

The following theorem states the soundness of our typing system.

Theorem 1. *Let us assume that* $\mathcal{AC}(\Gamma)$ *and* $\forall o \in X_O, \alpha(o) \not\sqsubseteq t$. *If* $p \vdash_\alpha \Gamma\{c\}\Gamma'$ *then* $c : \mathcal{I}(t, \Gamma) \Longrightarrow \mathcal{I}(t, \Gamma')$.

2.3 Soundness w.r.t. to Output-Sensitive Non-interference

In this section we show how we can use the typing system in order to prove that a program c is output-sensitive noninterferent. Let $Var^e = Var \cup \{\overline{o} \mid o \in X_O\}$. Let us define $\mathcal{L} \overset{def}{=} \{\tau_A \mid A \subseteq Var^e\}$. We denote $\bot = \tau_\emptyset$ and $\top = \tau_{Var^e}$ and we consider the lattice $(\mathcal{L}, \bot, \top, \sqsubseteq)$ with $\tau_A \sqcup \tau_{A'} \overset{def}{=} \tau_{A \cup A'}$ and $\tau_A \sqsubseteq \tau_{A'}$ iff $A \subseteq A'$. The following Theorem is a consequence of the Definition 1 and Theorem 1.

Theorem 2. *Let* $\mathcal{L}$ *be the lattice described above. Let* (Γ, α) *be defined by* $\Gamma(x) = \{\tau_x\}$, *for all* $x \in Var$ *and* $\alpha(o) = \{\tau_{\overline{o}}\}$, *for all* $o \in X_O$. *If* $\vdash_\alpha \Gamma\{c\}\Gamma'$ *and for all* $x_l \in X_L$, $\Gamma'(x_l) \sqsubseteq \Gamma(X_I) \sqcup \alpha(X_O)$, *then* c *is* (X_I, X_O, X_L)-*secure.*

3 Output-Sensitive Constant-Time

Following [1,4], we consider two types of cache-based information leaks: (1) disclosures that happen when secret data determine which parts of the program are executed; (2) disclosures that arise when access to memory is indexed by sensitive information. In order to model the latter category, we shall enrich the simple language from Sect. 2.2 with *arrays*:

$$c ::= x := e \mid x[e_1] := e \mid \text{skip} \mid c_1; c_2 \mid \text{If } e \text{ then } c_1 \text{ else } c_2 \text{ fi} \mid \text{While } e \text{ Do } c \text{ oD}$$

$$\frac{act \equiv \mathbf{r}(\sigma(\overrightarrow{f}))}{(x := e, \sigma) \overset{act}{\longrightarrow} \sigma[(x, 0) \mapsto \sigma(e)]}$$

$$\frac{act \equiv \mathbf{w}(\sigma(e_1)) : \mathbf{r}(\sigma(\overrightarrow{f}))}{(x[e_1] := e, \sigma) \overset{act}{\longrightarrow} \sigma[(x, \sigma(e_1)) \mapsto \sigma(e)]}$$

$$\frac{\sigma(e) \neq 1 \qquad act \equiv \mathbf{b}(\sigma(e)) : \mathbf{r}(\sigma(\overrightarrow{f}))}{(\text{While } e \text{ Do } c \text{ oD}, \sigma) \overset{act}{\longrightarrow} \sigma}$$

$$\frac{\sigma(e) = 1 \qquad act \equiv \mathbf{b}(\sigma(e)) : \mathbf{r}(\sigma(\overrightarrow{f}))}{(\text{While } e \text{ Do } c \text{ oD}, \sigma) \overset{act}{\longrightarrow} (c; \text{While } e \text{ Do } c \text{ oD}, \sigma)}$$

$$\frac{\sigma(e) = 1 \ ? \ i = 1 : \ i = 2 \qquad act \equiv \mathbf{b}(\sigma(e)) : \mathbf{r}(\sigma(\overrightarrow{f}))}{(\text{If } e \text{ then } c_1 \text{ else } c_2 \text{ fi}, \sigma) \overset{act}{\longrightarrow} (c_i, \sigma)}$$

Fig. 4. Syntax and labeled operational semantics

$$\text{As1'} \frac{x \notin X_O}{p \vdash_\alpha^{ct} \Gamma\{x := e\}\Gamma[x \mapsto p \sqcup \Gamma[\alpha](fv(e))][x_l \mapsto \Gamma(x_l) \sqcup \Gamma[\alpha](fv(\overrightarrow{f})))]}$$

$$\text{As1''} \frac{x \notin X_O \qquad p_1 = (\Gamma[\alpha](fv(e_1), fv(e)) \qquad p_l = (\Gamma[\alpha](fv(e_1), fv(\overrightarrow{f}))}{p \vdash_\alpha^{ct} \Gamma\{x[e_1] := e\}\Gamma[x \mapsto p \sqcup \Gamma(x) \sqcup p_1][x_l \mapsto \Gamma(x_l) \sqcup p_l]}$$

$$\text{If} \frac{\begin{array}{cc} p' = (\Gamma[\alpha](fv(e)), \Gamma) \lhd_\alpha \mathbf{aff}^O(c_1; c_2) & p \sqcup p' \vdash_\alpha^{ct} \Gamma\{c_i\}\Gamma_i \\ p_l = (\Gamma[\alpha](fv(\overrightarrow{f})), \Gamma) \lhd_\alpha \mathbf{aff}^O(c_1; c_2) & \Gamma' = \Gamma_1 \lhd_\alpha \mathbf{aff}^O(c_2) \sqcup \Gamma_2 \lhd_\alpha \mathbf{aff}^O(c_1) \end{array}}{p \vdash_\alpha^{ct} \Gamma\{\text{If } e \text{ then } c_1 \text{ else } c_2 \text{ fi}\}\Gamma'[x_l \mapsto \Gamma'(x_l) \sqcup p_l \sqcup p']}$$

Fig. 5. Typing rules for output sensitive constant time (excerpts)

To simplify notations, we assume that array indexes e_1 are basic expressions (not referring to arrays) and that X_O does not contain arrays. Moreover as in [4], a state or store σ maps array variables v and indices $i \in \mathbb{N}$ to values $\sigma(v, i)$. The labeled semantics of While programs are listed in Fig. 4. In all rules, we denote $\overrightarrow{f} = (f_i)_i$, where $x_i[f_i]$ are the indexed variables in e. The labels on the execution steps correspond to the information which is leaked to the environment ($\mathbf{r}()$ for a read access on memory, $\mathbf{w}()$ for a write access and $\mathbf{b}()$ for a branch operation). In the rules for (If) and (While) the valuations of branch conditions are leaked. Also, all indexes to program variables read and written at each statement are exposed. We give in Fig. 5 an excerpts of the new typing rules. As above, we denote $\overrightarrow{f} = (f_i)_i$, where $x_i[f_i]$ are the indexed variables in e. We add a fresh variable x_l, that is not used in programs, in order to capture the unintended leakage. Its type is always growing and it mirrors the information leaked by each command. In rule $(As1'')$ we take a conservative approach and we consider that the type of an array variable is the lub of all its cells. The information leaked by the assignment $x[e_1] := e$ is the index e_1 plus the set $\overrightarrow{f} = (f_i)_i$ of all indexes occurring in e. Moreover, the new type of the array variable x mirrors the fact that now the value of x depends also on the index e_1 and the right side e.

Definition 4. *An* **execution** *is a sequence of visible actions:* $\overset{a_1}{\longrightarrow} \overset{a_2}{\longrightarrow} \dots \overset{a_n}{\longrightarrow}$. *A program c is (X_I, X_O)-***constant time** *when all its executions starting with X_I-equivalent stores that lead to finally X_O-equivalent stores, are identical.*

•	$\omega(\bullet)$
$x := e$	$x_l := x_l : \mathbf{r}(\overrightarrow{f});\ \ x := e$
$x[e_1] := e$	$x_l := x_l : \mathbf{w}(e_1) : \mathbf{r}(\overrightarrow{f});\ \ x[e_1] := e$
$skip$	$skip$
$c_1; c_2$	$\omega(c_1); \omega(c_2)$
If e then c_1 else c_2 fi	$x_l := x_l : \mathbf{b}(e) : \mathbf{r}(\overrightarrow{f});\ \ $ If e then $\omega(c_1)$ else $\omega(c_2)$ fi
While e Do c oD	$x_l := x_l : \mathbf{b}(e) : \mathbf{r}(\overrightarrow{f}); $ While e Do $\omega(c); x_l := x_l : \mathbf{b}(e) : \mathbf{r}(\overrightarrow{f})$ oD

Fig. 6. Instrumentation for $\omega(\bullet)$

Following [4], given a set X of program variables, two stores σ and ρ are X-*equivalent* when $\sigma(x, i) = \rho(x, i)$ for all $x \in X$ and $i \in \mathbb{N}$. Two executions $\xrightarrow{a_1} \ldots \xrightarrow{a_n}$ and $\xrightarrow{b_1} \ldots \xrightarrow{b_m}$ are *identical* iff $n = m$ and $a_j = b_j$ for all $1 \le j \le n$. We can reduce the (X_I, X_O)-constant time security of a command c to the $(X_I, X_O, \{x_l\})$-security (see Sect. 2.3) of a corresponding command $\omega(c)$, obtained by adding a fresh variable x_l to the program variables $fv(c)$, and then adding recursively before each assignment and each boolean condition predicate, a new assignment to the leakage variable x_l that mirrors the leaked information. Let $:, \mathbf{b}(,)\mathbf{r}(,)\mathbf{w}()$ be some new abstract operators. The construction of the instrumentation $\omega(\bullet)$ is shown in Fig. 6. As above, we denote $\overrightarrow{f} = (f_i)_i$, where $x_i[f_i]$ are the indexed variables in e. Then, we extend, as in the rules $As1', Ass1''$ from Fig. 5, the typing system from Sect. 2.2 to take into account the array variables. The following lemma holds.

Lemma 1. *Let c a command such that $x_l \notin fv(c)$, σ, σ' two stores, tr some execution trace and $[]$ the empty trace.*

1. $p \vdash_\alpha^{ct} \Gamma\{c\}\Gamma'$ iff $p \vdash_\alpha \Gamma\{\omega(c)\}\Gamma'$.
2. $(c, \sigma) \xrightarrow{tr}^* \sigma'$ iff $(\omega(c), \sigma[x_l \mapsto []]) \longrightarrow^* \sigma'[x_l \mapsto tr]$.

Now combining Theorem 2 and Lemma 1 we get the following Theorem.

Theorem 3. *Let $\mathcal{L}$ be the lattice defined in the Sect. 2.3. Let (Γ, α) be defined by $\Gamma(x) = \{\tau_x\}$, for all $x \in Var$ and $\alpha(o) = \{\tau_{\bar{o}}\}$, for all $o \in X_O$ and $\Gamma(x_l) = \perp$. If $p \vdash_\alpha^{ct} \Gamma\{c\}\Gamma'$ and $\Gamma'(x_l) \sqsubseteq \Gamma(X_I) \sqcup \alpha(X_O)$, then c is (X_I, X_O)- constant time.*

4 Application to Low-Level Code

We show in this section how the type system we proposed to express output-sensitive constant-time non-interference on the *While* language can be lifted to a low-level program representation like the LLVM byte code [21].

$r \leftarrow op(Op, \overrightarrow{v})$	assign to r the result of Op applied to operands $\overrightarrow{v}$
$r \leftarrow load(v)$	load in r the value stored at address v
$store(v_1, v_2)$	store at address v_2 the value stored at address v_1
$cond(r, b_{then}, b_{else})$	branch to b_{then} if the value of r is true and to b_{false} otherwise
$goto\ b$	branch to b

Fig. 7. Syntax and informal semantics of simplified LLVM-IR

4.1   LLVM-IR

We consider a simplified LLVM-IR representation with four instructions: assignments from a temporary expression (register or immediate value) or from a memory location (load), writing to a memory location (store) and (un)conditional jump instructions. We assume that the program control flow is represented by a control-flow graph (CFG) $G = (\mathcal{B}, \rightarrow_E, b_{init})$ where $\mathcal{B}$ is the set of basic blocks, $\rightarrow_E$ the set of edges connecting the basic blocks, and $b_{init} \in \mathcal{B}$ the entry point. We denote by $Reach(b, b')$ the predicate indicating that there exists a path from b to b'. A program is a (partial) map from control points $(b, n) \in \mathcal{B} \times \mathbb{N}$ to instructions. Each basic block is terminated by a jump instruction. The memory model consists in a set of *registers* R and the memory M (including the execution stack). Val is the set of values and memory addresses. The informal semantics of our simplified LLVM-IR is given in Fig. 7, where $r \in R$ and $v \in R \cup Val$. We consider an operational semantics where execution steps are labelled with leaking data, i.e., addresses of store and load operations and branching conditions.

4.2   Type System

For a CFG $G = (\mathcal{B}, \rightarrow_E, b_{init})$:

1. Function $dep : \mathcal{B} \rightarrow 2^{\mathcal{B}}$ associates to each basic block its set of "depending blocks", i.e., $b' \in dep(b)$ iff b' dominates b and there is no block b'' between b' and b such that b'' post-dominates b'. We recall that a node b_1 dominates (*resp.* post-dominates) a node b_2 iff every path from the entry node to b_2 goes through b_1 (*resp.* every path from b_2 to the ending node goes through b_1).

2. Partial function $br : \mathcal{B} \rightarrow R$ returns the "branching register", i.e., the register r used to compute the branching condition leading outside b (b is terminated by an instruction $cond(r, b_{then}, b_{else})$). Note that in LLVM branching registers are always *fresh* and assigned only once before to be used.

3. Function $PointsTo : (\mathcal{B} \times \mathbb{N}) \times Val \rightarrow 2^R$ returns the set of registers containing memory locations pointed to by a given address at a given control point. For example, for a given address v, $r \in PointsTo(b, n)(v)$ means that register r contains a memory address pointed to by v.

We define a type system to express output-sensitive constant-time property on LLVM-IR. The main differences from the rules at the source level is that the control-flow is explicitly given by the CFG. For lack of space we describe only

$$A_m = PointsTo(b,n)(v_2)$$

$$p(b,n) = store(v_1, v_2) \qquad A_0 = A_m \cap X_0 \qquad \qquad \Gamma_1 = (\Gamma, \alpha) \triangleleft A_0$$

$$\tau_0 = \bigsqcup_{x \in br(dep(b))} \Gamma[\alpha](x) \qquad \tau_1 = \Gamma_1[\alpha](v_2) \sqcup \tau_0 \qquad \tau_2 = \Gamma_1[\alpha](v_1)$$

St ——

$$\vdash_\alpha (b,n) : \Gamma \Rightarrow \Gamma_1[x_l \to \Gamma_1(x_l) \sqcup \tau_1][v_{s \in A_m} \to \Gamma(v_s) \sqcup \tau_2 \sqcup \tau_0]$$

Fig. 8. Store instruction

the rule for the Store instruction (Fig. 8). It updates the type of v_1 by adding the dependencies of all memory locations pointed to by $v2$. In addition, the type of the leakage variable x_l is also updated with the dependencies of all these memory locations lying in A_m (since these locations are read).

4.3   Well Typed LLVM Programs Are Output-Sensitive Constant-Time

Definition 5. *An LLVM-IR program p is well typed with respect to an initial environment Γ_0 and final environment Γ' (written $\vdash_\alpha p : \Gamma_0 \Rightarrow \Gamma'$), if there is a family of well-defined environments $\{(\Gamma)_{(b,n)} \mid (b,n) \in (\mathcal{B}, \mathbb{N})\}$, such that for all nodes (b,n) and all its successors (b', n'), there exists a type environment γ and $A \subseteq X_O$ such that $\vdash_\alpha (b,n) : \Gamma_{(b,n)} \Rightarrow \gamma$ and $(\gamma \triangleleft_\alpha A) \sqsubseteq \Gamma_{(b',n')}$.*

In the above definition the set A is mandatory in order to prevent dependency cycles between variables in X_O. The following Theorem shows the soundness of the typing system with respect to output-sensitive constant-time.

Theorem 4. *Let $\mathcal{L}$ be the lattice from the Sect. 2.3. Let (Γ, α) be defined by $\Gamma(x) = \{\tau_x\}$, for all $x \in R \cup M$, $\alpha(o) - \{\tau_{\overline{o}}\}$, for all $o \in X_O$ and $\Gamma(x_l) = \bot$. If $\vdash_\alpha p : \Gamma \Rightarrow \Gamma'$ and $\Gamma'(x_l) \sqsubseteq \Gamma(X_I) \sqcup \alpha(X_O)$, then p is (X_I, X_O)-constant time.*

4.4   Implementation

We developed a prototype tool implementing the type system for LLVM programs. This type system consists in computing flow-sensitive dependency relations between program variables. Definition 5 provides the necessary conditions under which the obtained result is sound (Theorem 4). We give some technical indications regarding our implementation.

Output variables X_O are defined as function return values and global variables; we do not currently consider arrays nor pointers in X_O. Control dependencies cannot be deduced from the syntactic LLVM level, we need to explicitly compute the dominance relation between basic blocks of the CFG (the *dep* function). Definition 5 requires the construction of a set $A \subseteq X_O$ to update the environment produced at each control locations in order to avoid circular dependencies (when output variable are assigned in *alternative* execution paths). To identify the set of basic blocks belonging to such alternative execution paths

leading to a given block, we use the notion of *Hammock regions* [15]. More precisely, we compute function $Reg : (\mathcal{B} \times \mathcal{B} \times (\rightarrow_E)) \rightarrow 2^{\mathcal{B}}$, returning the set of *Hammock regions* between a basic block b and its immediate dominator b' with respect to an incoming edge e_i of b. Thus, $Reg(b', b, (c, b))$ is the set of blocks belonging to CFG paths going from b' to b without reaching edge $e_i = (c, b)$:
$Reg(b', b, (c, b)) = \{b_i \mid b' \rightarrow_E b_1 \cdots \rightarrow_E b_n \rightarrow_E b \wedge \forall i \in [1, n-1].\ \neg Reach(b_i, c)\}$.
Fix-point computations are implemented using Kildall's algorithm. To better handle real-life examples we are currently implementing the *PointsTo* function, an inter-procedural analysis, and a more precise type analysis combining both over- and under-approximations of variable dependencies (see Sect. 6).

5   Related Work

Information Flow. There is a large number of papers on language-based security aiming to prevent undesired information flows using type systems (see [26]). An information-flow security type system statically ensures noninterference, i.e. that sensitive data may not flow directly or indirectly to public channels [24, 28–30]. The typing system presented in Sect. 2.2 builds on ideas from Hunt and Sands' flow-sensitive static information-flow analysis [20].

As attractive as it is, noninterference is too strict to be useful in practice, as it prevents confidential data to have any influence on observable, public output: even a simple password checker function violates noninterference. Relaxed definitions of noninterference have been defined in order to support such intentional downward information flows [27]. Li and Zdancewic [22] proposed an expressive mechanism called *relaxed noninterference* for declassification policies that supports the extensional specification of secrets and their intended declassification. A declassification policy is a function that captures the precise information on a confidential value that can be *declassified*. For the password checker example, the following declassification policy $\lambda p.\lambda x.h(p) == x$, allows an equality comparison with the hash of password to be declassified (and made public), but disallows arbitrary declassifications such as revealing the password.

The problem of information-flow security has been studied also for low level languages. Barthe and Rezk [8, 9] provide a flow sensitive type system for a sequential bytecode language. As it is the case for most analyses, implicit flows are forbidden, and hence, modifications of parts of the environment with lower security type than the current context are not allowed. Genaim and Spoto present in [16] a compositional information flow analysis for full Java bytecode.

Information Flow Applied to Detecting Side-Channel Leakages. Information-flow analyses track the flow of information through the program but often ignore information flows through side channels. Side-channel attacks extract sensitive information about a program's state through its observable use of resources such as time or memory. Several approaches in language-based security use security type systems to detect timing side-channels [1, 18]. Agat [1] presents a type system sensitive to timing for a small While-language which includes a transformation which takes a program and transforms it into an equivalent program without timing leaks. Molnar et al. [23] introduce the program counter model, which is equivalent to path non-interference, and give a program transformation for making programs secure in this model.

FlowTracker [25] allows to statically detect time-based side-channels in LLVM programs. Relying on the assumption that LLVM code is in SSA form, they compute control dependencies using a sparse analysis [13] without building the whole Program Dependency Graph. Leakage at assembly-level is also considered in [6]. They propose a fine-grained information-flow analysis for checking that assembly programs generated by CompCert are constant-time. Moreover, they consider a stronger adversary which controls the scheduler and the cache.

All the above works do not consider publicly observable outputs. The work that is closest to ours is [4], where the authors develop a formal model for constant-time programming policies. The novelty of their approach is that it is distinguishing not only between public and private input values, but also between private and publicly observable output values. As they state, this distinction poses interesting technical and theoretical challenges. Moreover, constant-time implementations in cryptographic libraries like OpenSSL include optimizations for which paths and addresses can depend not only on public input values, but also on publicly observable output values. Considering only input values as non-secret information would thus incorrectly characterize those implementations as non-constant-time. They also develop a verification technique based on the self-composition based approach [7]. They reduce the constant time security of a program P to safety of a product program Q that simulates two parallel executions of P. The tool operates at the LLVM bytecode level. The obtained bytecode program is transformed into a product program which is verified by the Boogie verifier [5] and its SMT tool suite. Their approach is complete only if the public output is ignored. Otherwise, their construction relies on identifying the branches whose conditions can only be declared benign when public outputs are considered. For all such branches, the verifier needs to consider separate paths for the two simulated executions, rather than a single synchronized path and in the worst case this can deteriorate to an expensive product construction.

6   Conclusion and Perspectives

In this paper we proposed a static approach to check if a program is output-sensitive constant-time, i.e., if the leakage induced through branchings and/or memory accesses do not overcome the information produced by (regular) observable outputs. Our verification technique is based on a so-called output-sensitive non-interference property, allowing to compute the dependencies of a leakage variable from both the initial values of the program inputs and the final values of its outputs. We developed a type system on a high-level **While** language, and we proved its soundness. Then we lifted this type system to a basic LLVM-IR and we developed a prototype tool operating on this intermediate representation, showing the applicability of our technique.

This work could be continued in several directions. One limitation of our method arising in practice is that even if the two snippets $x_l = h; o = h$ and $o = h; x_l = o$ are equivalent, only the latter can be typed by our typing system. We are currently extending our approach by considering also an under-approximation $\beta(\bullet)$ of the dependencies between variables and using "symbolic dependencies" also for non-output variables. Then the safety condition from Theorem 2 can be improved to something like "$\exists V$ such that $(\Gamma'(x_l) \triangleleft_\alpha V) \sqsubseteq (\Gamma(X_I) \triangleleft_\alpha V) \sqcup (\beta'(X_O) \triangleleft_\alpha V) \sqcup \alpha(X_O)$". In the above example, we would obtain $\Gamma'(x_l) = \alpha(h) = \beta'(o) \sqsubseteq \alpha(o) \sqcup \beta'(o)$, meaning that the unwanted maximal leakage $\Gamma'(x_l)$ is less than the minimal leakage $\beta'(o)$ due to the normal output. From the implementation point of view, further developments are needed in order to extend our prototype to a complete tool able to deal with real-life case studies. This may require to refine our notion of arrays and to take into account arrays and pointers as output variables. We could also consider applying a sparse analysis, as in FlowTracker [25]. It may happen that such a pure static analysis would be too strict, rejecting too much "correct" implementations. To solve this issue, a solution would be to combine it with the dynamic verification technique proposed in [4]. Thus, our analysis could be used to find automatically which branching conditions are benign in the output-sensitive sense, which could reduce the product construction of [4]. Finally, another interesting direction would be to adapt our work in the context of quantitative analysis for program leakage, like in [14].

References

1. Agat, J.: Transforming out timing leaks. In: Proceedings of the 27th ACM SIGPLAN-SIGACT Symposium on Principles of Programming Languages, pp. 40–53. ACM (2000)
2. Al Fardan, N.J., Paterson, K.G.: Lucky thirteen: breaking the TLS and DTLS record protocols. In: 2013 IEEE Symposium on Security and Privacy (SP), pp. 526–540. IEEE (2013)
3. Albrecht, M.R., Paterson, K.G.: Lucky microseconds: a timing attack on Amazon's s2n implementation of TLS. In: Fischlin, M., Coron, J.-S. (eds.) EUROCRYPT 2016. LNCS, vol. 9665, pp. 622–643. Springer, Heidelberg (2016). https://doi.org/10.1007/978-3-662-49890-3_24
4. Almeida, J.B., Barbosa, M., Barthe, G., Dupressoir, F., Emmi, M.: Verifying constant-time implementations. In: 25th USENIX Security Symposium (USENIX Security 16), pp. 53–70. USENIX Association, Austin (2016). https://www.usenix.org/conference/usenixsecurity16/technical-sessions/presentation/almeida
5. Barnett, M., Chang, B.-Y.E., DeLine, R., Jacobs, B., Leino, K.R.M.: Boogie: a modular reusable verifier for object-oriented programs. In: de Boer, F.S., Bonsangue, M.M., Graf, S., de Roever, W.-P. (eds.) FMCO 2005. LNCS, vol. 4111, pp. 364–387. Springer, Heidelberg (2006). https://doi.org/10.1007/11804192_17
6. Barthe, G., Betarte, G., Campo, J., Luna, C., Pichardie, D.: System-level non-interference for constant-time cryptography. In: Proceedings of the 2014 ACM SIGSAC Conference on Computer and Communications Security, pp. 1267–1279. ACM (2014)

7. Barthe, G., D'Argenio, P.R., Rezk, T.: Secure information flow by self-composition. In: 2004 17th IEEE Proceedings of Computer Security Foundations Workshop, pp. 100–114. IEEE (2004)

8. Barthe, G., Rezk, T.: Secure information flow for a sequential JAVA virtual machine. In: Types in Language Design and Implementation, TLDI 2005. Citeseer (2003)

9. Barthe, G., Rezk, T., Basu, A.: Security types preserving compilation. Comput. Lang. Syst. Struct. **33**(2), 35–59 (2007)

10. Bernstein, D.J., Lange, T., Schwabe, P.: The security impact of a new cryptographic library. In: Hevia, A., Neven, G. (eds.) LATINCRYPT 2012. LNCS, vol. 7533, pp. 159–176. Springer, Heidelberg (2012). https://doi.org/10.1007/978-3-642-33481-8_9

11. Blazy, S., Pichardie, D., Trieu, A.: Verifying constant-time implementations by abstract interpretation. In: Foley, S.N., Gollmann, D., Snekkenes, E. (eds.) ESORICS 2017. LNCS, vol. 10492, pp. 260–277. Springer, Cham (2017). https://doi.org/10.1007/978-3-319-66402-6_16

12. Brumley, D., Boneh, D.: Remote timing attacks are practical. Comput. Netw. **48**(5), 701–716 (2005)

13. Choi, J.D., Cytron, R., Ferrante, J.: Automatic construction of sparse data flow evaluation graphs. In: Proceedings of the 18th ACM SIGPLAN-SIGACT Symposium on Principles of Programming Languages, POPL 1991, pp. 55–66. ACM (1991)

14. Doychev, G., Köpf, B., Mauborgne, L., Reineke, J.: CacheAudit: a tool for the static analysis of cache side channels. ACM Trans. Inf. Syst. Secur. **18**(1), 4:1–4:32 (2015). https://doi.org/10.1145/2756550

15. Ferrante, J., Ottenstein, K., Warren, J.: The program dependence graph and its use in optimization. TOPLAS **9**(3), 319–349 (1987)

16. Genaim, S., Spoto, F.: Information flow analysis for JAVA bytecode. In: Cousot, R. (ed.) VMCAI 2005. LNCS, vol. 3385, pp. 346–362. Springer, Heidelberg (2005). https://doi.org/10.1007/978-3-540-30579-8_23

17. Gullasch, D., Bangerter, E., Krenn, S.: Cache games-bringing access-based cache attacks on AES to practice. In: 2011 IEEE Symposium on Security and Privacy (SP), pp. 490–505. IEEE (2011)

18. Hedin, D., Sands, D.: Timing aware information flow security for a javacard-like bytecode. Electron. Notes Theor. Comput. Sci. **141**(1), 163–182 (2005)

19. Hunt, S., Sands, D.: Binding time analysis: a new perspective. In: Proceedings of the ACM Symposium on Partial Evaluation and Semantics-Based Program Manipulation (PEPM 1991), pp. 154–164. ACM Press (1991)

20. Hunt, S., Sands, D.: On flow-sensitive security types. In: ACM SIGPLAN Notices, vol. 41, pp. 79–90. ACM (2006)

21. Lattner, C., Adve, V.: LLVM: a compilation framework for lifelong program analysis & transformation. In: Proceedings of the International Symposium on Code Generation and Optimization: Feedback-directed and Runtime Optimization. CGO 2004. IEEE Computer Society, Washington (2004)

22. Li, P., Zdancewic, S.: Downgrading policies and relaxed noninterference. In: Proceedings of POPL, vol. 40, pp. 158–170. ACM (2005)

23. Molnar, D., Piotrowski, M., Schultz, D., Wagner, D.: The program counter security model: automatic detection and removal of control-flow side channel attacks. In: Won, D.H., Kim, S. (eds.) ICISC 2005. LNCS, vol. 3935, pp. 156–168. Springer, Heidelberg (2006). https://doi.org/10.1007/11734727_14

24. Myers, A.C.: JFlow: practical mostly-static information flow control. In: Proceedings of the 26th ACM SIGPLAN-SIGACT Symposium on Principles of Programming Languages, pp. 228–241. ACM (1999)
25. Rodrigues, B., Quintão Pereira, F.M., Aranha, D.F.: Sparse representation of implicit flows with applications to side-channel detection. In: Proceedings of the 25th International Conference on Compiler Construction, pp. 110–120. ACM (2016)
26. Sabelfeld, A., Myers, A.C.: Language-based information-flow security. IEEE J. Sel. Areas Commun. **21**(1), 5–19 (2003)
27. Sabelfeld, A., Sands, D.: Declassification: dimensions and principles. J. Comput. Secur. **17**(5), 517–548 (2009)
28. Swamy, N., Chen, J., Chugh, R.: Enforcing stateful authorization and information flow policies in FINE. In: Gordon, A.D. (ed.) ESOP 2010. LNCS, vol. 6012, pp. 529–549. Springer, Heidelberg (2010). https://doi.org/10.1007/978-3-642-11957-6_28
29. Vaughan, J.A., Zdancewic, S.: A cryptographic decentralized label model. In: 2007 IEEE Symposium on Security and Privacy, SP 2007, pp. 192–206. IEEE (2007)
30. Volpano, D., Irvine, C., Smith, G.: A sound type system for secure flow analysis. J. Comput. Secur. **4**(2–3), 167–187 (1996)

Component-aware Input-Output Conformance

Alexander Graf-Brill[1]([✉]) and Holger Hermanns[1,2]

[1] Saarland University, Saarland Informatics Campus, Saarbrücken, Germany
grafbrill@depend.uni-saarland.de, hermanns@depend.uni-saarland.de
[2] Institute of Intelligent Software, Guangzhou, China

Abstract. Black-box conformance testing based on a compositional
model of the intended behaviour is a very attractive approach to validate the correctness of an implementation. In this context, input-output
conformance is a scientifically well-established formalisation of the testing process. This paper discusses peculiar problems arising in situations
where the implementation is a monolithic black box, for instance for
reasons of intellectual property restrictions, while the specification is
compositional. In essence, tests need to be enabled to observe progress
in individual specification-level components. For that, we will reconsider
input-output conformance so that it can faithfully deal with such situations. Refined notions of quiescence play a central role in a proper
treatment of the problem. We focus on the scenario of parallel components with fully asynchronous communication covering very many notorious practical examples. We finally illustrate the practical implications
of component-aware conformance testing in the context of a prominent
example, namely networked embedded software.

Keywords: Model-based testing · Input-output conformance ·
Compositionality

1 Introduction

Component-based or *modular systems* are systems which are composed of several
components in order to provide a higher degree of functionality or just to offer the
ensemble of features offered by its components. From an implementation point
of view, component-based systems are very flexible since single components can
be updated or exchanged easily, or the system can be extended by additional
components, without having to touch the whole system.

When it comes to the verification of such systems, one usually tries to benefit from the compositional structure. Correctness of the components is easier
to verify in isolation and under appropriate conditions, correctness of the whole
system is derived from the correctness of all components. This reduces the overall verification effort. In particular, when updating a single component of the
system, one only has to verify the new component without the need to verify

J. A. Pérez and N. Yoshida (Eds.): FORTE 2019, LNCS 11535, pp. 111–128, 2019.
https://doi.org/10.1007/978-3-030-21759-4_7

the other components again. However, this approach is only applicable if the correctness properties are *compositional* [1,2,10,12,17,18,21].

Model-based testing is a validation technique where, based on a formal specification of a system, a suitable set of experiments (test suite) is generated in an automated manner and executed on the implementation of that system, so as to assert some notion of conformance between the implementation and its specification. In model-based testing, compositional testing is a research area of its own. Given a specification and an implementation under test (IUT), each as combinations of several components, a compositional conformance tester checks conformance between the components of the specification and the respective IUT components, so as to conclude conformance between the combined specification and IUT. If this implication holds, there is no need for further integration testing when combining the different IUT components [2,3,6,7,11]. Otherwise this is a costly and time-consuming step since the combined specification has to be taken into account which is notorious in size relative to the sizes of the individual components.

What all these approaches have obviously in common is the assumption that the IUT is indeed a combination of several components which can be accessed individually. Interestingly little attention has been payed to the situation where only the specification is composed of clearly distinguished components, but the IUT is a *single* black box, i.e. a monolithic object, or an object where components are not accessible in isolation.

We consider this as a mismatch, since the previously described scenario is pretty much the norm for black-box systems protected by intellectual property rights. Especially if such systems need to undergo a certification according to some well-structured component-based or scenario-based standard. This is the concrete problem motivating our work. But beyond that there are several other reasons for attacking this challenge.

Since there are no dedicated theoretical approaches targeting the testing of such scenarios, the standard input-output conformance [23] is the natural base methodology. Input-output conformance (**ioco**) is based on the idea that a reasonable implementation of a formally specified system should assure that

the IUT progresses as foreseen by the specification, and this progress is observable by the tester.

Since IUT progress corresponds to outputs of the IUT, this means that

1. any interaction sequence between tester and IUT possible according to the specification is followed only by IUT outputs foreseen according to the specification;
2. only in situations where no IUT output is foreseen, the IUT is allowed to be quiescent.

Quiescence, and especially the possibility to observe quiescence is a crucial ingredient to the theory of input-output conformance. It makes progress observable by refining classical testing equivalences and preorders [8,9] with concepts of refusal testing [19,22], thus enabling a more fine grained relation between systems based on their state-based capabilities to produce any output at all. In practice, quiescence is approximated by timeout mechanisms: If after some interaction sequence no IUT output is witnessed before the timeout, the IUT is interpreted as now being quiescent. The concept of quiescence therefore provides an implicit mechanism to test for absence as well as presence of progress, without an explicit reference to real time.

This paper explores the simple question what needs to change in the theory of input-output conformance in order to be able to test for the progress of components of a component-based specification. So, we add the idea that a reasonable implementation of a component-based system should assure that

the IUT progresses as foreseen by the *component-based* specification, and this progress is observable by the tester.

This then translates concretely to (the first item being unchanged),

1. any interaction sequence between tester and IUT possible according to the specification is followed only by IUT outputs foreseen according to the specification;
2. only in situations where no IUT output is foreseen *by some component*, the IUT is allowed to be quiescent *with respect to that component*.

The first requirement is indeed the standard **ioco** criterion considering *functional correctness* of an IUT. The second requirement is the core motivation for this paper. This requirement harvests the available information about the inner structure of a compositional specification. Since the specification is white-box, any observable behaviour of the system can be associated to the components possibly causing that behaviour. This provides the opportunity to deduce which components are taking part in an interaction, and effectively enables a fine-grained notion of quiescence. With this, we require an IUT to progress whenever possible not only on the system-level, but instead for each component of a composed system. Notably, we will apply this to monolithic black-box implementations, but we nevertheless ask them to respect the compositional nature of their specification. From a testing perspective this implies among others that we would reject an implementation which only exhibits the behaviour of a single component, in situations where other components can not stay quiescent i.e. they potentially can progress by observable behaviour. We make all this deducible by only looking at the compositional specification.

Organisation of the Paper. After setting the stage, we first argue why precisely standard input-output conformance is ill-suited for the problem at hand. We then focus on specifications that are fully asynchronous, so they are merely collections of behaviour descriptions where none of the behaviour emerges through interaction across components. This is a very widespread scenario in practice. We explain the details of a natural solution which comes with adaptations to the quiescence definition. On the practical side we discuss in how far the resulting notions can indeed be tested for, which leads to a well-motivated revision of the theory. We finally illustrate the practical implications of component-aware conformance testing in the context of networked embedded software.

2   Preliminaries

The basis for model-based testing is a precise specification of the IUT which unambiguously describes what an implementation may do, respectively not do.

Input-Output Transition Systems. A common semantic model to describe the behaviour of a system are labeled transition systems (LTS). In the presence of inputs and outputs, a suitable variation is provided by *Input-Output Transition Systems* (IOTS).

Definition 1. *An* input-output transition system *is a 5-tuple* $\langle Q, L_?, L_!, T, q_0 \rangle$ *where*

- *Q is a finite, non-empty set of* states;
- *$L_?$ and $L_!$ are disjoint countable sets ($L_? \cap L_! = \emptyset$) of* input labels *and* output labels, *respectively;*
- *$T \subseteq Q \times (L \cup \{\tau\}) \times Q$, with $\tau \notin L$, is the* transition relation, *where $L = L_? \cup L_!$;*
- *q_0 is the* initial state.

The class of input-output transition systems with inputs in $L_?$ and outputs in $L_!$ is denoted by $\mathcal{IOTS}(L_?, L_!)$.

As usual, τ represents an unobservable internal action of the system. We write $q \xrightarrow{\mu} q'$ if there is a transition labelled μ from state q to state q', i.e., $(q, \mu, q') \in T$. The composition of transitions $q_1 \xrightarrow{\mu_1 \cdot \mu_2 \cdot \ldots \cdot \mu_{n-1}} q_n$ expresses that the system, when in state q_1, may end in state q_n, after performing the sequence of actions $\mu_1 \cdot \mu_2 \cdot \ldots \cdot \mu_{n-1}$, i.e. $\exists (q_i, \mu_i, q_{i+1}) \in T, i \leq n-1$. Due to nondeterminism, it may be the case, that after performing the same sequence, the system may end in another state (or multiple such states): $q_1 \xrightarrow{\mu_1 \cdot \mu_2 \cdot \ldots \cdot \mu_{n-1}} q'_n$ with $q_n \neq q'_n$.

Traces and Derived Notions. Usually an IOTS can represent the entire behaviour of a system, including concrete interactions between system and environment. One such behaviour is represented by a so-called *trace*, of which we are only interested in its observable part, obtained by abstracting from internal actions of the system. Let $p = \langle Q, L_?, L_!, T, q_0 \rangle$ be an IOTS with $q, q' \in Q, L = L_? \cup L_!, a, a_i \in L$, and $\sigma \in L^*$. We write $q \xRightarrow{\epsilon} q'$ to express that $q = q'$ or $q \xrightarrow{\tau \ldots \tau} q'$. $q \xRightarrow{a} q'$ denotes the fact that $\exists q_1, q_2 \in Q : q \xRightarrow{\epsilon} q_1 \xrightarrow{a} q_2 \xRightarrow{\epsilon} q'$. This can be extended for a sequence of actions $q \xRightarrow{a_1 \cdot \ldots \cdot a_n} q'$ s.t. $\exists q_0, \ldots, q_n \in Q : q = q_0 \xRightarrow{a_1} q_1 \xRightarrow{a_2} \ldots \xRightarrow{a_n} q_n = q'$. $q \xRightarrow{\sigma}$ and $q \xnRightarrow{\sigma}$ are then defined as $\exists q' : q \xRightarrow{\sigma} q'$ and $\nexists q' : q \xRightarrow{\sigma} q'$, respectively.

Furthermore, $init(q)$ denotes the set of available transitions in a state q, i.e., $\{\mu \in L \cup \{\tau\} \mid q \xrightarrow{\mu}\}$. The set of traces starting in state q is defined as $traces(q) =_{\text{def}} \{\sigma \in L^* \mid q \xRightarrow{\sigma}\}$. For a given trace σ, the set of reachable states is given by the definition $q \textbf{ after } \sigma =_{\text{def}} \{q' \mid q \xRightarrow{\sigma} q'\}$. The extension for starting in a set of states Q' is Q' **after** σ $=_{\text{def}} \bigcup \{q\,\textbf{after}\,\sigma \mid q \in Q'\}$. With $der(q)$ we denote the set of all reachable states from q, i.e., $\{q' \mid \exists \sigma \in L^* : q \overset{\sigma}{\Longrightarrow} q'\}$. Following the standard literature, we restrict ourselves to *strongly convergent* IOTS i.e. there is no state that can perform an infinite sequence of internal transitions. An IOTS p is called *input-enabled*, if and only if all its reachable states q are input-enabled i.e. $\forall q \in der(p), \forall a \in L_?.q \overset{a}{\Longrightarrow}$. So, inputs can never be blocked (or come as surprises). It is common practice to work with specifications modelled as IOTS without requiring input-enabledness while IUTs are required to be represented as input-enabled IOTS. This is what we assume here, too.

Input-Output Conformance and Quiescence. A specific conformance relation, input-out conformance (**ioco**) [23] dominates theoretical as well as practical work on model-based testing. It relates implementations with specifications with respect to the possible output behaviour observed after executing traces of the specification. In **ioco**, the output behaviour includes a designated output *quiescence*, abbreviated with the special label δ. *Quiescence* represents the situation when there is no output to observe at all. A state q is said to be quiescent, denoted by $\delta(q)$, iff $init(q) \cap (L_! \cup \{\tau\}) = \emptyset$.

Assuming $\delta \notin (L \cup \{\tau\})$ it is technically convenient to encode quiescence wherever present into the transition structure at hand. For this a *suspension automaton* $\Delta(p)$ is constructed out of an IOTS p, where transitions $q \overset{\delta}{\longrightarrow} q$ are added to any quiescent state. The set of possible outputs of a state q is then defined as $out(q) =_{\text{def}} \{a \in L_! \mid q \overset{a}{\longrightarrow}\} \cup \{\delta \mid \delta(q)\}$, and this is lifted to sets of states P by $out(P) =_{\text{def}} \bigcup\{out(q) \mid q \in P\}$. Since quiescence is now interpreted as an additional observable output, we extend the definition for traces to *suspension traces*.

Definition 2. *Let* $p = \langle Q, L_?, L_!, T, q_0 \rangle \in \mathcal{IOTS}(L_?, L_!)$. *The* suspension traces *of* p *are given by* $Straces(p) =_{\text{def}} \{\sigma \in (L \cup \{\delta\})^* \mid q_0 \overset{\sigma}{\Longrightarrow}\}$.

The definition of **ioco** then looks as follows:

Definition 3. *Given a set of input labels* $L_?$ *and a set of output labels* $L_!$, *the relation* **ioco** $\subseteq \mathcal{IOTS}(L_?, L_!) \times \mathcal{IOTS}(L_?, L_!)$ *is defined for a specification* s *and an input-enabled implementation* i *as*

$$i\,\textbf{ioco}\,s \Leftrightarrow_{\text{def}} \forall \sigma \in Straces(s) : out(i\,\textbf{after}\,\sigma) \subseteq out(s\,\textbf{after}\,\sigma)$$

Partial Specifications. Since **ioco** is defined based on the suspension traces of the specification on the one hand, and only requires inclusion of the output behaviour of the IUT w.r.t. the specified outputs on the other hand, it is possible to have partial specifications. This means that an IUT does not have to implement all specified output transitions of a certain state, but these can be seen as output alternatives. Furthermore, there are no restrictions on the behaviour of an implementation once its execution left the suspension traces of the specifications i.e. it performs an *underspecified trace*. Since an underspecified trace always starts with an unspecified input action for a state input-enabled specifications do not have any underspecified trace.

Test Generation and Execution. Theoretically, a test case is a variant of an IOTS with two special trap states labeled **pass** and **fail**, whereby each other state represents all states of the specification which are reachable by the suspension trace corresponding to the trace that leads to this particular state of the test case. In order to detect quiescence, the special transition label θ is used in order to synchronise with δ. A test case is then generated based on the definition of **ioco** in an iterative manner. In each iteration step there are three options. (1) For all outputs in $L_!$ and quiescence a correspondingly labelled transition is added. If the output is not foreseen by the specification, the successor state is the special state **fail** and for all valid successor states the test case generation algorithm continues in the next iteration step. (2) An input action which is enabled in one of the encoded states of the specification is chosen and a correspondingly labeled transition is added to the test case. In order to handle interrupting outputs of the IUT, corresponding transitions are added as described in (1). (3) At any iteration step, the algorithm can be stopped by placing the special state **pass**.

An execution of a test case is then the parallel composition of the test case and the IUT. A *test run* is any trace of the parallel composition which ends in a state which is labeled with **pass** or **fail**. An IUT passes a test case if and only if all possible test runs lead to states labeled with **pass**. It fails the test case otherwise. By assuming some kind of fairness, an IUT will reveal sooner or later all its nondeterministic behaviour when repeatedly executed with a test case.

From a practical point of view, quiescence detection is realised by introducing a timer. This timer is restarted after every interaction with the IUT and upon its expiration, quiescence of the implementation is assumed and accordingly processed.

Before we delve deeper into conformance testing of component-based systems, we first give a formal definition of what we actually understand of a component-based system.

Definition 4. *A* component-based input-output transition system (CIOTS) *is a 6-tuple $\langle Q, L_?, L_!, T, q_0, C \rangle$ where*

- *the system is the composition of components in the non-empty vector $C = \langle s_0, \ldots, s_n \rangle$ with $n \in \mathbb{N}_0$*
- *each $s_k \in C$ is a finite input-output transition system $\langle Q_k, L_{?k}, L_{!k}, T_k, q_{0,k} \rangle \in \mathcal{IOTS}(L_{?k}, L_{!k})$*
- *all components are pairwise action-disjoint i.e. $\forall s_k. L_{?k} \cap \bigcup_{s_m \in C} L_{!m} = \emptyset \wedge L_{!k} \cap \bigcup_{s_m \in C} L_{?m} = \emptyset$*
- *the sets of input labels and output labels are $L_? = \bigcup_{s_k \in C} L_{?k}$ and $L_! = \bigcup_{s_k \in C} L_{!k}$*
- *the set of states Q is the cross product of the set of states of the components in C, i.e. $Q = \bigotimes_{s_k \in C} Q_k$*
- *the initial state q_0 is the cross product of the initial states of the components in C, i.e. $q_0 = \bigotimes_{s_k \in C} q_{k,0}$*
- *the transition relation T is the combination of the transition relations of the components s.t.*

$$T = \{(\hat{q}_0, \ldots, \hat{q}_k, \ldots, \hat{q}_n) \xrightarrow{\mu} (\hat{q}_0, \ldots, \hat{q}_k', \ldots, \hat{q}_n) \mid \hat{q}_k \xrightarrow{\mu} \hat{q}_k' \in T_k\}$$

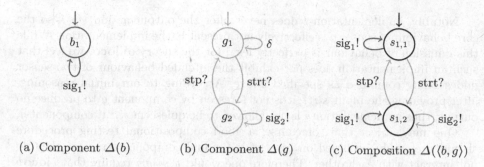

(a) Component $\Delta(b)$ (b) Component $\Delta(g)$ (c) Composition $\Delta(\langle b, g \rangle)$

Fig. 1. A simple component-based sensor node example.

The class of component-based input-output transition systems with inputs in $L_?$ and outputs in $L_!$ is denoted by $\mathcal{CIOTS}(L_?, L_!)$. We say that a system s is component-based, if and only if, $s \in \mathcal{CIOTS}(L_?, L_!)$ for some $L_?$ and $L_!$.

Notably, $\langle Q, L_?, L_!, T, q_0 \rangle$ is itself a finite input-output transition system in $\mathcal{IOTS}(L_?, L_!)$. Since a CIOTS is already completely defined by its components, we may use the abbreviation $\langle s_0, \ldots, s_n \rangle$ in order to refer to $s = \langle Q, L_?, L_!, T, q_0, \langle s_0, \ldots, s_n \rangle \rangle$.

Example 1. In Fig. 1 a very simple component-based specification is displayed. Figure 1a and b show the suspension automata of the IOTSs of components b and g, each specifying some kind of sensor. Sensor b can be thought of as continuously gathering some measurement data (not modelled) which it passes on to the environment via the action $sig_1!$. Sensor g works similarly using action $sig_2!$, but can be started (*strt?*) and stopped (*stp?*) from remote. Initially it is stopped – and hence quiescent.

Each IOTS $s = \langle Q, L_?, L_!, T, q_0 \rangle$ can be represented as a single-component CIOTS $\hat{s} = \langle Q, L_?, L_!, T, q_0, \langle s \rangle \rangle$ and vice versa.

3   Conformance and Component Behaviour

This section provides a motivation why the well-established general **ioco** testing procedure falls short when facing a component-based specification w.r.t. the conditions we postulated in Sect. 1.

Example 2. A potential candidate implementation i of the composed specification from Fig. 1 is displayed on the right. It is input enabled (w.r.t. the set $\{strt?, stp?\}$). Indeed, this implementation does conform to the specification, i.e. $i \, \textbf{ioco} \, \langle b, g \rangle$, since $\forall \sigma \in Straces(i) : out(i_1 \, \textbf{after} \, \sigma) = \{sig_1!\}$ and $\forall \sigma' \in Straces(\langle b, g \rangle) : out(s_{1,1} \, \textbf{after} \, \sigma')$ is either $\{sig_1!\}$ or $\{sig_1!, sig_2!\}$.

Notably, implementation i does never offer the output action $sig_2!$, so the core behaviour of sensor g is effectively not present in the implementation. While this omission of behaviour is perfectly legal for the theory of **ioco**, we feel that such an implementation does not exhibit the intended behaviour of two sensor nodes being combined as specified above. According to our initial reasoning, after providing the input $strt?$ it is not foreseen by component g to produce no output, thus implementation i is not allowed to be quiescent w.r.t. component g.

One may object that, of course, a good compositional testing procedure should preferably be based on tests of individual components in case they do not interact with each other. Therefore one would *a priori* require that i **ioco** b as well as i **ioco** g. Indeed, it turns out that i i̸**oco** g (due to the presence of the output action $sig_1!$, which is not foreseen by g) while i **ioco** b. So, from this perspective, the implementation i is not entirely convincing as a witness for the shortcoming of the classical **ioco** theory.

Example 3. Another implementation candidate j is displayed on the right. It correctly outputs $sig_1!$ in the initial state and starts and stops producing the output $sig_2!$ as intended by the inputs $strt?$ and $stp?$. However, the output $sig_1!$ is turned off in state j_2 where the output $sig_2!$ is produced only. Again it holds that j **ioco**$\langle b, g \rangle$.

The essence of the problem of implementation j is similar to the one of i appearing in Example 2. Contrary to what we assume reasonable, some valuable output behaviour of the specification of component b is not implemented, but here this is in a fragment of the state space reachable by transitions belonging to specification of component g. In this example, j **ioco** b as well as j **ioco** g provided we assume a suitable projection mechanism to filter the observable behaviour corresponding to the component under test.

As it stands, focusing on the behaviour of a single component, is no solution in a quest for a compositional testing theory. Instead one has to foresee arbitrary input actions of other components, in order to examine the full behaviour of an IUT. Unfortunately, "the full behaviour of an IUT" might include underspecified behaviour in case of specifications that are not input-enabled (which is not uncommon). This in turn might lead to outputs interfering with our current test run, thus, rendering such a testing approach useless, again. Hence, one has to adjust the provided inputs to the behaviour of the composed specification.

For now, we can conclude that the standard **ioco** approach is not well suited for testing scenarios involving compositional specifications. The problem is twofold. On the one hand, **ioco** is not aware of the underlying topology of the specification model. On the other hand, the relation is based on excluding unspecified output behaviour, rather than enforcing a certain output (set). We shall see that the concept of quiescence is the central leverage point regarding both aspects of the problem.

4   A Component-Aware Theory

The lesson learned in the previous section is that the **ioco** approach fails at considering simultaneously the specific output behaviour of the individual components embedded in the overall behaviour of a composed specification. Especially the absence of any output from a particular component can not be detected. This is however the only indicator at hand whether or not a specified component does take part in the interactions of the IUT, or not. Thus, a quiescence definition based on the output capabilities of single components is needed.

The composition setting has similarities to the **multi-ioco** (**mioco**) relation as presented in [16] where communication with a system is assumed to occur on multiple distinct interaction *interfaces* and quiescence is then redefined s.t. each interface is associated with a dedicated quiescence action. No component structure is considered, implying that this approach is not applicable right away to the problem we consider. However, it serves as a strong inspiration for our approach, in which we will indeed customise the definition of **mioco** to our component-based setting. To get started, we assume an indexed family of quiescence labels of the form δ_k for $k \in \mathbb{N}$. These will serve as means to signify quiescence per individual component.

Definition 5. *Let $p = (p_0, \ldots, p_n)$ be a state and P be a set of states of a CIOTS $s = \langle Q, L_?, L_!, T, q_0, C \rangle \in \mathcal{CIOTS}(L_?, L_!)$, where $C = \langle s_0, \ldots, s_n \rangle$ is the finite, non-empty set of component IOTS $s_k = \langle Q_k, L_{?k}, L_{!k}, T_k, q_{0,k} \rangle$. We define a vector $\hat{\boldsymbol{\delta}}$ (of dimension n) of quiescence labels by setting*

$$\hat{\delta}_k(p) =_{\text{def}} \delta(p_k) \text{ for } 0 \leq k \leq n \tag{1}$$

and we propagate this into the other elements of the theory by redefining

- *$out(p) =_{\text{def}} \{x \in L_! \mid p \xrightarrow{x}\} \cup \{\delta_k \mid \hat{\delta}_k(p)\}$,*
- *$\Delta(s) = \langle Q, L_?, L_! \cup \{\delta_k \mid 0 \leq k \leq n\}, T \cup \{p \xrightarrow{\delta_k} p \mid p \in Q, \hat{\delta}_k(p)\}, q_0, C \rangle$,*
- *$Straces(s) =_{\text{def}} \{\sigma \in (L \cup \{\delta_k \mid 0 \leq k \leq n\})^* \mid \Delta(s) \xRightarrow{\sigma}\}$.*

Definition 5 provides a component-specific version of quiescence and redefines *out*() and *Straces*() w.r.t. this quiescence definition, where the latter one is based on the corresponding redefinition for the suspension automaton $\Delta(s)$ of a CIOTS s.

The behaviour of an IUT is to be interpreted relative to a given specification CIOTS, which in essence means that the output alphabets of that CIOTS induce vectors of quiescence labels for the IOTS representing the IUT, too. But since IUTs are no CIOTSs themselves, the quiescence notion $\hat{\boldsymbol{\delta}}$ from Definition 5 can not be applied directly. Thus, we need a quiescence definition and a corresponding definition of the suspension automaton for input-enabled IOTSs, given the output alphabets of interest.

Definition 6. *Let p be a state and P be a set of states of an IOTS $s = \langle Q, L_?, L_!, T, q_0 \rangle \in \mathcal{IOTS}(L_?, L_!)$, and $L = (L_{!0}, \ldots, L_{!n})$ be a finite vector of*

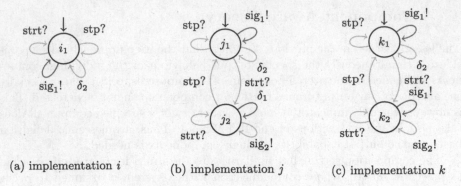

(a) implementation i (b) implementation j (c) implementation k

Fig. 2. Component-based testing with **mioco**

sets of output labels. We define a vector $\hat{\boldsymbol{\delta}}^L$ (of dimension n) of quiescence labels by setting, for $0 \le k \le n$,

$$\delta_k^L(p) =_{\text{def}} init(p) \cap (L_{!k} \cup \{\tau\}) = \emptyset \tag{2}$$

and we propagate this into the definition of the suspension automaton by setting
$\Delta^L(s) = \langle Q, L_?, L_! \cup \{\delta_k \mid 0 \le k \le n\}, T \cup \{p \xrightarrow{\delta_k} p \mid p \in Q, \delta_k^L(p)\}, q_0\rangle.$

Example 4. We revisit Fig. 1 from Example 1. In the presence of Definition 5, the loop $g_1 \xrightarrow{\delta} g_1$ from component g translates to a loop in $s_{1,1}$ labeled δ_2 in Fig. 1c. This is the only difference. Corresponding to Definition 6, implementation i from Example 2 is quiescent for component g in its initial state and so is implementation j appearing in Example 3. In addition, the latter is quiescent for component b in state j_2. Thus, their corresponding suspension automata for the vector of output label sets $\boldsymbol{L} = (\{\text{sig}_1!\}, \{\text{sig}_2!\})$ have loops labeled δ_2 at the initial states and δ_1 at j_2 of $\Delta^L(j)$. These suspension automata are depicted in Fig. 2a and b.

For a pair (CIOTS, IOTS) of specification and implementation, Definition 6 will be used on the implementation side and Definition 5 will be used on the specification side. Both are, of course, linked by the vector of output sets $\boldsymbol{L}$. We assume the component quiescence labels to be uniquely identifiable and consistently chosen throughout the definitions, s.t. indeed the label δ_k for a particular output set $L_{!k}$ is identical in each case and matches the quiescence label for the corresponding component s_k of the considered CIOTS. This enables us to drop the superscript ^{L}. For the remainder of this paper, we are (unless otherwise stated) working with the suspension automata without explicit reference, i.e. we use s and i instead of $\Delta(s)$ and $\Delta(i)$.

Based on the presented definitions and conventions, the definition for **mioco** in the context of component-based systems is as follows.

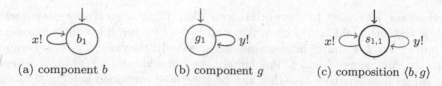

(a) component b (b) component g (c) composition $\langle b, g \rangle$

Fig. 3. Non-deterministic encoding of parallel component behaviour.

Definition 7. *Given a set of input labels $L_?$ and a set of output labels $L_!$, the relation* **mioco** $\subseteq \mathcal{IOTS}(L_?, L_!) \times \mathcal{CIOTS}(L_?, L_!)$ *for input-enabled implementation i and specification $s = \langle Q, L_?, L_!, T, q_0, C \rangle$, is defined as follows:*

$$i \textbf{ mioco } s \Leftrightarrow_{\text{def}} \forall \sigma \in Straces(s) : out(i \textbf{ after } \sigma) \subseteq out(s \textbf{ after } \sigma)$$

Example 5. We check **mioco**-conformance of the implementation candidates depicted in Fig. 2, with respect to the specification displayed in Fig. 1. Implementation i does not conform to $\langle b, g \rangle$ since $out(i \textbf{ after } \text{strt?}) = \{\text{sig}_1!, \delta_2\}$ which is not contained in $out(\langle b, g \rangle \textbf{ after } \text{strt?}) = \{\text{sig}_1!, \text{sig}_2!\}$. Likewise, implementation j is rejected again, since state j_2 is quiescent for component b i.e. $out(j \textbf{ after } \text{strt?}) = \{\text{sig}_2!, \delta_1\}$. Contrarily, implementation $k \textbf{ mioco} \langle b, g \rangle$, since it implements the missing $sig_2!$ transition of implementation j.

5 A Practical Theory

When it comes to the practical application of **ioco**-based testing approaches, the concept of quiescence is implemented by clock timeouts and resets. In the standard **ioco** setting, a single timer for the system is sufficient. Since **mioco** is a refinement of **ioco** one can basically use the standard test generation and execution algorithms [23], but with additional quiescence timers i.e. one timer per component. The timer for a specific component is then started or reset after each observable interaction with the IUT that belongs to this component, exactly as before when considering a single global component in **ioco**. This renders **ioco** testing as a special case of **mioco** testing. There are however some subtleties in the definition of **mioco** rooted in the fact that the quiescence definition used for the IUT is state-based.

Example 6. In Fig. 3, we have the specifications of two simple components b and g, always producing the output $x!$ and $y!$, respectively. Their composition (shown in Fig. 3c) is not quiescent for neither of the components. An implementation i which simply alternates between output $x!$ and $y!$ (shown on the right) is quiescent for both components at opposite states, by definition. As a result, i is not **mioco**-conformal to $\langle b, g \rangle$.

However, according to our initial motivation, there is no strong reason why such a system should be rejected. After all it does not produce any unforeseen output (w.r.t. $L_!$) and it implements the specified behaviour for both components, by producing $x!$ and $y!$ indefinitely. And in addition, a real physical system would pass any test case that can be generated, provided sufficiently large quiescence timeout values. So we are facing a testing *practice that matches our intuition very well, but it does not match the theory.* This gap between theory and practice is rooted in the different definition bases for quiescence. Theoretically, conformance is determined by a state-based definition of quiescence. But practical black-box testing does not have information about the internal state of the IUT. As a result, quiescence detection needs to be based on the observed behaviour of the system, i.e. be trace-based. So, what we are after is a fix of the theory on the implementation side, albeit accepting the approximative nature of quiescence being implemented by timers. At the same time we want to maintain the property of our theory refining **ioco**.

The crux lies in a relaxation $\delta_k^L(p)$ defined in (2) of Definition 6, so that an implementation that postpones outputs of component k for some finite time will not be considered quiescent. Therefore, an IUT will be declared quiescent w.r.t. component k whenever

- it is quiescent for *all* components, or
- it remains silent w.r.t. component k (unless triggered by an input).

This intuition is echoed in the following definition.

Definition 8. *The relation* **cioco** *is defined precisely as the relation* **mioco** *in Definition 7, but on the basis of (2) of Definition 6 replaced by*

$$\delta_k^L(p) =_{\text{def}} \delta(p) \vee (\forall \sigma \in traces(p) : \sigma \in (L_! \cup \{\tau\})^* \Rightarrow \sigma \in ((L_! \setminus L_{!k}) \cup \{\tau\})^* \\ \wedge \quad \tau \notin init(p) \ )$$

$$(3)$$

The last conjunct, enforcing non-quiescence if the implementation can step internally is needed in order to ensure that **cioco** is a conservative extension of **ioco**, as we will discuss right away. Standard input-output conformances considers states non-quiescent in the presence of outgoing internal transitions on both sides of the relation i.e. specification and implementation.

Example 7. Applying the quiescence notion to implementation i from Example 6 results in a suspension automaton without any quiescent transitions i.e. both states are neither quiescent for component b nor g. Thus, i **cioco**$\langle b, g \rangle$ as intended.

Theorem 1. *For specification $s \in \mathcal{CIOTS}(L_?, L_!)$, and input-enabled implementation $i \in \mathcal{IOTS}(L_?, L_!)$, the following holds:*

$$i \, \mathbf{cioco} \, s \Rightarrow i \, \mathbf{ioco} \, s$$

A converse result can be established, too:

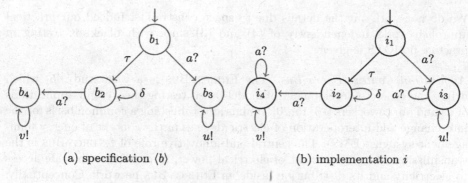

(a) specification $\langle b \rangle$ (b) implementation i

Fig. 4. Single components considered with **ioco** vs. **cioco**.

Theorem 2. *For action-disjoint specification components* $s_0, \ldots, s_n$ *and input-enabled implementations* $i_0, \ldots, i_n$ *with* $s_k, i_k \in \mathcal{IOTS}(L_{?k}, L_{!k})$ *for* $0 \leq k \leq n$, *the following holds:*

$$\forall k.\ i_k \ \mathbf{ioco}\ s_k \Rightarrow i_0 \otimes \ldots \otimes i_n \ \mathbf{cioco} \langle s_0, \ldots, s_n \rangle$$

Theorems 1 and 2 together imply that **ioco** and **cioco** are equivalent for single-component specifications.

Example 8. We consider the single component specification $\langle b \rangle$ in Fig. 4. According to **ioco**, state b_2 is quiescent while b_1 is not. Therefore the allowed outputs after the traces $a?$ and $\delta a?$ differ. The same difference applies to the states i_2 and i_1 of the input-enabled IOTS i (because the definition of δ is the same on both sides) and as a result $i\ \mathbf{ioco}\ b$ holds. The above theorems ensure that $i\ \mathbf{cioco} \langle b \rangle$, too. But Theorem 2 were broken if the conjunct $\tau \notin init(p)$ were dropped from (3) in Definition 8. In the example, state i_1 would be considered quiescent (for component b), as well, making it indistinguishable from i_2, while the difference between states b_1 and b_2 would remain, because (1) in Definition 5 reduces to the classic **ioco** quiescence definition.

So, Theorem 2 hinges on the fact that internal steps are considered non-quiescent in **ioco**. While this is a useful choice on the specification side [23], it could be considered a minor shortcoming on the implementation side, where internal steps are simply unobservable. This is rooted in the fact that the same quiescence definition is used on both sides in the standard **ioco** theory. As far as we are aware, the present work is the first to break with this tradition. If one would do the same for standard **ioco**, i.e. making internal steps quiescent on the implementation side, the two theorems above could be resurrected on the basis of the following definition replacing (3).

$$\delta_k^L(p) =_{\text{def}} \delta(p) \vee \forall \sigma \in traces(p) : \sigma \in (L_! \cup \{\tau\})^* \Rightarrow \sigma \in ((L_! \setminus L_{!k}) \cup \{\tau\})^*$$
$$(4)$$

We do not work out the details due to space constraints. Indeed our practical approach works independently of (4) and (3) since with blackbox testing in practice no IOTS is given.

Application Context EnergyBus. The ENERGYBUS is a case study [5] which drives the concrete development of model-based testing theory and applications of us and our coworkers [13–15,20]. It aims at establishing a common basis for the interchange and interoperation of electric devices in the context of energy management systems (EMS). The central and innovative role of ENERGYBUS is the transmission and management of electrical power, in particular the safe access to electricity and its distribution inside an ENERGYBUS network. Conceptually, ENERGYBUS extends the CANopen architecture in terms of *CANopen application profiles* endorsed by the CiA association [4]. Among these, the "Pedelec Profile 1" (PP1) is very elaborate, targeting a predominant business context, which is also at the centre of ongoing international standardisation efforts as part of IEC/IS/TC69/JPT61851-3. Alongside with the standardisation, a centralised certification procedure is to be set up, according to some well-structured component-based standard. The specifications themselves are provided as informal combinations of text, protocol flow charts, data tables, and finite state automata (FSA). The definitions include several data structures and various services for e.g. initial configuration, data exchange, and basic communication capability control. The ENERGYBUS introduces the notion of *virtual devices*, which encapsulate the functionality of a specific, dedicated role in an EMS, e.g. of a battery pack, a motor, or a sensor unit. A real (physical) device can combine several, not necessarily different, virtual devices. For example, a public charger can be considered as being composed of a voltage converter, a secondary EBC, and a load monitoring unit, each appearing as one virtual device to the protocol.

The specification of an ENERGYBUS-compliant system resembles a hierarchical, tree-like structure as sketched in Fig. 5. On top of this schematic structure, technically, a CANopen device might even consist of several ENERGYBUS devices. A real physical device (*field device*) might incorporate several CANopen device. The ENERGYBUS specification is a compositional specification by design. A generic CANopen and ENERGYBUS device has to deliver several services and continuously transmit contemporary runtime data. Furthermore, depending on the actually implemented virtual device(s), additional services have to be provided. All these protocols are concurrently running and are loosely coupled top-down and horizontally inside of a device. Depending on the chosen degree of abstraction, the involved components are purely asynchronous which holds especially for all device-level abstraction layers.

The theory developed in this paper improves the value of model-based testing in the ENERGYBUS context to an enormous extent. At the **cioco** core is a dedicated management of individual timers per specification-level component. The timer for a specific component is started or reset after each observable interaction with the IUT that belongs to this component, just as discussed for **mioco** in the beginning of Sect. 5, but now with the matching theoretical underpinning. The concrete difference to the standard, component-unaware testing approach

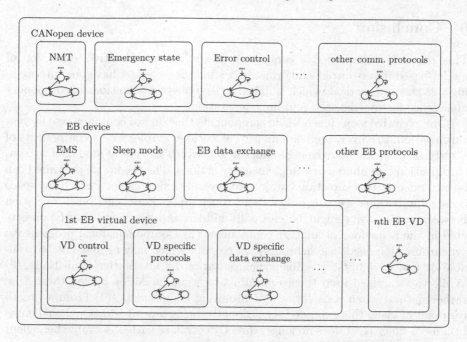

Fig. 5. Schematic view on the specification of an ENERGYBUS (EB) device

is that the latter is unable to cope with problems as simple as some components just stopping to work. Without our theory extension, these problems induce the need for a careful manual inspection of each seemingly passing test run, in order to double check for the absence of such unwanted behaviour. By using the presented component-aware approach of this paper, all needed checks are done mechanically, on the basis of timer mechanisms that are fully automated.

As an intermediate step, one can use the theory developed to justify a sound transfer of the observation mechanism of the critical circumstances from the tester to the adapter component, sitting between the actual IUT and the tester. The adapter is then equipped with a series of observer processes which maintain dedicated timers for each specific transmission expected from the IUT. The timers are started and stopped, according to the specification knowledge transferred into the adapter component. In case a time-out occurs, the adapter sends a special *absenceOfX!* output to the tester. Observing that output makes the tester stop with a **fail**-verdict. Indeed we performed our empirical evaluation successfully using this approach, too. It however has the drawback that the adapter component needs to be tailored to each case study variation manually. This is not needed if instead implementing the **cioco**-testing mechanisation as described.

6   Conclusion

This paper has developed a component-aware, yet conservative, extension of model-based input-output conformance testing. Some effort has gone into making this theory practical, which is linked to asymmetric definitions of component quiescence for specification and implementation.

Our exclusive focus has been on components that do not communicate by synchronisation. However, there are many real world examples where components of a system are meant to exchange information, which is usually modelled by synchronisation over shared or complementary actions. The theory we presented can be extended in this direction, subject to several design choices which for space constraint reasons we can only briefly touch upon here: (1) Synchronisation between components might be internally hidden and its effects may be observable in the behaviour of another component. (2) Component-local progress via synchronisation needs a synchronisation partner which may or may not be available or may preempt a possible synchronisation by alternative transitions. (3) While the standard ioco theory prohibits internal transition cycles, these arise rather natural when considering synchronising components. (4) From a practical point of view, this extended scenario introduces several additional challenges because a timer reset does no longer directly correlate with observable behaviour of a single component.

Acknowledgements. This work has received financial support by the ERC Advanced Investigators Grant 695614 (POWVER) and by the Deutsche Forschungsgemeinschaft (DFG, German Research Foundation) grant 389792660 as part of TRR 248, see https://perspicuous-computing.science.

References

1. Benes, N., Daca, P., Henzinger, T.A., Kretínský, J., Nickovic, D.: Complete composition operators for IOCO-testing theory. In: Proceedings of the 18th International ACM SIGSOFT Symposium on Component-Based Software Engineering, CBSE 2015, Montreal, QC, Canada, 4–8 May 2015, pp. 101–110 (2015). https://doi.org/10.1145/2737166.2737175
2. van der Bijl, M., Rensink, A., Tretmans, J.: Compositional testing with IOCO. In: Petrenko, A., Ulrich, A. (eds.) FATES 2003. LNCS, vol. 2931, pp. 86–100. Springer, Heidelberg (2004). https://doi.org/10.1007/978-3-540-24617-6_7
3. Braspenning, N.C.W.M., van de Mortel-Fronczak, J.M., Rooda, J.E.: A model-based integration and testing method to reduce system development effort. Electron. Notes Theor. Comput. Sci. **164**(4), 13–28 (2006). https://doi.org/10.1016/j.entcs.2006.09.003
4. CAN in Automation International Users and Manufacturers Group e.V.: CiA 301 CANopen Application Layer and Comm. Profile, v. 4.2.0, February 2011
5. CAN in Automation International Users and Manufacturers Group e.V., Energy-Bus e.V.: CiA 454 Draft Standard Proposal Application profile for energy management systems - doc. series 1–14, v. 2.0.0, June 2014

6. Carver, R., Lei, Y.: A modular approach to model-based testing of concurrent programs. In: Lourenço, J.M., Farchi, E. (eds.) MUSEPAT 2013. LNCS, vol. 8063, pp. 85–96. Springer, Heidelberg (2013). https://doi.org/10.1007/978-3-642-39955-8_8

7. Daca, P., Henzinger, T.A., Krenn, W., Nickovic, D.: Compositional specifications for IOCO testing. In: Seventh IEEE International Conference on Software Testing, Verification and Validation, ICST 2014, Cleveland, Ohio, USA, 31 March–4 April 2014, pp. 373–382. IEEE Computer Society (2014). https://doi.org/10.1109/ICST.2014.50

8. De Nicola, R.: Extensional equivalences for transition systems. Acta Inf. **24**(2), 211–237 (1987). https://doi.org/10.1007/BF00264365

9. De Nicola, R., Hennessy, M.: Testing equivalences for processes. Theor. Comput. Sci. **34**, 83–133 (1984). https://doi.org/10.1016/0304-3975(84)90113-0

10. Garavel, H., Lang, F., Mateescu, R.: Compositional verification of asynchronous-concurrent systems using CADP. Acta Inf. **52**(4–5), 337–392 (2015). https://doi.org/10.1007/s00236-015-0226-1

11. Gotzhein, R., Khendek, F.: Compositional testing of communication systems. In: Uyar, M.Ü., Duale, A.Y., Fecko, M.A. (eds.) TestCom 2006. LNCS, vol. 3964, pp. 227–244. Springer, Heidelberg (2006). https://doi.org/10.1007/11754008_15

12. Graf, S., Steffen, B., Lüttgen, G.: Compositional minimisation of finitestate systems using interface specifications. Formal Aspects Comput. **8**(5), 607–616 (1996). https://doi.org/10.1007/BF01211911

13. Graf-Brill, A., Hartmanns, A., Hermanns, H., Rose, S.: Modelling and certification for electric mobility. In: 15th IEEE International Conference on Industrial Informatics, INDIN 2017, Emden, Germany, 24–26 July 2017, pp. 109–114. IEEE (2017). https://doi.org/10.1109/INDIN.2017.8104755

14. Graf-Brill, A., Hermanns, H.: Model-based testing for asynchronous systems. In: Petrucci, L., Seceleanu, C., Cavalcanti, A. (eds.) FMICS/AVoCS -2017. LNCS, vol. 10471, pp. 66–82. Springer, Cham (2017). https://doi.org/10.1007/978-3-319-67113-0_5

15. Graf-Brill, A., Hermanns, H., Garavel, H.: A model-based certification framework for the EnergyBus standard. In: Ábrahám, E., Palamidessi, C. (eds.) FORTE 2014. LNCS, vol. 8461, pp. 84–99. Springer, Heidelberg (2014). https://doi.org/10.1007/978-3-662-43613-4_6

16. Heerink, L.: Ins and Outs in refusal testing. Ph.D. thesis, University of Twente, Enschede, Netherlands (1998)

17. Henzinger, T.A., Qadeer, S., Rajamani, S.K.: You assume, we guarantee: methodology and case studies. In: Hu, A.J., Vardi, M.Y. (eds.) CAV 1998. LNCS, vol. 1427, pp. 440–451. Springer, Heidelberg (1998). https://doi.org/10.1007/BFb0028765

18. Janssen, R., Tretmans, J.: Matching implementations to specifications: the corner cases of IOCO. In: ACM/SIGAPP Symp. on Applied Computing - Software Verification and Testing Track, pp. 2196–2205. ACM, USA (2019). https://sumbat.cs.ru.nl/Publications

19. Langerak, R.: A testing theory for LOTOS using Deadlock detection. In: Brinksma, E., Scollo, G., Vissers, C.A. (eds.) Protocol Specification, Testing and Verification IX, Proceedings of the IFIP WG6.1 Ninth International Symposium on Protocol Specification, Testing and Verification, Enschede, The Netherlands, 6–9 June, 1989, pp. 87–98. North-Holland (1989)

20. Marsso, L., Mateescu, R., Serwe, W.: TESTOR: a modular tool for On-the-Fly conformance test case generation. In: Beyer, D., Huisman, M. (eds.) TACAS 2018. LNCS, vol. 10806, pp. 211–228. Springer, Cham (2018). https://doi.org/10.1007/978-3-319-89963-3_13

21. Noroozi, N., Mousavi, M.R., Willemse, T.A.C.: Decomposability in input output conformance testing. In: Proceedings Eighth Workshop on Model-Based Testing, MBT 2013, Rome, Italy, 17th March 2013, pp. 51–66 (2013). https://doi.org/10.4204/EPTCS.111.5

22. Phillips, I.: Refusal testing. Theor. Comput. Sci. **50**, 241–284 (1987). https://doi.org/10.1016/0304-3975(87)90117-4

23. Tretmans, J.: Model based testing with labelled transition systems. In: Hierons, R.M., Bowen, J.P., Harman, M. (eds.) Formal Methods and Testing. LNCS, vol. 4949, pp. 1–38. Springer, Heidelberg (2008). https://doi.org/10.1007/978-3-540-78917-8_1

Declarative Choreographies and Liveness

Thomas T. Hildebrandt[1]([✉])(iD), Tijs Slaats[1](iD), Hugo A. López[2,3](iD),
Søren Debois[2](iD), and Marco Carbone[2](iD)

[1] Software, Data, People & Society Section, Department of Computer Science,
Copenhagen University, Copenhagen, Denmark
{hilde,slaats}@di.ku.dk
[2] Department of Computer Science, IT University of Copenhagen,
Copenhagen, Denmark
{hual,debois,maca}@itu.dk
[3] DCR Solutions, Copenhagen, Denmark

Abstract. We provide the first formal model for declarative choreographies, which is able to express general omega-regular liveness properties. We use the Dynamic Condition Response (DCR) graphs notation for both choreographies and end-points. We define end-point projection as a restriction of DCR graphs and derive the condition for end-point projectability from the causal relationships of the graph. We illustrate the results with a running example of a Buyer-Seller-Shipper protocol. All the examples are available for simulation in the online DCR workbench at http://dcr.tools/forte19.

Keywords: Choreographies · Liveness · Declarative models

1 Introduction

Choreographies are an important tool for the development of highly distributed applications. Using an "Alice-talks-to-Bob" notation, they permit to abstract away details of a distributed implementation and focus on how the different components interact. This has been a fundamental driver for the adoption of choreographies in industry standards such as Message Sequence Charts (MSC) [21], UML Sequence Diagrams [31], WS-CDL, and BPMN Choreography Notation [30]. Moreover, choreography notations have been used in a range of application areas, including web-service development [6,7], synthesis of protocol behaviour [25], monitoring [3], parallel programming [26] and cyber-physical systems [27]. Paired with static analysis techniques (e.g., behavioural type systems), they are capable of deriving distributed (endpoint) implementations where end-points generated from a choreography ascribe to all and only the behaviors defined by it. In practice, choreographies have "graduated" from the academic world, and several industrial programming languages implementing choreographies exist, e.g., [7,19,22].

© IFIP International Federation for Information Processing 2019
Published by Springer Nature Switzerland AG 2019
J. A. Pérez and N. Yoshida (Eds.): FORTE 2019, LNCS 11535, pp. 129–147, 2019.
https://doi.org/10.1007/978-3-030-21759-4_8

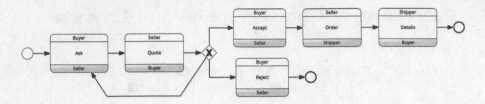

Fig. 1. BPMN Choreography for Buyer-Seller-Shipper example.

A central aspect of choreography languages is the notion of *interaction*. An interaction is a first class citizen in any choreography language and, as a minimum, it collects information regarding the sender, the receivers, and the action used to synchronize participants. In Fig. 1, we show an exemplary BPMN choreography, based on a variant of the Buyer-Seller protocol [6]. The choreography involves three participants, a Buyer, a Seller and a Shipper. After asking the Seller for a quote and getting the reply, the Buyer may either Accept, Reject or Ask again. If the Buyer accepts, the Seller sends an Order to the Shipper, which subsequently sends the detailed confirmation directly to the Buyer.

The second aspect considered in the design of choreography languages is the ordering of interactions. Typically, choreography languages are seen as imperative programs as the BPMN choreography above, that describe *how* interactions should occur. Any other flow not explicitly written in the language is considered forbidden. It has been observed that imperative notations are often insufficiently flexible for modelling business processes [1,33]. An imperative notation focuses on describing a small number of ideal flows through a process. Adding more flows to represent edge cases and less common solutions to the model tends to increase its complexity significantly. While this approach works for processes where the ideal case is all we are interested in, this does not suffice for knowledge and case work: knowledge workers tend to deal with highly variant scenarios for which they need to determine unique solutions. For instance, in the choreography above, we may in practice really want the *liveness property*, that a Quote is eventually followed by a decision, but that the Sellers can provide new quotes or the Buyer can ask again, any finite number of times, before accepting or rejecting a quote. The present imperative choreography languages do not allow to specify such general liveness property.

In the present paper, we propose using the declarative Dynamic Condition Response (DCR) graph notation [9,14,28,29,34] as a formal declarative notation for both choreographies and end-point specifications, allowing the specification of both safety and general liveness properties. The DCR graphs notation has been developed for the formalisation and digitalisation of collaborative, adaptive case management processes. The notation is both supported by a range of formal techniques, and serves as the formal base for the industrial (dcrgraphs.net) design and simulation tool. During the recent years, the DCR graphs technology has been employed in major industrial case management systems used in the public sector in Denmark. DCR graphs have been extended to include both data [35], time [18] and sub-processes [9]. In the present paper we consider only the core notation, which is expressive enough to represent both regular and omega-regular languages [9] as well as so-called true concurrency [10]. This means that we provide the first choreography model supporting end-point projection and general liveness properties. Definition and simulation of DCR graphs is supported by the on-line DCR Workbench [12] available at http://dcr.tools/forte19. DCR diagrams in this paper were all produced using the workbench.

One of the important reasons for using choreography languages is their correctness-by-design guarantees. Message-passing distributed systems consist of communicating endpoints whose behaviours are defined in terms of input/output actions. So if the choreography is to be implemented by a message-passing distributed system, it is necessary to translate choreographies into code that can be executed by these endpoints. Such a translation is referred to as an endpoint projection. The endpoint projection, paired with the global properties of the choreography, warrants the safety of the distributed execution of the endpoints (e.g. deadlock-freedom). A catch of this approach is, however, that the choreography language often allows specifications that are not well-formed, meaning that it is not possible to realise the choreography as the composition of end-point processes. A key result for any choice of choreography language and end-point language is therefore to provide criteria for the choreography to be well-formed.

A core property is that of local causality. Intuitively, local causality means that if a participant initiates an interaction, it must not have direct dependencies (or causal relationships) to interactions in which this participant is not involved. The criteria for end-point projectability is, however, highly dependent of the chosen languages. In BPMN 2.0.2 it is formulated as a constraint on sequencing

> "The Initiator of a Choreography Activity MUST have been involved (as Initiator or Receiver) in the previous Choreography Activity."

as well as a number of more complex constraints on the use of so-called branching gateways in BPMN for choices. Proving the correctness of such criteria requires a formal semantics, which is not yet provided for BPMN Choreographies, but for similar notations [5]. In the present paper, we will build upon the formal semantics and theory of safe projections [17,18] for DCR graphs to provide end-point projections for DCR choreographies.

Summary of Contributions: We provide a general end-point projection result for: (1) a declarative choreography model, (2) that can represent general omega-regular liveness properties [9], (3) supports a broad range of extensions such as dynamic process spanning and refinement [9], true-concurrency semantics [10] and time [18], and (4) is supported by both academic and industrial design and simulation tools.

2   Interactions and Dynamic Condition Response Graphs

In this section we first define the general concept of *interactions*, which are common to previous work on choreographies. We then recall the model of Dynamic Condition Response (DCR) graphs.

2.1 Interactions

Assume a fixed set of actions A, ranged over by a, b, c and a fixed set of roles R, ranged over by $r, r', r_1, r_2, \ldots$ (referred to as participants in [5]).

Definition 1. *An* interaction *is a triple* $(a, r \to R)$, *in which the action* $a \in A$ *is* initiated *by the role* r *and* received *by the roles* $R \subset_{\mathsf{fin}} R \backslash \{r\}$, *i.e a finite set of roles distinct from* r. *Define* $\mathsf{Initiator}((a, r \to R)) = r$. *We use the shorthand* $(a, r \to r')$ *for interactions between two participants* $(a, r \to \{r'\})$. *We denote by* IA *the set of all interactions.*

We proceed to define projections of interactions to actions for end-point processes. End-point processes describe the view of the process from a single participant r synchronising with the other participants via messages on channels: For each interaction $(a, r \to R)$ in the choreography, there will be channels $(a, r \to r')$ from r to r' for each $r' \in R$. To ease the definition of projections and avoid introducing new notation, we describe actions for an end-point also as interactions. That is, for the end-point process at role r, we use the interaction $(a, r \to R')$ to represent the action $!(a, r \to R')$ for sending a message on the channels $(a, r \to r')$ for all participants $r' \in R'$. The interaction $(a, r' \to r)$, represents the action $?(a, r' \to r)$ for receiving a message on the channel $(a, r' \to r)$. We apologize to the reader for the inconvenience this reuse of notation may cause.

Definition 2. *For an interaction* $\alpha = (a, r' \to R')$, *define the* end-point *projection of* α *at* r *by:*

$$\alpha_{|r} = \begin{cases} (a, r' \to r) & when \ r \in R' \\ (a, r' \to R') & when \ r' = r \\ \tau & otherwise \end{cases} \tag{1}$$

We extend end-point projections to sets and sequences of interactions by pointwise projection and removing τ actions, and finally to sets of sequences of interactions in the obvious way.

Definition 3. *A* choreographic language *is a triple* (C, A, R) *where* $A \subseteq A$, $R \subseteq_{fin} R$, *and* $C \subseteq \mathsf{IA}^\infty = \mathsf{IA}^* \cup \mathsf{IA}^\omega$. *That is, a set* C *of finite and infinite sequences of interactions for a given set of actions* A *and roles* R.

When A and R are obvious from the context, we shall take C as defining a choreographic language.

Definition 4. *The* end-point projection *of a choreographic language* (C, A, R) *is the family of languages* $(C_{|r})_{r \in R}$.

2.2 DCR Graphs

In this section we recall Dynamic Condition Response (DCR) graphs [10, 12–14, 28]. This paper follows the set-based formulation of [10, 14, 28].

As formally defined below, a DCR graph consists of a directed graph and a marking. The nodes of the graph are labelled events and the edges are relations of five kinds: conditions ($\rightarrow\bullet$), responses ($\bullet\rightarrow$), inclusions ($\rightarrow+$), exclusions ($\rightarrow\%$) and milestones ($\rightarrow\diamond$).

Definition 5. *A DCR graph is a tuple* $(E, M, L, \ell, \rightarrow\bullet, \bullet\rightarrow, \rightarrow\diamond, \rightarrow+, \rightarrow\%)$, *where*

- *E is a set of events*
- *$M \subseteq E \times E \times E$ is a* marking
- *L is a set of* labels
- *$\ell : E \rightarrow L$ is a* labelling function
- *$\phi \subseteq E \times E$ for $\phi \in \{\rightarrow\bullet, \bullet\rightarrow, \rightarrow\diamond, \rightarrow+, \rightarrow\%\}$ are* relations *between events.*

A DCR graph defines a process whose executions are finite and infinite sequences of (labelled) events. Note that an event may be executed several times. The three sets of events in the marking $M = (\mathsf{Ex}, \mathsf{Re}, \mathsf{In})$ defines the state of the DCR graph process, and are referred to as the **ex**ecuted events (Ex), the *pending* **re**sponse[1] events (Re) and the **in**cluded events (In). The relations define effects of the execution of events and constrain the executions of the process defined by the DCR graph as defined formally below. Briefly:

- An inclusion (respectively exclusion) relation $e \rightarrow+ e'$ (respectively $e \rightarrow\% e'$) means that if e is executed, then e' is included (respectively excluded).
- A condition relation $e \rightarrow\bullet e'$ means that e is a condition for e', i.e. if e is included, then e must have been executed for e' to be enabled for execution.
- A response relation $e \bullet\rightarrow e'$ means that whenever e is executed, e' becomes a pending response. During a process execution, a pending event must eventually be executed (which makes it no longer pending, unless it has a response relation to itself) or be excluded. We refer to e' as a response to e.
- A milestone relation $e \rightarrow\diamond e'$ means that if e is included it must not be pending for e' to be enabled for execution. We refer to e as a milestone for e'. Milestones are typically used in cyclic behaviour, when some earlier executed event e may be required to be executed again, i.e. it becomes pending, before the process can proceed executing event e'.

For DCR graph G with events E and marking $M = (\mathsf{Ex}, \mathsf{Re}, \mathsf{In})$ and event $e \in E$ we write $(\rightarrow\bullet e)$ for the set $\{e' \in E \mid e' \rightarrow\bullet e\}$, write $(e\bullet\rightarrow)$ for the set $\{e' \in E \mid e \bullet\rightarrow e'\}$ and similarly for $(e\rightarrow+)$, $(e\rightarrow\%)$ and $(\rightarrow\diamond e)$. We can now define when the events of a DCR graph are *enabled*.

---

[1] We often simply say "pending" instead of "pending response".

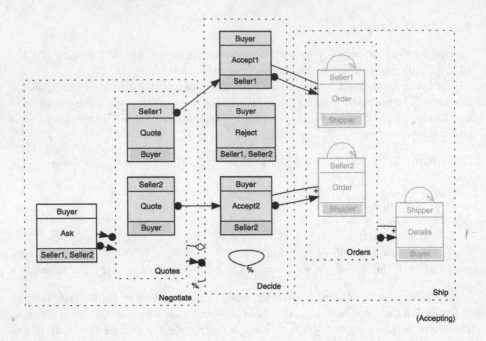

Fig. 2. Example DCR choreography

Definition 6 (Enabled events). *Let* $G = (E, M, L, \ell, \to\bullet, \bullet\to, \to\diamond, \to+, \to\%)$ *be a DCR graph, with marking* $M = (\mathsf{Ex}, \mathsf{Re}, \mathsf{In})$. *An event* $e \in \mathsf{E}$ *is* enabled, *written* $e \in \mathsf{enabled}(G)$, *iff (a)* $e \in \mathsf{In}$ *and (b)* $\mathsf{In} \cap (\to\bullet e) \subseteq \mathsf{Ex}$ *and (c)* $(\mathsf{Re} \cap \mathsf{In}) \cap (\to\diamond e) = \emptyset$.

That is, enabled events (a) are included, (b) their included conditions have already been executed, and (c) have no pending included milestones.

Example 7. We give an example of a DCR graph in Fig. 2 as visualised by the online-tool dcr.tools/forte19. Events are indicated by boxes with solid borders and collections of events are shown with dashed boxes. Relations are shown as arrows between the boxes. As formalised in [16], such collections are referred to as "nestings" and are just a visual shorthand, understanding arrows to (from) nestings to represent arrows to (from) *every* event inside the nesting.

Traditionally, the labels of DCR graphs only consist of an action and possibly a set of roles that may perform the action. In the present paper, however, the labels of the DCR graphs are interactions rather than just actions. Instead of labelling the boxes representing the events simply with the label, e.g., $(\mathsf{Ask}, \mathsf{Buyer} \to \{\mathsf{Seller1}, \mathsf{Seller1}\})$, we have split the label in three fields in the visualisation similarly to the notation for BPMN choreographies: The initiator (Buyer) is written in the field at the top of the box; the action (Ask) is written in the middle field, and the receiver(s) $(\mathsf{Seller1}, \mathsf{Seller2})$ in the bottom field with a grey background. When no confusion is possible, we refer to events by the action shown in middle field, speaking of, e.g., "the event Ask" rather than the more precise "the event labelled Buyer, Ask, Seller1, Seller2."

The marking of the graph and whether events are enabled or not is indicated visually: If the background of all fields is grey for a box, the event is included, but not enabled. For instance, the Ask event is enabled, but the two Quote events are not enabled (because the Ask event is a condition for the events and not yet executed). A box which is made opaque/dimmed out, such as the two Order events and the Details event, represents an event which is not included. When explaining Fig. 3 we describe the visualisation of executed and pending events.

The response relation ($\bullet\to$) from the event Ask to the nesting box around the Quote events means that the Quote events become pending when Ask is executed. This expresses the liveness constraint, that if the buyer asks, a quote must eventually be given by both sellers. The milestone relation ($\to\diamond$) from the box around the Quote events to the nesting box labelled Decide means that the events (Accept1, Accept2 and Reject) inside the Decide box cannot be executed if any of the Quote events are pending, not even if Quote happened in the past. This expresses the safety condition, that the buyer can not accept or reject if one of the sellers has not responded after the last time the buyer asked for a quote. The inclusion relation from e.g. Accept1 to Order for Seller 1 means that order event will be included if the buyer accepts the quote from Seller 1. The circular exclusion arrow in the Decide box means that any event inside the box is related by an exclude relation to any event inside the box, i.e. they are mutually and self-exclusive. That is, whenever one of the events inside the box happens, all three events inside the box are excluded. Moreover, due to the exclude relation from the Decide box to the Negotiate box, also the Ask and Quote events are excluded when a decision is made.

Below we formalise how the marking changes when an enabled event e is *executed*: (a) the event e is added to the set of executed events, (b) e is removed from the set of pending response events, and the responses to e are added to the set of pending response events, (c) the events excluded by e are removed from the set of included events, and the events included by e are added to the set of included events.

Definition 8 (Execution). *Let* $G = (E, M, L, \ell, \to\bullet, \bullet\to, \to\diamond, \to+, \to\%)$ *be a DCR graph, with marking* $M = (\text{Ex}, \text{Re}, \text{In})$. *When* $e \in \text{enabled}(G)$, *the result of executing* e, *written* $\text{execute}(G, e)$ *is a new DCR graph* G' *with the same events, labels, labelling function and relations, but a new marking* $M' = (\text{Ex}', \text{Re}', \text{In}')$, *where (a)* $\text{Ex}' = \text{Ex} \cup \{e\}$ *(b)* $\text{Re}' = (\text{Re}\backslash\{e\}) \cup (e\bullet\to)$, *and (c)* $\text{In}' = (\text{In}\backslash(e\to\%)) \cup (e\to+)$

Example 9. In the graph in Fig. 2, we may execute the event Ask. Following the relations in the graph, this will make the two Quote events enabled and pending: they were previously not enabled due to their condition relation from Ask and once Ask becomes "executed" in the marking, that condition is fulfilled, and Quote becomes enabled. Altogether, executing Ask yields the graph shown in Fig. 3. Red text and an exclamation mark after the action in the middle field

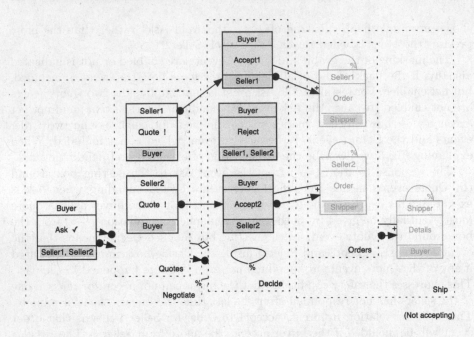

Fig. 3. DCR choreography after execution of Ask. (Color figure online)

represents an event which is pending, as is the case for the two Quote events. A box with a check mark after the label represents an event which is executed, as can be seen for the event Ask. Note that Ask may be executed again immediately, leaving the process in the same state, but the two Quote events must eventually be executed (without any intermediate Ask) in order for the run to be accepting.

From the definition of execution we can define a transition semantics for DCR graphs using labelled event transition system with responses.

Definition 10 (Transition semantics). *Let $G = (E, M, L, \ell, \to\bullet, \bullet\to, \to\diamond, \to+, \to\%)$ be a DCR graph. The Labelled Event Transition System with Responses (LETSR) for G is defined as $T(G) = (\mathcal{G}, G, E, L, \ell, \to, \rho)$, where the DCR graph G is the initial state, E is the set of events, L is the set of labels, ℓ is the labelling function, $\to \subseteq \mathcal{G} \times E \times \mathcal{G}$ is the transition relation, defined by $(G, e, G') \in \to$ iff $e \in \mathsf{enabled}(G)$ and $G' = \mathsf{execute}(G, e)$, and $\mathcal{G} = \{G' \mid G \to^* G'\}$, the set of states, is the graphs reachable from the initial graph G by execution of events, and finally ρ is the response function defined on DCR graphs by $\rho(G') = \mathsf{Re} \cap \mathsf{In}$, if $(\mathsf{Ex}, \mathsf{Re}, \mathsf{In})$ is the marking of G'.*

We say that two LETSR T and T' are isomorphic, written $T \equiv T'$, if there is an isomorphism between the sets of states preserving and respecting transitions and the response function.[2]

---

[2] Isomorphism could be defined more generally by also having an isomorphism on the set of events, but the given definition is sufficient for the present paper.

We define the language of a DCR graph as all finite and infinite sequences of such executions, where we demand that all pending responses are either eventually executed or excluded.

Definition 11 (Language of a DCR graph). *Let $G = (E, M, L, \ell, \rightarrow\bullet, \bullet\rightarrow,$ $\rightarrow\diamond, \rightarrow+, \rightarrow\%)$ be a DCR graph. A run of G is a finite or infinite sequence of events $e_0, e_1, \ldots$ such that $e_i \in$ enabled(G_i), execute$(G_i, e_i) = G_{i+1}$, and $G_0 = G$. We call a run accepting iff for each G_i with marking $M_i = (\mathsf{Ex}_i, \mathsf{Re}_i, \mathsf{In}_i)$ and $e \in \mathsf{Re}_i \cap \mathsf{In}_i$ there exists a $j \geq i$ such that $e_j = e$ or $e \notin \mathsf{Re}_j \cap \mathsf{In}_j$.*

The language lang$(G) \subseteq L^\infty$ *of G is the set of finite and infinite sequences of labels $l_0 l_1 \cdots$ such that there is an accepting run $e_0, e_1, \ldots$ where $\ell(e_i) = l_i$.*

It has been proven in [9] that DCR graphs can express exactly the languages that are the union of a regular and an ω-regular language. This means that one can express regular safety and liveness properties in DCR graphs.

Since the definition of accepting runs only depends on the included pending responses in the markings of the graphs and the events being executed during a run, it is easy to see that if two DCR graphs have isomorphic transition systems with responses then they also have the same languages.

Proposition 12. *Let G and G' be DCR graphs. If $T(G) \equiv T(G')$ then* lang$(G) =$ lang(G').

3   DCR Choreographies

Below we first account for how DCR Choreographies and DCR End-points can be defined using DCR graphs. We then derive the criteria for end-point projectability and provide the operational correspondence between an end-point projectable DCR graph and the synchronous composition of its end-points.

Definition 13. *Let $A \subseteq \mathsf{A}$ and $R \subset_{fin} \mathsf{R}$ be sets of roles and actions, respectively. A triple (G, A, R) is then a DCR choreography when G is a deadlock-free DCR graph such that the labels $L \subseteq \mathsf{IA}$ of G are interactions with actions in A and participants in R. For a role $r \in R$, a tuple (G, A, R, r) is a DCR End-point when the labels L of G are interactions either of the form $(a, r \rightarrow R')$ or $(a, r' \rightarrow r)$ with $a \in A$.*

Example 14. The DCR graph in Fig. 2 is the DCR graph G of a DCR choreography (G, A, R) where the actions A and roles R are given by:

$$A = \{\mathsf{Ask}, \mathsf{Quote}, \mathsf{Accept1}, \mathsf{Accept2}, \mathsf{Reject}, \mathsf{Order}, \mathsf{Details}\}$$
$$R = \{\mathsf{Buyer}, \mathsf{Seller}, \mathsf{Shipper}\}$$

Note that by virtue of being a general declarative notation, one may specify DCR graphs with deadlocks, e.g. by having a cycle of condition relations. It is easy to prove, that if $(\rightarrow\bullet \cup \rightarrow\diamond)$, i.e. the union of the condition and milestone relations, is acyclic, then the DCR graph is free of deadlocks. Moreover, such graphs can express all languages expressed by general DCR graphs, and in particular the complex behaviour in our running example.

We now turn to the key question for any choreography language: How do we project a global choreography description onto the intended behaviour of individual participants? And in particular, is this operation always possible, or are some global descriptions in fact not realisable by individual end-points?

Projections and distributed execution have been studied for DCR graphs in previous work [15,17,18], but in a rather different setting where events are only labeled by actions and initiating roles, not receiving roles. For this reason, it is safe in [15,17,18] to leave out an event in the projection to an end-point, if the execution of this event does not impact the state or enabledness of any event initiated by the participant responsible for that end-point. An example of such an event in our running example is the Details event for the Buyer end-point.

In the present paper we have explicit receivers and need to preserve all receiving events for a participant. Consequently, we can not directly use the notion of projection given in [15,17,18]. However, we may yet *build* on these projections to obtain one useful for DCR choreographies. The core idea in those papers was to project a graph G with events E to a network of local graphs for any division (not necessarily disjoint) of the events $\delta_1 \cup \delta_2 \cup \ldots \cup \delta_n = E$, then define synchronous composition of such networks of DCR graphs. Intuitively, shared events, i.e. events occurring in more than one graph, are executed synchronously in the network, representing communication. The projection then ensured that execution of the network formed by the local graphs would have a transition system isomorphic to that of the global graph, and thus in particular exhibit the same language as the global graph.

In the following we reconcile the notion of projection from [15,17,18] and then subsequently define end-point projections.

First, we characterise when the execution of an event may change the marking or enabledness of another. To this end, we define the notion of *direct dependency*.

Definition 15. *Let* $G = (E, M, L, \ell, \to\bullet, \bullet\to, \to\diamond, \to+, \to\%)$ *be a DCR graph and let* $e, e' \in E$ *be events of* E. *Then there is a* direct dependency $e' \preceq e$ *from* e' *to* e *iff either of the following conditions are true*

1. $e' = e$,
2. $e'(\to\bullet \cup \bullet\to \cup \to+ \cup \to\% \cup \to\diamond)e$,
3. $\exists e''. \ e'(\to+ \cup \to\%)e''(\to\bullet \cup \to\diamond)e$,
4. $\exists e''. \ e' \bullet\to e'' \to\diamond e$.

That is, $e' \preceq e$ iff either (1) they are the same, (2) there is a relation from e' to e, (3) e' includes or excludes an event which is itself a condition or milestone for e, or (4) e' has a response to a milestone for e.

The following proposition states that an event e *must* be directly dependent on any event e' whose execution may change the marking or enabledness of e.

Proposition 16. *Let* G *be a DCR graph with marking* $M = (\mathsf{Ex}, \mathsf{Re}, \mathsf{In})$. *Suppose* $e' \in \mathsf{enabled}(G)$, *and let* $G' = \mathsf{execute}(G, e')$ *and* $M' = (\mathsf{Ex}', \mathsf{Re}', \mathsf{In}')$ *be the marking of* G'. *If either of the following hold, then* $e' \preceq e$.

1. $e \in \mathsf{enabled}(G) \not\Leftrightarrow e \in \mathsf{enabled}(G')$,
2. $e \in \mathsf{Ex} \not\Leftrightarrow e \in \mathsf{Ex}'$,
3. $e \in \mathsf{Re} \not\Leftrightarrow e \in \mathsf{Re}'$,
4. $e \in \mathsf{In} \not\Leftrightarrow e \in \mathsf{In}'$.

Proof. (Sketch) For lack of space we just show why condition 2 above implies $e' \preceq e$, the other conditions follow from a similar inspection of the definitions. First note that the set Ex of executed events always grows, i.e. once executed an event can never become not executed. So we only need to consider the case $e \notin \mathsf{Ex}$ and $e \in \mathsf{Ex}'$. From the Definition 8 it is clear that the only event that can be included in the set Ex during execution is the event being executed, so it follows that $e = e'$ and thus $e' \preceq e$.

We note that this implication is not a bi-implication, e.g., in the DCR graph comprising just the two events e, f and the single relation $e \rightarrow\bullet f$ in a marking where e is already executed, we clearly have $e \preceq f$ (by Definition 15(2) because there is a relation from e to f), yet executing e in fact cause *no* changes to marking or enabledness of f.

Intuitively, we will obtain the end-point projection for a participant r by keeping (a) events labelled with interactions involving r, *as well as* (b) the direct dependencies of the events for which r is the initiator. We then interpret the interactions as end-point actions as described in Sect. 2.1. In order for the interactions to make sense as actions for the end-point process at r, the role r must be involved in its direct dependencies. We formalise this as follows.

Definition 17. *Let (G, A, R) be a DCR choreography and ℓ the labelling function of G; and let $r \in R$ be a role. This choreography is end-point projectable for r iff for all e, if $\mathsf{Initiator}(e) = r$ and $e' \preceq e$, then $\ell(e')_{|r} \neq \tau$,*

Example 18. Referring again to the example DCR choreography in Fig. 2, we find that this choreography is in fact *not* end-point projectable for the participants Seller1 and Seller2. We see in Fig. 2 that the Accept1 event causes Accept2 to be excluded, however, Seller2 is initiator of Accept2, but *not* participating in Accept1. To be precise, because of the exclusion we have Accept1 $\preceq$ Accept2 and $\ell(\mathsf{Accept2}) = (\mathsf{Accept2}, \mathsf{Buyer} \rightarrow \mathsf{Seller2})$ yet $\ell(\mathsf{Accept1}) = (\mathsf{Accept1}, \mathsf{Buyer} \rightarrow \mathsf{Seller1})$, so $\ell(\mathsf{Accept1})_{|\mathsf{Shipper}} = \tau$.

We fix this by redefining the choreography such that Seller2 is included in the Accept1 interaction, that is, so that Seller2 is notified that he lost the contract; and vice versa including Seller1 in the Accept2 interaction. We show the projectable process in Fig. 4. This choreography *is* end-point projectable.

We proceed by defining the end-point projection. We start by recalling the definition of projection in [15,17,18], adapted to keep all labels,

Definition 19 (Adapted DCR δ-Projection cf. [15,17]). *Given a DCR graph*

$$G = (E, M, L, \ell, \rightarrow\bullet, \bullet\rightarrow, \rightarrow\diamond, \rightarrow+, \rightarrow\%)$$

and a set of events $\delta \subseteq E$, define the projection of G to the events δ as the graph $G|_\delta = (E|_\delta, M|_\delta, L|_\delta, \ell|_\delta, \rightarrow\bullet|_\delta, \bullet\rightarrow|_\delta, \rightarrow\diamond|_\delta, \rightarrow+|_\delta, \rightarrow\%|_\delta)$ given by:

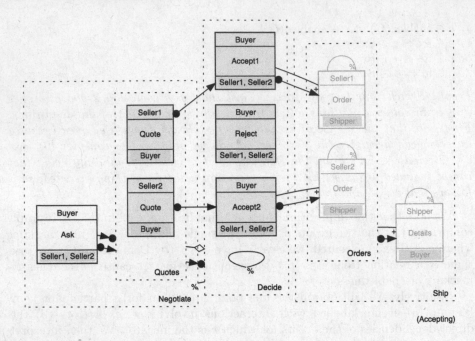

Fig. 4. End-point projectable DCR choreography

1. $E|_\delta = \{e \in E \mid \exists e' \in \delta. \ e \preceq e'\}$,
2. $M|_\delta = (\mathsf{Ex}|_\delta, \mathsf{Re}|_\delta, \mathsf{In}|_\delta)$ *where:*
    (a) $\mathsf{Ex}|_\delta = \mathsf{Ex} \cap E|_\delta$
    (b) $\mathsf{Re}|_\delta = \mathsf{Re} \cap E|_\delta$
    (c) $\mathsf{In}|_\delta = \big(\mathsf{In} \cap ((\to\bullet\, \delta) \cup (\to\diamond\, \delta) \cup\ \delta)\big) \cup \big(E|_\delta \setminus ((\to\bullet\delta) \cup (\to\diamond\delta) \cup \delta)\big)$.
3. $\ell|_\delta(e) = \ell(e)$,
4. $L|_\delta = \mathsf{img}(\ell)$
5. $\to\bullet|_\delta = \to\bullet \cap \big((\to\ \delta) \times \delta\big)$
6. $\to\diamond|_\delta = \to\diamond \cap \big((\to\diamond\ \delta) \times \delta\big)$
7. $\bullet\to|_\delta = \bullet\to \cap \big(((\bullet\to\to\diamond\ \delta) \times (\to\diamond\ \delta)) \cup ((\bullet\to\ \delta) \times \delta)\big)$
8. $\to+|_\delta = \to+ \cap\big(((\to+\to\bullet\ \delta) \times (\to\bullet\ \delta)) \cup ((\to+\to\diamond\ \delta) \times (\to\diamond\ \delta)) \cup ((\to+\ \delta) \times \delta)\big)$
9. $\to\%|_\delta = \to\% \cap\big(((\to\%\to\bullet\ \delta) \times (\to\bullet\ \delta)) \cup ((\to\%\to\diamond\ \delta) \times (\to\diamond\ \delta)) \cup ((\to\%\ \delta) \times \delta)\big)$.

The complexity in these rules arises mostly from the necessity of including events that may affect milestones or conditions for the events in δ. We see this particularly in the right-most half of 2(c), in the second clause in 7–9, and in the fourth clause in 8–9.

We now define the end-point projection for a DCR choreography with respect to a role r. The projection comes in two steps: first we compute the δ-projection, taking δ to be the set of events for which r is the initiator. Second, we simply add all events where r is a receiver. The latter step does not really change the behaviour in terms of sequences of actions, but it ensures that all receiving roles will be present for an interaction, even when it has no effect on other events in the end-point. As also described in the beginning of the section, this was not essential for the previous work, since receivers were not explicit.

Definition 20 (DCR end-point projection). *Let (G, A, R) be a DCR choreography with events E and labelling function ℓ. For any $r \in R$, define*

$$\delta = \{e \in E \mid \mathsf{Initiator}(e) = r\},$$

and let $G_{|\delta} = (E_{|\delta}, M, L, \ell_{|\delta}, \to\bullet, \bullet\to, \to\diamond, \to+, \to\%)$ be the δ-projection of G for r. Suppose $M = (\mathsf{Ex}, \mathsf{Re}, \mathsf{In})$ and define

$$E' = \{e \in E \mid \exists a\, r'.\, \ell(e)_{|r} = (a, r', r)\}$$
$$M' = (\emptyset, \emptyset, E' \backslash (E \backslash \mathsf{In}))$$

$$\ell'(e) = \begin{cases} \ell(e)_{|r} & \text{if } e \in E_{|\delta} \cup E' \\ \text{undefined} & \text{otherwise} \end{cases}$$

The end-point projection of (G, A, R) for r is then defined as the DCR end-point $(G_{|r}, A_{|r}, R, r)$ where

$$G_{|r} = (E_{|\delta} \cup E', M \cup M', \mathsf{img}(\ell'), \ell', \to\bullet, \bullet\to, \to\diamond, \to+, \to\%).$$

Example 21. The result of end-point projecting the corrected choreography in Fig. 4 can be seen in Figs. 5, 6 and 7.

Lemma 22. *Let (G, A, R) be a DCR choreography, let $r \in R$ be a role of R, and let $(G_{|r}, A_{|r}, R, r)$ be the projection of that choreography to r. If (G, A, R) is projectable for r, then every label in $G_{|r}$ is an interaction which has r as a participant.*

Proof. The set of events of $G_{|r}$ consists of the events $E_{|\delta}$ of the δ-projection for $\delta = \{e \in E_0 \mid \mathsf{Initiator}(e) = r\}$ and the events $E' = \{e \in E \mid \exists a\, r'.\, \ell(e)_{|r} = (a, r', r)\}$. Clearly, the events in E' by definition all have the role r among the receivers and thus as participant. According to Definition 19, we have $E_{|\delta} = \{e \in E \mid \exists e' \in \delta.\, e \preceq e'\}$. Now, since $\mathsf{Initiator}(e') = r$ for all $e' \in \delta$ it follows from the definition of end-point projectability in Definition 17 that $\ell(e)_{|r} \neq \tau$ when $e \preceq e'$ and thus r is also a participant in the interaction for all $e \in E_{|\delta}$.

As shown below, it follows easily, that if an event is shared between two end-points, it has the same initiator.

Lemma 23. *Let $C = (G, A, R)$ be an end-point projectable DCR choreography, $r, r' \subset R$ be roles of R, and $(G_{|r}, A_{|r}, R, r)$ and $(G_{|r'}, A_{|r'}, R, r')$ be the projections of C to r and r'. If $e \in E \cap E'$, where E and E' are the events of $G_{|r}$ and $G_{|r'}$ respectively, then $\mathsf{Initiator}(\ell(e)) = \mathsf{Initiator}(\ell(e'))$.*

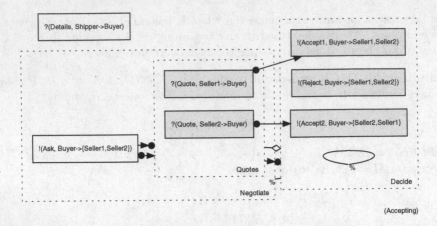

Fig. 5. End-point projection of Fig. 4 for Buyer.

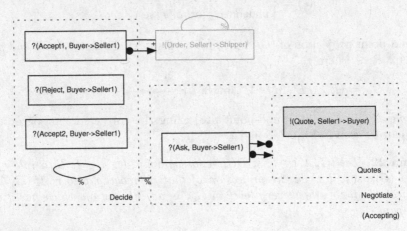

Fig. 6. End-point projection of Fig. 4 for Seller1.

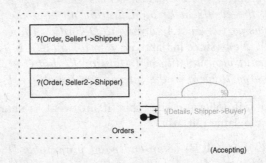

Fig. 7. End-point projection of Fig. 4 for Shipper.

Proof. According to Definition 20, the label of an event e in an end-point projection for role r is given by the restriction $\ell(e)_{|r}$. According to Definition 2 the initiator role is preserved by the restriction or the label is τ. However, by Definition 17 the label cannot be τ. Thus, being end-point projections of the same end-point projectable choreography C the event in the two end-point projections will have the same initiator role.

We now define the synchronous composition of a finite set of DCR end-points, for which the labels of shared events agree on the Initiator role. Intuitively, an event e is enabled in the synchronous composition, if it is enabled in all of the end-points in which it occurs. The execution of an event is then defined simply by executing the event in all of the components it occurs. Finally, the label is the interaction obtained by taking the union of receivers.

Definition 24 (Synchronous composition of DCR end-points). *For $R = \{r_1, r_2, \ldots, r_n\}$ and DCR end-points $P_i = (G_i, A_i, R, r_i)$ for $i \in \{1, .., n\}$ we write the synchronous parallel composition as $P = \Pi_{i \in \{1,..,n\}} P_i$. Define*

- $E = \bigcup_i \in \{1, .., n\} E_i$, *where E_i is the events of G_i.*
- $e \in \mathsf{enabled}(P)$ *iff $e \in E_i$ implies $e \in \mathsf{enabled}(G_i)$ for all $i \in \{1, .., n\}$.*
- $\mathsf{execute}(P, e) = \Pi_{i \in \{1,..,n\}} P_i'$, *if $e \in \mathsf{enabled}(P)$ and $P_i = (G_i', A_i, R, r_i)$ and $G_i' = \mathsf{execute}(G_i, e)$, if $e \in E_i$ and $P_i' = P_i$ otherwise.*
- $\ell_P(e) = (a, r \to R')$ *if $e \in E_i$ implies $\ell_i(e) = (a, r \to R_i')$ and $R' = \bigcup_i \in I$, where $I = \{i \in \{1, \ldots, n\} \mid e \in E_i\}$.*
- $\rho_P(P') = \bigcup_{i \in \{1,...,n\}} \mathsf{Re}_i \cap \mathsf{In}_i$ *if $P' = \Pi_{i \in \{1,..,n\}} P_i'$, $P_i' = (G_i', A_i, R, r_i)$ and the marking of G_i' is $(\mathsf{Ex}_i, \mathsf{Re}_i, \mathsf{In}_i)$.*

We now define the LETSR for P by $\mathcal{T}(P) = (\mathcal{P}, P, E, L, \ell_P, \to_P, \rho_P)$, where $(P', e, P'') \in \to_P$ if $e \in \mathsf{enabled}(P')$ and $P'' = \mathsf{execute}(P', e)$, and $\mathcal{P} = \{P' \mid P \to^* P'\}$.

The following theorem establishes the key property, that the synchronous composition of the end-points yields a transition system with responses isomorphic to the transition system for the choreography, and thus is in particular deadlock free.

Theorem 25. *Let $C = (G, A, R)$ be an end-point projectable DCR choreography, $R = \{r_1, \ldots, r_n\}$ and $P_i = (G_i, A_i, R, r_i)$ for $i \in \{1, \ldots, n\}$ the DCR end-points resulting from end-point projection of C. Then $\mathcal{T}(C) \equiv \mathcal{T}(\Pi_{i \in \{1,..,n\}} P_i)$ and thus $\Pi_{i \in \{1,..,n\}} P_i$ is deadlock free.*

Proof. (Sketch) The proof follows the same approach as the proof of Theorem 5.1 in [18] where a bisimulation is constructed between the original graph (in this case the choreography) and the network of synchronous parallel composition of projections. The reason why the same approach can be used is that the main difference between the present work and the work in [18] is that we have included also receiving events in the end-points that have no effect on the synchronous product, such as the Details event in Fig. 5.

We note that the isomorphism by Proposition 12 implies that the language of the choreography is the same as the language of the composition of the end-points.

4   Conclusion and Related Work

Based on the formal process notation of DCR graphs, we have provided the first declarative model for choreographies able to describe general liveness properties. We identified the local causality criteria for end-point projectability and defined end-point projections, using previous work on distributions of DCR graphs. We showed that the synchronous product of the end-point projections had the same behaviour as the original choreography. As future work we intend to extend the results to declarative timed choreographies, benefiting from projections already being defined for timed DCR graphs in [18].

Related Work. Properties for guaranteeing projectability are proposed in various settings and depend on the chosen choreography language. The results in [6] require three main properties: connectedness, well-threadedness, and coherence. While well-threadedness and coherence concern the behaviour of replicated servers, connectedness is the same as the projectability criterium of BPMN 2.0.2, which we also adopt in the present paper. The connectedness property occurs also in other works on choreography, e.g., [8,23]. In the theory of multiparty session types [20] and in Chor [7], such property is omitted at a price of a more flexible interpretation of sequencing.

To the authors' knowledge, this is the first work considering general liveness properties at the choreography-level. Other works in the literature have studied liveness for multiparty interactions from session types and contract development: Padovani et al. [32] propose a type system for session types to control liveness properties. However, the model considered is roleless since types describe interactions but without specifying which roles implement them. The work in [11] extends binary session types to specify response properties, that is applied to a variant of a collaborative BPMN process language to verify whether liveness for dead-lock free processes can be achieved. A recent paper by Lange et al. [24] investigates a bounded liveness property for GO programs, where protocols are specified as global types. Such property resembles a progress property and is not as general as our liveness. For instance, requiring that after a Quote we have eventually an Accept or a Reject cannot be expressed as bounded liveness. *Honesty* is a variant of liveness used in contract-oriented programming [2]. In short, an endpoint is honest if it abides the sequence of actions stipulated in its contract. Honesty will fail if the contract promises the execution of an action and the endpoint does not execute it. Contracts in this sense correspond to DCR responses. We differ from [2] in the sense that we do not require a session-type to verify liveness. It is specified in the model as a behavioural constraint only in the places that is required.

Our previous work in [4], presented a proof system for choreographies where properties such as liveness and connectedness can be expressed in terms of modal (may/must) operators. Apart from the difference on the languages explored (the global calculus in [4] and DCR in the present work), we differ from being able to express one-to-many communications. For DCR graphs, projections were studied in a different context in [15,17,18], where all participants were implicit receivers of actions and projections thus always defined.

Acknowledgments. Work supported by the Innovation Fund Denmark project *Eco-Know* (7050-00034A); the Danish Council for Independent Research project *Hybrid Business Process Management Technologies* (DFF-6111-00337), and the European Union's Horizon 2020 research and innovation programme under the Marie Sklodowska-Curie grant agreement BehAPI No. 778233.

References

1. van der Aalst, W.M.P., Pesic, M.: DecSerFlow: towards a truly declarative service flow language. In: Bravetti, M., Núñez, M., Zavattaro, G. (eds.) WS-FM 2006. LNCS, vol. 4184, pp. 1–23. Springer, Heidelberg (2006). https://doi.org/10.1007/11841197_1

2. Bartoletti, M., Scalas, A., Tuosto, E., Zunino, R.: Honesty by typing. Log. Methods Comput. Sci. **12**(4) (2016)

3. Bocchi, L., Chen, T.-C., Demangeon, R., Honda, K., Yoshida, N.: Monitoring networks through multiparty session types. In: Beyer, D., Boreale, M. (eds.) FMOODS/FORTE -2013. LNCS, vol. 7892, pp. 50–65. Springer, Heidelberg (2013). https://doi.org/10.1007/978-3-642-38592-6_5

4. Carbone, M., Grohmann, D., Hildebrandt, T.T., López, H.A.: A logic for choreographies. In: PLACES. EPTCS, vol. 69, pp. 29–43 (2010)

5. Carbone, M., Honda, K., Yoshida, N.: Structured communication-centred programming for web services. In: De Nicola, R. (ed.) ESOP 2007. LNCS, vol. 4421, pp. 2–17. Springer, Heidelberg (2007). https://doi.org/10.1007/978-3-540-71316-6_2

6. Carbone, M., Honda, K., Yoshida, N.: Structured communication-centered programming for web services. ACM Trans. Program. Lang. Syst. **34**(2), 8:1–8:78 (2012)

7. Carbone, M., Montesi, F.: Deadlock-freedom-by-design: multiparty asynchronous global programming. In: Symposium on Principles of Programming Languages, POPL 2013 pp. 263–274. ACM, New York (2013)

8. Cruz-Filipe, L., Montesi, F., Peressotti, M.: Communications in choreographies, revisited. In: ACM Symposium on Applied Computing, pp. 1248–1255. ACM (2018)

9. Debois, S., Hildebrandt, T., Slaats, T.: Safety, liveness and run-time refinement for modular process-aware information systems with dynamic sub processes. In: Bjørner, N., de Boer, F. (eds.) FM 2015. LNCS, vol. 9109, pp. 143–160. Springer, Cham (2015). https://doi.org/10.1007/978-3-319-19249-9_10

10. Debois, S., Hildebrandt, T., Slaats, T.: Concurrency and asynchrony in declarative workflows. In: Motahari-Nezhad, H.R., Recker, J., Weidlich, M. (eds.) BPM 2015. LNCS, vol. 9253, pp. 72–89. Springer, Cham (2015). https://doi.org/10.1007/978-3-319-23063-4_5

11. Debois, S., Hildebrandt, T.T., Slaats, T., Yoshida, N.: Type-checking liveness for collaborative processes with bounded and unbounded recursion. Log. Methods Comput. Sci. **12**(1) (2016)

12. Debois, S., Hildebrandt, T.: The DCR workbench: declarative choreographies for collaborative processes. In: Gay, S., Ravara, A. (eds.) Behavioural Types: from Theory to Tools, pp. 99–124. River Publishers, June 2017

13. Debois, S., Hildebrandt, T.T., Slaats, T.: Replication, refinement & reachability: complexity in dynamic condition-response graphs. Acta Inform. **55**(6), 489–520 (2018)
14. Hildebrandt, T.T., Mukkamala, R.R.: Declarative event-based workflow as distributed dynamic condition response graphs. In: PLACES. EPTCS, vol. 69, pp. 59–73 (2010)
15. Hildebrandt, T., Mukkamala, R.R., Slaats, T.: Declarative modelling and safe distribution of healthcare workflows. In: Liu, Z., Wassyng, A. (eds.) FHIES 2011. LNCS, vol. 7151, pp. 39–56. Springer, Heidelberg (2012). https://doi.org/10.1007/978-3-642-32355-3_3
16. Hildebrandt, T., Mukkamala, R.R., Slaats, T.: Nested dynamic condition response graphs. In: Arbab, F., Sirjani, M. (eds.) FSEN 2011. LNCS, vol. 7141, pp. 343–350. Springer, Heidelberg (2012). https://doi.org/10.1007/978-3-642-29320-7_23
17. Hildebrandt, T., Mukkamala, R.R., Slaats, T.: Safe distribution of declarative processes. In: Barthe, G., Pardo, A., Schneider, G. (eds.) SEFM 2011. LNCS, vol. 7041, pp. 237–252. Springer, Heidelberg (2011). https://doi.org/10.1007/978-3-642-24690-6_17
18. Hildebrandt, T.T., Mukkamala, R.R., Slaats, T., Zanitti, F.: Contracts for cross-organizational workflows as timed dynamic condition response graphs. J. Logic Algebraic Program. **82**(5–7), 164–185 (2013)
19. Honda, K., Mukhamedov, A., Brown, G., Chen, T.-C., Yoshida, N.: Scribbling interactions with a formal foundation. In: Natarajan, R., Ojo, A. (eds.) ICDCIT 2011. LNCS, vol. 6536, pp. 55–75. Springer, Heidelberg (2011). https://doi.org/10.1007/978-3-642-19056-8_4
20. Honda, K., Yoshida, N., Carbone, M.: Multiparty asynchronous session types. J. ACM **63**(1), 9:1–9:67 (2016)
21. ITU recommendation z.120 : Message Sequence Chart (MSC), August 2011. https://www.itu.int/rec/T-REC-Z.120-201102-I/en
22. Kouzapas, D., Dardha, O., Perera, R., Gay, S.J.: Typechecking protocols with Mungo and StMungo: a session type toolchain for Java. Sci. Comput. Program. **155**, 52–75 (2018)
23. Lanese, I., Guidi, C., Montesi, F., Zavattaro, G.: Bridging the gap between interaction- and process-oriented choreographies. In: International Conference on Software Engineering and Formal Methods, SEFM, pp. 323–332 (2008)
24. Lange, J., Ng, N., Toninho, B., Yoshida, N.: Fencing off go: liveness and safety for channel-based programming. In: POPL, pp. 748–761. ACM (2017)
25. Lange, J., Tuosto, E., Yoshida, N.: From communicating machines to graphical choreographies. In: POPL, pp. 221–232. ACM (2015)
26. López, H.A., et al.: Protocol-based verification of message-passing parallel programs. In: OOPSLA, pp. 280–298. ACM (2015)
27. López, H.A., Nielson, F., Nielson, H.R.: Enforcing availability in failure-aware communicating systems. In: Albert, E., Lanese, I. (eds.) FORTE 2016. LNCS, vol. 9688, pp. 195–211. Springer, Cham (2016). https://doi.org/10.1007/978-3-319-39570-8_13
28. Mukkamala, R.R.: A formal model for declarative workflows: dynamic condition response graphs. Ph.D. thesis, IT University of Copenhagen, June 2012
29. Mukkamala, R.R., Hildebrandt, T., Slaats, T.: Towards trustworthy adaptive case management with dynamic condition response graphs. In: EDOC, pp. 127–136. IEEE (2013)
30. Object Management Group BPMN Technical Committee: Business Process Model and Notation, version 2.0.2 (2014). http://www.omg.org/spec/BPMN/2.0.2/PDF

31. Object Management Group UML Technical Committee: Unified Modeling Language, version 2.5.1 (2017). http://www.omg.org/spec/UML/2.5.1/
32. Padovani, L., Vasconcelos, V.T., Vieira, H.T.: Typing liveness in multiparty communicating systems. In: Kühn, E., Pugliese, R. (eds.) COORDINATION 2014. LNCS, vol. 8459, pp. 147–162. Springer, Heidelberg (2014). https://doi.org/10.1007/978-3-662-43376-8_10
33. Reijers, H.A., Slaats, T., Stahl, C.: Declarative modeling–an academic dream or the future for BPM? In: Daniel, F., Wang, J., Weber, B. (eds.) BPM 2013. LNCS, vol. 8094, pp. 307–322. Springer, Heidelberg (2013). https://doi.org/10.1007/978-3-642-40176-3_26
34. Slaats, T.: Flexible process notations for cross-organizational case management systems. Ph.D. thesis, IT University of Copenhagen, January 2015
35. Strømsted, R., López, H.A., Debois, S., Marquard, M.: Dynamic evaluation forms using declarative modeling. In: Proceedings of the Dissertation Award and Demonstration, Industrial Track at BPM 2018 (2018). CEUR-WS.org

Model Checking HPnGs in Multiple Dimensions: Representing State Sets as Convex Polytopes

Jannik Hüls[✉] and Anne Remke

Westfälische Wilhelms-Universität, Münster, Germany
{jannik.huels,anne.remke}@uni-muenster.de

Abstract. Hybrid Petri Nets with general transitions (HPnG) include general transitions that fire after a randomly distributed amount of time. Stochastic Time Logic (STL) expresses properties that can be model checked using a symbolic representation for sets of states as convex polytopes. Model checking then performs geometric operations on convex polytopes. The implementation of previous approaches was restricted to two stochastic firings. This paper instead proposes model checking algorithms for HPnGs with an arbitrary but finite number of stochastic firings and features an implementation based on the library HYPRO.

1 Introduction

Hybrid systems combine continuous and discrete behavior and are used to model and verify safety-critical systems. Different approaches exist for the reachability analysis of Hybrid automata, e.g., flowpipe construction for different state-space representations [12,21,23]. Hybrid Petri nets form a subclass of Hybrid automata [2] and have further been extended to *Hybrid Petri nets with general transitions* (*HPnGs*) in [14], that fire stochastically after a random delay. They form a subclass of stochastic hybrid systems with piece-wise linear continuous behaviour without resets and a probabilistic resolution of discrete non-determinism. Albeit these restrictions, they have been applied successfully to critical infrastructures, like water and power distribution [8,18]. Several approaches for Hybrid automata extended with discrete probability distributions exist [20,28,29,31]. More general stochastic Hybrid systems often require a higher level of abstraction [1,19]. Related Petri net approaches are also restricted e.g., w.r.t. the number of continuous variables [15] or to Markovian jumps [5].

Stochastic Time Logic (STL) closely resembles MITL [3] or the *temporal layer* of STL/PSL [22] and is used to specify properties of HPnGs. Their piece-wise linear evolution of continuous variables allows to partition the state space into convex polytopes (so-called regions) with similar characteristics [9]. The idea of a polyhedra based representation of the state space has been explored before for model checking HPnGs [11], for (flowpipe) approximations [6,7] and to abstract uncountable-state stochastic processes [26,27]. Our approach explicitly includes

© IFIP International Federation for Information Processing 2019
Published by Springer Nature Switzerland AG 2019
J. A. Pérez and N. Yoshida (Eds.): FORTE 2019, LNCS 11535, pp. 148–166, 2019.
https://doi.org/10.1007/978-3-030-21759-4_9

the stochastic behaviour over time into the state representation; every stochastic firing adds a dimension to the state space. Model checking then identifies all realizations of the random variables, which satisfy a given STL formula. The satisfaction set of (the conjunction of) atomic properties is a single convex polytope, and negation requires a translation into a convex representation. A previous approach using Nef polyhedra was restricted to models with two stochastic firings [13] due to the restricted implementation of hyperplane arrangement in the corresponding CGAL library. Recently, we proposed the translation of the nodes of the *parametric location tree* (PLT) [17] into a geometric and symbolic system representation. This construction allows to circumvent the problem of hyperplane arrangement while still providing a geometric state set representation. Given the PLT of an HPnG model, this paper presents model checking for STL properties in HPnGs with an *arbitrary but finite number of stochastic firings*. For each STL operator an algorithm is introduced, based on geometric operations on symbolic state set representations. Our implementation relies on the library HyPro [25], which offers efficient implementations for operations on convex polytopes [32] in higher dimensions. Being aware of other implementations [4,30], we like HyPro's convenient interfaces and conversion functions.

Model checking recursively follows the parse tree of the formula. Per region a convex representation of its satisfying parts is returned. A simple but scalable example is used to showcase the feasibility of the approach. Note that the resulting satisfaction sets implicitly contain the stochastic evolution and allow to compute the probability that a HPnG satisfies a specific STL by integrating over the density of each random variable.

Organisation: Section 2 discusses the modeling formalism, Sect. 3 illustrates the state-space generation using HyPro. Section 4 describes the logic STL, for which Sect. 5 introduces the region-based model checking approach.

2   Hybrid Petri Nets with General Transitions

HPnGs are defined according to [14] with the extension to *multiple* stochastic firings that fire after a randomly distributed amount of time as in [10].

Their key components are: Discrete or continuous *Places* which contain a number of tokens or an amount of fluid. A *marking* $\mathbf{M} = (\mathbf{m}, \mathbf{x})$ combines the discrete marking $\mathbf{m} = (m_1, ..., m_{n_d})$, and the continuous marking $\mathbf{x} = (x_1, ..., x_{n_c})$, for n_d discrete and n_c continuous places. The number of tokens in the i-th discrete place is denoted m_i and x_i contains the value of the i-th continuous place.

Transitions change the content of places upon firing. Discrete transitions (general, deterministic and immediate) change the number of tokens in discrete places. Transitions may only fire if all enabling criteria are met. Deterministic transitions fire after being enabled for a constant predefined amount time. Immediate transitions fire after zero time. The random firing delay of a general transition is distributed according to an arbitrary continuous probability distribution. Continuous transitions change the fluid level of connected input and output places with a constant nominal rate. [14]. *Arcs* connect places and transitions and define via weights and priorities how their content changes, when a transition fires. Guard arcs enable transitions based on the discrete or continuous marking of connected places.

Definition 1. *An HPnG is defined as a tuple* $(\mathcal{P}, \mathcal{T}, \mathcal{A}, \mathbf{M}_0, \Phi)$. $\mathcal{P}$ *is the set of places,* $\mathcal{T}$ *the set of transitions and* $\mathcal{A}$ *the set of arcs. The initial marking is denoted as* $\mathbf{M}_0$ *and the tuple of mappings* Φ, *further defines the model evolution. The finite set* $\mathcal{P} = \mathcal{P}^d \cup \mathcal{P}^c$ *combines discrete and continuous places. The finite set of transitions* $\mathcal{T} = \mathcal{T}^I \cup \mathcal{T}^D \cup \mathcal{T}^G \cup \mathcal{T}^F$ *holds immediate, deterministic, general and continuous transitions,* $\mathcal{T}\backslash\mathcal{T}^F$ *holds the set of discrete transitions. The set* $\mathcal{A}$ *is divided into three subsets: (i) The set of discrete arcs* $\mathcal{A}^d \subseteq ((\mathcal{P}^d \times \mathcal{T}^D) \cup (\mathcal{T}^D \times \mathcal{P}^d))$ *connects discrete places and transitions. (ii) The set of continuous arcs* $\mathcal{A}^f \subseteq ((\mathcal{P}^c \times \mathcal{T}^F) \cup (\mathcal{T}^F \times \mathcal{P}^c))$ *connects continuous places and transitions. (iii) The set of guard arcs* $\mathcal{A}^t \subseteq (((\mathcal{T}^D \cup \mathcal{T}^I \cup \mathcal{T}^G) \times (\mathcal{P}^d \cup \mathcal{P}^c)) \cup (\mathcal{T}^C \times \mathcal{P}^d))$ *connects discrete and continuous places to all kind of transitions. The initial marking* $\mathbf{M}_0 = (\mathbf{m}_0, \mathbf{x}_0)$ *denotes the initial number of tokens and fluid levels in the places. Parameter functions defining the specifics of enabling and model evolution are collected in:*

$$\Phi = (\Phi_b^{\mathcal{P}}, \Phi_p^{\mathcal{T}}, \Phi_d^{\mathcal{T}}, \Phi_{st}^{\mathcal{T}}, \Phi_g^{\mathcal{T}}, \Phi_n^{\mathcal{A}}, \Phi_u^{\mathcal{A}}, \Phi_s^{\mathcal{A}})$$

Example 1. Figure 1 shows a HPnG, which models a buffer (B) as continuous place (double circle) with a varying number of continuous input transitions and one continuous output transition (double rectangle). The buffer has a max. capacity of C = 100, starts with L = 10 and can be filled using producer pumps $I_1 \ldots I_n$ and is drained by one demand pump D, each with nominal rate $r_i \cup r_d = 5$. The general transitions (rectangle) $G_1, \ldots, G_n, G_d$ disable the pumps connected via guard arcs (two arrowheads) with weight 1 to the discrete places (circle).

Enabling Rules. Every continuous place has an upper boundary defined in $\Phi_b^{\mathcal{P}} : \mathcal{P}^c \to \mathbb{R}^+ \cup \infty$. (The lower boundary is always zero.) $\Phi_{st}^{\mathcal{T}} : \mathcal{T}^C \to \mathbb{R}^+$ defines the constant nominal flow rate for each continuous transition. $\Phi_g^{\mathcal{T}} : \mathcal{T}^G \to CDF$ assigns a unique cumulative distribution function (CDF) to each general transition, which does not depend on the number of firings. $\Phi_p^{\mathcal{T}} : \mathcal{T}^D \cup \mathcal{T}^C \cup \mathcal{T}^G \to \mathbb{N}_{>0}$

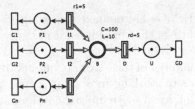

Fig. 1. Scalable HPnG model.

defines a priority for each type of transition. Using $\Phi_u^{\mathcal{A}} : \mathcal{A}^t \to \{\lhd, \mathbb{R}\}$ with $\lhd = \{\geq, <\}$ assigns a comparison operator and a weight to each guard arc. $\Phi_n^{\mathcal{A}} : \mathcal{A}^d \to \mathbb{R}^+$ determines the number of tokens moved when the transition fires and $\Phi_s^{\mathcal{A}} : \mathcal{A}^C \to \mathbb{R}^+$ defines a share for conflicting continuous transitions.

For transition T we define the set of input places $\mathcal{I}_\mathcal{P}(T)$, the set of output places $\mathcal{O}_\mathcal{P}(T)$ and the set of places connected via guard arcs $\mathcal{G}_\mathcal{P}(T)$. Let $\mathcal{P}_i^d \in P^d$

denote the i-th discrete place and $\mathcal{P}_i^c \in P^c$ the i-th continuous place, respectively. A discrete transition $T_j \in \mathcal{T} \setminus \mathcal{T}^C$ is enabled if the following conditions hold: (i) Discrete guard arcs satisfy: $\forall P_i^d \in \mathcal{P}^d \cap \mathcal{G}_\mathcal{P}(T_j), (\vartriangleleft, q) = \Phi_u^A(\langle T_j, P_i^d \rangle) : m_i \vartriangleleft q$, (ii) Continuous guard arcs satisfy: $\forall P_i^c \in \mathcal{P}^c \cap \mathcal{G}_\mathcal{P}(T_j), (\vartriangleleft, q) = \Phi_u^A(\langle T_j, P^c \rangle) : x_i \vartriangleleft q$, (iii) Connected input places satisfy: $\forall P_i^d \in \mathcal{I}_\mathcal{P}(T_j) : m_i \geq \Phi_n^A(\langle P_i^d, T_j \rangle)$.

Continuous transitions may only be connected to discrete places via guard arcs. The following needs to hold for a continuous transition $T_j^F \in \mathcal{T}^F$ to be enabled: (i) Discrete guard arcs satisfy: $\forall P_i^d \in \mathcal{P}^d \cap \mathcal{G}_\mathcal{P}(T_j^F), (\vartriangleleft, q) = \Phi_u^A(\langle T_j^F, P_i^d \rangle) : m_i \vartriangleleft q$, and (ii) connected input places hold fluid: $\forall P_i^c \in \mathcal{I}_\mathcal{P}(T_j^F) : x_i > 0$.

Model Evolution. Discrete transitions are associated with clocks. Let c_j be the clock associated with transition $T_j \in \mathcal{T} \setminus \mathcal{T}^F$. If transition T_j is enabled c_j evolves with $\delta c_j / \delta t = 1$, otherwise $\delta c_j / \delta t = 0$. A deterministic transition fires when c_j reaches the transitions firing time defined by $\Phi_d^\mathcal{T} : \mathcal{T} \setminus \mathcal{T}^F \to \mathbb{R}^+$. A firing of a discrete transition changes the corresponding marking according to the weights specified in $\Phi_n^A : \mathcal{A} \to \mathcal{R}^+$. A general transition may fire at any point in time, if enabled, and changes the discrete marking similarly to the discrete transitions. The probability that a general transition fires at the scheduled firing time of a discrete transition is zero, hence, model evolution needs to consider all enabled general transitions firing before or after the next scheduled deterministic event.

For a continuous transition $P_i^c \in \mathcal{P}^c$ we define the set of input transitions $\mathcal{I}_\mathcal{T}(P_i^c)$, the set of output places $\mathcal{O}_\mathcal{T}(P_i^c)$. An enabled continuous transition fires with its nominal rate. If a continuous place is at either boundary *rate adaptation* is performed to connected continuous transitions. This decreases the inflow to match the outflow if the place is full (or the other way around). Let $r(T_j^F)$ be the actual rate of the continuous transition $T_j^F \in \mathcal{T}^F$ after adaptation. The in-flow $f_{in}(P_i^c)$ of $P_i^c \in \mathcal{P}^c$ is defined as $f_{in}(P_i^c) = \sum_{T_j^F \in \mathcal{I}_\mathcal{T}(P_i^c)} r(T_j^F)$, i.e., the sum of all incoming rates. The out-flow is the defined as $f_{out}(P_i^c) = \sum_{T_j^F \in \mathcal{O}_\mathcal{T}(P_i^c)} r(T_j^F)$. A continuous place evolves with *drift* $d(P_i^c) = f_{in}(P_i^c) - f_{out}(P_i^c)$.

Example 2. The enabling of the continuous transitions in Fig. 1 depends on the marking of the discrete places. Initially, each discrete place contains one token, which satisfies the condition of the guard arc connecting them to I_i and D, respectively, hence enabling them. Each general transition G_i is initially enabled and when firing after a random delay, it disables input pump I_i. The initial marking of place B is 10, and its drift depends on the number of enabled producer pumps (and the enabling of D): $d = \sum_{1 \leq i \leq n} r_i - r_d$. Since all r_i and r_d have the same rate 5, the initial drift is $d = 5(n - 1)$.

3   State Space Representation Using HyPro

The state of an HPnG contains all information required by the time-bounded analysis, as well as model checking an HPnG. It is defined as $\Gamma = (\mathbf{m}, \mathbf{x}, \mathbf{c}, \mathbf{d}, \mathbf{g})$, where $\mathbf{m}$ and $\mathbf{x}$ are the discrete and continuous marking, respectively, and $\mathbf{c} = (c_1, \ldots, c_{|T^D|})$ is the vector of discrete clocks, $\mathbf{d} = (d_1, \ldots, d_{|T^C|})$ contains the drift of each continuous place. Furthermore, $\mathbf{g} = (g_1, \ldots, g_{|T^G|})$ indicates the time each general transition has been enabled. The state space $S = \{\Gamma = (\mathbf{m}, \mathbf{x}, \mathbf{c}, \mathbf{d}, \mathbf{g})\}$ contains all reachable HPnG states w.r.t. the initial state $\Gamma_0 = (\mathbf{m}_0, \mathbf{x}_0, \mathbf{0}, \mathbf{d}_0, \mathbf{0})$. The continuous marking $\mathbf{x}$ changes with derivative $\mathbf{d}$. The discrete clocks $\mathbf{c}$ and the enabling time of general transitions $\mathbf{g}$ change with derivative 1 for all enabled transitions. The discrete marking $\mathbf{m}$ and the drift of the continuous places $\mathbf{d}$ change with *events*: (i) A continuous place reaching its lower or upper boundary. (ii) A continuous place reaches the weight of a connected guard arc. (iii) An enabled discrete transition fires. Events do not move time forward.

Although the state of the system Γ changes continuously with time, its bounded evolution up to some maximum time $\tau_{\max}$ can be described symbolically using a *parametric location tree* (PLT) [14,17]. Nodes are so-called parametric locations and symbolically represent all states, whose continuous marking only differ due to the evolution of time. The occurrence of events results in branching to new locations. A location is defined as a tuple $\Lambda = (t_e, \Gamma, \mathbf{S}, p)$. At time t_e the system enters the parametric location and the state Γ follows the Definition presented before. The potential domain $\mathbf{S}$ provides the bounds for each general transition firing. The real number p is a probability assigned to each location in case of a conflict. The number of random variables present in the system n corresponds to the number of stochastic firings that occurred plus the number of general transitions that are currently enabled but have not fired before $\tau_{\max}$. All random variables are collected in the vector $\mathbf{s} = (s_0, \ldots, s_n)$ and the domain $\mathbf{S} = ([l_0, r_0], \ldots, [l_n, r_n])$ contains all possible values for the random variables per parametric location. We define $\mathbf{s} \in \mathbf{S}$ iff $s_i \in [l_i, r_i]$ for all $0 \leq i \leq n$.

The PLT is generated using a depth-first search by extending all parametric locations until $\tau_{\max}$. We start from the initial parametric location, which extends the initial state Γ_0 by $t_e = 0$, $p = 1$ and $\mathbf{S}_0 = ([0, \tau_{\max}], \ldots, [0, \tau_{\max}])$. In each location the time until the next event is computed relatively to the entry time t_e of that location. Note that the number of events that occur at the *next minimum event time* $\tau_{\min}$ is finite [14], and for each possible event e, a new parametric location is created with a marking adapted according to the causing event. Additionally, each enabled general transition may fire before that point in time. Hence, additional successors are scheduled for each enabled general transition and the potential domains have to be set accordingly. The next minimum event time is unique before the first stochastic firing. After a single stochastic firing s_i, the entry time of a location, the clocks, the continuous marking and the potential domains may linearly depend on the value of the corresponding random variable s_i. The case of multiple general transition firings leads to multi-dimensional linear equations and the domains $\mathbf{S}$ may linearly depend on the vector of random variables $\mathbf{s}$. For each successor, the procedure is called recursively and the domains are adapted to ensure the order of events. The intervals denote the values of $\mathbf{s}$, for which the causing event is the minimum next event.

Geometric Representation of Locations. We propose model checking algorithms for HPnGs that combine the tree-based approach of parametric locations with the geometric representation of stochastic time diagrams (STD). The implementation of the presented algorithm allows the analysis of HPnGs with multiple general transition firings. For each parametric location, we construct a $n + 1$-dimensional geometric representation, one dimension for each random variable and one for time. This corresponds to a region in an STD, as defined in [9].

For a given time t and a valuation of vector $\mathbf{s}$, $\Gamma(\mathbf{s}, t)$ defines a specific system state. For all system states in a region, the initial marking $\Gamma(\mathbf{s}, t).\mathbf{m}$ and the drift $\Gamma(\mathbf{s}, t).\mathbf{d}$ do not change. As shown in [9], the amount of fluid and the clock valuations are linear equations of $\mathbf{s}$ and t.

Definition 2. *A region R is a maximal connected set of $(\mathbf{s}, t)$ points, for which:*

$$\forall(\mathbf{s}_1, t_1), (\mathbf{s}_2, t_2) \in R \begin{cases} \Gamma(\mathbf{s}_1, t_1).\mathbf{m} = \Gamma(\mathbf{s}_2, t_2).\mathbf{m}, \\ \Gamma(\mathbf{s}_1, t_1).\mathbf{d} = \Gamma(\mathbf{s}_2, t_2).\mathbf{d}. \end{cases}$$

The boundaries between regions, which represent the occurrence of an event, are also characterized by linear functions of $\mathbf{s}$ and t and represent a multi dimensional *hyperplane*. We denote the hyperplane between regions R and R' that corresponds to event e as $H_{R,R'}^e$. Using halfspace intersection, convex polytopes are created as geometric representation of regions [9].

Time Evolution. Starting from a tuple $(\mathbf{s}, t)$ the time evolution is deterministic within a region, such that a time step τ is defined through the forward time closure as $\mathcal{T}_R^+(\mathbf{s}, t) = \{(\mathbf{s}, t') \mid (\mathbf{s}, t') \in R \wedge t' \geq t\}$. The occurrence of an event e does not advance time, but may lead to branching between locations, e.g. in case multiple events are scheduled at the same time. Hence, a discrete step caused by event e to other regions R' is defined for all tuples that lie on the hyperplane $H_{R,R'}^e$, for $R \neq R'$. The discrete successors of $(\mathbf{s}, t)$ are then defined as $\mathcal{D}^+(\mathbf{s}, t) = \{R' \mid \exists e.(\mathbf{s}, t) \in H_{R,R'}^e\}$. For a fixed valuation $\mathbf{s}$, a finite path σ, starting at time t_0 is denoted as $\sigma(\mathbf{s}, t_0)$ and defined as alternating sequence $((\mathbf{s}, t_0) \in R_0) \xrightarrow{\tau_1} ((\mathbf{s}, t_1) \in R_0) \xrightarrow{e_1} ((\mathbf{s}, t_1) \in R_1) \xrightarrow{\tau_2} \dots \xrightarrow{\tau_n} ((\mathbf{s}, t_n) \in R_{n-1}) \xrightarrow{e_n} ((\mathbf{s}, t_n) \in R_n)$, such that $(\mathbf{s}, t_i) \in \mathcal{T}_{R_{i-1}}^+(\mathbf{s}, t_{i-1})$ and $R_i \in \mathcal{D}^+(\mathbf{s}, t_i)$ and $t_i = t_0 + \sum_{j \geq 1}^i \tau_j$ for all $0 \leq i \leq n$. A state is on path σ if it is in the forward time closure of a region in step i of σ:

$$(\mathbf{s}, t) \in \sigma \text{ iff } \exists R.\exists i.(\mathbf{s}, t) \in \mathcal{T}_R^+(\mathbf{s}, t_i). \tag{1}$$

For a definition of the resulting probability space, we refer to [24]. Note that Zeno-behaviour is excluded by prohibiting cycles which potentially take no time, i.e. cycles of only immediate and general transitions. This together with the restriction to time-bounded reachability analysis ensures that a path is always finite. The exclusion of cycles of general transition firings is mostly technical, as the probability of infinitely many firings in finite time is zero with continuous distributions.

The Use of HYPRO. The algorithm presented in [17] to transform locations into the graphical representation of regions heavily relies on the C++ library HYPRO [25]. Amongst other data structures, HYPRO contains an implementation for convex polytopes [32] as well as a wrapper class to the well-known Parma polyhedra library (PPL) [4]. We use the so-called $\mathcal{H}$-representation for convex polytopes, where H is defined as the intersection of a finite set of halfspaces. Note that previous implementations [10,13] used Nef-polyhedra by CGAL, but were limited to three dimensions. While Nef-polyhedra are closed under the set operations union, intersection and set difference, they are not necessarily convex. Convex polytopes are only closed under intersection. Section 5 will present model checking algorithms that only deal with convex state set representations.

Note that HYPRO is restricted to closed convex polytopes, that also need to be bounded. This leads to difficulties when performing operations that are not closed w.r.t. this representation, as e.g. negation. The restriction to bounded polytopes however naturally fits our analysis and model checking approach, as the state space is bounded by the maximum time of analysis.

Example 3. The running example focuses on the core complexity of the HPnG formalism, i.e. the number of general transition firings. As shown in [8,18], analyzing larger models with few random variables is not prohibitive. The random variables modeling pump failures compete and hence increase model complexity. In general, the resulting state space has $n + 2$ dimensions.

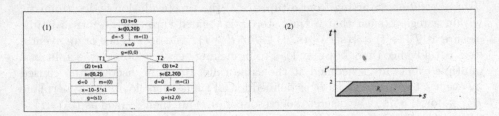

Fig. 2. A PLT and the region R_1 of the root location.

Figure 2 shows the root location and the first level of child locations of the PLT for $n = 0$. PLTs for all settings are available online[1]. The root location has the entry time $t = 0$ and neither the potential domain is restricted nor any clock has evolved. Since no input pump is present in this system, only the demand pump is enabled, initially. The initial drift is $d = -5$ and given the initial level $L = 10$ of place B, it takes 2 time units until B is empty. Hence, two events may occur, i.e. either the demand is disabled first or B is empty. The entry times of the child locations thus are $t = s_1$ and $t = 2$, respectively. Their potential domains are restricted s.t. the locations are only valid for $s \in [0, 2]$, if the general transition fires before the place is empty, and $s \in [2, \tau_{max}]$ otherwise.

---

[1] https://uni-muenster.sciebo.de/s/A3mNHLclM8233T5.

The geometric representation of the root location is shown in the right part of Fig. 2. The region R_1 is created by halfspace intersection: Every region is first restricted by the entry time of the location and τ_{max} and the potential domain of the random variables. Hence for the root location the halfspaces defined by $t \geq 0$ and $t \leq \tau_{max}$ as well as $s \geq 0$ and $s \geq \tau_{max}$ are intersected. Intersecting the halfspaces defined by the entry time of the respective locations, i.e. $t \geq 0$, $t \leq s_1$ and $t \leq 2$, then creates R_1.

4   Stochastic Time Logic

A logic for expressing properties of interest for HPnGs at a certain time was introduced in [11] and denoted as Stochastic Time Logic (STL). This paper concentrates on computing those subsets of the domain $\mathbf{S}$ for which Φ holds at a given point in time. An STL formula Φ is built according to Eq. 2:

$$\Phi ::= x_P \geq c \mid m_P = a \mid \neg\Phi \mid \Phi \wedge \Phi \mid \Phi\mathcal{U}^{[0,T]}\Phi, \tag{2}$$

where $x_P \geq c$ and $m_P = a$ are continuous and discrete atomic properties and $T \in \mathbb{R}^+$ a time bound. The satisfaction relation from [11] is adapted, to cover branching between locations:

$$\Gamma(\mathbf{s},t) \models x_P \geq c \qquad \text{iff } \Gamma(\mathbf{s},t).x_P \geq c, \tag{3}$$

$$\Gamma(\mathbf{s},t) \models m_P = a \qquad \text{iff } \Gamma(\mathbf{s},t).m_P = a, \tag{4}$$

$$\Gamma(\mathbf{s},t) \models \neg\Phi \qquad \text{iff } \Gamma(\mathbf{s},t) \not\models \Phi, \tag{5}$$

$$\Gamma(\mathbf{s},t) \models \Phi_1 \wedge \Phi_2 \qquad \text{iff } \Gamma(\mathbf{s},t) \models \Phi_1 \wedge \Gamma(\mathbf{s},t) \models \Phi_2, \tag{6}$$

$$\Gamma(\mathbf{s},t) \models \Phi_1\mathcal{U}^{[0,T]}\Phi_2 \quad \text{iff } \exists\sigma(\mathbf{s},t).\exists\tau \in [t,t+T].\Gamma(\mathbf{s},\tau) \models \Phi_2 \wedge (\mathbf{s},\tau) \in \sigma(\mathbf{s},t)$$
$$\wedge \ (\forall\tau' \in [t,\tau].\Gamma(\mathbf{s},\tau') \models \Phi_1 \wedge (\mathbf{s},\tau') \in \sigma(\mathbf{s},t)). \tag{7}$$

The *until* operator holds if a path σ starting in $(\mathbf{s},t)$ exists, such that a point in time $\tau \geq t$ exists, for which Φ_2 holds and that for all time points in $\tau' \in [t,\tau]$ the formula Φ_1 holds and all corresponding states $(\mathbf{s},\tau')$ lie on σ, according to Eq. 1. We define the satisfaction set for time t', denoted $Sat^{t'}$ and the satisfaction set for a region Sat^R as follows:

$$Sat^{t'}(\Phi) = \{\mathbf{s} \in \mathbf{S} \mid \Gamma(\mathbf{s},t') \models \Phi\} \text{ and } Sat^R(\Phi) = \{(\mathbf{s},t) \in R \mid \Gamma(\mathbf{s},t) \models \Phi\}. \tag{8}$$

The former satisfaction set contains all possible stochastic firing times, such that their time evolution from t' on satisfies a given STL formula Φ. These subsets of the domain of all random variables present in the system are also called *validity intervals*. The latter satisfaction set contains all points $(\mathbf{s},t) \in R$, such that $\Gamma(\mathbf{s},t)$ satisfies Φ. Note that Φ can also be wrapped into a probability operator $\varphi ::= P_{\bowtie p}(\Phi)$, where $\bowtie \in \{<,>,\leq,\geq\}$ is a comparison operator and $p \in [0,1]$ a probability bound. This expresses that for a given point in time, the probability that a formula Φ holds matches the threshold p. This probability can be computed from the resulting satisfaction sets, which implicitly includes information about the stochastic behaviour. This computation is however not covered in this paper. We also exclude the nesting of multiple until operators.

Example 4. All states with a disabled consumer pump are identified by $\Phi_1 :=$ $(m_U = 0)$ and $\Phi_2 := \neg(x_B \leq 2)$ ensures that the buffer does not have less than two units of fluid. Checking whether the buffer is emptied within 4 time units, while the output pump stays on, is formulated as $\Phi_3 := (m_U = 1)U^{[0,4]}(x_B \leq 0)$.

5   Model Checking STL

This section presents STL model checking algorithms for HPnGs. To obtain $Sat^{t'}(\Phi)$, first all regions the model can be in at time t' are identified. Geometrically, these regions all have a non-empty intersection with hyperplane $H_{t'}$. Then the general model checking function is called per candidate region for the overall STL formula and returns a satisfaction set $Sat^R(\Phi)$ per region R. Following the recursive definition of STL formulas, operator-specific algorithms are called to compute satisfaction sets along the parse tree of the STL formula. Model checking discrete and continuous atomic formulae as well as their conjunction solely relies on the intersection of regions with halfspaces. However, model checking negation and the time-bounded until operator requires the set operations complement, set difference and union, which may result in non-convex polytopes. We use sets of convex polytopes instead of performing the operation union to ensure that the model checking algorithms are closed w.r.t. the state representation.

5.1   Model Checking Algorithms per Operator

Model checking STL is performed along the parse tree of the formula for all regions in which the system can be at time t'. Negation and conjunction are independent of time t', and return the set of convex polytopes $Sat^R(\Phi)$. Because of the relative definition of the time bound $[0, T]$, the algorithm for until is executed only for t', and returns the satisfaction set w.r.t. time t' and region R:

$$Sat^{t',R}(\Phi_1 U^{[0,T]}\Phi_2) = \{\mathbf{s} \in \mathbf{S} \mid (\mathbf{s}, t') \in R \wedge \Gamma(\mathbf{s}, t') \models \Phi_1 U^{[0,T]}\Phi_2\}. \quad (9)$$

Note that the interplay between the different kind of satisfaction sets is explained in Sect. 5.2. Recall that polytopes are represented as the intersection of a finite number of halfspaces. We create a polyope representation P by intersecting m_P halfspaces:

$$P = \bigcap_{i=1}^{m_P} h_{i,P}, \text{ where } h_{i,P} = \{x \in \mathbb{R}^d | c_i^T \cdot x \leq d_i\}. \quad (10)$$

Restricting polytopes to their intersection with R allows defining satisfaction sets per region as the finite union of n_Φ non-necessarily disjoint polytopes P_i^R:

$$P^R = P \cap R, \text{ and } Sat^R(\Phi) = \bigcup_{j=1}^{n_\Phi} P_j^R = \{(\mathbf{s}, t) \in R \mid \Gamma(\mathbf{s}, t) \models \Phi\}. \quad (11)$$

Atomic Formula. Model checking discrete and continuous atomic formula is shown in [17] and [11]. For completeness, we present the algorithm per region, as shown in Listing 1. It takes as input a specific region R and a discrete or continuous atomic property Φ and outputs a satisfaction set, which contains all states in R that satisfy Φ. For a continuous atomic formula Φ, the region has to be intersected with the halfspace representing the continuous level $h_{x_P \geq c}$ (Line 3). A discrete formula is satisfied in the entire region or not at all, hence, a test whether the considered regions meets the marking specified by the formula Φ is sufficient (Line 4).

Theorem 1. *The satisfaction set $Sat^R(\Phi)$ w.r.t. a region R is empty or a convex polytope in case Φ is an atomic property.*

Proof. Let $\Phi := m_p = a$. A discrete atomic property is satisfied in the whole region or not at all. In either case, $Sat^R(\Phi)$ is a convex polytope. Let $\Phi := x_p \geq c$. A continuous atomic formula may only be satisfied in part of the region. The boundary c implies a halfspace $h_{x_P \geq c}$ which after intersection with R again results in a convex polytope as convex polytopes are closed under intersection.

Negation. According to the semantics of STL and as implemented in [13], negation is defined as set difference. Convex polytopes are not closed under set difference, hence, the satisfaction set of $\Phi = \neg\Phi_1$ is in general not a convex polytope. We obtain a representation in terms of sets of convex polytopes, as follows. The complement of a convex polytope with respect to a region $\mathbf{R}$ is a not necessarily convex polytope P_C and can be computed as the union of the inverted halfspaces which define P. However, inverting halfspaces results in turning a non-strict comparison operator in the halfspace definition into a strict comparison. This results in an open polytope, which HYPRO currently does not support. Hence, we define a non-disjunct complement w.r.t. region R:

$$P_{\tilde{C}}^R = (\bigcup_{i=1}^{m_P} h_{i,P}^{\sim})\cap R \text{ and } h_{i,P}^{\sim} = \begin{cases} \{\mathbf{x} \in \mathbb{R}^d | c_i^T \cdot X \geq d_i\} \text{ iff } h_{i,P} = \{\mathbf{x} \in \mathbb{R}^d | c_i^T \cdot x \leq d_i\}, \\ \{\mathbf{x} \in \mathbb{R}^d | c_i^T \cdot X \leq d_i\} \text{ iff } h_{i,P} = \{\mathbf{x} \in \mathbb{R}^d | c_i^T \cdot x \geq d_i\}. \end{cases}$$
$$(12)$$

such that $P_{\tilde{C}}^R \cap P^R \neq \varnothing$ and results exactly in the facets of P^R. Note that this definition also results in non-disjunct satisfaction sets and imprecise borders of the validity intervals that are computed after model checking each region. This is currently circumvented by additionally storing in a separate vector whether a halfspace is open or closed. In case the satisfaction set already consists of more than one polytope, the negation of the respective formula requires building the complement over a set of polytopes.

Listing 2 illustrates the general algorithm for the negation of an STL formula with respect to region R. After instantiating the satisfaction set for $\neg\Phi$ (Line 1), the general model checking routine is called for Φ (Line 2). The resulting satisfaction set consists of a set of convex polytopes, each created by the intersection of halfspaces. Hence, when computing the satisfaction set of $\neg\Phi$, for each polytope all creating halfspaces need to be inverted (Line 5–6) and collected. Then, the

Listing 1. Satisfaction set $Sat^R(\Phi)$ for atomic formula Φ and a region R.

```
1: SatR(Φ) ← ∅
2: if isContinuous(Φ) then
3:     SatR(Φ) ← R ∩ hxp≥c
4: if isDiscrete(Φ) ∧ Γ.m = Φ.m then
5:     SatR(Φ) ← R
6: return SatR(Φ)
```

Listing 2. Satisfaction set $Sat^R(\Phi)$ of a negated formula $Sat(\neg\Phi)$ for region R.

```
1: SatR(Φ) ← modelcheck(R, Φ)
2: for all Pj ∈ SatR(Φ) do
3:     H~Pj ← ∅                          ▷ Set of convex polytopes that fulfill ¬Φ in R.
4:     for all hi,Pj ∈ Pj do             ▷ For all halfspaces defining P.
5:         H~Pj ← H~Pj ∪ hi,Pj.invert()
6: for all x ∈ ✗(H~Pj) do  ▷ For all elements in the cross product over all sets H~Pj.
7:     P ← x1 ∩ R
8:     for j ← 0; j > 1; j + + do        ▷ For all halfspaces in the cross product.
9:         P ← P ∩ xj
10:    SatR(Φ) ← SatR(Φ) ∪ P
11: return SatR(Φ)
```

cross product over all these sets of inverted halfspaces per polytope is required (Line 7), whereas each entry in the resulting tuple indicates an inverted halfspace from a specific polytope. For each element of the cross product, a new polytope is constructed by successively intersecting the halfspaces that correspond to each entry of the tuple with the region (Lines 8–10), ensuring the intersection of all possible combinations of inverted halfspaces per polytope.

The resulting polytope, representing a part of the region satisfying $\neg\Phi$, is then added to the list of (not necessarily disjoint) convex polytopes, forming the satisfaction set of $\neg\Phi$ (Line 11), which then is returned (Line 12).

Conjunction. In case of a conjunction $\Phi = \Phi_1 \wedge \Phi_2$ both satisfaction sets with respect to a specific region R, namely $Sat^R(\Phi_1)$ and $Sat^R(\Phi_2)$, are required and intersected to compute the satisfaction set $Sat(\Phi)$. Listing 3 illustrates the algorithm using the representation as sets of convex polytopes. First, the model checking algorithm is called recursively for Φ_1 and Φ_2. Then, each of the polytopes in $Sat(\Phi_1)$ is intersected with each of the polytopes in $Sat(\Phi_2)$ (Line 4–5) and the result (if non-empty) is added to the resulting satisfaction set. (Line 6)

Theorem 2. *The satisfaction set $Sat^R(\Phi)$ w.r.t. a region R, for an STL formula Φ that consists of negation and conjunction only, is a set of not necessarily disjunct convex polytopes.*

Proof. We prove the above Theorem by structural induction over the parse tree of the formula Φ, using the notation introduced throughout this section.

Listing 3. Satisfaction set computation of $\Phi_1 \wedge \Phi_2$ for a region R.

```
1: Sat^R(Φ) ← ∅
2: Sat(Φ_1) ← modelcheck(R, Φ_1)
3: Sat(Φ_2) ← modelcheck(R, Φ_2)
4: for all P_i ∈ Sat(Φ_1) do                  ▷ For all polytopes in Sat(Φ_1)
5:     for all P_j ∈ Sat(Φ_2) do              ▷ For all polytopes in Sat(Φ_2)
6:         Sat^R(Φ) ← Sat^R(Φ) ∪ (P_i ∩ P_j)
7: return Sat^R(Φ)
```

Inductive Hypothesis: Suppose the theorem holds for arbitrary sub-formulas Φ_1 and Φ_2, which only consist of negation and conjunction.

Inductive Case 1: For an atomic formula Φ follows directly from Theorem 1 that $Sat(\Phi)$ contains at most one convex polytope.

Inductive Case 2: In the following we distinguish between a formula Φ, where the highest binding operator is a conjunction or a negation. Let $\Phi = \Phi_1 \wedge \Phi_2$ be a conjunction. Using the constructor case, it follows that both satisfaction sets $Sat(\Phi_1)$ and $Sat(\Phi_2)$ are sets of convex polytopes, which can be rewritten according to Eq. 11. When intersecting those unions of polytopes, applying the distributive law yields again the union (of a union) of convex polytopes, as the intersection of two convex polytopes P_i^R and P_j^R will always be convex again.

$$Sat^R(\Phi_1 \cap \Phi_2) = Sat^R(\Phi_1) \cap Sat^R(\Phi_2) = \bigcup_{i=1}^{n_{\Phi_1}} P_i^R \cap \bigcup_{j=1}^{n_{\Phi_2}} P_j^R = \bigcup_{i=1}^{n_{\Phi_1}} \bigcup_{j=1}^{n_{\Phi_2}} (P_i^R \cap P_j^R).$$
(13)

Let $\Phi = \neg\Phi_1$ be a negation. According to Eq. 11, let $Sat(\Phi_1) = Sat^R(\Phi_1) = \bigcup_{j=1}^{n_{\Phi_1}} P_j^R$ be a finite set of convex polytopes which all satisfy Φ_1 in R. Then, it follows that:

$$Sat^R(\neg\Phi_1) := R \backslash Sat^R(\Phi_1) = R \backslash (\bigcup_{j=1}^{n_{\Phi_1}} P_j^R) = R \cap \neg(\bigcup_{j=1}^{n_{\Phi_1}} P_j^R) = R \cap \bigcap_{j=1}^{n_{\Phi_1}} P_{\tilde{C},j}^R. \quad (14)$$

Note that the above definition also results in non-disjunct sets $Sat^R(\Phi) \cap Sat^R(\neg\Phi) \neq \varnothing$. Using Eq. 12, we can rewrite Eq. 14 as the intersection of R with the intersection over all polytopes in $Sat(\Phi_1)$ over the union of all inverted halfspaces per polytope:

$$Sat^R(\neg\Phi_1) = \left(\bigcap_{j=1}^{n_{\Phi_1}} \bigcup_{i=1}^{m_P} h_{i,P}^{\tilde{\,}}\right) \cap R = \left(\bigcup_{\varnothing \subset X} \bigcap_{j-1}^{m_P} h_{i,P}^{\tilde{\,}}\right) \cap R = \bigcup_{x \in X} \left(\bigcap_{j=1}^{m_P} h_{i,P}^{\tilde{\,}} \cap R\right),$$
(15)

where the Cartesian product over all sets H_{P_i} of defining halfspaces for polytopes P_i in $Sat(\Phi_1)$ is defined as $X = \bigtimes_{i=1}^{n_{\Phi_1}} H_{P_i}$, forall $P_i^R \in Sat^R(\Phi_1)$.

The second equality follows from the distributive law for families of sets. The last equality results in a set of convex polytopes, restricted to region R.

Listing 4. check_until: satisfaction set $Sat^{t',R}(\Phi)$ w.r.t. region R, time hyperplane H and remaining time halfspace $h_{t'+T}$ for $\Phi = \Phi_1 U^{[0,T]}\Phi_2$.

```
1: set<interval> I1, I2, I3 ← ∅          ▷ Intervals validating Φ in the respective region.
2: Sat^R(Φ₁) ← modelcheck(R, Φ₁)
3: Sat^R(Φ₂) ← modelcheck(R, Φ₂)
4: R ← R ∩ h_{t'+T}
5: I1 ← project(Sat^R(Φ₂) ∩ H)                    ▷ Intervals validating Φ₂ immediately.
6: C ← project(Sat^R(Φ₁) ∩ H)       ▷ Candidate intervals validating Φ₁ immediately.
7: C_{Φ₁∩Φ₂} ← project(Sat^R(Φ₁) ∩ Sat^R(Φ₂))
8: C_F ← project(Sat^R(Φ₁) ∩ Sat^R(¬Φ₁ ∧ ¬Φ₂))     ▷ Projection of boundary states.
9: I2 ← C \ (C_F ∩ C_{Φ₁∩Φ₂})              ▷ Set of intervals validating Φ₁UΦ₂ in R.
10: C_N ← C \ C_F \ I2               ▷ Removing the non-convex parts of Sat^R(Φ₁)
11: if C_N! = ∅ then  ▷ Call function for children intersecting remaining candidates.
12:    for all R_C ∈ R.children() : H^e_{R,R_c} ∩ box(C_N, R)! = ∅ do
13:        I3 = I3 ∪ (C_N ∩ check_until(R_c, Φ₁, Φ₂, h_{t+T}, H^e_{R,R_c})))
14: return I1 ∪ I2 ∪ I3
```

Together, both cases show that the satisfaction set of an STL formula, which does not contain the until operator, can be expressed as a set of convex polytopes.

Time-Bounded Until. The time-bounded until operator $\Phi := \Phi_1 U^{[0,T]}\Phi_2$ describes a property for paths within the time interval $[0,T]$ relative to time t', hence the algorithm potentially calls all regions that can be reached from the initially called region within the time interval $[t', t' + T]$. Geometrically, these are all regions that lie between the halfspaces h_t and $h^{\sim}_{t+T}$. Recall from Sect. 3 that each location is reached through a so-called source event. In the geometric representation, this corresponds to a halfspace h_R. Also, a region can be left through its other facets, which mark the entrance into the children of that region in the PLT.

According to Eq. 9, a state in region R satisfies Φ if (i) it immediately satisfies Φ_2 or if (ii) a state Φ_2 is reached inside R only via Φ_1-states or if (iii) a Φ_2-state outside region R is reached, also only via Φ_1-states. The first two cases can be determined per region and the third case recursively model checks each child until the property is satisfied or time $t' + T$ is reached. As the time bound T is relative to time t', computing the satisfaction of an until operator within a region not only depends on $Sat(\Phi_1)$ and $Sat(\Phi_2)$, but also on their relative distance with respect to time, which may vary within the region. To simplify the matter, we compute $Sat^{t',R}(\Phi_1 U^{[0,T]}\Phi_2)$, (c.f., Eq. 9) which corresponds to fixing the t-component for all tuples $(\mathbf{s}, t)$ in a region to time t'.

Listing 4 describes the model checking process and first reduces the identified region to the part that lies before the end of the time interval $[0,T]$, (Line 4) which is reached at time $t' + T$. The remainder of the algorithm operates on families of multi-dimensional intervals which satisfy different combinations of Φ_1 and Φ_2. They are obtained by projecting convex polytopes that are subsets of region R onto the domain of the random variables $\mathbf{S}$. We say that an interval I

validates a formula Φ at time t, if $\Gamma(\mathbf{s}, t) \models \Phi \forall \mathbf{s} \in I$. All intervals that immediately validate the until property are obtained by intersecting the satisfaction set of Φ_2 with the hyperplane H and then projecting the results onto the $\mathbf{S}$-space (Line 5), as indicated by the function project. Initially, check_until is called for region R in which the model can be at time t', the hyperplane H is instantiated as $t = t'$. Hence, $I1$ identifies all points in the region that satisfy Φ_2 at time t'.

The algorithm then proceeds to identify those intervals that validate $\Phi_1 U^{[0,T]} \Phi_2$ within the region R. This corresponds to case (ii) in the above explanation. First, a family C of candidate intervals is computed by projecting those states that satisfy Φ_1 when entering the region. This is done by intersecting the satisfaction set of Φ_1 again with hyperplane H (Line 6). Another family of candidate intervals $C_{\Phi_1 \cap \Phi_2}$ is formed by the projection of goal states, i.e., all $(\mathbf{s}, t) \in R$ which satisfy $\Phi_1 \cap \Phi_2$ (Line 7). However, only those candidates $\mathbf{s}$ which, from time t' on, continuously fulfill Φ_1 on their path to a goal state belong to the satisfaction set. Hence, we need to identify boundaries between $Sat^R(\Phi_1)$ and $Sat^R(\neg\Phi_1)$. C_F contains the projection of those facets that do not fulfill Φ_2 (Line 8) and can be computed as the projection of the intersection of $Sat^R(\Phi_1) \cap Sat^R(\neg\Phi_1)$. According to Eq. 14, the above intersection returns precisely the points on the boundary between both satisfaction sets, due to the non-disjunct definition of complement.

$I2$ then is computed (Line 9), i.e., the family of intervals validating the until formula within region R by only taking those candidates $\mathbf{s}$ whose time evolution $(\mathbf{s}, t)$ for $t \geq t'$ continuously satisfies Φ_1 and finally reaches a Φ_2-state within region R before $t = t' + T$. To compute the family of intervals which validate the until formula by reaching a Φ_2-state in another region, first, the family of intervals whose time evolution continuously satisfies Φ_1 and which do not reach a Φ_2-state within region R is computed (Line 10). If this collection is non-empty (Line 11), the model checking algorithm is called for each child of R, restricting the potential domain to the box defined by C_N and the states that can be reached only via Φ_1-states in R (Line 12–13). For each child, we collect those candidates which reach a Φ_2-state before time $t' + T$ within that child and intersect them with the candidates whose time evolution continuously satisfies Φ_1 and does not satisfy Φ_2 within the current region. Calling algorithm check_until (Line 13) instantiates hyperplane H as source event for each child location to account for different possible entrance times of child locations. The algorithm returns the family of intervals of the $\mathbf{S}$ domain (Line 14), which validate the until formula in that region from time t' on.

The approach is illustrated for three regions in Fig. 3. The model checking algorithm is called for an until formula $\Phi_1 U^{[0,T]} \Phi_2$ and for region R_1, where H is initiated as hyperplane $H_{t'} = h_{t'} \cap h_{t'}^*$. The intersection of $H_{t'}$ and $Sat^R(\Phi_2)$ is empty, hence $I1$, containing those states that immediately satisfy the until formula, is empty. The candidate intervals are computed by projecting the intersection of $H_{t'}$ and $Sat^R(\Phi_1)$ and indicated in Fig. 3.

Φ_2 does not hold in Region R_1, hence $C_{\Phi_1 \cap \Phi_2}$ and $I2$ are empty. In the next step the facets between the polytopes representing $Sat^R(\Phi_1)$ and $Sat^R(\Phi_2)$ are projected as C_F (also shown below). They represent those parts of the domain whose time evolution after t' not continuously satisfies Φ_1. Hence, they have to be subtracted from the candidate intervals, yielding C_N. Since the latter is not empty, model checking is called recursively for the children that have a non-empty intersection with C_N. In this example, the function is only called

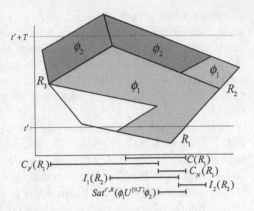

Fig. 3. Intervals for time-bounded until.

for R_2, where H is initiated as hyperplane representing the occurrence time of its source event. First, $I1$ is the projection of H with $Sat^R(\Phi_2)$, as indicated below the state space. Then $I2$ is obtained as the intersection of the projection of all candidates with the projection of the facets between the polytopes representing $Sat^R(\Phi_1)$ and $Sat^R(\Phi_2)$. Note that the computation of check_until for region R_2 requires calling the function again for the child of R_2 which lies above the polytope representing $Sat^R(\Phi_1)$ (not illustrated in the figure). For this part of the candidates a Φ_2-state cannot be reached in R_2, nor is the end of the time bound reached. The result of the function call for R_2 is intersected with the intervals in C_N of region R_1 and returned as $Sat^{t'}(\Phi)$.

5.2 Computing $Sat^{t'}(\Phi)$ for nested formula and complexity

We have shown that model checking atomic and compound formulas Φ generally results in a set of convex polytopes, containing all tuples $(\mathbf{s}, t)$ that satisfy Φ. Model checking an until operator, however returns a set of intervals, i.e. all $\mathbf{s} \in \mathbf{S}$, which validate the formula at time t'. To enable the conjunction of an until operator with another arbitrary STL formula, its satisfaction set needs to be lifted back into the region, by adding time t' to all elements $\mathbf{s} \in Sat^{t'}(\Phi_1 U^{[0,T]} \Phi_2)$. This results in one convex polytope per interval. Convexity results directly from the use of intersection, set difference and projection.

The general routine modelcheck(R, Φ) recursively calls the operator-specific functions, as introduced above, along the parse tree of the formula. To compute the overall satisfaction set $Sat^{t'}(\Phi)$, the satisfaction sets of all candidate regions $Sat^R(\Phi)$ have to be intersected with the hyperplane representing time $H_{t'}$. The results are projected onto the $\mathbf{S}$-space and the resulting validity intervals are combined for all candidate regions. If the STL formula Φ is wrapped inside a probability operator, multi-dimensional integration is performed over the resulting set $Sat^{t'}(\Phi)$ using the density function of each random variable combined with the branching probabilities. The computation of the PLT and the multi-dimensional integration are explained in [16].

The complexity of the overall model checking routine depends on the number of regions in the PLT $|R|$ and the number of operators in the STL formula $|L|$. Negation requires geometric operations on the cross product of polytopes, which is cubic in the number of halfspaces ($\mathcal{O}(|H_P|^3)$). Model checking Until relies on a series of geometric operations, where polytope inversion has the worst case complexity (similar to negation) and accesses at most $|R|$ children. The worst case complexity of the overall model checking routine is then $\mathcal{O}(|H_P|^3 \times |R|^2 \times |L|)$, as it might be called for all regions. The dimensionality of halfspaces and regions influences the complexity of the geometric operations.

Model checking nested formula might result in a large list of convex polytopes, caused by negating non-atomic formulas (c.f. Sect. 5). This effect can be reduced by rewriting the propositional parts of an STL formula in disjunctive normal form. When negation is applied directly to atomic properties, it does not increase the number of convex polytopes in the representation.

Example 5. Table 1 shows results for checking Φ_1 and Φ_2 at time $t' = 4$ and Φ_3 at time $t' = 0$, for a varying number of input pumps. The computations have been performed on a MacBook Pro with 2.5 GHz i7 and 16 GByte RAM. The number of locations generated before $\tau_{max} = 20$ is indicated by $|L|$. Per formula, we provide the number of candidate locations ($|C_R|$), the number of intervals stored in the satisfaction set ($|Sat^{t'}|$), and the respective computation times. The number of candidate regions grows considerably with the number of random variables present in the system. The computation times are much larger for the until formula, $n = 4$ required 34 min and $n = 5$ could not be solved. The large computation times for model checking an until formula are due to the required geometric operations within a region and the recursive call for child regions. In contrast model checking Φ_1 only requires to check the discrete marking, with is done in constant time per region. Checking Φ_2 is more time consuming, due to negation, but results for $n = 5$ can be obtained. The number of candidates is slightly smaller for checking Φ_3 at $t' = 0$, as less branching has taken place. Due to space limitations, this number is not included in the table.

Table 1. Results for model checking $\Phi_1, \Phi_2,$ and $\Phi_3 := (m_U = 1)\mathcal{U}^{[0,T]}(x_B \leq 0)$.

| n | $|L|$ | $|C_R|$ | $\Phi_1 := (m_U = 0), t' = 4$ | | $\Phi_2 := \neg(x_B \leq 2), t' = 4$ | | $\Phi_3, t' = 0$ | |
			$|Sat^{t'}(\Phi_1)|$	t_c [ms]	$|Sat^{t'}(\Phi_2)|$	t_c [ms]	$|Sat^{t'}(\Phi_3)|$	t_c[ms]
1	9	7	4	3	4	112	5	208
2	31	20	7	12	14	2327	3	3200
3	139	97	68	61	63	37337	4	69218
4	667	456	327	306	320	897511	7	2055254
5	3683	2338	1797	2100	1961	26790200	N/A	N/A

6   Conclusions

We proposed model checking algorithms for STL operators that can be used to check properties of HPnGs with an arbitrary but finite number of stochastic firings, working only on convex state set representations. While the current paper does not provide a framework to compute the probability that an STL formula holds, the current results in terms of validity intervals can be used to synthesize parameters for the timing of general transitions, which validate a specific formula. To the best of our knowledge, we present a model checking approach for a type of Hybrid Petri nets, that is neither restricted in the number of continuous variables, nor in the number of stochastic firings. Future work will present an algorithm to compute the complete satisfaction set $Sat^R(\Phi)$ for the until operator and compare computational complexities and efficiency of both approaches, as well as an algorithm to evaluate the probability operator, taking into account branching probabilities between locations. Furthermore, we plan to conduct a large-scale case study, to evaluate the efficiency of the current implementation. The transformation of a PLT to hybrid automata is being investigated.

References

1. Abate, A., Katoen, J.-P., Lygeros, J., Prandini, M.: Approximate model checking of stochastic hybrid systems. Eur. J. Control **6**, 624–641 (2010)
2. Alla, H., David, R.: Continuous and hybrid Petri nets. J. Circuits Syst. Comput. **8**(01), 159–188 (1998)
3. Alur, R., Feder, T., Henzinger, T.A.: The benefits of relaxing punctuality. J. ACM **43**(1), 116–146 (1996)
4. Bagnara, R., Hill, P.M., Zaffanella, E.: The parma polyhedra library: toward a complete set of numerical abstractions for the analysis and verification of hardware and software systems. Sci. Comput. Program. **72**(1–2), 3–21 (2008)
5. Everdij, M.H.C., Blom, H.A.P.: Piecewise deterministic Markov processes represented by dynamically coloured Petri nets. Stochastics **77**(1), 1–29 (2005)
6. Frehse, G., Han, Z., Krogh, B.: Assume-guarantee reasoning for hybrid I/O-automata by over-approximation of continuous interaction. In: 43rd IEEE Conference on Decision and Control, pp. 479–484 (2004)
7. Frehse, G., Kateja, R., Le Guernic, C.: Flowpipe approximation and clustering in space-time. In 16th International Conference on Hybrid Systems: Computation and Control, pp. 203–212. ACM (2013)
8. Ghasemieh, H., Remke, A., Haverkort, B.R.: Survivability analysis of a sewage treatment facility using hybrid Petri nets. In: Performance Evaluation, vol. 97, pp. 36–56. Elsevier (2016)
9. Ghasemieh, H., Remke, A., Haverkort, B., Gribaudo, M.: Region-based analysis of hybrid Petri nets with a single general one-shot transition. In: Jurdziński, M., Ničković, D. (eds.) FORMATS 2012. LNCS, vol. 7595, pp. 139–154. Springer, Heidelberg (2012). https://doi.org/10.1007/978-3-642-33365-1_11
10. Ghasemieh, H., Remke, A., Haverkort, B.R.: Hybrid petri nets with multiple stochastic transition firings. In: 2014 8th International Conference on Performance Evaluation Methodologies and Tools, pp. 217–224. ICST (2014)

11. Ghasemieh, H., Remke, A., Haverkort, B.R.: Survivability evaluation of fluid critical infrastructures using hybrid Petri nets. In IEEE 19th Pacific Rim International Symposium on Dependable Computing, pp. 152–161. IEEE (2013)
12. Girard, A.: Reachability of uncertain linear systems using zonotopes. In: Morari, M., Thiele, L. (eds.) HSCC 2005. LNCS, vol. 3414, pp. 291–305. Springer, Heidelberg (2005). https://doi.org/10.1007/978-3-540-31954-2_19
13. Godde, A., Remke, A.: Model checking the STL time-bounded until on hybrid Petri nets using nef polyhedra. In: Reinecke, P., Di Marco, A. (eds.) EPEW 2017. LNCS, vol. 10497, pp. 101–116. Springer, Cham (2017). https://doi.org/10.1007/978-3-319-66583-2_7
14. Gribaudo, M., Remke, A.: Hybrid Petri nets with general one-shot transitions. Perform. Eval. **105**, 22–50 (2016)
15. Horton, G., Kulkarni, V.G., Nicol, D.M., Trivedi, K.S.: Fluid stochastic Petri nets: theory, applications, and solution techniques. J. Oper. Res. **105**(1), 184–201 (1998)
16. Hüls, J., Pilch, C., Schinke, P., Delicaris, J., Remke, A.: State-space construction of hybrid Petri nets with multiple stochastic firings. Technical report, Westfälische Wilhelms-Universität Münster (2018). https://uni-muenster.sciebo.de/s/BMwdh25rHgmDvb6
17. Hüls, J., Schupp, S., Remke, A., Abraham, E.: Analyzing hybrid Petri nets with multiple stochastic firings using HyPro. In 11th International Conference on Performance Evaluation Methodologies and Tools (2017)
18. Jongerden, M.R., Hüls, J., Remke, A., Haverkort, B.R.: Does your domestic photovoltaic energy system survive grid outages? Energies **9**(9), 736 (2016)
19. Julius, A.A.: Approximate abstraction of stochastic hybrid automata. In: Hespanha, J.P., Tiwari, A. (eds.) HSCC 2006. LNCS, vol. 3927, pp. 318–332. Springer, Heidelberg (2006). https://doi.org/10.1007/11730637_25
20. Kwiatkowska, M., Norman, G., Segala, R., Sproston, J.: Automatic verification of real-time systems with discrete probability distributions. Theor. Comput. Sci. **282**(1), 101–150 (2002)
21. Le Guernic, C., Girard, A.: Reachability analysis of linear systems using support functions. Nonlinear Anal.: Hybrid Syst. **4**(2), 250–262 (2010)
22. Maler, O., Nickovic, D.: Monitoring temporal properties of continuous signals. In: Lakhnech, Y., Yovine, S. (eds.) FORMATS/FTRTFT -2004. LNCS, vol. 3253, pp. 152–166. Springer, Heidelberg (2004). https://doi.org/10.1007/978-3-540-30206-3_12
23. Moore, R.E., Kearfott, R.B., Cloud, M.J.: Introduction to Interval Analysis. SIAM (2009)
24. Pilch, C., Remke, A.: Statistical model checking for hybrid Petri nets with multiple general transitions. In: 47th International Conference on Dependable Systems and Networks, pp. 475–486. IEEE (2017)
25. Schupp, S., Ábrahám, E., Makhlouf, I.B., Kowalewski, S.: HyPro: a C++ library of state set representations for hybrid systems reachability analysis. In: Barrett, C., Davies, M., Kahsai, T. (eds.) NFM 2017. LNCS, vol. 10227, pp. 288–294. Springer, Cham (2017). https://doi.org/10.1007/978-3-319-57288-8_20
26. Esmaeil Zadeh Soudjani, S., Abate, A.: Adaptive and sequential gridding procedures for the abstraction and verification of stochastic processes. SIAM J. Appl. Dyn. Syst. **12**(2), 921–956 (2013)
27. Soudjani, S.E.Z., Gevaerts, C., Abate, A.: FAUST²: formal abstractions of uncountable-STate STochastic processes. In: Baier, C., Tinelli, C. (eds.) TACAS 2015. LNCS, vol. 9035, pp. 272–286. Springer, Heidelberg (2015). https://doi.org/10.1007/978-3-662-46681-0_23

28. Sproston, J.: Decidable model checking of probabilistic hybrid automata. In: Joseph, M. (ed.) FTRTFT 2000. LNCS, vol. 1926, pp. 31–45. Springer, Heidelberg (2000). https://doi.org/10.1007/3-540-45352-0_5
29. Teige, T., Fränzle, M.: Constraint-based analysis of probabilistic hybrid systems. IFAC Proc. Vol. **42**(17), 162–167 (2009)
30. The CGAL Project. CGAL User and Reference Manual. CGAL Editorial Board, 4.10 edition (2017)
31. Zhang, L., She, Z., Ratschan, S., Hermanns, H., Hahn, E.M.: Safety verification for probabilistic hybrid systems. Eur. J. Control **18**(6), 572–587 (2012)
32. Ziegler, G.M.: Lectures on Polytopes, vol. 152. Springer, New York (2012). https://doi.org/10.1007/978-1-4613-8431-1

Causal-Consistent Replay Debugging for Message Passing Programs

Ivan Lanese[1], Adrián Palacios[2], and Germán Vidal[2(✉)]

[1] Focus Team, University of Bologna/Inria, Bologna, Italy
ivan.lanese@gmail.com
[2] MiST, DSIC, Universitat Politècnica de València, Valencia, Spain
{apalacios,gvidal}@dsic.upv.es

Abstract. Debugging of concurrent systems is a tedious and error-prone activity. A main issue is that there is no guarantee that a bug that appears in the original computation is replayed inside the debugger. This problem is usually tackled by so-called replay debugging, which allows the user to record a program execution and replay it inside the debugger. In this paper, we present a novel technique for replay debugging that we call *controlled causal-consistent replay*. Controlled causal-consistent replay allows the user to record a program execution and, in contrast to traditional replay debuggers, to reproduce a visible misbehavior inside the debugger including all *and only* its causes. In this way, the user is not distracted by the actions of other, unrelated processes.

1 Introduction

Debugging is a main activity in software development. According to a 2014 study [24], the cost of debugging is \$312 billions annually. Another recent study [2] estimates that the time spent in debugging is 49.9% of the total programming time. The situation is not likely to improve in the near future, given the increasing demand of concurrent and distributed software. Indeed, distribution is inherent in current computing platforms, such as the Internet or the Cloud, and concurrency is a must to overcome the advent of the power wall [25]. Debugging concurrent and distributed software is clearly more difficult than debugging sequential code [9]. Furthermore, misbehaviors may depend, e.g., on the execution speed of the different processes, showing up only in some (sometimes rare) cases.

This work has been partially supported by the EU (FEDER) and the *Spanish Ministerio de Ciencia, Innovación y Universidades*/AEI (MICINN) under grant TIN2016-76843-C4-1-R, by the *Generalitat Valenciana* under grants PROMETEO-II/2015/013 (SmartLogic) and Prometeo/2019/098 (DeepTrust), and by the COST Action IC1405 on Reversible Computation - extending horizons of computing. The first author has been also partially supported by French ANR project DCore ANR-18-CE25-0007. The second author has been also supported by the EU (FEDER) and the Spanish *Ayudas para contratos predoctorales para la formación de doctores* (MICINN) under FPI grant BES-2014-069749.

J. A. Pérez and N. Yoshida (Eds.): FORTE 2019, LNCS 11535, pp. 167–184, 2019.
https://doi.org/10.1007/978-3-030-21759-4_10

A particularly unfortunate situation is when a program exhibits a misbehavior in its usual execution environment, but it runs smoothly when re-executed in the debugger. This problem is usually tackled by so-called replay debugging, which allows the user to record a program execution and replay it inside the debugger. However, in concurrent programs, part of the execution may not be relevant: some processes may not have interacted with the one showing a misbehavior, or may have interacted with it only at the very beginning of their execution, hence most of their execution is not relevant for the debugging session. Having to replay all these behaviors is both time and resource consuming as well as distracting for the user.

Our main contribution in this paper is a novel technique for replay debugging that we call *controlled causal-consistent replay*. It extends the techniques in the literature as follows: given a log of a (typically faulty) concurrent execution, we do not replay exactly the same execution step by step (as traditional replay debuggers), but we allow the user to select any action in the log (e.g., one showing a misbehavior) and to replay the execution up to this action, including all *and only* its causes. This allows one to focus on those processes where (s)he thinks the bug(s) might be, disregarding the actual interleaving of processes. To the best of our knowledge, the notion of controlled causal-consistent replay is new.

We fully formalize causal-consistent replay for (a subset of) a realistic functional and concurrent programming language based on message-passing: Erlang. Moreover, we prove relevant properties, e.g., that misbehaviors in the original computation are always replayed, and that we guarantee minimal replay of observable behaviors. This is in contrast with most approaches to replay in the literature, that, beyond considering different languages, are either fully experimental (like, e.g., [1,18,19,27]), or present limited theoretical results, as in [8,10,21].

Causal-consistent replay can be seen as the dual of causal-consistent rollback, a technique for reversible computing which allows one to select an action in a computation and undo it, including all *and only* its consequences. Indeed, the two techniques integrate well, giving rise to a framework to explore back and forward a given concurrent computation, always concentrating on the actions of interest and avoiding unrelated actions. By lack of space, we will only present causal-consistent replay in this paper. More details, including the integration with causal-consistent rollback, proofs of technical results, and a description of an implemented reversible replay debugger for Erlang [16] that follows the ideas in this paper, can be found in an accompanying technical report [17]. While not technically needed, printing the paper in color may help the understanding.

2   The Language

We present below the considered language: a first-order functional and concurrent language based on message passing that mainly follows the actor model.

$$program ::= fun_1 \ \dots \ fun_n \qquad\qquad fun ::= fname = \mathsf{fun}\ (X_1,\dots,X_n) \to expr$$
$$fname ::= Atom/Integer \qquad\qquad\quad lit ::= Atom \mid Integer \mid Float \mid [\,]$$
$$expr ::= Var \mid lit \mid fname \mid [expr_1 | expr_2] \mid \{expr_1,\dots,expr_n\}$$
$$\mid \ \mathsf{call}\ expr\ (expr_1,\dots,expr_n) \mid \mathsf{apply}\ expr\ (expr_1,\dots,expr_n)$$
$$\mid \ \mathsf{case}\ expr\ \mathsf{of}\ clause_1;\dots;clause_m\ \mathsf{end}$$
$$\mid \ \mathsf{let}\ Var = expr_1\ \mathsf{in}\ expr_2 \mid \mathsf{receive}\ clause_1;\dots;clause_n\ \mathsf{end}$$
$$\mid \ \mathsf{spawn}(expr,[expr_1,\dots,expr_n]) \mid expr_1\ !\ expr_2 \mid \mathsf{self}()$$
$$clause ::= pat\ \mathsf{when}\ expr_1 \to expr_2 \qquad pat ::= Var \mid lit \mid [pat_1|pat_2] \mid \{pat_1,\dots,pat_n\}$$

Fig. 1. Language syntax rules

Language Syntax. The syntax of the language is in Fig. 1. A program is a sequence of function definitions, where each function name f/n (atom/arity) has an associated definition fun $(X_1,\dots,X_n) \to e$, where $X_1,\dots,X_n$ are (distinct) fresh variables and are the only variables that may occur free in e. The body of a function is an *expression*, which can include variables, literals, function names, lists (using Prolog-like notation: $[\,]$ is the empty list and $[e_1|e_2]$ is a list with head e_1 and tail e_2), tuples (denoted by $\{e_1,\dots,e_n\}$),[1] calls to built-in functions (mainly arithmetic and relational operators), function applications, case expressions, let bindings, receive expressions, spawn (for creating new processes), "!" (for sending a message), and self. As is common practice, we assume that X is a fresh variable in let $X = expr_1$ in $expr_2$.

In this language, we distinguish expressions, patterns, and values, ranged over respectively by $e, e', e_1, \dots$, by $pat, pat', pat_1, \dots$ and by $v, v', v_1, \dots$. In contrast to expressions, *patterns* are built from variables, literals, lists, and tuples. Patterns can only contain fresh variables. Finally, *values* are built from literals, lists, and tuples. Atoms (i.e., constants with a name) are written in roman letters, while variables start with an uppercase letter. A *substitution* θ is a mapping from variables to expressions, and $\mathcal{D}om(\theta)$ is its domain. Substitutions are usually denoted by (finite) sets of bindings like, e.g., $\{X_1 \mapsto v_1,\dots,X_n \mapsto v_n\}$. The identity substitution is denoted by id. Composition of substitutions is denoted by juxtaposition, i.e., $\theta\theta'$ denotes a substitution θ'' such that $\theta''(X) = \theta'(\theta(X))$ for all $X \in Var$. Substitution application $\sigma(e)$ is also denoted by $e\sigma$.

In a case expression "case e of pat_1 when $e_1 \to e'_1; \ \dots; \ pat_n$ when $e_n \to e'_n$ end", we first evaluate e to a value, say v; then, we find (if it exists) the first clause pat_i when $e_i \to e'_i$ such that v matches pat_i, i.e., such that there exists a substitution σ for the variables of pat_i with $v = pat_i\sigma$, and $e_i\sigma$ (the *guard*) reduces to *true*; then, the case expression reduces to $e'_i\sigma$.

In our language, a running system is a pool of processes that can only interact through message sending and receiving (i.e., there is no shared memory). Received messages are stored in the queues of processes until they are consumed; namely, each process has one associated local (FIFO) queue. Each process is uniquely identified by its *pid* (process identifier). Message sending is

---

[1] As in Erlang, the only data constructors in the language (besides literals) are the predefined functions for lists and tuples.

asynchronous, while receive instructions block the execution of a process until an appropriate message reaches its local queue (see below).

$$\begin{aligned}
&\mathsf{main}/0 = \mathsf{fun}\ () \rightarrow \mathsf{let}\ S = \mathsf{spawn}(\mathsf{server}/0, [\,])\\
&\qquad\qquad\qquad\quad \mathsf{in}\ \mathsf{let}\ P = \mathsf{spawn}(\mathsf{proxy}/0, [\,])\ \mathsf{in}\ \mathsf{apply}\ \mathsf{client}/2\ (P, S)\\
&\mathsf{server}/0 = \mathsf{fun}\ () \rightarrow \mathsf{receive}\\
&\qquad\qquad\qquad\quad \{C, N\} \rightarrow \mathsf{receive}\\
&\qquad\qquad\qquad\qquad\qquad M \rightarrow \mathsf{let}\ X = C\,!\,\mathsf{call} + (N, M)\ \mathsf{in}\ \mathsf{apply}\ \mathsf{server}/0\ ()\\
&\qquad\qquad\qquad\qquad \mathsf{end};\\
&\qquad\qquad\qquad\quad E \rightarrow \mathsf{error}\\
&\qquad\qquad\quad \mathsf{end}\\
&\mathsf{proxy}/0 = \mathsf{fun}\ () \rightarrow \mathsf{receive}\ \{T, M\} \rightarrow \mathsf{let}\ W = T\,!\,M\ \mathsf{in}\ \mathsf{apply}\ \mathsf{proxy}/0\ ()\ \mathsf{end}\\
&\mathsf{client}/2 = \mathsf{fun}\ (P, S) \rightarrow \mathsf{let}\ X = P\,!\,\{S, \{\mathsf{self}(), 40\}\}\ \mathsf{in}\ \mathsf{let}\ Y = S\,!\,2\ \mathsf{in}\ \mathsf{receive}\ N \rightarrow N\ \mathsf{end}
\end{aligned}$$

Fig. 2. A simple client/server program

In the paper, $\overline{o_n}$ denotes a sequence of syntactic objects $o_1, \ldots, o_n$.

We consider the following functions with side-effects: self, "!", spawn, and receive. The expression $\mathsf{self}()$ returns the pid of a process, while $p\,!\,v$ sends a message v to the process with pid p, which will be eventually stored in p's local queue. New processes are spawned with a call of the form $\mathsf{spawn}(a/n, [\overline{v_n}])$, so that the new process begins with the evaluation of apply $a/n\ (\overline{v_n})$. Finally, an expression "receive $\overline{pat_n}$ when $e_n \rightarrow e'_n$ end" should find the *first* message v in the process' queue (if any) such that case v of $\overline{pat_n}$ when $e_n \rightarrow e'_n$ end can be reduced to some expression e''; then, the receive expression evaluates to e'', with the side effect of deleting the message v from the process' queue. If there is no matching message, the process *suspends* until a matching message arrives.

Our language models a significant subset of Core Erlang [3], the intermediate representation used during the compilation of Erlang programs. Therefore, our developments can be directly applied to Erlang (as can be seen in the technical report [17], where the development of a practical debugger is described).

Example 1. The program in Fig. 2 implements a simple client/server scheme with one server, one client and a proxy. The execution starts with a call to function main/0. It spawns the server and the proxy and finally calls function client/2. Both the server and the proxy then suspend waiting for messages. The client makes two requests $\{C, 40\}$ and 2, where C is the pid of client (obtained using self()). The second request goes directly to the server, but the first one is sent through the proxy (which simply resends the received messages), so the client actually sends $\{S, \{C, 40\}\}$, where S is the pid of the server. Here, we expect that the server first receives the message $\{C, 40\}$ and, then, 2, thus sending back 42 to the client C (and calling function server/0 again in an endless recursion). If the first message does not have the right structure, the catch-all clause "$E \rightarrow$ error" returns error and stops.

A High-Level Semantics. Now, we present an (asynchronous) operational semantics for our language. Following [26], we introduce a *global mailbox* (there called "ether") to guarantee that our semantics generates all admissible message interleavings. In contrast to previous semantics [15, 22, 26], our semantics abstracts away from processes' queues. We will see in Sect. 2 that this decision simplifies both the semantics and the notion of independence, while still modeling the same potential computations (see the technical report [17]).

Definition 1 (process). *A process is a configuration* $\langle p, \theta, e \rangle$, *where* p *is its pid,* θ *an environment (a substitution of values for variables), and* e *an expression.*

In order to define a *system* (roughly, a pool of processes interacting through message exchange), we first need the notion of global mailbox.

Definition 2 (global mailbox). *We define a global mailbox,* Γ, *as a multiset of triples of the form* $(sender\_pid, target\_pid, message)$. *Given a global mailbox* Γ, *we let* $\Gamma \cup \{(p, p', v)\}$ *denote a new mailbox also including the triple* (p, p', v), *where we use "$\cup$" as multiset union.*

In Erlang, the order of two messages sent directly from process p to process p' is kept if both are delivered; see [5, Section 10.8].[2] To enforce such a constraint, we could define a global mailbox as a collection of FIFO queues, one for each sender-receiver pair. In this work, however, we keep Γ a multiset. This solution is both simpler and more general since FIFO queues serve only to select those computations satisfying the constraint. Nevertheless, if our logging approach is applied to a computation satisfying the above constraint, then our replay computation will also satisfy it, thus replay does not introduce spurious computations.

Definition 3 (system). *A system is a pair* $\Gamma; \Pi$, *where* Γ *is a global mailbox and* Π *is a pool of processes, denoted as* $\langle p_1, \theta_1, e_1 \rangle \mid \cdots \mid \langle p_n, \theta_n, e_n \rangle$; *here "$\mid$" represents an associative and commutative operator. We often denote a system as* $\Gamma; \langle p, \theta, e \rangle \mid \Pi$ *to point out that* $\langle p, \theta, e \rangle$ *is an arbitrary process of the pool.*
    A system is initial *if it has the form* $\{\}; \langle p, id, e \rangle$, *where* $\{\}$ *is an empty global mailbox,* p *is a pid,* id *is the identity substitution, and* e *is an expression.*

Following the style in [22], the semantics of the language is defined in a modular way, so that the labeled transition relations $\rightarrow$ and $\hookrightarrow$ model the evaluation of *expressions* and the reduction of *systems*, respectively. Given an environment θ and an expression e, we denote by $\theta, e \xrightarrow{l} \theta', e'$ a one-step reduction labeled with l. The relation $\xrightarrow{l}$ follows a typical call-by-value semantics for side-effect free expressions; for expressions with side-effects, we label the reduction with the information needed to perform the side-effects within the system rules of Fig. 3. We refer to the rules of Fig. 3 as the *logging* semantics, since the relation is labeled with some basic information used to log the steps of a computation (see Sect. 3). For now, the reader can safely ignore these labels (actually, labels

---

[2] Current implementations only guarantee this restriction within the same node.

(Seq)
$$\dfrac{\theta, e \xrightarrow{\tau} \theta', e'}{\Gamma; \langle p, \theta, e \rangle \mid \Pi \hookrightarrow_{p,\mathsf{seq}} \Gamma; \langle p, \theta', e' \rangle \mid \Pi}$$

$(Send)$
$$\dfrac{\theta, e \xrightarrow{\mathsf{send}(p',v)} \theta', e' \text{ and } \ell \text{ is a fresh symbol}}{\Gamma; \langle p, \theta, e \rangle \mid \Pi \hookrightarrow_{p,\mathsf{send}(\ell)} \Gamma \cup \{(p, p', \{v, \ell\})\}; \langle p, \theta', e' \rangle \mid \Pi}$$

$(Receive)$
$$\dfrac{\theta, e \xrightarrow{\mathsf{rec}(\kappa, \overline{cl_n})} \theta', e' \text{ and } \mathsf{matchrec}(\theta, \overline{cl_n}, v) = (\theta_i, e_i)}{\Gamma \cup \{(p', p, \{v, \ell\})\}; \langle p, \theta, e \rangle \mid \Pi \hookrightarrow_{p,\mathsf{rec}(\ell)} \Gamma; \langle p, \theta'\theta_i, e'\{\kappa \mapsto e_i\} \rangle \mid \Pi}$$

$(Spawn)$
$$\dfrac{\theta, e \xrightarrow{\mathsf{spawn}(\kappa, a/n, [\overline{v_n}])} \theta', e' \text{ and } p' \text{ is a fresh pid}}{\Gamma; \langle p, \theta, e \rangle \mid \Pi \hookrightarrow_{p,\mathsf{spawn}(p')} \Gamma; \langle p, \theta', e'\{\kappa \mapsto p'\} \rangle \mid \langle p', id, \mathsf{apply}\ a/n\ (\overline{v_n}) \rangle \mid \Pi}$$

$(Self)$
$$\dfrac{\theta, e \xrightarrow{\mathsf{self}(\kappa)} \theta', e'}{\Gamma; \langle p, \theta, e \rangle \mid \Pi \hookrightarrow_{p,\mathsf{self}} \Gamma; \langle p, \theta', e'\{\kappa \mapsto p\} \rangle \mid \Pi}$$

Fig. 3. Logging semantics

will be omitted when irrelevant). The topics of this work are orthogonal to the evaluation of expressions, thus we refer the reader to [17] for the formalization of the rules of $\xrightarrow{l}$. Let us now briefly describe the interaction between the reduction of expressions and the rules of the logging semantics:

- A one-step reduction of an expression without side-effects is labeled with τ. In this case, rule *Seq* in Fig. 3 is applied to update correspondingly the environment and expression of the considered process.
- An expression $p'\,!\,v$ is reduced to v, with label $\mathsf{send}(p', v)$, so that rule *Send* in Fig. 3 can add the triple $(p, p', \{v, \ell\})$ to Γ (p is the process performing the send).
  The message is *tagged* with some fresh (unique) identifier ℓ. These tags allow us to track messages and avoid confusion when several messages have the same value (these tags are similar to the timestamps used in [21]).
- The remaining functions, receive, spawn and self, pose an additional problem: their value cannot be computed locally. Therefore, they are reduced to a fresh distinguished symbol κ, which is then replaced by the appropriate value in the system rules. In particular, a receive statement receive $\overline{cl_n}$ end is reduced to κ with label $\mathsf{rec}(\kappa, \overline{cl_n})$. Then, rule *Receive* in Fig. 3 nondeterministically checks if there exists a triple $(p', p, \{v, \ell\})$ in the global mailbox that matches some clause in $\overline{cl_n}$; pattern matching is performed by the auxiliary function matchrec. If the matching succeeds, it returns the pair (θ_i, e_i) with the matching substitution θ_i and the expression in the selected branch e_i. Finally, κ is bound to the expression e_i within the derived expression e'.
- For a spawn, an expression $\mathsf{spawn}(a/n, [\overline{v_n}])$ is also reduced to κ with label $\mathsf{spawn}(\kappa, a/n, [\overline{v_n}])$. Rule *Spawn* in Fig. 3 then adds a new process with a fresh pid p' initialized with an empty environment id and the application apply $a/n\ (v_1, \ldots, v_n)$. Here, κ is bound to p', the pid of the spawned process.
- Finally, the expression $\mathsf{self}()$ is reduced to κ with label $\mathsf{self}(\kappa)$ so that rule *Self* in Fig. 3 can bind κ to the pid of the given process.

$\{\,\}$; $\langle c, \_, \textsf{apply main/0 ()}\rangle$

$\hookrightarrow \{\,\}$; $\langle c, \_, \textsf{let } S = \textsf{spawn(server/0, [\,])} \textsf{ in } \ldots\rangle$

$\hookrightarrow \{\,\}$; $\langle c, \_, \textsf{let } P = \textsf{spawn(proxy/0, [\,])} \textsf{ in apply client/2 } (P, s)\rangle \mid \langle s, \_, \textsf{apply server/0 ()}\rangle$

$\hookrightarrow.\{\,\}$; $\langle c, \_, \textsf{apply client/2 (p, s)}\rangle \mid \langle s, \_, \textsf{apply server/0 ()}\rangle \mid \langle p, \_, \textsf{apply proxy/0 ()}\rangle$

$\hookrightarrow \{\,\}$; $\langle c, \_, \textsf{let } X = \textsf{p ! } \{s, \{\underline{\textsf{self}()}, 40\}\} \textsf{ in } \ldots\rangle \mid \langle s, \_, \textsf{apply server/0 ()}\rangle \mid \langle p, \_, \textsf{apply proxy/0 ()}\rangle$

$\hookrightarrow \{\,\}$; $\langle c, \_, \textsf{let } X = \textsf{p ! } \{s, \{c, 40\}\} \textsf{ in } \ldots\rangle \mid \langle s, \_, \underline{\textsf{apply server/0 ()}}\rangle \mid \langle p, \_, \textsf{apply proxy/0 ()}\rangle$

$\hookrightarrow \{\,\}$; $\langle c, \_, \textsf{let } X = \textsf{p ! } \{s, \{c, 40\}\} \textsf{ in } \ldots\rangle \mid \langle s, \_, \textsf{receive } \ldots\rangle \mid \langle p, \_, \underline{\textsf{apply proxy/0 ()}}\rangle$

$\hookrightarrow \{\,\}$; $\langle c, \_, \textsf{let } X = \underline{\textsf{p ! } \{s, \{c, 40\}\}} \textsf{ in } \ldots\rangle \mid \langle s, \_, \textsf{receive } \ldots\rangle \mid \langle p, \_, \textsf{receive } \ldots\rangle$

$\hookrightarrow \{(c, p, \{\{s, \{c, 40\}\}, \ell_1\})\}$; $\langle c, \_, \textsf{let } Y = \underline{\textsf{s ! 2}} \textsf{ in } \ldots\rangle \mid \langle s, \_, \textsf{receive } \ldots\rangle \mid \langle p, \_, \textsf{receive } \ldots\rangle$

$\hookrightarrow \{(c, p, \{\{s, \{c, 40\}\}, \ell_1\}), (c, s, \{2, \ell_2\})\}$; $\langle c, \_, \textsf{receive } \ldots\rangle \mid \langle s, \_, \textsf{receive } \ldots\rangle \mid \langle p, \_, \underline{\textsf{receive } \ldots}\rangle$

$\hookrightarrow \{(c, s, \{2, \ell_2\})\}$; $\langle c, \_, \textsf{receive } \ldots\rangle \mid \langle s, \_, \textsf{receive } \ldots\rangle \mid \langle p, \_, \textsf{let } W = \underline{\textsf{s ! } \{c, 40\}} \textsf{ in } \ldots\rangle$

$\hookrightarrow \{(c, s, \{2, \ell_2\}), (p, s, \{\{c, 40\}, \ell_3\})\}$; $\langle c, \_, \textsf{receive } \ldots\rangle \mid \langle s, \_, \underline{\textsf{receive } \ldots}\rangle \mid \langle p, \_, \textsf{apply proxy/0 ()}\rangle$

$\hookrightarrow \{(p, s, \{\{c, 40\}, \ell_3\})\}$; $\langle c, \_, \textsf{receive } \ldots\rangle \mid \langle s, \_, \textsf{error}\rangle \mid \langle p, \_, \textsf{apply proxy/0 ()}\rangle$

Fig. 4. Faulty derivation with the client/server of Example 1

We often refer to reduction steps derived by the system rules as *actions* taken by the chosen process.

Example 2 Let us consider the program of Example 1 and the initial system $\{\,\}$; $\langle c, id, \textsf{apply main/0 ()}\rangle$, where c is the pid of the process. A possible (faulty) computation from this system is shown in Fig. 4 (the selected expression at each step is underlined).[3] Here, we ignore the labels of the relation $\hookrightarrow$. Moreover, we skip the steps that just bind variables and we do not show the bindings of variables but substitute them for their values for clarity.

Independence. In order to define a causal-consistent replay semantics we need not only an interleaving semantics such as the one we just presented, but also a notion of causality or, equivalently, the opposite notion of independence. To this end, we use the labels of the logging semantics (see Fig. 3). These labels include the pid p of the process that performs the transition, the rule used to derive it and, in some cases, some additional information: a message tag ℓ in rules *Send* and *Receive*, and the pid p' of the spawned process in rule *Spawn*.

Before formalizing the notion of independence, we need to introduce some notation and terminology. Given systems s_0, s_n, we call $s_0 \hookrightarrow^* s_n$, which is a shorthand for $s_0 \hookrightarrow_{p_1, r_1} \ldots \hookrightarrow_{p_n, r_n} s_n$, $n \geq 0$, a *derivation*. One-step derivations are simply called *transitions*. We use $d, d', d_1, \ldots$ to denote derivations and $t, t', t_1, \ldots$ for transitions. Given a derivation $d = (s_1 \hookrightarrow^* s_2)$, we define $\textsf{init}(d) = s_1$. Two derivations, d_1 and d_2, are said *coinitial* if $\textsf{init}(d_1) = \textsf{init}(d_2)$.

For simplicity, in the following, we consider derivations up to renaming of bound variables. Under this assumption, the semantics is *almost* deterministic, i.e., the main sources of non-determinism are the selection of a process p and of the message to be retrieved by p in rule *Receive*. Choices of the fresh identifier ℓ for messages and of the pid p' of new processes are also non-deterministic.

---

[3] Roughly speaking, the problem comes from the fact that the messages reach the server in the wrong order. Note that this faulty derivation is possible even by considering Erlang's policy on the order of messages, since they follow a different path.

Note that each process can perform at most one transition for each label, i.e., $s \hookrightarrow_{p,r} s_1$ and $s \hookrightarrow_{p,r} s_2$ trivially implies $s_1 = s_2$.

We now instantiate to our setting the well-known *happened-before* relation [11], and the related notion of *independent* transitions:[4]

Definition 4 (happened-before, independence). *Given transitions $t_1 = (s_1 \hookrightarrow_{p_1,r_1} s_1')$ and $t_2 = (s_2 \hookrightarrow_{p_2,r_2} s_2')$, we say that t_1 happened before t_2, in symbols $t_1 \rightsquigarrow t_2$, if one of the following conditions holds:*

- *they consider the same process, i.e., $p_1 = p_2$, and t_1 comes before t_2;*
- *t_1 spawns a process p, i.e., $r_1 = \mathsf{spawn}(p)$, and t_2 is performed by process p, i.e., $p_2 = p$;*
- *t_1 sends a message ℓ, i.e., $r_1 = \mathsf{send}(\ell)$, and t_2 receives the same message ℓ, i.e., $r_2 = \mathsf{rec}(\ell)$.*

Furthermore, if $t_1 \rightsquigarrow t_2$ and $t_2 \rightsquigarrow t_3$, then $t_1 \rightsquigarrow t_3$ (transitivity). Two transitions t_1 and t_2 are independent *if $t_1 \not\rightsquigarrow t_2$ and $t_2 \not\rightsquigarrow t_1$.*

Switching consecutive independent transitions does not change the final state:

Lemma 1 (switching lemma). *Let $t_1 = (s_1 \hookrightarrow_{p_1,r_1} s_2)$ and $t_2 = (s_2 \hookrightarrow_{p_2,r_2} s_3)$ be consecutive independent transitions. Then, there are two consecutive transitions $t_{2 \langle\!\langle t_1} = (s_1 \hookrightarrow_{p_2,r_2} s_4)$ and $t_{1 \rangle\!\rangle t_2} = (s_4 \hookrightarrow_{p_1,r_1} s_3)$ for some system s_4.*

The happened-before relation gives rise to an equivalence relation equating all derivations that only differ in the switch of independent transitions. Formally,

Definition 5 (causally equivalent derivations). *Let d_1 and d_2 be derivations under the logging semantics. We say that d_1 and d_2 are* causally equivalent, *in symbols $d_1 \approx d_2$, if d_1 can be obtained from d_2 by a finite number of switches of pairs of consecutive independent transitions.*

Causal equivalence is an instance of the *trace equivalence* in [20].

3   Logging Computations

In this section, we introduce a notion of *log* for a computation. Basically, we aim to analyze in a debugger a faulty behavior that occurs in some execution of a program. To this end, we need to extract from an actual execution enough information to replay it inside the debugger. Actually, we do not want to replay necessarily the exact same execution, but a causally equivalent one. In this way, the programmer can focus on some actions of a particular process, and actions of other processes are only performed if needed (formally, if they happened-before these actions). As we will see in the next section, this ensures that the considered misbehaviors will still be replayed.

---

[4] Here, we use the term *independent*, instead of *concurrent* as in [11], since the latter has a slightly different meaning in the literature of causal-consistency.

In a practical implementation (see the technical report [17]), one should instrument the program so that its execution in the actual environment produces a collection of sequences of logged events (one sequence per process). In the following, though, we exploit the logging semantics and, in particular, part of the information provided by the labels. The two approaches are equivalent, but the chosen one allows us to formally prove a number of properties in a simpler way.

One could argue (as in, e.g., [21]) that logs should only store information about the receive events, since this is the only nondeterministic action (once a process is selected). However, this is not enough in our setting, where:

- We need to log the sending of a message since this is where messages are tagged, and we need to know its (unique) identifier to be able to relate the sending and receiving of each message.
- We also need to log the spawn events, since the generated pids are needed to relate an action to the process that performed it (spawn events are not considered in [21] and, thus, their set of processes is fixed).

We note that other nondeterministic events, such as input from the user or from external services, should also be logged in order to correctly replay executions involving them. One can deal with them by instrumenting the corresponding primitives to log the input values, and then use these values when replaying the execution. Essentially, they can be dealt with as the receive primitive. Hence, we do not present them in detail to keep the presentation as simple as possible.

In the following, (ordered) sequences are denoted by $w = (r_1, r_2, \ldots, r_n)$, $n \geq 1$, where () denotes the empty sequence. Concatenation is denoted by $+$. We write $r+w$ instead of $(r)+w$ for simplicity.

Definition 6 (log). *A log is a (finite) sequence of events $(r_1, r_2, \ldots)$ where each r_i is either* spawn(p), send(ℓ) *or* rec(ℓ), *with p a pid and ℓ a message identifier. Logs are ranged over by ω. Given a derivation $d = (s_0 \hookrightarrow_{p_1, r_1} s_1 \hookrightarrow_{p_2, r_2} \ldots \hookrightarrow_{p_n, r_n} s_n)$, $n \geq 0$, under the logging semantics, the log of a pid p in d, in symbols $\mathcal{L}(d, p)$, is inductively defined as follows:*

$$\mathcal{L}(d, p) = \begin{cases} () & \text{if } n = 0 \text{ or } p \text{ docs not occur in } d \\ r_1 + \mathcal{L}(s_1 \hookrightarrow^* s_n, p) & \text{if } n > 0, \ p_1 = p, \text{ and } r_1 \notin \{\text{seq}, \text{self}\} \\ \mathcal{L}(s_1 \hookrightarrow^* s_n, p) & \text{otherwise} \end{cases}$$

The log of d, written $\mathcal{L}(d)$, is defined as: $\mathcal{L}(d) = \{(p, \mathcal{L}(d, p)) \mid p \text{ occurs in } d\}$. We sometimes call $\mathcal{L}(d)$ the global log of d to avoid confusion with $\mathcal{L}(d, p)$. Note that $\mathcal{L}(d, p) = \omega$ if $(p, \omega) \in \mathcal{L}(d)$ and $\mathcal{L}(d, p) = ()$ otherwise.

Example 3. Consider the derivation shown in Example 2, here referred to as d. If we run it under the logging semantics, we get the following logs:

$$\mathcal{L}(d, c) = (\text{spawn}(s), \text{spawn}(p), \text{send}(\ell_1), \text{send}(\ell_2))$$
$$\mathcal{L}(d, s) = (\text{rec}(\ell_2)) \qquad \mathcal{L}(d, p) = (\text{rec}(\ell_1), \text{send}(\ell_3))$$

In the following we only consider finite derivations under the logging semantics. This is reasonable in our context where the programmer wants to analyze in the debugger a finite (possibly incomplete) execution showing a faulty behavior.

An essential property of our semantics is that causally equivalent derivations have the same log, i.e., the log depends only on the equivalence class, not on the selection of the representative inside the class. The reverse implication, namely that (coinitial) derivations with the same global log are causally equivalent, holds provided that we establish the following convention on when to stop a derivation:

Definition 7 (fully-logged derivation). *A derivation d is* fully-logged *if, for each process p, its last transition $s_1 \hookrightarrow_{p,r} s_2$ in d (if any) is a* logged *transition, i.e., $r \notin \{\mathsf{seq}, \mathsf{self}\}$. In particular, if a process performs no logged transition, then it performs no transition at all.*

Restricting to fully-logged derivations is needed since only logged transitions contribute to logs. Otherwise, two derivations d_1 and d_2 could produce the same log, but differ simply because, e.g., d_1 performs more non-logged transitions than d_2. Restricting to fully-logged derivations, we include the minimal amount of transitions needed to produce the observed log.

Finally, we present a key result of our logging semantics. It states that two derivations are causally equivalent iff they produce the same log.

Theorem 1. *Let d_1, d_2 be coinitial fully-logged derivations. $\mathcal{L}(d_1) = \mathcal{L}(d_2)$ iff $d_1 \approx d_2$.*

4   A Causal-Consistent Replay Semantics

In this section, we introduce an *uncontrolled* replay semantics. It takes a program and the log of a given derivation, and allows us to replay any causally equivalent derivation. This semantics constitutes the kernel of our replay framework. The term uncontrolled indicates that the semantics specifies how to perform replay, but there is no policy to select the applicable rule when more than one is enabled. The uncontrolled semantics is suitable to set the basis of our replay mechanism, but does not allow one to focus on the causes of a given action. For this reason, in Sect. 5, we build on top of this semantics a *controlled* one, where the selection of actions is driven by the queries from the user.

In the following, we introduce a transition relation $\rightharpoonup$ to specify replay. Transition $\rightharpoonup$ is similar to the logging semantics $\hookrightarrow$ (Fig. 3) but it is now driven by the considered log. Thus, processes have the form $\langle p, \omega, \theta, e \rangle$, with ω a log.

The uncontrolled causal-consistent replay semantics is shown in Fig. 5. For technical reasons, labels of the replay semantics contain the same information as the labels of the logging semantics. Moreover, the labels now also include a set of replay *requests*. The reader can ignore these elements until the next section. For simplicity, we also consider that the log $\mathcal{L}(d, p)$ of each process p in the original derivation d is a fixed global parameter of the transition rules (see rule *Spawn*).

$$(Seq) \quad \frac{\theta, e \xrightarrow{\tau} \theta', e'}{\Gamma; \langle p, \omega, \theta, e \rangle \mid \Pi \rightarrow_{p, \mathsf{seq}, \{\mathsf{s}\}} \Gamma; \langle p, \omega, \theta', e' \rangle \mid \Pi}$$

$$(Send) \quad \frac{\theta, e \xrightarrow{\mathsf{send}(p', v)} \theta', e'}{\Gamma; \langle p, \mathsf{send}(\ell) + \omega, \theta, e \rangle \mid \Pi \rightarrow_{p, \mathsf{send}(\ell), \{\mathsf{s}, \ell \Uparrow\}} \Gamma \cup \{(p, p', \{v, \ell\})\}; \langle p, \omega, \theta', e' \rangle \mid \Pi}$$

$$(Receive) \quad \frac{\theta, e \xrightarrow{\mathsf{rec}(\kappa, \overline{cl_n})} \theta', e' \text{ and } \mathsf{matchrec}(\theta, \overline{cl_n}, v) = (\theta_i, e_i)}{\Gamma \cup \{(p', p, \{v, \ell\})\} \langle p, \mathsf{rec}(\ell) + \omega, \theta, e \rangle \mid \Pi \\ \rightarrow_{p, \mathsf{rec}(\ell), \{\mathsf{s}, \ell \Downarrow\}} \Gamma; \langle p, \omega, \theta' \theta_i, e' \{\kappa \mapsto e_i\} \rangle \mid \Pi}$$

$$(Spawn) \quad \frac{\theta, e \xrightarrow{\mathsf{spawn}(\kappa, a/n, [\overline{v_n}])} \theta', e' \text{ and } \omega' = \mathcal{L}(d, p')}{\Gamma; \langle p, \mathsf{spawn}(p') + \omega, \theta, e \rangle \mid \Pi \rightarrow_{p, \mathsf{spawn}(p'), \{\mathsf{s}, \mathsf{sp}_{p'}\}} \Gamma; \langle p, \omega, \theta', e' \{\kappa \mapsto p'\} \rangle \\ \mid \langle p', \omega', id, \mathsf{apply} \; a/n \; (\overline{v_n}) \rangle \mid \Pi}$$

$$(Self) \quad \frac{\theta, e \xrightarrow{\mathsf{self}(\kappa)} \theta', e'}{\Gamma; \langle p, \omega, \theta, e \rangle \mid \Pi \rightarrow_{p, \mathsf{self}, \{\mathsf{s}\}} \Gamma; \langle p, \omega, \theta', e' \{\kappa \mapsto p\} \rangle \mid \Pi}$$

Fig. 5. Uncontrolled replay semantics

The rules for expressions are the same as in the logging semantics (an advantage of the modular design). The replay semantics is similar to the logging semantics, except that logs fix some parameters: the fresh message identifier in rule *Send*, the message received in rule *Receive*, and the fresh pid in rule *Spawn*.

Example 4. Consider the logs of Example 3. Then, we have, e.g., the replay derivation in Fig. 6. The actions performed by each process are the same as in the original derivation in Example 2, but the interleavings are slightly different. Moreover, after ten steps, the server is waiting for a message, the global mailbox contains a matching message but, in contrast to the logging semantics, receive cannot proceed since the message identifier in the log does not match (ℓ_2 vs ℓ_3).

Basic Properties of the Replay Semantics. Here, we show that the uncontrolled replay semantics is consistent and we relate it with the logging semantics. We need the following auxiliary functions:

Definition 8. *Let $d = (s_1 \hookrightarrow^* s_2)$ be a derivation under the logging semantics, with $s_1 = \Gamma; \langle p_1, \theta_1, e_1 \rangle \mid \ldots \mid \langle p_n, \theta_n, e_n \rangle$. The system corresponding to s_1 in the replay semantics is defined as follows:*

$$addLog(\mathcal{L}(d), s_1) = \Gamma; \langle p_1, \mathcal{L}(d, p_1), \theta_1, e_1 \rangle \mid \ldots \mid \langle p_n, \mathcal{L}(d, p_n), \theta_n, e_n \rangle$$

Conversely, given a system $s = \Gamma; \langle p_1, \omega_1, \theta_1, e_1 \rangle \mid \ldots \mid \langle p_n, \omega_n, \theta_n, e_n \rangle$ in the replay semantics, we let $del(s)$ be the system obtained from s by removing logs, i.e., $del(s) = \Gamma; \langle p_1, \theta_1, e_1 \rangle \mid \ldots \mid \langle p_n, \theta_n, e_n \rangle$, and similarly for derivations.

In the following, we extend the notions of log and coinitial derivations, as well as function init, to replay derivations in the obvious way. Furthermore, we

$\{\,\}$; $\langle$c, (spawn(s), spawn(p), send(ℓ_1), send(ℓ_2)), -, apply main/0 ()$\rangle$
$\rightharpoonup$ $\{\,\}$; $\langle$c, (spawn(s), spawn(p), send(ℓ_1), send(ℓ_2)), -, let S = spawn(server/0, [ ]) in ...$\rangle$
$\rightharpoonup$ $\{\,\}$; $\langle$c, (spawn(p), send(ℓ_1), send(ℓ_2)), -, let P = spawn(proxy/0, [ ]) in
    apply client/2 $(P, s)\rangle$ | $\langle$s, (rec(ℓ_2)), -, apply server/0 ()$\rangle$
$\rightharpoonup$ $\{\,\}$; $\langle$c, (spawn(p), send(ℓ_1), send(ℓ_2)), -, let P = spawn(proxy/0, [ ]) in
    apply client/2 $(P, s)\rangle$ | $\langle$s, (rec(ℓ_2)), -, receive ...$\rangle$
$\rightharpoonup$ $\{\,\}$; $\langle$c, (send(ℓ_1), send(ℓ_2)), -, apply client/2 (p, s)$\rangle$
    | $\langle$s, (rec(ℓ_2)), -, receive ...$\rangle$ | $\langle$p, (rec(ℓ_1), send(ℓ_3)), -, apply proxy/0 ()$\rangle$
$\rightharpoonup$ $\{\,\}$; $\langle$c, (send(ℓ_1), send(ℓ_2)), -, let X = p ! {s, {self(), 40}} in ...$\rangle$
    | $\langle$s, (rec(ℓ_2)), -, receive ...$\rangle$ | $\langle$p, (rec(ℓ_1), send(ℓ_3)), -, apply proxy/0 ()$\rangle$
$\rightharpoonup$ $\{\,\}$; $\langle$c, (send(ℓ_1), send(ℓ_2)), -, let X = p ! {s, {c, 40}} in ...$\rangle$
    | $\langle$s, (rec(ℓ_2)), -, receive ...$\rangle$ | $\langle$p, (rec(ℓ_1), send(ℓ_3)), -, apply proxy/0 ()$\rangle$
$\rightharpoonup$ $\{$(c, p, {{s, {c, 40}}, ℓ_1})$\}$; $\langle$c, (send(ℓ_2)), -, let Y = s ! 2 in ...$\rangle$ | $\langle$s, (rec(ℓ_2)), -, receive ...$\rangle$
    | $\langle$p, (rec(ℓ_1), send(ℓ_3)), -, apply proxy/0 ()$\rangle$
$\rightharpoonup$ $\{$(c, p, {{s, {c, 40}}, ℓ_1})$\}$; $\langle$c, (send(ℓ_2)), -, let Y = s ! 2 in ...$\rangle$ | $\langle$s, (rec(ℓ_2)), -, receive ...$\rangle$
    | $\langle$p, (rec(ℓ_1), send(ℓ_3)), -, receive ...$\rangle$
$\rightharpoonup$ $\{\,\}$; $\langle$c, (send(ℓ_2)), -, let Y = s ! 2 in ...$\rangle$ | $\langle$s, (rec(ℓ_2)), -, receive ...$\rangle$
    | $\langle$p, (send(ℓ_3)), -, let s ! {c, 40} in ...$\rangle$
$\rightharpoonup$ $\{$(p, s, {{c, 40}, ℓ_3})$\}$; $\langle$c, (send(ℓ_2)), -, let Y = s ! 2 in ...$\rangle$ | $\langle$s, (rec(ℓ_2)), -, receive ...$\rangle$
    | $\langle$p, (), -, apply proxy/0 ()$\rangle$
$\rightharpoonup$ $\{$(p, s, {{c, 40}, ℓ_3}), (c, s, {2, ℓ_2})$\}$; $\langle$c, (), -, receive ...$\rangle$ | $\langle$s, (rec(ℓ_2)), -, receive ...$\rangle$
    | $\langle$p, (), -, apply proxy/0 ()$\rangle$
$\rightharpoonup$ $\{$(p, s, {{c, 40}, ℓ_3})$\}$; $\langle$c, (), -, receive ...$\rangle$ | $\langle$s, (), -, error$\rangle$ | $\langle$p, (), -, apply proxy/0 ()$\rangle$

Fig. 6. Uncontrolled replay derivation with the traces of Example 3

now call a system s' *initial* under the replay semantics if there exists a derivation d under the logging semantics, and s' = $addLog(\mathcal{L}(d), \text{init}(d))$.

We extend the notion of fully-logged derivations to our replay semantics:

Definition 9 (fully-logged replay derivation). *A derivation d under the replay semantics is* fully-logged *if, for each process p, the log is empty and its last transition (if any) is a logged transition.*

Note that, in addition to Definition 7, we now require that processes *consume* all their logs.

We will only consider systems reachable from the execution of a program:

Definition 10 (reachable systems). *A system s is* reachable *if there exists an initial system s_0 such that $s_0 \rightharpoonup^* s$.*

Since only reachable systems are of interest (non-reachable systems are ill-formed), in the following we assume that all systems are reachable.

Now, we can tackle the problem of proving that our replay semantics preserves causal equivalence, i.e., that the original and the replay derivations are always causally equivalent.

Theorem 2. *Let d be a fully-logged derivation under the logging semantics. Let d' be any finite fully-logged derivation under the replay semantics such that $\text{init}(d')$ = $addLog(\mathcal{L}(d), \text{init}(d))$. Then $d \approx del(d')$.*

Usefulness for Debugging. Now, we show that our replay semantics is indeed useful as a basis for designing a debugging tool. In particular, we prove that a (faulty) behavior occurs in the logged derivation iff any replay derivation also exhibits the same *faulty* behavior, hence replay is correct and complete.

In order to formalize such a result we need to fix the notion of faulty behavior we are interested in. For us, a misbehavior is a wrong system, but since the system is possibly distributed, we concentrate on misbehaviors visible from a "local" observer. Given that our systems are composed of processes and messages in the global mailbox, we consider that a (local) misbehavior is either a wrong message in the global mailbox or a process with a wrong configuration.

Theorem 3 (Correctness and completeness). *Let d be a fully-logged derivation under the logging semantics. Let d' be any fully-logged derivation under the uncontrolled replay semantics such that* $\mathsf{init}(d') = addLog(\mathcal{L}(d), \mathsf{init}(d))$. *Then:*

1. *there is a system $\Gamma; \Pi$ in d with a configuration $\langle p, \theta, e \rangle$ in Π iff there is a system $\Gamma'; \Pi'$ in d' with a configuration $\langle p, \theta, e \rangle$ in $del(\Gamma'; \Pi')$;*
2. *there is a system $\Gamma; \Pi$ in d with a message $(p, p', \{v, \ell\})$ in Γ iff there is a system $\Gamma'; \Pi'$ in d' with a message $(p, p', \{v, \ell\})$ in Γ'.*

The result above is very strong: it ensures that a misbehavior occurring in a logged execution is replayed in *any* possible fully-logged derivation. This means that any scheduling policy is fine for replay. Furthermore, this remains true whatever actions the user takes: either the misbehavior is reached, or it remains in any possible forward computation.

One may wonder whether more general notions of misbehavior make sense. Above, we consider just "local" observations. One could ask for more than one local observation to be replayed. By applying the result above to multiple observations we get that all of them will be replayed, but, if they concern different processes or messages, we cannot ensure that they are replayed *at the same time or in the same order*. For instance, in the derivation of Fig. 4, process c sends the message with identifier ℓ_2 before process p receives the message with identifier ℓ_1, while in the replay derivation of Fig. 6 the two actions are executed in the opposite order. Only a *super user* able to see the whole system at once could see such a (mis)behavior, which are thus not relevant in our context.

5 Controlled Replay Semantics

In this section, we introduce a controlled version of the replay semantics. The semantics in the previous section allows one to replay a given derivation and be guaranteed to replay, sooner or later, any local misbehavior. In practice, though, one normally knows in which process p the misbehavior appears, and thus (s)he wants to focus on a process p or even on some of its actions. However, to correctly replay these actions, one also needs to replay the actions that happened before them. We present in Fig. 7 a semantics where the user can specify which actions (s)he wants to replay, and the semantics takes care of replaying them. Replaying

$$\frac{\Gamma;\Pi \rightarrow_{p,r,\Psi'} \Gamma';\Pi' \;\wedge\; \psi \in \Psi'}{\lVert\Gamma;\Pi\rVert_{\{p,\psi\}+\Psi} \rightsquigarrow \lVert\Gamma';\Pi'\rVert_{\Psi}} \qquad \frac{\Gamma;\Pi \rightarrow_{p,r,\Psi'} \Gamma';\Pi' \;\wedge\; \psi \notin \Psi'}{\lVert\Gamma;\Pi\rVert_{\{p,\psi\}+\Psi} \rightsquigarrow \lVert\Gamma';\Pi'\rVert_{\{p,\psi\}+\Psi}}$$

$$\frac{\Gamma;\langle p,\mathsf{rec}(\ell)+\omega,\theta,e\rangle \mid \Pi \not\rightarrow_{p,r,\Psi'} \;\wedge\; sender(\ell) = p'}{\lVert\Gamma;\langle p,\mathsf{rec}(\ell)+\omega,\theta,e\rangle \mid \Pi\rVert_{\{p,\psi\}+\Psi} \rightsquigarrow \lVert\Gamma;\langle p,\mathsf{rec}(\ell)+\omega,\theta,e\rangle \mid \Pi\rVert_{(\{p',\ell^{\Uparrow}\},\{p,\psi\})+\Psi}}$$

$$\frac{\not\exists p \text{ in } \Pi \;\wedge\; parent(p) = p'}{\lVert\Gamma;\Pi\rVert_{\{p,\psi\}+\Psi} \rightsquigarrow \lVert\Gamma;\Pi\rVert_{(\{p',\mathsf{sp}_p\},\{p,\psi\})+\Psi}}$$

Fig. 7. Controlled replay semantics

an action requires to replay all *and only* its causes. Notably, the bug causing a misbehavior causes the action showing the misbehavior.

Here, given a system s, we want to start a replay until a particular action ψ is performed on a given process p. We denote such a replay request with $\lVert s \rVert_{(\{p,\psi\})}$. In general, the subscript of $\lVert\ \rVert$ is a stack of requests, where the first element is the most recent one. In this paper, we consider the following replay requests:

- $\{p,\mathsf{s}\}$: one step of process p (the extension to n steps is straightforward);
- $\{p,\ell^{\Uparrow}\}$: request for process p to send the message tagged with ℓ;
- $\{p,\ell^{\Downarrow}\}$: request for process p to receive the message tagged with ℓ;
- $\{p,\mathsf{sp}_{p'}\}$: request for process p to spawn the process p'.

Variable creations as not valid targets for replay requests, since variable names are not known before their creation (variable creations are not logged). The requests above are *satisfied* when a corresponding uncontrolled transition is performed. Indeed, the third element labeling the relations of the replay semantics in Fig. 5 is the set of requests satisfied in the corresponding step.

Let us explain the rules of the controlled replay semantics in Fig. 7. Here, we assume that the computation always starts with a single request.

- If the desired process p can perform a step satisfying the request ψ on top of the stack, we do it and remove the request from the stack (first rule).
- If the desired process p can perform a step, but it does not satisfy the request ψ, we update the system but keep the request in the stack (second rule).
- If a step on the desired process p is not possible, then we track the dependencies and add a new request on top of the stack. We have two rules: one for adding a request to a process to send a message we want to receive and another one to spawn the process we want to replay if it does not exist. Here, we use the auxiliary functions *sender* and *parent* to identify, respectively, the sender of a message and the parent of a process. Both functions *sender* and *parent* are easily computable from the logs in $\mathcal{L}(d)$.

The relation $\rightsquigarrow$ can be seen as a controlled version of the uncontrolled replay semantics in the sense that each derivation of the controlled semantics corresponds to a derivation of the uncontrolled one, while the opposite is not generally true. Notions for derivations and transitions are easily extended to controlled derivations. We also need a notion of projection from controlled systems to uncontrolled systems: $uctrl(\lfloor\!\lfloor \Gamma; \Pi \rfloor\!\rfloor_\Psi) = \Gamma; \Pi$. The notion of projection trivially extends to derivations.

Theorem 4 (Soundness). *For each controlled derivation d, $uctrl(d)$ is an uncontrolled derivation.*

While simple, this result allows one to recover many relevant properties from the uncontrolled semantics. For instance, by using the controlled semantics, if starting from a system $s = addLog(\mathcal{L}(d), \mathsf{init}(d))$ for some logging derivation d we find a wrong message $(p, p', \{v, \ell\})$, then we know that the same message exists also in d (from Theorem 3).

Our controlled semantics is not only sound but also minimal: causal-consistent replay redoes the minimal amount of actions needed to satisfy the replay request.

Here, we need to restrict the attention to requests that ask to replay transitions which are in the future of the process.

Definition 11. *A controlled system $c = \lfloor\!\lfloor s \rfloor\!\rfloor_{(\{p, \psi\})}$ is well initialized iff there are a derivation d under the logging semantics, a system $s_0 = addLog(\mathcal{L}(d), \mathsf{init}(d))$, an uncontrolled derivation $s_0 \rightharpoonup^* s$, and an uncontrolled derivation from s satisfying $\{p, \psi\}$.*

The existence of a derivation satisfying the request can be efficiently checked. For replay requests $\{p, \mathsf{s}\}$ it is enough to check that process p can perform a step, for other replay requests it is enough to check the process log.

Theorem 5 (Minimality). *Let d be a controlled derivation such as $\mathsf{init}(d) = \lfloor\!\lfloor s \rfloor\!\rfloor_{(\{p, \psi\})}$ is well-initialized. Derivation $uctrl(d)$ has minimal length among all uncontrolled derivations d' with $\mathsf{init}(d') = s$ including at least one transition satisfying the request $\{p, \psi\}$.*

6   Related Work and Conclusion

In this work, we have introduced (controlled) causal-consistent replay. It is strongly related (indeed dual) to the notion of causal-consistent reversibility, and its instance on debugging, causal-consistent reversible debugging, introduced in [6] for the *toy* language μOz. Beyond this, it has only been used so far in the CauDEr [13,14] debugger for Erlang, which we took as a starting point for our prototype implementation (see [17]). Causal-consistent rollback has also been studied in the context of the process calculus HOπ [12] and the coordination language Klaim [7]. We refer to [6] for a description of the relations between causal-consistent debugging and other forms of reversible debugging.

The basic ideas in this paper are also applicable to other message-passing languages and calculi. In principle, the approach could also be applied to shared memory languages, yet it would require to log all interactions with shared memory (which may give rise, in principle, to an inefficient scheme).

An approach to record and replay for actor languages is introduced in [1]. While we concentrate on the theory, they focus on low-level issues: dealing with I/O, producing compact logs, etc. Actually, we could consider some of the ideas in [1] to produce more compact logs and thus reduce our instrumentation overhead.

At the semantic level, the work closest to ours is the reversible semantics for Erlang in [15]. However, all our semantics abstract away local queues in processes and their management. This makes the notion of independence much more natural, and it avoids some spurious conflicts between deliveries of different messages present in [15]. Moreover, our replay semantics is driven by the log of an actual execution, while the one in [15] is not. Finally, our controlled semantics, built on top of the uncontrolled reversible semantics, is much simpler than the low-level controlled semantics in [15] which, anyway, is based on undoing the actions of an execution up to a given checkpoint (rollback requests appeared later, in [13]).

None of the works above treats causal-consistent replay and, as far as we know, such notion has never been explored. For instance, no reference to it appears in a recent survey [4]. The survey classifies our approach as a message-passing multi-processor scheme (the approach is studied in a single-processor multi-process setting, but it makes no use of the single-processor assumption). It is in between content-based schemes (that record the content of the messages) and ordering-based schemes (that record the source of the messages), since it registers just unique identifiers for messages. This reduces the size of the log (content of long messages is not stored) w.r.t. content-based schemes, yet differently from ordering-based schemes it does not necessarily require to replay the system from a global checkpoint (but we do not yet consider checkpoints).

A related ordering-based scheme is [21]: it uses race detection to avoid logging all message exchanges, and we may try to integrate it in our approach in the future (though it considers only systems with a fixed number of processes). A content-based work is [19] for MPI programs, which does not replay calls to MPI functions, but just takes the values from the log. By applying this approach in our case, the state of Γ would not be replayed, and causal-consistent replay would not be possible since no relation between send and receive is kept.

Our work is also related to slicing, and in particular to [23], since it also deals with concurrent systems. Both approaches are based on causal consistency, but slicing considers the whole computation and extracts the fragment of it needed to explain a visible behavior, while we instrument the computation so to be able to go back and forward. Other differences include the considered languages—pi calculus vs Erlang—, the style of the semantics—labelled transitions vs reductions—, etc.

References

1. Aumayr, D., Marr, S., Béra, C., Boix, E.G., Mössenböck, H.: Efficient and deterministic record & replay for actor languages. In: Tilevich, E., Mössenböck, H. (eds.) Proceedings of the 15th International Conference on Managed Languages & Runtimes (ManLang 2018), pp. 15:1–15:14. ACM (2018)
2. Britton, T., Jeng, L., Carver, G., Cheak, P., Katzenellenbogen, T.: Reversible debugging software - quantify the time and cost saved using reversible debuggers (2012). http://www.roguewave.com
3. Carlsson, R., et al.: Core Erlang 1.0.3. Language specification (2004). https://www.it.uu.se/research/group/hipe/cerl/doc/core_erlang-1.0.3.pdf
4. Chen, Y., Zhang, S., Guo, Q., Li, L., Wu, R., Chen, T.: Deterministic replay: a survey. ACM Comput. Surv. **48**(2), 17:1–17:47 (2015)
5. Frequently Asked Questions about Erlang (2018). http://erlang.org/faq/academic.html
6. Giachino, E., Lanese, I., Mezzina, C.A.: Causal-consistent reversible debugging. In: Gnesi, S., Rensink, A. (eds.) FASE 2014. LNCS, vol. 8411, pp. 370–384. Springer, Heidelberg (2014). https://doi.org/10.1007/978-3-642-54804-8_26
7. Giachino, E., Lanese, I., Mezzina, C.A., Tiezzi, F.: Causal-consistent rollback in a tuple-based language. J. Log. Algebr. Methods Program. **88**, 99–120 (2017)
8. Huang, J., Liu, P., Zhang, C.: LEAP: lightweight deterministic multi-processor replay of concurrent Java programs. In: 2010 Proceedings of the 18th ACM SIGSOFT International Symposium on Foundations of Software Engineering, Santa Fe, NM, USA, 7–11 November 2010, pp. 385–386. ACM (2010)
9. Huang, J., Zhang, C.: Debugging concurrent software: advances and challenges. J. Comput. Sci. Technol. **31**(5), 861–868 (2016)
10. Jiang, Y., Gu, T., Xu, C., Ma, X., Lu, J.: CARE: cache guided deterministic replay for concurrent Java programs. In: 36th International Conference on Software Engineering, ICSE 2014, Hyderabad, India, 31 May–07 June 2014, pp. 457–467. ACM (2014)
11. Lamport, L.: Time, clocks, and the ordering of events in a distributed system. Commun. ACM **21**(7), 558–565 (1978)
12. Lanese, I., Mezzina, C.A., Schmitt, A., Stefani, J.-B.: Controlling reversibility in higher-order Pi. In: Katoen, J.-P., König, B. (eds.) CONCUR 2011. LNCS, vol. 6901, pp. 297–311. Springer, Heidelberg (2011). https://doi.org/10.1007/978-3-642-23217-6_20
13. Lanese, I., Nishida, N., Palacios, A., Vidal, G.: CauDEr: a causal-consistent reversible debugger for Erlang. In: Gallagher, J.P., Sulzmann, M. (eds.) FLOPS 2018. LNCS, vol. 10818, pp. 247–263. Springer, Cham (2018). https://doi.org/10.1007/978-3-319-90686-7_16
14. Lanese, I., Nishida, N., Palacios, A., Vidal, G.: CauDEr website (2018). https://github.com/mistupv/cauder
15. Lanese, I., Nishida, N., Palacios, A., Vidal, G.: A theory of reversibility for Erlang. J. Log. Algebr. Methods Program. **100**, 71–97 (2018)
16. Lanese, I., Palacios, A., Vidal, G.: CauDEr, causal-consistent reversible replay debugger. Logger. https://github.com/mistupv/tracer, debugger. https://github.com/mistupv/cauder/tree/replay
17. Lanese, I., Palacios, A., Vidal, G.: Causal-consistent replay debugging for message passing programs. Technical report, DSIC, Universitat Politècnica de València (2019). http://personales.upv.es/gvidal/german/forte19tr/paper.pdf

18. LeBlanc, T.J., Mellor-Crummey, J.M.: Debugging parallel programs with instant replay. IEEE Trans. Comput. **36**(4), 471–482 (1987)

19. Maruyama, M., Tsumura, T., Nakashima, H.: Parallel program debugging based on data-replay. In: Zheng, S.Q. (ed.) Proceedings of the IASTED International Conference on Parallel and Distributed Computing and Systems (PDCS 2005), pp. 151–156. IASTED/ACTA Press (2005)

20. Mazurkiewicz, A.: Trace theory. In: Brauer, W., Reisig, W., Rozenberg, G. (eds.) ACPN 1986. LNCS, vol. 255, pp. 278–324. Springer, Heidelberg (1987). https://doi.org/10.1007/3-540-17906-2_30

21. Netzer, R.H., Miller, B.P.: Optimal tracing and replay for debugging message-passing parallel programs. J. Supercomput. **8**(4), 371–388 (1995)

22. Nishida, N., Palacios, A., Vidal, G.: A reversible semantics for Erlang. In: Hermenegildo, M.V., Lopez-Garcia, P. (eds.) LOPSTR 2016. LNCS, vol. 10184, pp. 259–274. Springer, Cham (2017). https://doi.org/10.1007/978-3-319-63139-4_15

23. Perera, R., Garg, D., Cheney, J.: Causally consistent dynamic slicing. In: Desharnais, J., Jagadeesan, R. (eds.) CONCUR. LIPIcs, vol. 59, pp. 18:1–18:15. Schloss Dagstuhl - Leibniz-Zentrum fuer Informatik (2016)

24. Undo Software: Increasing software development productivity with reversible debugging (2014). https://undo.io/media/uploads/files/Undo_ReversibleDebugging_Whitepaper.pdf

25. Sutter, H.: The free lunch is over: a fundamental turn toward concurrency in software. Dr. Dobb's J. **30**(3), 202–210 (2005)

26. Svensson, H., Fredlund, L.A., Earle, C.B.: A unified semantics for future Erlang. In: 9th ACM SIGPLAN Workshop on Erlang, pp. 23–32. ACM (2010)

27. Veeraraghavan, K., et al.: DoublePlay: parallelizing sequential logging and replay. ACM Trans. Comput. Syst. **30**(1), 3:1–3:24 (2012)

Correct and Efficient Antichain Algorithms for Refinement Checking

Maurice Laveaux(✉), Jan Friso Groote, and Tim A. C. Willemse

Eindhoven University of Technology, Eindhoven, The Netherlands
{m.laveaux,j.f.groote,t.a.c.willemse}@tue.nl

Abstract. Refinement checking plays an important role in system verification. This means that the correctness of the system is established by showing a refinement relation between two models; one for the implementation and one for the specification. In [21], Wang *et al.* describe an algorithm based on antichains for efficiently deciding stable failures refinement and failures-divergences refinement. We identify several issues pertaining to the correctness and performance in these algorithms and propose new, correct, antichain-based algorithms. Using a number of experiments we show that our algorithms outperform the original ones in terms of running time and memory usage.

1 Introduction

Refinement is often an integral part of a mature engineering methodology for designing a (software) system in a stepwise manner. It allows one to start from a high-level specification that describes the permitted and desired behaviours of a system and arrive at a detailed implementation that behaves as originally specified. While in many settings, refinement is often used rather informally, it forms the mathematical cornerstone in the theoretical development of the process algebra CSP (Communicating Sequential Processes) by Hoare [12,17,18].

This formal view on refinement—as a mathematical relation between a specification and its implementation—has been used successfully in industrial settings [10], and it has been incorporated in commercial Formal Model-Driven Engineering tools such as *Dezyne* [3]. In such settings there are a variety of refinement relations, each with their own properties. In particular, each notion of refinement offers specific guarantees on the (types of) behavioural properties of the specification that carry over to correct implementations. For the theory of CSP, the—arguably—most prominent refinement relations are *stable failures refinement* [2,18] and *failures-divergences refinement* [18]. Both are implemented in the tool FDR [6] for specifying and analysing CSP processes.

Both stable failures refinement and failures-divergences refinement are computationally hard problems; deciding whether there is a refinement relation between an implementation and a specification, both represented by CSP processes or labelled transition systems, is PSPACE-hard [13]. In practice, however,

Published by Springer Nature Switzerland AG 2019
J. A. Pérez and N. Yoshida (Eds.): FORTE 2019, LNCS 11535, pp. 185–203, 2019.
https://doi.org/10.1007/978-3-030-21759-4_11

tools such as FDR are able to work with quite large state spaces. The basic algorithm for deciding a stable failures refinement or a failures-divergences refinement between an implementation and a specification relies on a *normalisation* of the specification. This normalisation is achieved by a subset construction that is used to obtain a deterministic transition system which represents the specification.

As observed in [21] and inspired by successes reported, *e.g.*, in [1], *antichain* techniques can be exploited to improve on the performance of refinement checking algorithms. Unfortunately, a closer inspection of the results and algorithms in [21], reveals several issues. First, the definitions of stable failures refinement and failures-divergences refinement used in [21] do not match the definitions of [2,18], nor do they seem to match known relations from the literature [8].

Second, as we demonstrate in Example 2 in this paper, the results [21, Theorems 2 and 3] claiming correctness of their algorithms for deciding both refinement relations are incorrect. We do note that their algorithm for checking stable failures refinement correctly decides the refinement relation defined by [2,18].

Third, unlike claimed by the authors in [21], their algorithms violate the antichain property as we demonstrate in Example 4. Fourth, their algorithms suffer from severely degraded performance due to suboptimal decisions made when designing the algorithms, leading to an overhead of a factor $|\Sigma|$, where Σ is the set of events. When using a FIFO queue to realise a breadth-first search strategy instead of the stack used by default for a depth-first search this factor is even greater, *viz.* $|\Sigma|^{|S|}$, where S is the set of states of the implementation, see our Example 3. Note that there are compelling reasons for using a breadth-first strategy [17]; *e.g.*, the conciseness of counterexamples to refinement.

The contributions of the current paper are as follows. Apart from pointing out the issues in [21], we propose new antichain-based algorithms for deciding stable failures refinement and failures-divergences refinement and we prove their correctness. We compare the performance of the stable failures refinement algorithm of [21] to ours. Due to the flaw in their algorithm for checking failures-divergences refinement, a comparison for this refinement relation makes little sense. Our results indicate a small improvement in run time performance for practical models when using depth-first search, whereas our experiments using breadth-first search illustrate that decision problems intractable using the algorithm of [21] generally become quite easy using our algorithm.

The remainder of this paper is organised as follows. We recall the necessary mathematics in Sect. 2 and we describe the essence of refinement checking algorithms in Sect. 3. In Sect. 4, we analyse the algorithms of [21] and in Sect. 5, we propose new antichain-based refinement algorithms, claim their correctness and provide proof sketches. In Sect. 6, we compare the performance of our algorithm to that of [21]. Full proofs of our claims can be found in a technical report [14], which also contains additional experiments, showing that further speed improvements can be obtained by applying divergence-preserving branching bisimulation [7] minimisation before checking refinement.

2   Preliminaries

In this section the preliminaries of labelled transition systems, stable failures refinement and failures-divergences refinement checking are introduced.

2.1   Labelled Transition Systems

Let Σ be a finite set of event labels that does not contain the constant τ, modelling *internal* events.

Definition 1. *A labelled transition system is a tuple $\mathcal{L} = (S, \iota, Act, \to)$ where S is a set of states; $\iota \in S$ is an initial state; $Act = \Sigma$ or $Act = \Sigma \cup \{\tau\}$ is a set of actions and $\to \subseteq S \times Act \times S$ is a labelled transition relation.*

The following definitions are in the context of a given labelled transition system $\mathcal{L} = (S, \iota, Act, \to)$. We typically use letters s, t, u to denote states, U, V to denote *sets* of states, a to denote an arbitrary action, e to denote an arbitrary event and $\sigma, \rho \in Act^*$ to denote a sequence of actions.

We adopt the following conventions and notation. Whenever $(s, a, t) \in \to$, we write $s \xrightarrow{a} t$; we write $s \xrightarrow{a}$ just whenever there is some t such that $s \xrightarrow{a} t$, and $s \not\xrightarrow{a}$ holds iff not $s \xrightarrow{a}$. The set of actions that can be executed in s is given by the set $\mathsf{enabled}(s)$, defined as $\mathsf{enabled}(s) = \{a \in Act \mid s \xrightarrow{a} \}$. We generalise the relation $\to$ in the usual manner to sequences of actions as follows: $s \xrightarrow{\epsilon} t$ holds iff $s = t$, and $s \xrightarrow{a\sigma} t$ holds iff there is some u such that $s \xrightarrow{a} u$ and $u \xrightarrow{\sigma} t$. Finally, the *weak* transition relation $\leadsto \subseteq S \times \Sigma^* \times S$ is the least relation satisfying:

- $s \overset{\epsilon}{\leadsto} t$ if there is some $\sigma \in \tau^*$ such that $s \xrightarrow{\sigma} t$,
- if $s \xrightarrow{a} t$ then $s \overset{a}{\leadsto} t$,
- if $s \overset{\rho}{\leadsto} t$ and $t \overset{\sigma}{\leadsto} u$ then $s \overset{\rho\sigma}{\leadsto} u$.

Definition 2. *Traces, weak traces and reachable states are defined as follows:*

- *$\sigma \in Act^*$ is a* trace *starting in s iff $s \xrightarrow{\sigma} t$ for some t. We denote the set of all traces starting in s by $\mathsf{traces}(s)$, and we define $\mathsf{traces}(\mathcal{L}) = \mathsf{traces}(\iota)$,*
- *$\sigma \in \Sigma^*$ is a* weak trace *starting in s iff $s \overset{\sigma}{\leadsto} t$ for some t. The set of all weak traces starting in s is denoted by $\mathsf{traces}_w(s)$, and we define $\mathsf{traces}_w(\mathcal{L}) = \mathsf{traces}_w(\iota)$,*
- *the set of states, reachable from s is defined as $\mathsf{reachable}(s) = \{t \in S \mid \exists \sigma \in \Sigma^* : s \overset{\sigma}{\leadsto} t\}$; we define $\mathsf{reachable}(\mathcal{L}) = \mathsf{reachable}(\iota)$.*

The semantics of the CSP process algebra builds on observations of *failures* and *divergences*. A failure is a set of event labels that the system observably refuses following an experiment on that system, *i.e.*, after executing a weak trace on that system.

By assumption, refusals can only be observed when the system has *stabilised*. Formally, a state s is *stable*, denoted $\mathsf{stable}(s)$, if and only if $s \not\xrightarrow{\tau}$. A divergence can be understood as the potential inability of a system to stabilise. In effect, this means that a divergence is an infinite sequence of τ-actions; formally, a state s is a diverging state, denoted $\text{div}(s)$, if and only if there is an infinite sequence of states s_i such that $s \xrightarrow{\tau} s_1 \xrightarrow{\tau} s_2 \xrightarrow{\tau} \cdots$. For a set of states U, we write $\text{div}(U)$ iff $\text{div}(s)$ for some $s \in U$.

Definition 3. *Let $s \in S$ be a stable state. The* refusals *of s are defined as*[1] *the set* $\text{refusals}(s) = \mathcal{P}(\Sigma \setminus \text{enabled}(s))$. *For a set of (not necessarily stable) states U, we define* $\text{refusals}(U) = \{X \subseteq \Sigma \mid \exists s \in U : \text{stable}(s) \wedge X \in \text{refusals}(s)\}$.

We are now in a position to formally define the set of divergences and the set of failures of an LTS; we here follow the standard conventions and definitions of [4,9,18]. Note that in [14] we instead have adopted the notational conventions of [21] to allow for an easier comparison of our results to theirs.

Definition 4. *The set of all* divergences *of a state s, denoted by* $\text{divergences}(s)$, *is defined as* $\{\sigma\rho \in \Sigma^* \mid \exists t \in S : s \xrightarrow{\sigma} t \wedge \text{div}(t)\}$. *We define* $\text{divergences}(\mathcal{L}) = \text{divergences}(\iota)$.

Observe that a divergence is not only a weak trace that can reach a diverging state, but also any suffix of a weak trace that can reach a diverging state. This is based on the assumption that divergences lead to *chaos*. In theories in which divergences are considered chaotic, such chaos obscures all information about the behaviours involving a diverging state; we refer to this as obscuring *post-divergences details*.

Definition 5. *The set of all* stable failures *of a state s, denoted* $\text{failures}(s)$, *is defined as* $\{(\sigma, X) \in \Sigma^* \times \mathcal{P}(\Sigma) \mid \exists t \in S : s \xrightarrow{\sigma} t \wedge \text{stable}(t) \wedge X \in \text{refusals}(t)\}$. *The set of stable failures of a state s with post-divergences details obscured, denoted* $\text{failures}_\perp(s)$, *is defined as* $\text{failures}(s) \cup \{(\sigma, X) \in \Sigma^* \times \mathcal{P}(\Sigma) \mid \sigma \in \text{divergences}(s)\}$.

The two standard models of CSP are the *stable failures* model and the *failures-divergences* model. The refinement relations on LTSs, induced by these models, are called the *stable failures refinement* and the *failures-divergences refinement*. We remark that the LTS that is refined is commonly referred to as the *specification*, whereas the LTS that refines the specification is often referred to as the *implementation*.

Definition 6. *Let $\mathcal{L}_1$ and $\mathcal{L}_2$ be two LTSs. We say that $\mathcal{L}_2$ is a stable failures refinement of $\mathcal{L}_1$, denoted by $\mathcal{L}_1 \sqsubseteq_{sfr} \mathcal{L}_2$, iff* $\text{traces}_w(\mathcal{L}_2) \subseteq \text{traces}_w(\mathcal{L}_1)$ *and* $\text{failures}(\mathcal{L}_2) \subseteq \text{failures}(\mathcal{L}_1)$. *LTS $\mathcal{L}_2$ is a failures-divergences refinement of $\mathcal{L}_1$, denoted by $\mathcal{L}_1 \sqsubseteq_{fdr} \mathcal{L}_2$, iff* $\text{failures}_\perp(\mathcal{L}_2) \subseteq \text{failures}_\perp(\mathcal{L}_1)$ *and* $\text{divergences}(\mathcal{L}_2) \subseteq \text{divergences}(\mathcal{L}_1)$.

---

[1] We remark that [21] states the following, non-standard, definition: $\text{refusals}(s) = \{X \mid \exists s' \in S : s \xrightarrow{\varepsilon} s' \wedge \text{stable}(s') \wedge X \subseteq \Sigma \setminus \text{enabled}(s')\}$, suggesting that refusals are also defined for unstable states. As we discuss in Sect. 4, this has consequences for the performance of the algorithms for deciding the various refinement relations.

Remark 1. The notions defined above appear in different formulations in [21]. Their stable failures refinement omits the clause for weak trace inclusion, and their failures-divergences refinement replaces failures$_\perp$ with failures. This yields refinement relations different from the standard ones and neither relation seems to appear in the literature [8].

We finish this section with a small example, illustrating the difference between failures-divergences refinement and stable failures refinement.

Example 1. Consider the two transition systems (named after their initial states s_0 and t_0) depicted below.

Observe that we have $s_0 \sqsubseteq_{\mathrm{fdr}} t_0$, but not $s_0 \sqsubseteq_{\mathrm{sfr}} t_0$. The latter fails because aa is a trace of t_0, but not of s_0; the same goes for the stable failure $(a, \{b\})$ of t_0. The failures-divergences refinement holds because the divergent trace a obfuscates the observations of traces of the form aa^+: since divergence is chaos, anything is permitted. We do have $t_0 \sqsubseteq_{\mathrm{sfr}} s_0$ but not $t_0 \sqsubseteq_{\mathrm{fdr}} s_0$. The latter fails because of the divergent trace a not being present in t_0. Stable failures refinement holds because all traces and stable failure pairs of s_0 are included in those of t_0; in particular, the instability of state s_1 causes s_1 not to contribute to the stable failures set of s_0. □

3 Refinement Checking

In general, the set of failures and divergences of an LTS can be infinite. Therefore, checking inclusion of the set of failures or divergences is not viable. In [17,18], an algorithm to decide refinement between two labelled transition systems is sketched. As a preprocessing to this algorithm, all diverging states in both LTSs are marked. The algorithm then relies on exploring the cartesian product of the *normal form* representation of the specification, *i.e.*, the LTS that is to be refined, and the implementation. We remark that what we refer to as *cartesian product*, defined in [17], is called a *synchronous product* in [21]. For each pair in the product it checks whether it can locally decide non-refinement of the implementation state with the normal form state. A pair for which non-refinement holds is referred to as a *witness*.

Following [18,21] and specifically the terminology of [17], we formalise the cartesian product between LTSs that is explored by the procedure.

Definition 7. Let $\mathcal{L}_1 = (S_1, \iota_1, \Sigma, \rightarrow_1)$ and $\mathcal{L}_2 = (S_2, \iota_2, Act, \rightarrow_2)$ be LTSs. The cartesian product of $\mathcal{L}_1$ and $\mathcal{L}_2$ is the LTS $\mathcal{L}_1 \times \mathcal{L}_2 = (S, \iota, Act, \rightarrow)$ satisfying $S = S_1 \times S_2$; $\iota = (\iota_1, \iota_2)$; and the transition relation $\rightarrow$ is the smallest relation satisfying the following conditions for all $s_1, t_1 \in S_1$, and $s_2, t_2 \in S_2$ and $e \in \Sigma$:

- If $s_2 \xrightarrow{\tau}_2 t_2$ then $(s_1', s_2) \xrightarrow{\tau} (s_1, t_2)$,
- If $s_1 \xrightarrow{e}_1 t_1$ and $s_2 \xrightarrow{e}_2 t_2$ then $(s_1, s_2) \xrightarrow{e} (t_1, t_2)$.

We remark that Σ is used in $\mathcal{L}_1$ to indicate that it has no transitions labelled with τ, whereas, $\mathcal{L}_2$ might contain τ-transitions. A key property of the cartesian product, provable by induction on the length of sequence σ, is the following:

Proposition 1. *Let* $\mathcal{L}_1 = (S_1, \iota_1, \Sigma, \rightarrow_1)$ *and* $\mathcal{L}_2 = (S_2, \iota_2, Act, \rightarrow_2)$ *be LTSs, and let* $\mathcal{L}_1 \times \mathcal{L}_2 = (S, \iota, Act, \rightarrow)$ *be their cartesian product. For all* $s_1 \in S_1$, $s_2 \in S_2$ *and all* $\sigma \in Act^*$, $\iota \overset{\sigma}{\leadsto} (s_1, s_2)$ *iff* $\iota_1 \overset{\sigma}{\leadsto}_1 s_1$ *and* $\iota_2 \overset{\sigma}{\leadsto}_2 s_2$.

The normal form LTS is obtained using a typical subset construction as is common when determinising a transition system. Although all states in an LTS in normal form are stable, the states of the original LTS comprising a normal form state may not be. To avoid confusion when we wish to reason about the stability and divergences of states U in the LTS $\mathcal{L}$ underlying a normal form LTS, rather than the state of the normal form LTS, we write $\llbracket U \rrbracket_{\mathcal{L}}$ to indicate we refer to the set of states in $\mathcal{L}$. Stable failures refinement and failures-divergences refinement require different normal forms.

Definition 8. *Let* $\mathcal{L} = (S, \iota, Act, \rightarrow)$ *be a labelled transition system. Set* $S' = \mathcal{P}(S)$, $\iota' = \{s \in S \mid \iota \overset{\epsilon}{\leadsto} s\}$. *The stable failures refinement normal form of* $\mathcal{L}$ *is the LTS* $\mathrm{norm}_{sfr}(\mathcal{L}) = (S', \iota', \Sigma, \rightarrow')$, *where* $\rightarrow'$ *is defined as* $U \xrightarrow{e}' V$ *if and only if* $V = \{t \in S \mid \exists s \in U : s \overset{e}{\leadsto} t\}$ *for all* $U, V \subseteq S$ *and* $e \in \Sigma$. *The failures-divergences refinement normal form of* $\mathcal{L}$ *is the LTS* $\mathrm{norm}_{fdr}(\mathcal{L}) = (S', \iota', \Sigma, \rightarrow'')$ *where* $\rightarrow''$ *is defined as* $U \xrightarrow{e}'' V$ *if and only if* $U \xrightarrow{e}' V$ *and not* $\mathsf{div}(\llbracket U \rrbracket_{\mathcal{L}})$.

We remark that we deliberately permit the empty set to be a state in a normal form LTS. Clearly, a normal form LTS satisfies $\emptyset \xrightarrow{e} \emptyset$ for all actions e. Moreover, note that a normal form LTS is *deterministic*; in particular, for all σ, and states U, T, V of a normal form LTS $U \overset{\sigma}{\leadsto} T$ and $U \overset{\sigma}{\leadsto} V$ implies $T = V$.

The structure explored by the refinement checking procedure of [17,18] is essentially the cartesian product $\mathrm{norm}_{sfr}(\mathcal{L}_1) \times \mathcal{L}_2$ in case of stable failures refinement, or $\mathrm{norm}_{fdr}(\mathcal{L}_1) \times \mathcal{L}_2$ in case of failures-divergences refinement. For these structures the related witnesses, where the reachability of such a witness indicates non-refinement, are then as follows:

Definition 9. *Let* $\mathcal{L}_1$ *and* $\mathcal{L}_2$ *be LTSs.*

- *A state* (U, s) *in* $\mathrm{norm}_{sfr}(\mathcal{L}_1) \times \mathcal{L}_2$ *is called an SFR-witness iff* $U = \emptyset$; *or* $\mathsf{stable}(s)$ *and not* $\mathsf{refusals}(s) \subseteq \mathsf{refusals}(\llbracket U \rrbracket_{\mathcal{L}_1})$,
- *a state* (U, s) *in* $\mathrm{norm}_{fdr}(\mathcal{L}_1) \times \mathcal{L}_2$ *is called an FDR-witness iff not* $\mathsf{div}(\llbracket U \rrbracket_{\mathcal{L}_1})$, *and either* $\mathsf{div}(s)$; *or* $U = \emptyset$; *or* $\mathsf{stable}(s)$ *and not* $\mathsf{refusals}(s) \subseteq \mathsf{refusals}(\llbracket U \rrbracket_{\mathcal{L}_1})$.

The following statement formalises the insights of [17]; both results follow from Proposition 1 and the characteristics of the normal form LTSs.

Theorem 1. *Let* $\mathcal{L}_1$ *and* $\mathcal{L}_2$ *be LTSs. Then:*

- $\mathcal{L}_1 \sqsubseteq_{sfr} \mathcal{L}_2$ *iff no SFR-witness is reachable in* $\mathrm{norm}_{sfr}(\mathcal{L}_1) \times \mathcal{L}_2$,
- $\mathcal{L}_1 \sqsubseteq_{fdr} \mathcal{L}_2$ *iff no FDR-witness is reachable in* $\mathrm{norm}_{fdr}(\mathcal{L}_1) \times \mathcal{L}_2$.

4   Antichain Algorithms for Refinement Checking

The normalisation of the specification LTS in refinement checking dominates the theoretical worst-case run time complexity of refinement checking, which itself is a PSPACE-hard problem. In practice, however, refinement checking can often be done quite effectively. Nevertheless, as observed in [21], there is room for improvement by exploiting an antichain approach to keep the size of the normal form LTS of the specification in check.

An antichain is a set $\mathcal{A} \subseteq X$ of a partially ordered set $(X, \leq)$ in which all distinct $x, y \in \mathcal{A}$ are incomparable: neither $x \leq y$ nor $y \leq x$. Given a partially ordered set $(X, \leq)$ and an antichain $\mathcal{A}$, the operation $\Subset$ checks whether $\mathcal{A}$ 'contains' an element x; that is, $x \Subset \mathcal{A}$ holds true if and only if there is some $y \in \mathcal{A}$ such that $y \leq x$. We write $Y \Subset^\forall \mathcal{A}$ iff $y \Subset \mathcal{A}$ for all $y \in Y$. Antichain $\mathcal{A}$ can be extended by inserting an element $x \in X$, denoted $\mathcal{A} \uplus x$, which is defined as the set $\{y \mid y = x \vee (y \in \mathcal{A} \wedge x \not\leq y)\}$. Note that this operation only yields an antichain whenever $x \not\Subset \mathcal{A}$.

As [1,21] suggest, the state space of the cartesian product $(S, \iota, Act, \rightarrow)$ between the normal form of LTS $\mathcal{L}_1$ and the LTS $\mathcal{L}_2$ induces a partially ordered set as follows. For $(U, s), (V, t) \in S$, define $(U, s) \leq (V, t)$ iff $s = t$ and $[\![U]\!]_{\mathcal{L}_1} \subseteq [\![V]\!]_{\mathcal{L}_1}$. Then the set $(S, \leq)$ is a partially ordered set. The fundamental property underlying the reason why an antichain approach to refinement checking works is expressed by the following proposition, stating that the traces of any state (V, s) in the cartesian product can be executed from all states smaller than (V, s). We remark that this is due to including the empty set as a state in the normal form LTS.

Proposition 2. *For all $(U, s) \leq (V, s)$ of a normal form LTS $\mathrm{norm}_{sfr}(\mathcal{L}_1) \times \mathcal{L}_2$ or $\mathrm{norm}_{fdr}(\mathcal{L}_1) \times \mathcal{L}_2$ and for every sequence $\sigma \in Act^*$ such that $(V, s) \xrightarrow{\sigma}\!\!\twoheadrightarrow (V', t)$, there is some (U', t) such that $(U, s) \xrightarrow{\sigma}\!\!\twoheadrightarrow (U', t)$ and $(U', t) \leq (V', t)$.*

The proof of this proposition proceeds by induction on the length of σ and is routine.

The main idea of the antichain algorithm is now as follows: the set of states of the cartesian product explored is recorded in an antichain. Whenever a new state of the cartesian product is found that is already included in the antichain (w.r.t. the membership test $\Subset$), further exploration of that state is unnecessary, thereby pruning the state space of the cartesian product. Note that it is not immediate that doing so is also 'safe' for refusals and divergences. Algorithm 1 is the pseudocode for checking stable failures refinement and failures-divergences refinement as presented in [21, Algorithms 2 and 3]; we remark that we combined these algorithms, as their check for failures-divergences refinement only requires an additional check for divergences (enabled by the Boolean *CheckDiv*).

Algorithm 1. Antichain-based refinement checking algorithm from [21]. The algorithm is claimed to return *true* iff LTS $\mathcal{L}_1 = (S_1, \iota_1, Act_1, \rightarrow_1)$ is refined by $\mathcal{L}_2 = (S_2, \iota_2, Act_2, \rightarrow_2)$. The refinement check conducted checks for stable failures refinement when *CheckDiv* is *false* and failures-divergences refinement otherwise.

```
 1: procedure REFINES(L₁, L₂, CheckDiv)
 2:     let working be a stack containing a pair ({s | ι₁ ↝ᵉ₁ s}, ι₂)
 3:     let antichain := ∅
 4:     while working ≠ ∅ do
 5:         pop (spec, impl) from working
 6:         antichain := antichain ⊎ (spec, impl)
 7:         if CheckDiv and div(impl) then
 8:             if not div(spec) then
 9:                 return false
10:         else
11:             if refusals(impl) ⊈ refusals(spec) then
12:                 return false
13:             for impl ⟶ᵃ₂ impl' do
14:                 if a = τ then
15:                     spec' := spec
16:                 else
17:                     spec' := {s' | ∃s ∈ spec : s ↝ᵃ₁ s'}
18:                 if spec' = ∅ then
19:                     return false
20:                 if (spec', impl') ∈ antichain is not true then
21:                     push (spec', impl') into working
22:     return true
```

Let us first stress that the algorithm correctly decides stable failures refinement but it fails to correctly decide failures-divergences refinement. Second, the algorithm also fails to decide the non-standard relations used in [21], see also Remark 1. All three issues are illustrated by the example below.

Example 2. Consider the four transition systems depicted below.

Let us first observe that the algorithm correctly decides that $s_1 \sqsubseteq_{\mathrm{sfr}} s_0$ does not hold, which follows from a violation of $\mathsf{traces}_w(s_0) \subseteq \mathsf{traces}_w(s_1)$. Next, observe that we have $s_0 \sqsubseteq_{\mathrm{fdr}} s_1$, since the divergence of the root state s_0 implies chaotic behaviour of s_0 and, hence, any system refines such a system. However, Algorithm 1 returns *false* when *CheckDiv* holds.

With respect to the refinement relations defined in [21], we observe the following. Since s_0 is not stable, we have $\mathsf{failures}(s_0) = \emptyset$ and hence $\mathsf{failures}(s_0) \subseteq \mathsf{failures}(s_1)$. Consequently, stable failures refinement as defined in [21] should hold, but as we already concluded above, the algorithm returns *false* when checking for $s_1 \sqsubseteq_{\mathrm{sfr}} s_0$. Next, observe that the algorithm returns *true* when checking for $s_2 \sqsubseteq_{\mathrm{fdr}} s_3$. The reason is that for the pair $(\{s_2\}, s_3)$, it detects that state s_3 diverges and concludes that since also the normal form state of the specification $\{s_2\}$ diverges, it can terminate the iteration and return *true*. This is a consequence of splitting the divergence tests over two **if**-statements in lines 7 and 8. According to the failures-divergences refinement of [21], however, the algorithm should return *false*, since failures(s_3) $\subseteq$ failures(s_2) fails to hold: we have $(a, \{a\}) \in$ failures(s_3) but not $(a, \{a\}) \in$ failures(s_2).   □

We note that the algorithm explores the cartesian product between the normal form of a specification, and an implementation in a depth-first, on-the-fly manner. While depth-first search is typically used for detecting divergences, [17] states a number of reasons for running the refinement check in a breadth-first manner. A compelling argument in favour of using a breadth-first search is conciseness of the counterexample in case of a non-refinement.

Algorithm 1 can be made to run in a breadth-first fashion simply by using a FIFO *queue* rather than a stack as the data structure for *working*. However, our implementation of this algorithm suffers from a severely degraded performance. We can trace this back to the following three additional problems in the original algorithm, which also are present (albeit less pronounced in practice) when utilising a depth-first exploration:

1. The refusal check on line 11 is also performed for unstable states, which, combined with the definition of **refusals** in [21] (see also our remark in Footnote 1 on page 4), results in a repeated, potentially expensive, search for stable states;
2. Adding the pair (*spec, impl*) that is taken from *working* to *antichain* might result in duplicate pairs in *working* since *working* is filled with all successors of that pair in line 21, regardless of whether these pairs are already scheduled for exploration, *i.e.*, included in *working*, or not;
3. Contrary to the explicit claim in [21, Section 2.2], the set *antichain* is *not* guaranteed to be an antichain.

The first problem is readily seen to lead to undesirable overhead. The second and third problem are more subtle. We first illustrate the second problem: the following pathological example shows that the algorithm stores an excessive number of pairs in *working*.

Example 3. Consider the family of LTSs $\mathcal{L}_n^k = (S_n, \iota_n, Act_k, \rightarrow_n)$ with states $S_n = \{s_1, \ldots, s_n\}$, event labels $Act_k = \{e_1, \ldots, e_k\}$ and transitions $s_i \xrightarrow{e_j}_n s_{i-1}$ for all $1 \leq j \leq k$, $1 < i \leq n$ and $\iota_n = s_n$; see also the transition system depicted below. Note that each LTS that belongs to this family is completely deterministic.

Suppose one checks for refinement between an implementation and specification both of which are given by $\mathcal{L}_n^k$; *i.e.*, we test for $\mathcal{L}_n^k \sqsubseteq_{\mathrm{sfr}} \mathcal{L}_n^k$. Then the stack *working* will contain exactly $i \cdot (k-1)+1$ pairs at the end of the i-*th* iteration (when $i \leq n$), resulting in a working stack size of $\mathcal{O}(n \cdot k)$ entries. At the end of the n-*th* iteration *antichain* contains all reachable pairs of the cartesian product, *i.e.*, *antichain* $= \{(\{s_j\}, s_j) \mid 1 \leq j \leq n\}$ at that point. Emptying *working* after the n-*th* iteration will involve k antichain membership tests per entry. Consequently, $\mathcal{O}(n \cdot k^2)$ antichain membership tests are required. A breadth-first search strategy requires even more antichain membership tests, *viz.*, $\mathcal{O}(k^n)$.   □

The example below illustrates the third problem of the algorithm, *viz.*, the violation of the antichain property.

Example 4. Consider the two left-most labelled transition systems depicted below, along with the (normal form) cartesian product (the LTS on the right).

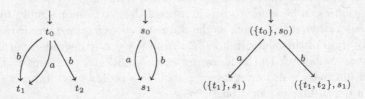

Algorithm 1 starts with *working* containing pair $(\{t_0\}, s_0)$ and *antichain* $= \emptyset$. Inside the loop, the pair $(\{t_0\}, s_0)$ is popped from *working* and added to *antichain*. The successors of the pair $(\{t_0\}, s_0)$ are the pairs $(\{t_1\}, s_1)$ and $(\{t_1, t_2\}, s_1)$. Since *antichain* contains neither of these, both successors are added to *working* in line 21. Next, popping $(\{t_1\}, s_1)$ from *working* and adding this pair to *antichain* results in *antichain* consisting of the set $\{(\{t_0\}, s_0), (\{t_1\}, s_1)\}$. In the final iteration of the algorithm, the pair $(\{t_1, t_2\}, s_1)$ is popped from *working* and added to *antichain*, resulting in the set $\{(\{t_0\}, s_0), (\{t_1\}, s_1), (\{t_1, t_2\}, s_1)\}$. Clearly, since $(\{t_1\}, s_1) \leq (\{t_1, t_2\}, s_1)$, the set *antichain* no longer is a proper antichain.   □

5   A Correct and Improved Antichain Algorithm

We address the identified performance problems by rearranging the computations that are conducted. Note that in order to solve the first performance problem, we only perform the check to compare the refusals of the implementation and the normal form state of the specification in case the implementation state is stable.

Solving the second performance problem is more involved. The essential observation here is that in order for the information in *antichain* to be most effective, states of the cartesian product must be added to *antichain* as soon as these are discovered, even if these have not yet been fully explored. This is achieved by maintaining, as an invariant, that *working* $\in^\forall$ *antichain*; the states in *working* then essentially compose the *frontier* of the exploration. We achieve this by initialising *working* and *antichain* to consist of exactly the initial state of the cartesian product, and by extending *antichain* with all (not already discovered) successors for the state (*spec, impl*) that is popped from *working*. As a side effect, this also resolves the third issue, as now both *working* and *antichain* are only extended with states that have not yet been discovered, *i.e.*, for which the membership test in *antichain* fails, and for which insertion with such states does not invalidate the antichain property.

Algorithm 2. The corrected antichain-based refinement checking algorithm. The algorithm returns *true* iff. LTS $\mathcal{L}_1 = (S_1, \iota_1, Act_1, \rightarrow_1)$ is refined by $\mathcal{L}_2 = (S_2, \iota_2, Act_2, \rightarrow_2)$. The refinement check conducted checks for stable failures refinement when *CheckDiv* is *false* and failures-divergences refinement otherwise.

```
 1: procedure REFINES_new(L_1, L_2, CheckDiv)
 2:     let working be a stack containing a pair ({s | ι_1 ⇝^ε_1 s}, ι_2)
 3:     let antichain := ∅ ⊎ ({s | ι_1 ⇝^ε_1 s}, ι_2)
 4:     while working ≠ ∅ do
 5:         pop (spec, impl) from working
 6:         if not div(spec) or not CheckDiv then
 7:             if CheckDiv and div(impl) then
 8:                 return false
 9:             else
10:                 if stable(impl) then
11:                     if refusals(impl) ⊈ refusals(spec) then
12:                         return false
13:                 for impl →^a_2 impl' do
14:                     if a = τ then
15:                         spec' := spec
16:                     else
17:                         spec' := {s' | ∃s ∈ spec : s ⇝^a_1 s'}
18:                     if spec' = ∅ then
19:                         return false
20:                     if (spec', impl') ∈ antichain is not true then
21:                         antichain := antichain ⊎ (spec', impl')
22:                         push (spec', impl') into working
23:     return true
```

Algorithm 2 shows the corrected antichain procedure for checking stable failures refinement and failures-divergences refinement. Since the algorithm fundamentally differs (in the relations that it computes) from the one in [21], we cannot reuse their arguments in our proof of correctness, which are based on invariants that do not hold in our case.

In the remainder of this section, we sketch the proof of correctness of Algorithm 2 as claimed below by Theorem 2. We focus on the proof of correctness w.r.t. failures-divergences refinement; for stable failures refinement the proof is almost the same except that it does not have to consider divergences.

Theorem 2. *Let $\mathcal{L}_i = (S_i, \iota_i, Act_i, \rightarrow_i)$ where $i \in \{1, 2\}$ be two labelled transition systems. Then:*

- REFINES$_{new}(\mathcal{L}_1, \mathcal{L}_2, false)$ *returns* true *if and only if* $\mathcal{L}_1 \sqsubseteq_{sfr} \mathcal{L}_2$;
- REFINES$_{new}(\mathcal{L}_1, \mathcal{L}_2, true)$ *returns* true *if and only if* $\mathcal{L}_1 \sqsubseteq_{fdr} \mathcal{L}_2$;

For the remainder of this section we fix the two LTSs $\mathcal{L}_i = (S_i, \iota_i, Act_i, \rightarrow_i)$ where $i \in \{1, 2\}$. First we show termination of Algorithm 2. A crucial observation of the antichain operations is that adding elements to an antichain does not affect the membership test of elements already included; see the lemma below.

Lemma 1. *Let $(X, \leq)$ be a partially ordered set, $A \subseteq X$ an antichain, and let $x, y \in X$. If $x \in A$ and $y \notin A$ then $x \in (A \uplus y)$.*

Termination now follows from the observation that all states of the cartesian product that have been processed occur in *antichain* and do not get added back to *working*; for this we rely on Lemma 1. To reason formally about the states that have been processed, we introduce a ghost variable *done*; *i.e.*, *done* is intialised as the empty set and each pair $(spec, impl)$ that is popped from *working* in line 5 is added to *done* after line 22. We have the following invariants.

Lemma 2. *Let $\mathcal{L}_n = \text{norm}_{fdr}(\mathcal{L}_1)$ if CheckDiv holds and $\mathcal{L}_n = \text{norm}_{sfr}(\mathcal{L}_1)$ otherwise. The while loop (lines 4–22) of Algorithm 2 satisfies the following invariants: $done \cup working \subseteq \text{reachable}(\mathcal{L}_n \times \mathcal{L}_2)$, $done \cap working = \emptyset$, $done \cup working \in^\forall$ antichain and working contains no duplicates.*

Theorem 3. *Algorithm 2 terminates for finite state, finitely branching LTSs.*

Proof. The total number of pairs present in $\text{norm}_{sfr}(\mathcal{L}_1) \times \mathcal{L}_2$ and $\text{norm}_{fdr}(\mathcal{L}_1) \times \mathcal{L}_2$ are finite since $\mathcal{L}_1$ and $\mathcal{L}_2$ are finite state. By Lemma 2 we find that, when not *CheckDiv*, $working \cup done \subseteq \text{reachable}(\text{norm}_{sfr}(\mathcal{L}_1) \times \mathcal{L}_2)$. Likewise, we conclude $working \cup done \subseteq \text{reachable}(\text{norm}_{fdr}(\mathcal{L}_1) \times \mathcal{L}_2)$ when *CheckDiv*. Furthermore, as $done \cap working = \emptyset$, *done* strictly increases in size each iteration and so only a finite number of iterations of the outer for-loop are possible. Termination of the inner for-loop follows from the assumption that $\mathcal{L}_1$ and $\mathcal{L}_2$ are finitely branching. □

The correctness of the algorithm requires a lemma that shows anti-monotonicity of witnesses (*cf.* Definition 9); see below. Combined with Proposition 2 (see page 7) this allows us to conclude that the distance (defined below) from a state in the cartesian product to a witness is at least the distance to a witness from smaller states.

Lemma 3. *Let* $(U, s), (V, s)$ *be states of* $\mathrm{norm}_{sfr}(\mathcal{L}_1) \times \mathcal{L}_2$ *satisfying* $(U, s) \le (V, s)$. *If* (V, s) *is an SFR-witness then* (U, s) *is an SFR-witness. Likewise, if* (V, s) *is an FDR-witness in* $\mathrm{norm}_{fdr}(\mathcal{L}_1) \times \mathcal{L}_2$ *and* $(U, s) \le (V, s)$ *then* (U, s) *is an FDR-witness.*

For a set of states $\mathcal{U}$ in the cartesian product, let $SFR(\mathcal{U})$ be a predicate that is true if and only if $\mathcal{U}$ contains an SFR-witness; likewise, $FDR(\mathcal{U})$ holds if and only if $\mathcal{U}$ contains an FDR-witness. We denote the set of all reachable SFR-witnesses in the cartesian product $\mathrm{norm}_{sfr}(\mathcal{L}_1) \times \mathcal{L}_2$ by $\mathcal{S}$, and the set of all reachable FDR-witnesses in $\mathrm{norm}_{fdr}(\mathcal{L}_1) \times \mathcal{L}_2$ by $\mathcal{F}$. For a state (U, s) in the cartesian product, we define the *distance* to a set $\mathcal{U}$ of the cartesian product by $Dist_{\mathcal{U}}(U, s)$ as the shortest distance from state (U, s) to a state in $\mathcal{U}$. If $\mathcal{U}$ is unreachable, the distance is set to infinity. Formally, $Dist_{\mathcal{U}}(U, s) = \min\{|\sigma| \mid \exists (V, t) \in \mathcal{U} : (U, s) \xrightarrow{\sigma} (V, t)\}$. We generalise this to a set of states $\mathcal{V}$ as follows: $Dist_{\mathcal{U}}(\mathcal{V}) = \min\{Dist_{\mathcal{U}}(U, s) \mid (U, s) \in \mathcal{V}\}$.

Proposition 3. *For* $(U, s), (V, s)$ *in* $\mathrm{norm}_{sfr}(\mathcal{L}_1) \times \mathcal{L}_2$ *satisfying* $(U, s) \le (V, s)$ *we have* $Dist_{\mathcal{S}}(U, s) \le Dist_{\mathcal{S}}(V, s)$. *Likewise, for* $(U, s), (V, s)$ *in* $\mathrm{norm}_{fdr}(\mathcal{L}_1) \times \mathcal{L}_2$ *satisfying* $(U, s) \le (V, s)$ *we have* $Dist_{\mathcal{F}}(U, s) \le Dist_{\mathcal{F}}(V, s)$.

Proof. Follows from Lemma 3 and Proposition 2. □

We conclude with a sketch of the proof of correctness of the algorithm. The full proof can be found in [14].

Proof (Theorem 2). We prove both implications, by contraposition, for the case of failures-divergences refinement. The proof of correctness for stable failures refinement proceeds along the same lines.

- Assume that Algorithm 2 returns *false*. This occurs when the pair (*spec, impl*) satisfies the conditions of an FDR-witness, as follows from lines 7, 11 and 18 of Algorithm 2. Since *working* $\subseteq$ reachable($\mathrm{norm}_{fdr}(\mathcal{L}_1) \times \mathcal{L}_2$) and (*spec, impl*) $\in$ *working*, the FDR-witness is reachable. By Theorem 1 we find that $\mathcal{L}_1 \sqsubseteq_{fdr} \mathcal{L}_2$ fails to hold.
- Assume that an FDR-witness is reachable in $\mathrm{norm}_{fdr}(\mathcal{L}_1) \times \mathcal{L}_2$, i.e., $\mathcal{F} \ne \emptyset$. Then the following invariant holds in the while loop (lines 4–22):

$$Dist_{\mathcal{F}}(done) > Dist_{\mathcal{F}}(working) \text{ and } Dist_{\mathcal{F}}(working) = Dist_{\mathcal{F}}(antichain).$$

Towards a contradiction, assume Algorithm 2 returns *true*. This can only be the case when *working* is empty. Upon termination of the while loop, $Dist_{\mathcal{F}}(working) = Dist_{\mathcal{F}}(\emptyset) = \infty$. By the above invariants, $Dist_{\mathcal{F}}(working) = Dist_{\mathcal{F}}(antichain)$. Since $\iota = (\{s \in S_1 \mid \iota_1 \xrightarrow{\epsilon}_1 s\}, \iota_2) \in antichain$ and $Dist_{\mathcal{F}}(\iota) < \infty$, we also have $Dist_{\mathcal{F}}(antichain) < \infty$. Contradiction. □

We remark that the correctness of the algorithm is independent of the search order that is used. That is, replacing the data structure for *working* with a FIFO queue results in a breadth-first search strategy and does not impair the correctness of the algorithm. As explained in [17], breadth-first search has the advantage to yield the shortest possible counterexamples. Reconstructing such counterexamples can be done efficiently by recording, for each state stored in *working*, its breadth-first search level. We close this section by briefly returning to Example 3.

Example 5 Reconsider the family of transition systems of Example 3. Contrary to the original algorithm, the improved algorithm will, in each iteration, only add a single successor state to *working*, because every other successor will already be part of *antichain*. This results in *working* containing $\mathcal{O}(1)$ entries; *antichain* will be queried $\mathcal{O}(n \cdot k)$ times. Compared to the original algorithm, this reduces overhead for the depth-first search strategy by a factor $n \cdot k$ in the working stack size and by a factor k in the number of antichain checks. For the breadth-first search strategy, the *working* size is reduced by a factor k^n and the *antichain* checks by a factor k^n/n.   □

6   Experimental Validation

We have conducted several benchmarks to compare the run time of both algorithms to show that solving the identified issues actually improves the run time performance in practice.

For this purpose we have implemented a depth-first and breadth-first variant of both Algorithms 1 and 2 in a branch of the mCRL2[2] tool set [5] as part of the `ltscompare` tool, which is implemented in C++. The implementation of the *working* and *antichain* operations are the same. For the implementation of refusals in Algorithm 1 we follow the definition of [21] (see also Footnote 1 on page 4), implementing refusals for any state, whereas for Algorithm 2 we follow Definition 3. The source modifications and experiments can be obtained from the downloadable package [15].

The experiments we consider are taken from three sources. First, Example 3 for exposing the performance overhead of the original algorithm. Second, several *linearisability tests* of concurrent data structures for more practical benchmarks. These models have been taken from [16], and consist of six implementations of concurrent data types that, when *trace-refining* their specifications, are guaranteed to be linearisable. As in [21], we approximate trace-refinement by the stronger stable failures refinement. For these models, the implementation and specification pairs are based on the same descriptions; the difference between the two is that the specification uses a simple construct to guarantee that each method of the concurrent data structure executes atomically. This significantly reduces the non-determinism and the number of transitions in the specification models.

Finally, an industrial model of a control system modelled in the Dezyne language [3] that first exposed the performance issues in practice. The industrial example is of a more traditional flavour in which the specification is an abstract

---

[2]   www.mcrl2.org.

description of the behaviours at the external interface of a control system, and the implementation is a detailed model that interacts with underlying services to implement the expected interface. For reasons of confidentiality, the industrial model cannot be made available.

All measurements have been performed on a machine with an Intel Core i7-7700HQ CPU 2.80 Ghz and a 16 GiB memory limit imposed by `ulimit -Sv 16777216`.

6.1 Benchmarking Example 3

Example 3 has been benchmarked for all combinations of $k, n \leq 500$, where k and n are multiples of 10, checking stable failures refinement between equivalent LTSs, i.e., $\mathcal{L}_n^k \sqsubseteq_{\text{sfr}} \mathcal{L}_n^k$. Figure 1 shows the run time performance (in seconds) of the depth-first variant of Algorithm 1 on the left and Algorithm 2 on the right.

The plots match the asymptotic growth as stated in Example 3, illustrating a factor k speed-up of our algorithm compared to the original one. A comparison of the performance of breadth-first search is infeasible as the original algorithm already runs into the memory limit for small k and n, whereas for Algorithm 2 there is only little difference between the depth-first and breadth-first variants.

Note that due to the absence of τ-transitions, there is no performance difference in the computation of refusals in both algorithms. Consequently, the difference in performance is entirely due to the different way of inspecting and extending *working*.

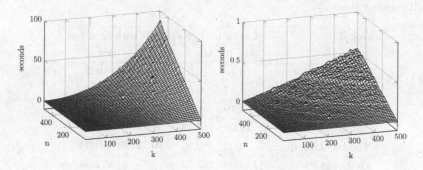

Fig. 1. The run time performance (in seconds) of Example 3 for depth-first search (left: original algorithm, right: our improved algorithm).

6.2 Benchmarking Practical Examples

Our next batch of experiments consists of more typical refinement checks, assessing whether the behaviours of the implementations are in line with the behaviours prescribed by their specifications. Characteristics of the state spaces are listed in Table 1.

Table 1. The size of the state space for each specification and associated implementation.

Model	Ref.	Specification		$\sqsubseteq_{sfr}$	Implementation	
		#states	#transitions		#states	#transitions
Coarse set	[11]	50 488	64 729	Yes	55 444	145 043
Fine-grained set	[11]	3 720	3 305	Yes	5 077	9 006
Lazy set	[11]	3 565	3 980	Yes	24 496	41 431
Optimistic set	[11]	25 435	28 154	Yes	234 332	389 344
Non-blocking queue	[19]	1 248	1 473	No	3 030	5 799
Treiber stack	[20]	87 389	124 740	Yes	205 634	564 862
Industrial		24	45	Yes	24 551	45 447

The run time performance of both algorithms (both depth-first and breadth-first) can be found in Table 2. The run times we report are averages obtained from five runs. As illustrated by the figures in that table, we see small improvements of our algorithm over the original algorithm for depth-first search, whereas the improvements for breadth-first search are dramatic.

Table 2. Run time comparison between Algorithms 1 and 2 using both a depth-first and breadth-first search strategy. All run times are in seconds; † indicates an out-of-memory issue indicating that the algorithm failed to complete within the imposed 16 GiB memory limit.

Model	Depth-first (sec.)		Breadth-first (sec.)	
	Alg. 1	Alg. 2	Alg. 1	Alg. 2
Coarse set	9.15	8.61	†	9.06
Fine-grained set	0.37	0.32	†	0.46
Lazy set	1.19	1.02	†	1.26
Optimistic set	16.96	14.13	†	22.67
Non-blocking queue	0.03	0.02	0.17	0.09
Treiber stack	148.39	137.52	†	352.59
Industrial	1.36	0.15	296.29	0.17

To better understand the reason behind the performance gains we obtain, we report on the maximal size of *working* and *antichain*, and the number of successful and unsuccessful antichain membership tests; see Table 3. We only report on metrics for the breadth-first search strategy; the figures for the depth-first search strategy for both algorithms are similar; see [14].

Table 3. Metrics for the breadth-first search strategy experiments. For the original algorithm most of these figures are *under-approximations* due to the out-of-memory issue. All values we report on are in thousands (*i.e.*, the actual number is obtained by multiplying with 10^3).

Model	max size *working*		max size *antichain*		*antichain*-hits		*antichain*-misses	
	Alg. 1	Alg. 2	Alg. 1	Alg. 2	Alg. 1	Alg. 2	Alg. 1	Alg. 2
Coarse set	4 710.3	3.4	3.6	55.4	13.9	96.2	7 807.4	60.3
Fine-grained set	6 604.5	0.4	1.9	5.1	180.7	7.2	15 547.9	9.7
Lazy set	6 726.4	1.7	4.3	24.5	130.5	24.3	14 852.8	35.2
Optimistic set	6 366.5	15.2	4.4	234.4	38.7	292.5	14 238.0	434.2
Non-blocking queue	6.3	0.3	0.3	2.7	3.1	342.6	14.6	4.0
Treiber stack	5 829.9	139.2	4.8	214.8	76.1	2 411.6	8 340.6	1 523.8
Industrial	549.2	224.3	43.1	43.1	54 591.1	36.4	12 888.4	43.1

For the breadth-first search strategy, the fact that the original algorithm delays adding state pairs to the antichain induces an enormous overhead in the size of *working* due to the many failing antichain checks. This can be seen from the large size of *working* and the small size of *antichain*. Because of these differences in size, most antichain membership tests fail in the original algorithm. The situation is largely reversed in our improved algorithm, explaining the substantial performance improvements we observe. Since the original algorithm for failures-divergences refinement is incorrect, we only compared the performance of both algorithms for stable failures refinement. The performance of our failures-divergences refinement algorithm is comparable to our stable failures refinement algorithm; we refer to [14] for further details. In [14], we also performed additional experiments which show that further run time improvements can be obtained by applying divergence-preserving branching bisimulation [7] minimisation as a preprocessing step to refinement checking.

7   Conclusions

Our study of the antichain-based algorithms for deciding stable failures refinement and failures-divergences refinement presented in [21] revealed that the failures-divergences refinement algorithm is incorrect; both algorithms perform suboptimally when implemented using a depth-first search strategy and poorly when implemented using a breadth-first search strategy. Moreover, both violate the claimed antichain property. We have proposed alternative algorithms for which we showed correctness and which utilise proper antichains. Our experiments indicate significant performance improvements for deciding stable failures refinement and a performance of deciding failures-divergences refinement that is comparable to deciding stable failures refinement.

References

1. Abdulla, P.A., Chen, Y.-F., Holík, L., Mayr, R., Vojnar, T.: When simulation meets antichains. In: Esparza, J., Majumdar, R. (eds.) TACAS 2010. LNCS, vol. 6015, pp. 158–174. Springer, Heidelberg (2010). https://doi.org/10.1007/978-3-642-12002-2_14
2. Bergstra, J.A., Klop, J.W., Olderog, E.: Failures without chaos: a new process semantics for fair abstraction. In: Wirsing, M. (ed.) IFIP TC 2/WG 2.2 1986, pp. 77–104, North-Holland (1987)
3. van Beusekom, R., et al.: Formalising the Dezyne modelling language in mCRL2. In: Petrucci, L., Seceleanu, C., Cavalcanti, A. (eds.) FMICS/AVoCS -2017. LNCS, vol. 10471, pp. 217–233. Springer, Cham (2017). https://doi.org/10.1007/978-3-319-67113-0_14
4. Brookes, S.D., Roscoe, A.W.: An improved failures model for communicating processes. In: Brookes, S.D., Roscoe, A.W., Winskel, G. (eds.) CONCURRENCY 1984. LNCS, vol. 197, pp. 281–305. Springer, Heidelberg (1985). https://doi.org/10.1007/3-540-15670-4_14
5. Bunte, O., et al.: The mCRL2 toolset for analysing concurrent systems. In: Vojnar, T., Zhang, L. (eds.) TACAS 2019. LNCS, vol. 11428, pp. 21–39. Springer, Cham (2019). https://doi.org/10.1007/978-3-030-17465-1_2
6. Gibson-Robinson, T., Armstrong, P., Boulgakov, A., Roscoe, A.W.: FDR3—a modern refinement checker for CSP. In: Ábrahám, E., Havelund, K. (eds.) TACAS 2014. LNCS, vol. 8413, pp. 187–201. Springer, Heidelberg (2014). https://doi.org/10.1007/978-3-642-54862-8_13
7. van Glabbeek, R.J., Luttik, B., Trcka, N.: Branching bisimilarity with explicit divergence. Fundam. Inform. 93(4), 371–392 (2009). https://doi.org/10.3233/FI-2009-109
8. van Glabbeek, R.J.: Personal Communication, 7 January 2019
9. Glabbeek, R.: A branching time model of CSP. In: Gibson-Robinson, T., Hopcroft, P., Lazić, R. (eds.) Concurrency, Security, and Puzzles. LNCS, vol. 10160, pp. 272–293. Springer, Cham (2017). https://doi.org/10.1007/978-3-319-51046-0_14
10. Gomes, A.O., Butterfield, A.: Modelling the haemodialysis machine with Circus. In: Butler, M., Schewe, K.-D., Mashkoor, A., Biro, M. (eds.) ABZ 2016. LNCS, vol. 9675, pp. 409–424. Springer, Cham (2016). https://doi.org/10.1007/978-3-319-33600-8_34
11. Herlihy, M., Shavit, N.: The Art of Multiprocessor Programming. Morgan Kaufmann (2008)
12. Hoare, C.: Communicating Sequential Processes. Prentice-Hall, Upper Saddle River (1985)
13. Kanellakis, P.C., Smolka, S.A.: CCS expressions, finite state processes, and three problems of equivalence. Inf. Comput. 86(1), 43–68 (1990). https://doi.org/10.1016/0890-5401(90)90025-D
14. Laveaux, M., Groote, J.F., Willemse, T.A.C.: Correct and efficient antichain algorithms for refinement checking. CoRR abs/1902.09880 (2019)
15. Laveaux, M.: Downloadable sources and benchmarks for the experimental validation (2019). https://doi.org/10.5281/zenodo.2573095
16. Paval, R.: Modeling and verifying concurrent data structures. Master's thesis, Eindhoven University of Technology (2018). https://research.tue.nl/files/93882157/Thesis_Roxana_Paval.pdf

17. Roscoe, A.W.: Model-checking CSP. In: Roscoe, A.W. (ed.) A Classical Mind: Essays in Honour of C.A.R. Hoare, Chap. 21, pp. 353–378. Prentice Hall International (UK) Ltd. (1994)
18. Roscoe, A.W.: Understanding Concurrent Systems. Texts in Computer Science. Springer, London (2010). https://doi.org/10.1007/978-1-84882-258-0
19. Shann, C., Huang, T., Chen, C.: A practical nonblocking queue algorithm using compare-and-swap. In: ICPADS 2000, pp. 470–475. IEEE Computer Society (2000). https://doi.org/10.1109/ICPADS.2000.857731
20. Treiber, R.K.: Systems programming: coping with parallelism. International Business Machines Incorporated. Thomas J. Watson Research (1986)
21. Wang, T., et al.: More anti-chain based refinement checking. In: Aoki, T., Taguchi, K. (eds.) ICFEM 2012. LNCS, vol. 7635, pp. 364–380. Springer, Heidelberg (2012). https://doi.org/10.1007/978-3-642-34281-3_26

Towards Verified Blockchain Architectures: A Case Study on Interactive Architecture Verification

Diego Marmsoler[(✉)]

Technische Universität München, Munich, Germany
diego.marmsoler@tum.de

Abstract. With the emergence of cryptocurrencies, Blockchain architectures have become more and more important. In such architectures, components maintain and exchange a list of records in a way which makes the entries persistent, i.e., resistant to modifications. Thereby, the architecture is dynamic in the sense that components may join or leave the network and connections between them may change over time. The dynamic nature of Blockchain architectures makes their verification a challenge, since it involves reasoning about potentially unbounded number of components. To this end, we developed FACTUM, an approach for the specification and interactive verification of dynamic architectures based on the interactive theorem prover Isabelle. In this paper we report on the outcome of applying the approach to formally specify a version of Blockchain architectures and verify that the list entries of such architectures are indeed persistent.

Keywords: Blockchain · Interactive theorem proving ·
Dynamic architectures · FACTUM · Isabelle

1 Introduction

The concept of Blockchain was first introduced with the invention of the Bitcoin cryptocurrency by a person (or group) known as Nakamoto in 2008 [1]. Since then, the technology found several other applications, especially in the domain of cryptocurrencies [2]. However, the technology seems promising also for other domains, such as the medical [3], land management [4], business process management [5], or even identity management [6]. Usually, the term *"blockchain"* refers to a list of records, so-called *blocks*, which contain actual data elements. A *Blockchain architecture*, on the other hand, consists of a network of so-called *nodes*, in which every node maintains a copy of the blockchain and continuously exchanges its copy with other nodes. Thereby, blockchains are required to be *persistent*, i.e., entries should be resistant to modifications. To achieve this, nodes are required to follow a certain protocol consisting of several, so-called, *consensus rules*.

© IFIP International Federation for Information Processing 2019
Published by Springer Nature Switzerland AG 2019
J. A. Pérez and N. Yoshida (Eds.): FORTE 2019, LNCS 11535, pp. 204–223, 2019.
https://doi.org/10.1007/978-3-030-21759-4_12

Blockchain architectures are an instance of a more general class of architectures called dynamic architectures [7]. In such architectures, components may join or leave the architecture and connections between components can change over time. This dynamics makes the verification of such architectures a challenge, since it involves reasoning about an unbounded number of components.

In an attempt to address this problem, we developed FACTUM [8], an approach for the specification and verification of such architectures. A FACTUM specification consists of three main parts:

- A specification of the involved data types in terms of abstract datatypes.
- A specification of the involved types of components in terms of interfaces and corresponding assertions about the behavior of components of a certain type.
- A set of architectural assertions to specify component activation and reconfiguration of connections between components.

A FACTUM specification can be systematically transferred to a corresponding Isabelle [9] theory where it is subject to interactive verification.

While the general FACTUM approach was already introduced in [8], the focus of [8] was the presentation and discussion of the specification techniques and the algorithm to map a FACTUM specification to a corresponding Isabelle locale. To this end, we demonstrated the algorithm by means of three simple examples: a Singleton architecture, a Publisher-Subscriber architecture, and a Blackboard architecture, amounting up to 500 lines of Isabelle code. With this paper, we build on the work described in [8] and evaluate the approach on a larger case study. To this end, we applied the approach to specify Blockchain architectures based on the description provided in [1] and verify persistency of confirmed blocks. With this paper, we report on the outcome of applying FACTUM for the specification and verification of Blockchain architectures according to [1]. Thus, the contribution of the paper is twofold:

- It describes a case study for FACTUM, which reveals important insights about the use of FACTUM for the verification of dynamic architectures.
- It provides a formal specification of Blockchain architectures, which is guaranteed to resist double spend attacks.

In total, the specification consists of 12 assumptions for Blockchain architectures and verification required roughly 3500 lines of Isabelle/HOL code.

In the next section, we provide some background on Blockchains (Sect. 2) and the FACTUM approach (Sect. 3). We then present a possible specification of Blockchain architectures (Sect. 4) and describe our formalization and verification of the persistence property for blockchain entries (Sect. 5). We continue with a discussion of related work (Sect. 7) in the area of formalizations of blockchain-related concepts and verification of consensus algorithms. We conclude our presentation with a summary of major results and a discussion of its implications as well as directions for future work (Sect. 8).

2   Blockchain Architectures

Blockchain architectures were first introduced with the invention of the Bitcoin cryptocurrency [1]. In cryptocurrencies, a digital coin is usually passed from one owner to the next one by digitally signing an electronic transaction. To ensure that coins are only spent once, a payee has to know whether a received coin is already spent or not at the time he receives it. This problem is known as the *double spend problem* and before the invention of Blockchain, it was solved using a central, trusted identity, which knew every transaction of the system and confirmed that a coin was not already spent. In an attempt to avoid such central authorities, Bitcoin proposed a system called Blockchain to solve the double spend problem in a distributed, peer-to-peer network. To this end, the network stores a continuously growing list of persistent entries, which contain the actual money transactions. The list is shared among all participants of the network and by inspecting it, a node can independently verify that a coin was not already spent. In this paper, we call such a network a *Blockchain architecture* and in the following we summarize some basic concepts of such architectures. Thereby, we follow the informal description provided in [1].

Blockchain. The term "blockchain" usually refers to the major data structure involved in a Blockchain architecture: a list of records aka. *blocks*. Blocks, on the other hand, contain the actual data elements, for example, money transactions in cryptocurrency applications. Blocks can be added on top of the chain and verified by a process known as *mining*. In Bitcoin, for example, mining involves the guessing of a random number (a so-called *nonce*), adding it to a candidate block and checking whether the corresponding hash exhibits a certain form (starting with a certain number of zeros). This makes mining of a new block computationally expensive, since it usually requires many guesses (and subsequent hashings) to find a number which produces the right hash. On the other hand, ensuring that a given block was indeed successfully mined remains computationally cheap (it only requires a single hashing).

Consensus. In a Blockchain architecture, every node maintains a local copy of the blockchain, which it exchanges with its peers. Due to the distributed nature, it may happen that two different blocks are added concurrently, resulting in two different versions of the blockchain available in the network. In order to reach a *consensus* on which version is the "right" one, a Blockchain architecture usually comes with a strategy of how to select the right version from a set of competing blockchains. This rule is applied by every *honest* node of the network and should guarantee that the nodes eventually reach a consensus.

Consensus Rules. There are several different types of strategies used to reach consensus, such as proof-of-work [1] or proof-of-stake [2]. In the proposed specification, we rely on the *proof-of-work* concept also used by Bitcoin and related applications. It is based on the observation that the number of blocks in a blockchain usually represents the amount of computing power involved to build this chain. Thus, the largest chain from a set of competing blockchains must be the one accepted by the majority of the network. Thus, if a honest node is facing two versions of a blockchain, it is required to always choose the longer one.

Confirmation Blocks. In a proof-of-work network, every CPU gets one vote and majority decisions can usually only be manipulated if one entity owns more than 50% of the computing power of the network. This might not be true, however, for blocks added to the blockchain only recently. A single node may just be lucky and guess the right nonce fast, without investing a lot of computational power. To cope with such lucky guesses, one usually waits for some blocks to be mined on top of the block containing a certain transaction, to accept this transaction as completed. These blocks are called *confirmation blocks* and in Bitcoin, for example, it is suggested to wait for at least six confirmation blocks to accept a transaction as completed [10].

3 FACTum

FACTUM [8] is an approach for the formal specification and interactive verification of dynamic architectures. It consists of a formal system model for dynamic architectures, techniques to specify architectures over this model, an algorithm to map the specification to a corresponding Isabelle theory, and an Isabelle-based framework to support the interactive verification of architecture specifications. FACTUM is also implemented in terms of an Eclipse/EMF application called FACTUM Studio [11] which supports a user in the development of architecture specifications.

3.1 System Model

In FACTUM, an architecture is modeled in terms of *sets* of so-called *architecture traces* [7, 12], i.e., streams [13] of architecture snapshots. Thereby, an *architecture snapshot* consists of a set of (active) components with their ports valuated by messages and connections between the ports of the components. Moreover, components of a certain type may be parameterized by a set of messages.

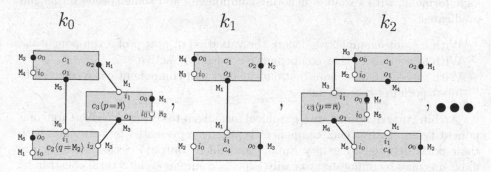

Fig. 1. Architecture trace with its first three architecture snapshots.

Example 1 (Architecture trace). Assuming that M_1, M_2, ... are sets of messages. Figure 1 depicts an architecture trace t with corresponding architecture snapshots $t(0) = k_0$, $t(1) = k_1$, and $t(2) = k_2$. Architecture snapshot k_0, for example, consists of three active components: c_1, c_2, and c_3. Component c_3 is parameterized with a parameter p with value M. It has two input ports i_0 and i_1, valuated with messages M_2 and M_1, respectively. Moreover, it has two output ports o_0 and o_1, valuated with messages M_1 and M_3, respectively.   □

Note that the model allows components to be valuated by a set of messages, rather than just a single message, at each point in time. Moreover, components can be activated and deactivated and connections between them may change over time. The model of architecture traces is also implemented by a corresponding Isabelle/HOL theory, which is described in [14].

3.2   Specifying Dynamic Architectures

FACTUM provides several techniques to support the formal specification of dynamic architectures [8]:

- First, the data types involved in an architecture are specified in terms of algebraic specifications [15].
- Then, a set of interfaces is specified graphically using architecture diagrams.
- Component types are then created by adding constraints about component behavior to the corresponding interfaces.
- Finally, a set of architectural assertions is added to specify constraints about component activation and deactivation as well as interconnection.

A FACTUM specification comes with a formal semantics in a denotational style, which is described in [16]. To this end, each specification is interpreted by a corresponding set of architecture traces.

Constraints about component behavior are specified in terms of *behavior trace assertions*, i.e., first order linear temporal logic formulæ using ports of the interfaces as free variables. Architectural constraints are specified in terms of *architecture trace assertions*. These are also a type of first order linear temporal logic formulæ, with variables denoting components and some special terms and predicates:

- With $c.p$, for example, we denote the valuation of port p of a component c.
- With ⸨c⸩ we denote that component c is currently active.
- With $c.o \rightsquigarrow c'.i$ we denote that output port o of component c is connected to input port i of component c'.

Architecture diagrams are a graphical formalism to specify interfaces for component types. To this end, component types are represented by rectangles with their ports denoted by empty (input) and filled (output) circles. Architecture diagrams may be annotated to easily express common architectural constraints:

Activation annotations can be added to component types, to specify upper and lower bounds for the number of active components of the corresponding type.

Connection annotations are expressed in terms of annotated lines between the ports of component types, to express upper and lower bounds for connections between the ports of corresponding components.

Note that activation and connection annotations are actually just synonyms for certain architectural assertions and may also be expressed using architecture trace assertions described above.

3.3 Verifying Dynamic Architectures

FACTUM comes with an algorithm to map a given specification to a corresponding Isabelle theory, where it is subject to formal verification. To support the verification, FACTUM provides a framework for the interactive verification of architecture specifications in Isabelle/HOL [14]. Among other things, the framework implements a calculus to support reasoning about component behavior in a dynamic environment [17].

4 Formalizing Blockchain Architectures

In the following, we present our formalization of Blockchain architectures in FACTUM.

4.1 Data Types and Ports

As described in Sect. 2, a key data type for Blockchain architectures is the *blockchain* itself. In the following, we first formalize a blockchain data structure by means of algebraic datatypes. Then, we specify two types of ports to send and receive blockchains, respectively.

Blockchains. A blockchain is modeled as a parametric list, in which the nature of the list entries (the blocks) depends on the concrete application context of the pattern. In cryptocurrency applications, for example, a block is usually a set of transactions. In other applications, however, blocks could be of a different type.

Figure 2a depicts a specification of blockchains by means of an abstract data type specification. First, a parametric sort $\langle B \rangle BC$ is introduced as a synonym for a corresponding list. Thereby, the type of blocks is denoted with type parameter B. In addition, we specify a function symbol MAX for blockchains, which takes a set of blockchains, and returns a blockchain with maximal length. Thus, we require two characteristic properties for MAX. Eq. (1) requires that a maximal blockchain of a set of blockchains BC is part of BC itself. In addition, Eq. (2) requires that MAX is indeed maximal, i.e., that the length of every other blockchain of the corresponding set BC is less or equal to the length of MAX. Note that $MAX(BC)$ is guaranteed to exist, whenever $BC \neq \emptyset$ and BC is *finite*.

Port Types. Figure 2b specifies two types of ports which can be used to exchange blockchains: *pin* for input ports and *pout* for output ports. They, will be used later on for the specification of component type interfaces.

DTSpec Blockchain	imports ⟨B⟩LIST as ⟨B⟩BC
MAX :	$\wp(\langle B\rangle BC) \to \langle B\rangle BC$
flex BC :	$\wp(\langle B\rangle BC)$
bc :	BC
$MAX(BC) \in BC$	(1)
$\forall bc \in BC : \#bc \le \#MAX(BC)$	(2)

(a) Data type specification.

PSpec BPort	
pin :	⟨B⟩BC
$pout$:	⟨B⟩BC

(b) Port specification.

Fig. 2. Data types and ports for Blockchain architectures.

4.2 Component Types

As described in Sect. 2, the components involved in a Blockchain architecture are called *nodes*. In the following, we first describe the syntactic interface of such a node component. Then, we introduce some auxiliary definitions for nodes. Finally, we provide a set of characteristic properties for a node's behavior.

Interfaces. The architecture diagram depicted in Fig. 3 is parameterized by a number of confirmation blocks *cb* and specifies the syntactic interface of Blockchain nodes. Actually, the diagram also contains a graphical representation of a connection constraint as well as the definition of three auxiliary definitions for nodes. For now, we may just ignore these additional aspects and focus on the description of the interface. We will, however, come back to the auxiliary definitions in the next section and we will discuss the connection constraint later on in Sect. 4.3.

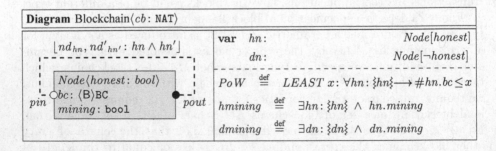

Fig. 3. Architecture diagram for Blockchain architectures.

Recall that a node in a Blockchain may either be honest or dishonest. Thus, a node is parameterized by a boolean value *honest*, which means that every component of type node is associated with a boolean value, which determines its trustworthiness. In addition, a node has two state variables: variable *bc* keeps a local copy of the blockchain and variable *mining* signals the mining of a new block. Finally, a node may exchange blockchains via its input port *pin* and output port *pout*.

Auxiliary Definitions. To support subsequent development, the right hand side of Fig. 3 introduces three auxiliary definitions for nodes: honest proof-of-work and honest/dishonest mining.

Honest Proof-of-Work. Honest proof-of-work (*PoW*) represents the *maximal* proof-of-work, currently available in the honest community. Since proof-of-work corresponds to the length of a blockchain (Sect. 2), honest proof-of-work is defined as the least upper bound for the length of honest blockchains, i.e. blockchains of active ($\{hn\}$) and honest (*Node[honest]*) nodes. Note the use of the definite description operator *LEAST* to denote the *least* element x which satisfies a certain condition.

Honest and Dishonest Mining. Honest mining (*hmining*) is a predicate to denote the successful mining by some honest node. Similarly, dishonest mining (*dmining*) signals the mining by some dishonest node. Both predicates are interpreted over an architecture state and require the existence of a honest/dishonest node, which currently finished mining. Honest and dishonest mining play an important role for the formalization of a fundamental assumption for Blockchain architectures later on.

Behavior. The behavior of nodes is formalized in terms of behavior trace assertions (described in Sect. 3).

Honest Nodes. The behavior of honest nodes is specified in Fig. 4 (with $\bigcirc P$ and $\Box P$ we denote taht P is true in the next state or in all future states, respectively). First, we introduce several variables to denote single blocks (b) and blockchains (c and c'). Note the distinction between "flexible" and "rigid" variables: while "flexible" variables may be newly interpreted at each point in time, "rigid" variables keep their value over time. Then, we require three assertions for a honest node's behavior: Eq. (3) requires that a new node is initialized by the empty blockchain while Eq. (4) requires that every honest node always forwards a copy of its local blockchain to the network through its output port *pout*. Equation (5) formalizes the consensus rule for honest nodes, which (according to Sect. 2) requires that a honest node always takes the blockchain with maximal proof-of-work as the current one, i.e, if a honest node receives a blockchain on its input with more proof-of-work than its own blockchain, then it will accept that blockchain as the current one. Its formalization consists of two parts: The antecedent characterizes the blockchain taken by a honest node:

$$c = \begin{cases} MAX(pin) & \text{if } \exists c' \in pin \colon \#c' > \#bc, \\ bc & \text{else.} \end{cases}$$

Since the proof-of-work for a blockchain is given by its length, the property fixes a blockchain c, which is either a maximal blockchain from its input port *pin* (for the case that it is strictly longer than its own blockchain), or its own blockchain bc (for the case that no blockchain from its input is longer than its own blockchain). The consequent formalizes the mining process:

$$\bigcirc\left(\neg mining \wedge bc = c \vee mining \wedge \exists b \colon bc = c@b\right).$$

Thereby, a honest node may either mine a new block (*mining*), append it to c and take the resulting chain as its current blockchain bc, or it may not mine any new block ($\neg mining$) and just set c as its current blockchain bc.

BSpec Blockchain	**for** *Node⟨honest⟩* **of** Blockchain
flex b :	B
c' :	BC⟨B⟩
rig c :	BC⟨B⟩
$bc = []$	(3)
$\square(pout = bc)$	(4)
$\square\left(c = \begin{cases} MAX(pin) & \text{if } \exists c' \in pin \colon \#c' > \#bc, \\ bc & \text{else.} \end{cases}\right.$ $\longrightarrow \bigcirc\left(\neg mining \wedge bc = c \vee mining \wedge \exists b \colon bc = c@b\right)\Big)$	(5)

Fig. 4. Specification of behavior for honest nodes.

Dishonest Nodes. The attacker model is given by the specification of the behavior for dishonest nodes in Fig. 5. Similar as for honest nodes, Eq. (6) requires that a new node is initialized by the empty blockchain. Additional behavior is characterized by Eq. (7). Note that, compared to honest nodes, dishonest nodes may not follow the consensus rules. Thus, while honest nodes always take the blockchain with the most proof-of-work as their current blockchain, dishonest nodes may take every blockchain from its input as their current one. Moreover, in contrast to honest nodes, dishonest nodes may also drop elements from a blockchain, thus trying to modify a blockchain's history. The formalization consists of two parts. The antecedent first characterizes a blockchain c:

$$c \in (pin \cup \{bc\})$$

The consequent is similar to the one for honest nodes:

$$\bigcirc\big(\neg mining \wedge bc \sqsubseteq c \vee mining \wedge \exists b\colon \ bc = c@b\big)$$

Note that, due to computing restrictions, even dishonest nodes may at most mine one single block at a time. Thus, the mining case is indeed the same as for honest nodes. The difference, however, comes with the case in which no new block is mined. While, for such a case, honest nodes are required to take c as their current blockchain, dishonest nodes may take an arbitrary prefix of c as their current blockchain.

BSpec Blockchain	**for** $Node\langle\neg honest\rangle$ **of** Blockchain
flex $\quad b\colon$	B
rig $\quad c\colon$	BC$\langle$B$\rangle$
$bc = []$	(6)
$\square\Big(c \in (pin \cup \{bc\}) \longrightarrow \bigcirc\big(\neg mining \wedge bc \sqsubseteq c \vee mining \wedge \exists b\colon \ bc = c@b\big)\Big)$	(7)

Fig. 5. Specification of behavior for dishonest nodes.

4.3 Architectural Constraints

Architectural constraints restrict activation and deactivation of components and connections between component ports [7,12]. They are mainly formulated in terms of architecture trace assertions, i.e., linear temporal logic formulæ, formulated over component ports[1]. Certain constraints, however, can be expressed more easily in a graphical manner, by annotating the pattern's architecture diagram. In the following, we first discuss connection constraints for Blockchain architectures. Then, we present some basic activation constraints for such architectures. Finally, we conclude the section with a description of a fundamental constraint for Blockchain architectures, which is essential to guarantee persistence of blockchain entries.

Connection Constraints. Connection constraints restrict connections between component ports and therefore they affect the topology of an architecture. For our pattern of Blockchain architectures, we require a single connection constraint, which is expressed graphically by an annotation of the architecture diagram, depicted in Fig. 3. The dashed connection between a nodes input and output ports expresses a conditional connection between ports $pout$ and pin of

---

[1] Architecture trace assertions are summarized in Sect. 3.

two (possible different) components of type node. The *minimal* condition for the connection to happen is expressed by the annotation

$$\lfloor nd_{hn}, nd'_{hn'} : hn \wedge hn' \rfloor.$$

The condition essentially requires the ports to be connected, whenever two components are *honest*. Roughly speaking, the constraint requires that every honest node is connected to every other honest node of the network. While this constraint is indeed a strong requirement, it is necessary to guarantee persistence of blockchain entries.

ASpec Basic		**for Blockchain**
flex	$bc:$	$BC\langle B \rangle$
	$nd:$	$Node\langle hn \rangle$
	$nd':$	$Node\langle hn' \rangle$
rig	$hn:$	$Node[honest]$

$$\Box\left(finite\left(\{\,nd \mid \!\!\{nd\!\}\,\}\right)\right) \tag{8}$$

$$\Box\left(\exists hn : \!\!\{hn\!\} \wedge \bigcirc\!\!\{hn\!\}\right) \tag{9}$$

$$\Box\left(\!\!\{hn\!\} \wedge hn.mining \longrightarrow \ominus\!\!\{hn\!\}\right) \tag{10}$$

$$\Box\left(\!\!\{nd\!\} \wedge bc \in nd.pin \longrightarrow \exists nd' : \!\!\{nd'\!\} \wedge nd'.bc = bc\right) \tag{11}$$

Fig. 6. Basic activation constraints for Blockchain architectures.

Basic Activation Constraints. Activation constraints affect the activation and deactivation of components of a certain type. We require four basic activation constraints for Blockchain architectures, summarized in Fig. 6 (with $\ominus P$ we denote that P was true in the previous state) and explained in more detail in the following. *Finite number of active nodes.* Our first activation property for Blockchain architectures is more of technical nature and restricts the number of active components at each point in time. By Eq. (8), we require that at each point in time, only a finite number of node components can be active. The property should be satisfied by every architecture found in practice. However, it is needed to guarantee that at every point in time, a node component receives only a finite number of blockchains which, in turn, is required to guarantee the existence of a maximal blockchain for a component's input port.

Keeping the Honest Blockchain. The second activation property we require for Blockchain architectures is needed to guarantee that the honest blockchain, i.e., the blockchain accepted by honest nodes as the "correct" one, is not lost. It is formalized by Eq. (9) and requires that at every point in time, there exists an active and honest node, which stays active for at least one time step. Thus, it is guaranteed that the current honest blockchain is stored by the honest network and does not get lost.

Mining on Most Recent Blockchain. Another basic activation property for Blockchain architectures is needed to ensure that the honest network indeed collaborates in the mining process. The property is formalized by Eq. (10) using the previous operator: it requires that whenever a honest node is mining a new block, this node was active at the time point right before the mining happened. This ensures that the node had indeed access to the most recent version of the honest blockchain and works on extending this version instead of an older one.

Closed Architecture. The last basic activation property for Blockchain architectures requires such an architecture to be closed. Equation (11) formalizes the property and requires that for every blockchain available at the input of any active node component at any point in time, there exists a corresponding active node component which provides the blockchain at its output. In other words, the property guarantees that every blockchain available in the architecture was build up by the network via the mining process and not injected from the outside.

A Fundamental Assumption for Blockchain Architectures. In the following section, we present a fundamental constraint for Blockchain architectures. Since its specification requires to express mining frequencies, we first introduce an operator to express such frequencies in LTL. The operator can be used to express statements of the form: "for every time span in which at least x states can be observed which satisfy a certain property φ, at least y states can be observed to satisfy a certain property φ'".

Definition 1 (Weak until for relative frequencies). *A truce t satisfies* $\varphi_{\ \lceil x \rceil} \mathcal{W}_{\lfloor y \rfloor} \varphi'$, *for state predicates φ and φ', at time point n, iff*

$$\exists n' \geq n \colon cc(t, n, n', \varphi') \geq y \ \wedge \ (\forall n \leq i < n' \colon cc(t, n, i, \varphi) \leq x)$$
$$\vee \ (\forall n' \geq n \colon cc(t, n, n', \varphi) \leq x),$$

with $cc(t, n, n', p) \ \overset{def}{=} \ |\{i \mid i > n \wedge i \leq n' \wedge p(t(i))\}|.$

ASpec Blockchain	for Blockchain
$\square \left(umining_{\ \lceil cb \rceil} \mathcal{W}_{\ \lfloor cb+1 \rfloor} tmining \right)$	(12)

Fig. 7. Fundamental assumption for Blockchain architectures.

In Fig. 7 we use the newly introduced operator to formalize a fundamental requirement for Blockchain architectures. Roughly speaking, the property requires that for every time span in which we can observe a number of dishonest minings which is *greater or equal* to the number of confirmation blocks cb, then we can also observe a number of honest minings which is *greater* than the number of confirmation blocks. Note that this is an important requirement needed to guarantee persistence of blockchain entries.

5   Verifying Blockchain Architectures

We verified an important property for Blockchain architectures which ensures persistence of blockchain entries.

5.1   Persistence of Blockchain Entries

As described in the introduction, Blockchain architectures were invented to solve the double spend problem in a distributed peer-to-peer network. In order to do so, blockchain entries, once accepted by the network, must be resistant to future modifications. This property is summarized by the following theorem:

Theorem 1 (Persistence of blockchain entries). *In a Blockchain architecture, the entries of honest blockchains, which are confirmed by a number of blocks greater or equal to the number of confirmation blocks, are resistant to future modifications.*

The theorem is formally specified by the architectural assertion depicted in Fig. 8 (with $\boxminus P$ we denote that P was true in all previous states). To this end, sbc denotes a blockchain which contains the entries supposed to be persistent and Eqs. (13)–(16) characterize a time point n_s, for which the property actually holds.

ASpec Save		**for Blockchain**
flex	$hn:$	$Node[honest]$
	$dn:$	$Node[\neg honest]$
	$nd:$	$Node$
rig	$hn':$	$Node[honest]$
	$sbc:$	$\langle B \rangle BC$

$$\Box\left(\left(\forall hn: (\neg\{hn'\})\; \mathcal{W}\; (\{hn'\} \wedge sbc \sqsubseteq hn'.bc)\right) \wedge \right. \tag{13}$$

$$PoW \geq \#sbc + cb\; \wedge \tag{14}$$

$$\left(\forall dn: \{dn\} \longrightarrow \#dn.bc < \#sbc\right) \wedge \tag{15}$$

$$\ominus\boxminus\left(\forall nd: \{nd\} \longrightarrow \#nd.bc < \#sbc \vee sbc \sqsubseteq nd.bc\right) \wedge \tag{16}$$

$$\longrightarrow \quad \Box\left.\left(\forall hn: \{hn\} \longrightarrow sbc \sqsubseteq hn.bc\right)\right) \tag{17}$$

Fig. 8. Specification of persistence property for Blockchain architectures.

Equation (13) requires that sbc is indeed a prefix of the blockchain of every honest node hn' at hn''s first activation after n_s. It basically ensures that the honest network is initialized with blockchains extending sbc.

Equation (14) requires the proof-of-work at time point n_s to be greater or equal to the length of sbc, increased by the number of confirmation blocks cb. This equation is required to provide the honest network with some lead over a potential attacker, which might want to change sbc. Note, however, that the assumption is indeed feasible, since Theorem 1 ensures persistence only of entries which were confirmed by cb number of blocks.

Equation (15) requires the length of the blockchain of every active and dishonest node dn to be less than the length of sbc. Together with Eq. (16), this equation ensures that a potential attacker did not prepare a "false" blockchain before time point n_s, which he could then use later on to cheat the honest network.

Equation (16) requires for every node's blockchain $nd.bc$, at every time point before n_s, that sbc is either a prefix of $nd.bc$ or that the length of $nd.bc$ is smaller than the length of sbc.

For every time point n_s, for which the above conditions hold, the property depicted in Fig. 8 guarantees that sbc will always be a prefix of every honest node's blockchain (formalized by Eq. (17)).

5.2 Verification Effort

The pattern's specification (as presented in Sect. 4) was formalized in three different Isabelle/HOL theories, which are available via the Archive of Formal Proofs in [18]:

- a theory `Auxiliary`, which contains some auxiliary results, such as custom induction rules;
- a theory `RF_LTL`, which contains a calculus for Blockchain architectures, based on counting LTL;
- a theory `Blockchain`, which is the main theory containing the actual formalization of the pattern.

Theorem 1 was then formalized as theorem *blockchain-save* in theory `Blockchain` and mechanically verified in Isabelle. Its proof consists of roughly 3 500 lines of Isabelle/Isar code and required an effort of roughly three person months (by a person with around two years of experience in using Isabelle).

6 Discussion

We admit that the specification presented in Sect. 4 is somehow idealized and some of the assumptions may not always hold. Thus, to better understand when the results can be applied, we discuss some of these assumptions in more detail.

Cryptographic Aspects. Cryptography is an important aspect when it comes to Blockchain. For example, some Blockchain implementations make extensive use of Merkle tree's [19] to ensure integrity of blockchains. With the work presented in this paper, we abstracted from cryptographic aspects. Rather, we assumed integrity of blockchains and focused on the problem of building consensus in a way to resist double spend attacks. Of course, flaws in the implementation of the integrity mechanism might lead to situations in which the results presented in this paper are not valid anymore. Thus, for such applications, one first needs to verify correctness of the employed integrity mechanism. Only then, our results can be applied to support the verification.

Probabilistic Aspects. In Blockchain, the process of mining new blocks is usually of probabilistic nature and thus, it is actually difficult to provide any "hard" guarantees. The reason why we could provide such a guarantee here, is the probabilistic nature of the assumption provided by Eq. (12). In a real-world setting, the assumption is usually only valid with a certain probability. Thus, also the corresponding guarantee, provided by Theorem 1, is only valid with a certain probability. Hence, to use the results presented in this paper for a concrete setting, one first needs to verify (or estimate) the probability of Eq. (12) to be true in this setting. This is then also the probability of Theorem 1 to be true in this setting.

Broadcast. Another limitation of the specification presented in this paper is the connection constraint provided by Fig. 3, which requires honest nodes to be always connected. While this may seem too strict, it indeed reflects a real problem in Blockchain networks, such as Bitcoin, in which "resilience to the double spending attack relies strongly on the assumption that Bitcoin's P2P network is connected, and that honest nodes are able to communicate" [20]. Thus, to ensure that Theorem 1 holds, and thus the corresponding Blockchain network indeed resists double spend attacks, the network needs to employ mechanisms to ensure a high degree of connectivity for the honest sub-network.

The Attacker Model. The attacker model presented in Fig. 5 does not allow the instantaneous modification of blocks within a blockchain. Rather, modifying an entry can only be done by first removing corresponding entries from the top of the blockchain and then to add new blocks over time. This assumption is based on two fundamental design decisions inherent in bitcoin-like Blockchain applications: First, as already discussed above, such Blockchain applications usually employ Merkle tree's to ensure integrity of blockchains. Second, adding new blocks to a blockchain is done through mining, which usually requires some time and cannot happen instantaneous.

7 Related Work

This paper provides a formalization of Blockchain architectures and a mechanized proof of an important safety property regarding integrity of blockchain entries. Thus, related work can be found in formalizations of Blockchain architectures in general, as well as verification of consensus algorithms, specifically.

7.1   Formalizations of Blockchain Concepts

There has been some work in formalizing and investigating different aspects of Blockchain technologies. A lot of research in this area is devoted to the formalization of concrete technological implementations. The Ethereum Virtual Machine and its contract language Solidity, for example, are formalized in Coq [21] and Isabelle/HOL [22], respectively. Another interesting branch of research in this area concerns the study of so-called smart contracts. Such contracts can be used to associate transactions with code, which execution is triggered by certain events. A proposal to formalize such contracts is provided by Bhargavan [23]. Approaches for their verification were made based on behavior models [24], Finite State Machines [25], or interactive theorem proving [26].

Relation to Our Work: The studies described so far report on the formalization of various types of concepts found in Blockchain technology. Thus, they provide many insights into the formalization and even mechanization of various concepts used in Blockchain. The main difference to our work lies in the scope of these studies: while they focus on the details of these different concepts, we try to integrate them at a more abstract level in a so-called Blockchain architecture. One exception here is Pirlea's recent work [27] which goes in a similar direction to our work. The authors try to come up with an abstract model of Blockchain, which we would consider a Blockchain architecture, in Coq. What is interesting is that they identify important aspects of Blockchain architectures and provide abstract notions for them. Specifically, they introduce an abstract notion of proof object and a so-called validator acceptance function, which is used to ensure validity of a block w.r.t. a specific proof object. Moreover, they abstract from the concrete consensus agreement, called Fork Choice Rule in an abstract function, which they require to form a total order between blockchains. These abstractions allow their model to be applied to various scenarios. While, with our work, we follow a similar approach, there are some notable differences: (i) First, with our implementation in Isabelle/HOL we provide an alternative framework for Isabelle/HOL users. (ii) A more important difference, however, concerns the scope of the proved property: In their work, the authors verified that a Blockchain architecture, in a consistent state, will eventually reach a consistent state again. In our work, we were rather interested in blockchain integrity, i.e., that additions to the blockchain are guaranteed to be persistent. (iii) Finally, in their work, they do not consider possible attackers. As shown in this work, these nodes may have different behavior and we were interested whether this could influence integrity.

7.2   Verification of Consensus Algorithms

Consensus mechanisms for Blockchain architectures are actually an instance of more traditional, distributed fault tolerance protocols. Such protocols were intensively studied over the last decades and mechanical verifications exist, for example, for Paxos [28,29], Raft [30,31], and the classical Two-Phase Commit [32]. More recently, work in this area focuses on the verification of more Blockchain-specific protocols. Kiayias [33], for example, proposes a verified consensus protocol based on proof-of-stake.

Relation to Our Work: The work discussed so far provides formalizations of various protocols, useful for the implementation of distributed trust. The pattern proposed and verified in this paper, however, uses a mechanism called "proof-of-work". Thus, approaches using proof-of-work are most closely related to our work and are discussed in more detail. The idea of applying proof-of-work to the problem of establishing distributed trust goes back to Nakamoto in its original bitcoin paper [1]. Here the author provides a mathematical description of the theory behind Blockchain technology and provides probabilistic bounds about certain security concerns. Garay [34,35] and Pass [36] elaborate on these ideas and identify and verify two properties of proof-of-work: *common prefix* and *chain quality*. The former is actually similar to Theorem 1 proved in this paper. While these works provide similar results to ours, there are two notable differences to our work: (i) First, the above approaches exclusively focus on probabilistic boundaries. While such boundaries are important in the area of Blockchain, we try to identify the preconditions which are required in order to establish these properties. (ii) Second, the above works were not mechanized, so far.

8   Conclusion

In this paper, we reported on the outcome of applying FACTum to specify a variant of Blockchain architectures [1] and verify that blockchains are guaranteed to be persistent for architectures implementing the specification:

- The blockchain itself is modeled as a parametric list over blocks.
- Nodes represent the types of components. They either keep a blockchain and forward copies to other nodes or they may add at most one new block through mining. Thereby, we distinguish between two types of nodes: **Honest nodes** strictly follow the consensus rules and when faced with different copies of a blockchain, they always take the longest one (containing the most amount of work) as the "correct" one. **Dishonest nodes** on the other hand, do not necessarily follow the consensus rules and may also remove blocks from any blockchain they receive, in order to attempt to modify a certain entry.
- A Blockchain architecture is parameterized by a number of confirmation blocks, i.e., a value which determines the number of blocks which need to be mined on top of a block in order to consider this block to be save.

We also propose a formalization of a desired safety property: *persistence of blockchain entries*. Finally, we (mechanically) verified the property from the specification.

Throughout the paper, we describe 11 characteristic properties for Blockchain architectures and one fundamental assumption about relative mining frequencies, which guarantee persistence of blockchain entries. The properties can be used to support the verification of Blockchain architectures. To this end, an architecture specification is verified to satisfy the properties and in return, persistence of blockchain entries is guaranteed by Theorem 1. For the case that nodes are implemented by means of statemachines, this step could even be automated using model checking techniques. In addition, the paper presents a case study about the use of FACTUM for the verification of dynamic architectures. Thereby it reveals interesting insights to direct future research. On the positive side, it shows feasibility of verifying properties for dynamically evolving architectures, even if we need to reason about unbounded number of components. On the negative side, we discovered two main weaknesses: Since the approach is based on interactive theorem proving, the effort required to verify an architecture is still relatively high. For example, the verification of the property presented in this paper required a total effort of roughly three person months. Another weakness concerns the usability of the approach in practice since verification requires expertise in interactive theorem proving, which is not always available.

Based on the outcome of this study, we derive two directions for future work: (i) One direction should focus on extending the preliminary analysis of Blockchain architectures presented in this paper. To this end it should mainly address the limitations identified in Sect. 6: partial broadcasts, cryptographic aspects, explicit consideration of probabilities. (ii) Another direction should address to extend the FACTUM approach based on the lessons learned from this case study. In particular possibilities for proof automation and proof modeling should be investigated.

Acknowledgments. We would like to thank Manfred Broy, Alexander Knapp, Maximilian Junker, and Andreas Lochbihler for their comments and helpful suggestions on earlier versions of this paper. In addition, we are grateful to all the anonymous reviewers of FORTE 2019 for suggesting many improvements to the presentation. Parts of the work on which we report in this paper was funded by the German Federal Ministry of Education and Research (BMBF) under grant no. 01Is16043A.

References

1. Nakamoto, S.: Bitcoin: a peer-to-peer electronic cash system (2008)
2. Bentov, I., Gabizon, A., Mizrahi, A.: Cryptocurrencies without proof of work. In: Clark, J., Meiklejohn, S., Ryan, P.Y.A., Wallach, D., Brenner, M., Rohloff, K. (eds.) FC 2016. LNCS, vol. 9604, pp. 142–157. Springer, Heidelberg (2016). https://doi.org/10.1007/978-3-662-53357-4_10
3. Azaria, A., Ekblaw, A., Vieira, T., Lippman, A.: MedRec: using blockchain for medical data access and permission management. In: International Conference on Open and Big Data (OBD), pp. 25–30. IEEE (2016)
4. Chavez-Dreyfuss, G.: Sweden tests blockchain technology for land registry. http://web.archive.org/web/20161024065806/www.reuters.com/article/us-sweden-blockchain-idUSKCN0Z22KV

5. Mendling, J., et al.: Blockchains for business process management-challenges and opportunities. ACM Trans. Manag. Inf. Syst. (TMIS) **9**(1), 4 (2018)

6. Yurcan, B.: How blockchain fits into the future of digital identity. http://web. archive.org/web/20170119054131/https://www.americanbanker.com/news/how-blockchain-fits-into-the-future-of-digital-identity

7. Marmsoler, D., Gleirscher, M.: Specifying properties of dynamic architectures using configuration traces. In: Sampaio, A., Wang, F. (eds.) ICTAC 2016. LNCS, vol. 9965, pp. 235–254. Springer, Cham (2016). https://doi.org/10.1007/978-3-319-46750-4_14

8. Marmsoler, D.: Hierarchical specification and verification of architectural design patterns. In: Russo, A., Schürr, A. (eds.) FASE 2018. LNCS, vol. 10802, pp. 149–168. Springer, Cham (2018). https://doi.org/10.1007/978-3-319-89363-1_9

9. Nipkow, T., Paulson, L.C., Wenzel, M.: Isabelle/HOL: A Proof Assistant for Higher-Order Logic, vol. 2283. Springer, Heidelberg (2002). https://doi.org/10. 1007/3-540-45949-9

10. The Bitcoin Community: The bitcoin wiki. http://web.archive.org/web/20181106124036/https://en.bitcoin.it/wiki/Confirmation

11. Marmsoler, D., Gidey, H.K.: FACTUM studio: a tool for the axiomatic specification and verification of architectural design patterns. In: Bae, K., Ölveczky, P.C. (eds.) FACS 2018. LNCS, vol. 11222, pp. 279–287. Springer, Cham (2018). https://doi. org/10.1007/978-3-030-02146-7_14

12. Marmsoler, D., Gleirscher, M.: On activation, connection, and behavior in dynamic architectures. Sci. Ann. Comput. Sci. **26**(2), 187–248 (2016)

13. Broy, M.: A logical basis for component-oriented software and systems engineering. Comput. J. **53**(10), 1758–1782 (2010)

14. Marmsoler, D.: A framework for interactive verification of architectural design patterns in Isabelle/HOL. In: Sun, J., Sun, M. (eds.) ICFEM 2018. LNCS, vol. 11232, pp. 251–269. Springer, Cham (2018). https://doi.org/10.1007/978-3-030-02450-5_15

15. Wirsing, M.: Algebraic specification. In: van Leeuwen, J., (ed.): Handbook of Theoretical Computer Science, vol. B, pp. 675–788. MIT Press, Cambridge, MA, USA (1990)

16. Marmsoler, D.: Axiomatic specification and interactive verification of architectural design patterns in FACTum. Dissertation, Technische Universität München, München (2019)

17. Marmsoler, D.: Towards a calculus for dynamic architectures. In: Hung, D.V., Kapur, D. (eds.) ICTAC 2017. LNCS, vol. 10580, pp. 79–99. Springer, Heidelberg (2017). https://doi.org/10.1007/978-3-319-67729-3_6

18. Marmsoler, D.: A theory of architectural design patterns. Archive of Formal Proofs, March 2018. Formal proof development. http://isa-afp.org/entries/Architectural_Design_Patterns.html

19. Merkle, R.C.: A digital signature based on a conventional encryption function. In: Pomerance, C. (ed.) CRYPTO 1987. LNCS, vol. 293, pp. 369–378. Springer, Heidelberg (1988). https://doi.org/10.1007/3-540-48184-2_32

20. Zohar, A.: Bitcoin: under the hood. Commun. ACM **58**(9), 104–113 (2015)

21. Hirai, Y.: Ethereum virtual machine for Coq (v0. 0.2). Published online on, 5 March 2017

22. Hirai, Y.: Defining the ethereum virtual machine for interactive theorem provers. In: Brenner, M., et al. (eds.) FC 2017. LNCS, vol. 10323, pp. 520–535. Springer, Cham (2017). https://doi.org/10.1007/978-3-319-70278-0_33

23. Bhargavan, K., et al.: Formal verification of smart contracts: short paper. In: Proceedings of the 2016 ACM Workshop on Programming Languages and Analysis for Security, pp. 91–96. ACM (2016)

24. Abdellatif, T., Brousmiche, K.: Formal verification of smart contracts based on users and blockchain behaviors models. In: 2018 9th IFIP International Conference on New Technologies, Mobility and Security (NTMS), pp. 1–5, February 2018

25. Mavridou, A., Laszka, A.: Tool demonstration: FSolidM for designing secure ethereum smart contracts. In: Bauer, L., Küsters, R. (eds.) POST 2018. LNCS, vol. 10804, pp. 270–277. Springer, Cham (2018). https://doi.org/10.1007/978-3-319-89722-6_11

26. Amani, S., Bégel, M., Bortin, M., Staples, M.: Towards verifying ethereum smart contract bytecode in Isabelle/HOL. In: Proceedings of the 7th ACM SIGPLAN International Conference on Certified Programs and Proofs, pp. 66–77. ACM (2018)

27. Pîrlea, G., Sergey, I.: Mechanising blockchain consensus. In: Proceedings of the 7th ACM SIGPLAN International Conference on Certified Programs and Proofs, pp. 78–90. ACM (2018)

28. Drăgoi, C., Henzinger, T.A., Zufferey, D.: PSYNC: a partially synchronous language for fault-tolerant distributed algorithms. In: Proceedings of the 43rd Annual ACM SIGPLAN-SIGACT Symposium on Principles of Programming Languages, POPL 2016, pp. 400–415. ACM, New York (2016)

29. Jaskelioff, M., Merz, S.: Proving the correctness of disk Paxos. The Archive of Formal Proofs (2005). http://afp.sf.net/entries/DiskPaxos.shtml

30. Wilcox, J.R., et al.: Verdi: a framework for formally verifying distributed system implementations. In: Proceedings of the 2015 ACM SIGPLAN Conference on Programming Language Design and Implementation (PLDI), Portland, OR (2015)

31. Woos, D., Wilcox, J.R., Anton, S., Tatlock, Z., Ernst, M.D., Anderson, T.: Planning for change in a formal verification of the raft consensus protocol. In: Proceedings of the 5th ACM SIGPLAN Conference on Certified Programs and Proofs, pp. 154–165. ACM (2016)

32. Sergey, I., Wilcox, J.R., Tatlock, Z.: Programming and proving with distributed protocols. Proc. ACM Program. Lang. 2(POPL), 28 (2017)

33. Kiayias, A., Russell, A., David, B., Oliynykov, R.: Ouroboros: a provably secure proof-of-stake blockchain protocol. In: Katz, J., Shacham, H. (eds.) CRYPTO 2017. LNCS, vol. 10401, pp. 357–388. Springer, Cham (2017). https://doi.org/10.1007/978-3-319-63688-7_12

34. Garay, J., Kiayias, A., Leonardos, N.: The bitcoin backbone protocol: analysis and applications. In: Oswald, E., Fischlin, M. (eds.) EUROCRYPT 2015. LNCS, vol. 9057, pp. 281–310. Springer, Heidelberg (2015). https://doi.org/10.1007/978-3-662-46803-6_10

35. Garay, J., Kiayias, A., Leonardos, N.: The bitcoin backbone protocol with chains of variable difficulty. In: Katz, J., Shacham, H. (eds.) CRYPTO 2017. LNCS, vol. 10401, pp. 291–323. Springer, Cham (2017). https://doi.org/10.1007/978-3-319-63688-7_10

36. Pass, R., Seeman, L., Shelat, A.: Analysis of the blockchain protocol in asynchronous networks. In: Coron, J.-S., Nielsen, J.B. (eds.) EUROCRYPT 2017. LNCS, vol. 10211, pp. 643–673. Springer, Cham (2017). https://doi.org/10.1007/978-3-319-56614-6_22

Unfolding-Based Dynamic Partial Order Reduction of Asynchronous Distributed Programs

The Anh Pham[ID], Thierry Jéron[✉][ID], and Martin Quinson[ID]

Univ. Rennes, Inria, CNRS, IRISA, Rennes, France
{the-anh.pham,thierry.jeron}@inria.fr,
martin.quinson@irisa.fr

Abstract. Unfolding-based Dynamic Partial Order Reduction (UDPOR) is a recent technique mixing Dynamic Partial Order Reduction (DPOR) with concepts of concurrency such as unfoldings to efficiently mitigate state space explosion in model-checking of concurrent programs. It is optimal in the sense that each Mazurkiewicz trace, *i.e.* a class of interleavings equivalent by commuting independent actions, is explored exactly once. This paper shows that UDPOR can be extended to verify asynchronous distributed applications, where processes both communicate by messages and synchronize on shared resources. To do so, a general model of asynchronous distributed programs is formalized in TLA+. This allows to define an independence relation, a main ingredient of the unfolding semantics. Then, the adaptation of UDPOR, involving the construction of an unfolding, is made efficient by a precise analysis of dependencies. A prototype implementation gives promising experimental results.

Keywords: Partial order · Unfolding · Distributed program · Asynchronous

1 Introduction

Developing distributed applications that run on parallel computers and communicate by message passing is hard due to their size, heterogeneity, asynchronicity and dynamicity. Besides performance, their correction is crucial but very challenging due to the complex interactions of parallel components.

Model-checking (see *e.g.* [4]) is a set of techniques allowing to verify automatically and effectively some properties on models of such systems. The principle is usually to explore all possible behaviors (states and transitions) of the system model. However, state spaces increase exponentially with the number of concurrent processes. *Unfoldings* and *Partial order reduction (POR)* are two candidate

This work has been supported by INRIA collaborative project IPL HAC-SPECIS (http://hacspecis.gforge.inria.fr/).

© IFIP International Federation for Information Processing 2019
Published by Springer Nature Switzerland AG 2019
J. A. Pérez and N. Yoshida (Eds.): FORTE 2019, LNCS 11535, pp. 224–241, 2019.
https://doi.org/10.1007/978-3-030-21759-4_13

alternative techniques born in the 90's to mitigate this state space explosion and scale to large applications.

Unfoldings (see *e.g.* [6]) is a concept of concurrency theory providing a representation of the behaviors of a model in the form of an *event structure* aggregating causal dependencies or concurrency between events (occurrence of actions), and conflicts that indicate choices in the evolution of the program. This representation may be exponentially more compact than an interleaving semantics, while still allowing to verify some properties, such as safety.

POR comprises a set of exploration techniques (see *e.g.* [8]), sharing the idea that, to detect deadlocks (and, by extension, for checking safety properties) it is sufficient to cover each *Mazurkiewicz trace*, *i.e.* a class of interleavings equivalent by commutation of consecutive *independent* actions. This state space reduction is obtained by choosing at each state, based on the independence of actions, only a subset of actions to explore (ample, stubborn or persistent sets, depending on the method), or to avoid (sleep set). *Dynamic partial order reduction* (DPOR) [7] was later introduced to combat state space explosion for stateless model-checking of software. In this context, while POR relies on a statically defined and imprecise independence relation, DPOR may be much more efficient by dynamically collecting it at run-time. Nevertheless, redundant explorations, named *sleep-set blocked* (SSB) [1], may still exist that would lead to an already visited interleaving, and detected by using sleep sets.

In the last few years, two research directions were investigated to improve DPOR. The first one tries to refine the independence relation: the more precise, the less Mazurkiewicz traces exist, thus the more efficient could be DPOR. For example [2] proposes to consider conditional independence relations where commutations are specified by constraints, while in [3] independence is built lazily, conditionally to future actions called *observers*. The other direction proposes alternatives to persistent sets, in order to minimize the number of explored interleavings. Optimality is obtained when exactly one interleaving per Mazurkiewicz trace is built. In [1] authors propose *source sets* that outperform DPOR, but optimality requires expensive computations of *wake-up trees* to avoid SSB explorations. In [16] the authors propose *unfolding-based DPOR* (UDPOR), an optimal DPOR method combining the strengths of PORs and unfoldings with the notion of *alternatives*. The approach is generalized [13] with a notion of *k-partial alternative* allowing to balance between optimal DPOR and sometimes more efficient sub-optimal DPOR.

Some approaches already try to use DPOR techniques for the verification of asynchronous distributed applications, such as MPI programs (Message Passing Interface). In the absence of model, determining global states of the system and checking equality [15] are already challenging. In [14], an approach is taken that is tight to MPI. A significant subset of MPI primitives is considered, formally specified in order to define the dependency relation, and then to use the DPOR technique of [7]. In [18], the efficiency is improved by focusing on particular deadlocks, but at the price of incompleteness.

We propose first steps to adapt UDPOR for asynchronous distributed applications. In [17] authors proposed an abstract model of distributed applications with a small set of primitives, sufficient to express most communication actions. We revise and extend this model with synchronization primitives and formally specify it in TLA+ [11]. A clear advantage of this model is its abstraction: it remains concise, but its generality allows *e.g.* the encoding of MPI primitives. Already defining a correct independence relation from this formal model is difficult, due to the variety and complex semantics of actions. In addition, making UDPOR and in particular the computation of unfoldings and extensions efficient cannot directly rely on solutions of [13], which are tuned for concurrent programs with only mutexes, thus clever algorithms need to be designed. For now we prototyped our solutions in a simplified context, but we target the Sim-Grid tool which allows to run HPC code (in particular MPI) in a simulation environment [5]. The paper is organized as follows. Section 2 recalls notions of interleaving and concurrency semantics, and how a transition system is unfolded into an event structure with respect to an independence relation. In Sect. 3 the programming model is presented together with a sketch of the independence relation. Section 4 presents the UDPOR algorithm, its adaptation to our programming model, and how to make it efficient. Finally we present a prototype implementation and its experimental evaluation.

2   Interleaving and Unfolding Semantics

The behaviors of a distributed program can be described in an interleaving semantics by a labelled transition system, or in a true concurrency semantics by an event structure. An LTS equipped with an independence relation can be unfolded into an event structure [16]. This is a main step for UDPOR.

Definition 1 (Labelled transition system). *A labelled transition system (LTS) is a tuple $T = \langle S, s_0, \Sigma, \rightarrow \rangle$ where S is the set of states, $s_0 \in S$ the initial state, Σ is the alphabet of actions, and $\rightarrow \subseteq S \times \Sigma \times S$ is the transition relation.*

We note $s \xrightarrow{a} s'$ when $(s, a, s') \in \rightarrow$ and extend the notation to execution sequences: $s \xrightarrow{a_1 \cdot a_2 \cdots a_n} s'$ if $\exists s_0 = s, s_1, \ldots s_n = s'$ with $s_{i-1} \xrightarrow{a}_i s_i$ for $i \in [1, n]$. For a state s in S, we denote by $enabled(s) = \{a \in \Sigma : \exists s' \in S, s \xrightarrow{a} s'\}$ the set of actions enabled at s.

Independence is a key notion in both POR techniques and unfoldings, linked to the possibility to commute actions:

Definition 2 (Commutation and independence). *Two actions a_1, a_2 of an LTS $T = \langle S, s_0, \Sigma, \rightarrow \rangle$ commute in a state s if they satisfy the two conditions:*

– executing one action does not enable nor disable the other one:

$$a_1 \in enabled(s) \wedge s \xrightarrow{a_1} s' \implies (a_2 \in enabled(s) \Leftrightarrow a_2 \in enabled(s')) \quad (1)$$

– *their execution order does not change the overall result:*

$$a_1, a_2 \in enabled(s) \implies (s \xrightarrow{a_1 \cdot a_2} s' \wedge s \xrightarrow{a_2 \cdot a_1} s'' \implies s' = s'') \qquad (2)$$

A relation $I \subseteq \Sigma \times \Sigma$ *is a* valid independence relation *if it under-approximates commutation, i.e.* $\forall a_1, a_2, I(a_1, a_2)$ *implies that* a_1 *and* a_2 *commute in all states. Conversely* a_1 *and* a_2 *are* dependent *and we note* $D(a_1, a_2)$ *when* $\neg(I(a_1, a_2))$.

A *Mazurkiewicz trace* is an equivalence class of executions (or interleavings) of an LTS $\mathcal{T}$ obtained by commuting adjacent independent actions. By the second item of Definition 2, all these interleavings reach a unique state. The principle of all DPOR approaches is precisely to reduce the state space exploration while covering at least one execution per Mazurkiewicz trace. If a deadlock exists, a Mazurkiewicz trace leads to it and will be discovered. More generally, safety properties are preserved.

The UDPOR technique that we consider also uses concurrency notions. A classical model of true concurrency is prime event structures:

Definition 3 (Prime event structure). *Given an alphabet of actions* Σ, *a* Σ-prime event structure *(Σ-PES) is a tuple* $\mathcal{E} = \langle E, <, \#, \lambda \rangle$ *where E is a set of events, $<$ is a partial order relation on E, called the* causality relation, $\lambda : E \rightarrow \Sigma$ *is a function labelling each event e with an action $\lambda(e)$, $\#$ is an irreflexive and symmetric relation called the* conflict relation *such that, the set of causal predecessors or* history *of any event e,* $\lceil e \rceil = \{e' \in E : e' < e\}$ *is finite, and conflicts are inherited by causality:* $\forall e, e', e'' \in E, e\#e' \wedge e' < e'' \implies e\#e''$.

Intuitively, $e < e'$ means that e must happen before e', and $e\#e'$ that those two events cannot belong to the same execution. Two distinct events that are neither causally ordered nor in conflict are said *concurrent*. The set $[e] := \lceil e \rceil \cup \{e\}$ is called the *local configuration* of e. An event e can be characterized by a pair $< \lambda(e), H >$ where $\lambda(e)$ is its action, and $H = \lceil e \rceil$ its history.

We note $conf(E)$ the *set of configurations* of $\mathcal{E}$, where a *configuration* is a set of events $C \subseteq E$ that is both *causally closed* ($e \in C \implies \lceil e \rceil \subseteq C$) and *conflict free* ($e, e' \in C \implies \neg(e\#e')$). A configuration C is characterized by its causally maximal events $maxEvents(C) = \{e \in C : \nexists e' \in C, e < e'\}$, since it is exactly the union of local configurations of these events: $C = \bigcup_{e \in maxEvents(C)} [e]$; conversely a conflict free set K of incomparable events for $<$ defines a configuration $config(K)$ and $C = config(maxEvents(C))$.

A configuration C, together with the causal and independence relations defines a *Mazurkiewicz trace*: all interleavings are obtained by causally ordering all events in the configuration C but commuting concurrent ones. The *state* of a configuration C denoted by $state(C)$ is the state in $\mathcal{T}$ reached by any of these executions, and it is unique as discussed above. We write $enab(C) = enabled(state(C)) \subseteq \Sigma$ for the set of actions enabled at $state(C)$, while $actions(C)$ denotes the set of actions labelling events in C, i.e. $actions(C) = \{\lambda(e) : e \in C\}$.

The set of *extensions* of C is $ex(C) = \{e \in E \setminus C : \lceil e \rceil \subseteq C\}$, *i.e.* the set of events not in C but whose causal predecessors are all in C. When appending an extension to C, only resulting conflict-free sets of events are indeed configurations. These extensions constitute the set of *enabled* events $en(C) = \{e \in ex(C) : \nexists e' \in C, e\#e'\}$ while the other ones are *conflicting extensions* $cex(C) := ex(C) \setminus en(C)$.

Parametric Unfolding Semantics. Given an LTS $\mathcal{T}$ and an independence relation I, one can build a prime event structure $\mathcal{E}$ such that each linearization of a maximal (for inclusion) configuration represents an execution in $\mathcal{T}$, and conversely, to each Mazurkiewicz trace in $\mathcal{T}$ corresponds a configuration in $\mathcal{E}$ [13].

Definition 4 (Unfolding). *The* unfolding *of an LTS* $\mathcal{T}$ *under an independence relation* I *is the* Σ-*PES* $\mathcal{E} = \langle E, <, \#, \lambda, \rangle$ *incrementally constructed from the initial* Σ-*PES* $\langle \emptyset, \emptyset, \emptyset, \emptyset \rangle$ *by the following rules until no new event can be created:*

- *for any configuration* $C \in conf(E)$, *any action* $a \in enabled(state(C))$, *if for any* $e' \in maxEvents(C)$, $\neg I(a, \lambda(e'))$, *add a new event* $e = \langle a, C \rangle$ *to* E;
- *for any such new event* $e = \langle a, C \rangle$, *update* $<$, $\#$ *and* λ *as follows:* $\lambda(e) := a$ *and for every* $e' \in E \setminus \{e\}$, *consider three cases:*
  (i) *if* $e' \in C$ *then* $e' < e$,
  (ii) *if* $e' \notin C$ *and* $\neg I(a, \lambda(e'))$, *then* $e\#e'$,
  (iii) *otherwise, i.e. if* $e' \notin C$ *and* $I(a, \lambda(e'))$, *then* e *and* e' *are concurrent.*

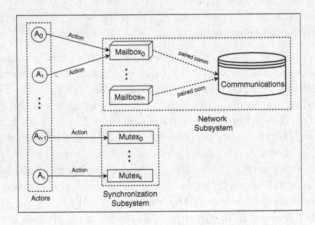

Fig. 1. Main elements of the model: Actors, Network and Synchronization

3   Programming Model and Independence Relation

In this section we introduce the abstract model of asynchronous distributed systems that we consider. While abstract, this model is sufficient to represent concrete MPI programs, as it encompasses all building blocks of the SMPI implementation of the standard [5]. We formalized this model in the specification language TLA+ [11], to later infer an independence relation (Fig. 1).

3.1   Abstract Model

In our model an asynchronous distributed system P consists in a set of n actors Actors $= \{A_1, A_2, ... A_n\}$ that perform local actions, communicate asynchronously with each others, and share some resources. We assume that the program is terminating, which implies that all actions are terminating. All local actions are abstracted into a unique one *LocalComp*. Communication actions are of four types: *AsyncSend*, *AsyncReceive*, *TestAny*, and *WaitAny*. Actions on shared resources called *synchronizations* are of four types: *AsyncMutexLock*, *MutexUnlock*, *MutexTest* and *MutexWait*.

At the semantics level, P is a tuple $P = \langle$Actors, Network, Synchronization$\rangle$ where Network and Synchronization respectively describe the abstract objects, and the effects on these of the communication and synchronizations actions. The Network subsystem provides facilities for the Actors to asynchronously communicate with each others, while the subsystem Synchronization allows the synchronization of actors on access to shared resources.

Network Subsystem. The state of the Network subsystem is defined as a pair $\langle$Mailboxes, Communications$\rangle$, where Mailboxes is a set of mailboxes storing unpaired communications, while Communications stores only paired ones. Each communication c has a status in $\{send, receive, done\}$, ids of source and destination actors, data addresses for those. A mailbox is a rendez-vous point where *send* and *receive* communications meet. It is modelled as an unbounded FIFO queue that is either empty, or stores communications with all same *send* or *receive* status, waiting for a matching opposite communication. When matching occurs, this paired communication gets a *done* status and is appended to the set Communications. We now detail the effect in actor A_i of the communication actions on Mailboxes and Communications:

- $c = AsyncSend(m, data)$ drops an asynchronous *send* communication c to the mailbox m. If pending *receive* communications exist in the mailbox, c is paired with the oldest one c' to form a communication with *done* status in Communications, the *receive* communication is removed from m and the *data* is copied from the source to the destination. Otherwise, a pending communication with *send* status is appended to m.
- $c = AsyncReceive(m, d)$ drops an asynchronous *receive* communication to mailbox m; the way a *receive* communication is processed is similar to *send*. If pending *send* communications exist, c is paired with the oldest one c' to form a communication with *done* status in Communications, the *send* communication is removed from m, and the data of the *send* is copied to d. Otherwise, a pending communication with *receive* status is appended to m.
- *TestAny(Com)* tests a set of communications *Com* of A_i. It returns a boolean, *true* if and only if some communication in *Com* with *done* status exists.
- *WaitAny(Com)* waits for a set of communications *Com* of A_i. The action is blocking until at least one communication in *Com* has a *done* status.

Synchronization Subsystem. The Synchronization subsystem consists in a pair ⟨Mutexes, Requests⟩ where Mutexes is a set of asynchronous mutexes used to synchronize the actors, and Requests is a vector indexed by actors ids of sets of requested mutexes. Each mutex m_j is represented by a FIFO queue of actors ids i who declared their interest on a mutex m_j by executing the action AsyncMutexLock(m_j). A mutex m_j is *free* if its queue is empty, *busy* otherwise. The *owner* is the actor whose id is the first in the queue. In actor A_i, the effect of the synchronization actions on Mutexes and Requests is as follows:

- *AsyncMutexLock*(m_j) requests a mutex m_j with the effect of appending the actor id i to m_j's queue and adding j to Requests[i]. A_i is *waiting* until *owning* m_j but, unlike classical mutexes, waiting is not necessarily blocking.
- *MutexUnlock*(m_j) removes its interest to a mutex m_j by deleting the actor id i from the m_j's queue and removing j from Requests[i].
- *MutexTest*(M) returns *true* if actor A_i owns some previously requested mutex m_j in M (i is first in FIFO $m_j \in M$ s.t. j in Requests[i]).
- *MutexWait*(M) blocks until A_i owns some mutex m_j in M. Note that *Mutex-Test* (resp. *MutexWait*) are similar to *TestAny* (resp. *WaitAny*) and could be merged. We keep them separate here for simplicity of explanations.

Beside those actions, a program can have local computations named *Local-Comp* actions. Such actions do not intervene with shared objects (Mailboxes, Mutexes and Communications), and they can be responsible for I/O tasks.

We specified our model of asynchronous distributed systems in the formal language TLA+ [11]. Our TLA+ model[1] focuses on how actions transform the global state of the system. An instance P of a program is described by a set of actors and their actions (representing their source code). Following the semantics of TLA+, and since programs are terminating, the interleaving semantics of a program P can be described by an acyclic LTS representing all its behaviors. Formally, the LTS of P is a tuple $\mathcal{T}_P = \langle S, s_0, \Sigma, \rightarrow \rangle$ where Σ represent the actions of P; a state $s =< l, g >$ in S consists of the local state l of all actors (*i.e.* local variables, Requests) and g the state of all shared objects including Mutexes, Mailboxes and Communications; in the initial state s_0 all actors are in their initial local state, sets and FIFO queues are empty; a transition $s \xrightarrow{a} s'$ is defined if, according to the TLA+ model, the action encoded by a is enabled at s and executing a transforms the state from s to s'.

Notice that when verifying a real program, we only observe its actions and assume that they respect the proposed TLA+ model and the independence relation discussed below. These assumptions are necessary to suppose that the LTS correctly models the actual program behaviors.

3.2 Additional Property of the Model

The model presented in the previous section may appear unusual, because the lock action on mutexes is split into an *AsyncMutexLock* and a *MutexWait* while

---

[1] https://github.com/pham-theanh/simixNetworks

most works in the literature consider atomic locks. Our model does not induce any loss of generality, since synchronous locks can trivially be simulated with asynchronous locks. One reason to introduce this specificity is that this entails the following lemma, that is the key to the efficiency of UDPOR in our model.

Lemma 1 (Persistence). *Let u be a prefix of an execution v of a program in our model. If an action a is enabled after u, it is either executed in v or still enabled after v.*

Intuitively, persistence says that once enabled, actions are never disabled by any subsequent action, thus remain enabled until executed. Persistence does not hold for classical synchronous locks, as some enabled *lock(m)* action of an actor may become disabled by the *lock(m)* of another actor. This persistence property has been early introduced by Karp and Miller [9], and later studied for Petri Nets [12]. It should not be confused with the notion of persistent set used in DPOR[2]. Persistent sets are linked to independence, while persistence is not.

Proof. When *a* is a *LocalComp*, *AsyncSend*, *AsyncReceive*, *TestAny*, *AsyncMutexLock*, *MutexUnlock*, or *MutexTest* action, *a* cannot be disabled by any new action. Indeed, these actions are never blocking (*e.g.* *AsyncMutexLock* comes down to the addition of an element in a FIFO, which is always enabled) and only depend on the execution of the action right before them by the same actor.

WaitAny and *MutexWait* may seem more complex. If *a* is a *WaitAny*, being enabled after *u* means that one communication it refers to was paired. Similarly, if *a* is a *MutexWait*, being enabled after *u* means that the corresponding actor is first in the FIFO of a mutex it refers to. In both cases these facts cannot be modified by any subsequent action, so *a* remains enabled until executed.

3.3 Independence Theorems

In order to use DPOR algorithms for our model of distributed programs, and in particular UDPOR that is based on the unfolding semantics, we need to define a valid independence relation for this model. Intuitively, two actions in distinct actors are independent when they do not compete on shared objects, namely Mailboxes, Communications, or Mutexes. This relation is formally expressed in TLA+ as so-called "independence theorems". We use the term "theorem" since the validity of the independence relation with respect to commutation should be proved. We proved them manually and implemented them as rules in the model-checker. These independence theorems are as follows[3]:

---

[2] A set of transitions T is called persistent in a state s if all transitions not in T and, either enabled in T or enabled in a state reachable by transitions not in T, are independent with all transitions in T. As a consequence, exploring only transitions in persistent sets is sufficient to detect all deadlocks.

[3] Some independence theorems could be enlarged but we give these ones for simplicity.

1. A *LocalComp* is independent with any other action of another actor.
2. Any synchronization action is independent of any communication action of a distinct actor.
3. Any pair of communication actions in distinct actors concerning distinct mailboxes are independent.
4. An *AsyncSend* is independent of an *AsyncReceive* of another actor.
5. Any pair of actions in { *TestAny*, *WaitAny* } in distinct actors is independent.
6. Any action in { *TestAny*(*Com*), *WaitAny*(*Com*) } is independent with any action of another actor in { *AsyncSend*, *AsyncReceive* } as soon as they do not both concern the first paired communication in the set *Com*[4].
7. Any pair of synchronization actions of distinct actors concerning distinct mutexes are independent.
8. An *AsyncMutexLock* is independent with a *MutexUnlock* of another actor.
9. Any pair of actions in { *MutexWait*, *MutexTest* } of distinct actors is independent.
10. A *MutexUnlock* is independent of a *MutexWait* or *MutexTest* of another actor, except if the same mutex is involved and one of the two actors owns it.
11. An *AsyncMutexLock* is independent of any *MutexWait* and *MutexTest* of another actor.

4   Adapting UDPOR

This section first recalls the UDPOR algorithm of [16] and then explains how it may be adapted to our context, in particular how the computation of extensions, a key operation, can be made efficient in our programming model.

4.1   The UDPOR Algorithm

Algorithm 1 presents the UDPOR exploration algorithm of [16]. Like other DPOR algorithms, it explores only a part of the LTS of a given terminating distributed program P according to an independence relation I, while ensuring that the explored part is sufficient to detect all deadlocks. The particularity of UDPOR is to use the concurrency semantics explicitly, namely unfoldings, which makes it both complete and optimal: it explores exactly one interleaving per Mazurkiewicz trace, never reaching any sleep-set blocked execution.

The algorithm works as follows. Executions are represented by configurations, thus equivalent to their Mazurkiewicz traces. The set U, initially empty, contains all events met so far in the exploration. The procedure *Explore* has three parameters: a configuration C encoding the current execution; a set D (for *disabled*) of events to avoid (playing a role similar to a sleep set in [8]), thus preventing revisits of configurations; a set A (for *add*) of events conflicting with

---

[4] Intuitively, *WaitAny*(*Com*) needs only one done communication (the first paired (*AsyncSend*, *AsyncReceive*)) in *Com* to become enabled. Similarly, the effect of *TestAny*(*Com*) only depends on this first done communication.

Algorithm 1. Unfolding-based POR exploration

```
1  Set U := ∅
2  call Explore(∅, ∅, ∅)
3  Procedure Explore(C, D, A)
4  |   Compute ex(C), and add all events in ex(C) to U
5  |   if en(C) ⊆ D then
6  |   |   Return
7  |   if (A = ∅) then
8  |   |   chose e from en(C) \ D
9  |   else
10 |   |   choose e from A ∩ en(C)
11 |   Explore(C ∪ {e}, D, A \ {e})
12 |   if ∃J ∈ Alt(C, D ∪ {e}) then
13 |   |   Explore(C, D ∪ {e}, J \ C)
14 |   U := U ∩ Q_{C,D}
```

D and used to guide the search to events in conflicting configurations in $cex(C)$ to explore alternative executions.

First, all extensions of C are computed and added to U (line 4). The search backtracks (line 6) in two cases: when C is maximal ($en(C) = ∅$), i.e. a deadlock (or the program end) is reached, or when all events enabled in C should be avoided ($en(C) ⊆ D$), which corresponds to a redundant call, thus a sleep-set blocked execution. Otherwise, an enabled event e is chosen (line 7–10), in A if this guiding information is non empty (line 10), and a "left" recursive exploration $Explore(C ∪ \{e\}, D, A \setminus \{e\})$ is called (line 11) from this extended configuration $C ∪ \{e\}$, it continues trying to avoid D, but e is removed from A in the guiding information. When this call is completed, all configurations containing C and e have been explored, thus it remains to explore those that contain C but not e. In this aim *alternatives* are computed (line 12) with the function call $Alt(C, D ∪ \{e\})$. Alternatives play a role similar to "backtracking sets" in the original DPOR algorithm, i.e. sets of actions that must be explored from the current state. Formally, an alternative to $D' = D ∪ \{e\}$ after C in U is a subset J of U that, does not intersect D', forms a configuration $C ∪ J$ after C, and such that all events in D' conflict with some event in J. If an Alternatives J exists, a right "recursive" exploration is called $Explore(C, D ∪ \{e\}, J \setminus C)$: C is still the configuration to extend, but e is now also to be avoided, thus added to D, while events in $J \setminus C$ are used as guides. Upon completion (line 14), U is intersected with $Q_{C,D}$ which includes all events in C and D as well as every event in U conflicting with some events in $C ∪ D$.

In order to avoid sleep-set blocked executions (SSB) and obtain the optimality of DPOR, the function $Alt(C, D ∪ \{e\})$ has to solve an NP-complete problem [13]: find a subset J of U that can be used for backtracking, conflicts with all $D ∪ \{e\}$ thus necessarily leading to a configuration $C ∪ J$ that is not already visited. In this case $en(C) ⊆ D$ can then be replaced by $en(C) = ∅$ in line 5. Note that with a different encoding, Optimal DPOR must solve the same problem [1] as explained in [13]. In [13], a variant of the algorithm is proposed for the function Alt that computes k-*partial alternatives* rather than alternatives, i.e. sets of events J conflicting with only k events in D, not necessarily all of them. Depending on k, (e.g. $k = \infty$ (or $k = |D| + 1$) for alternatives, $k = 1$ for source sets of [1]) this variant allows to tune between an optimal or a quasi-optimal algorithm that may be more efficient.

4.2   Computing Extensions Efficiently

Computing the extensions $ex(C)$ of a configuration C may be costly in general. It is for example an NP-complete problem for Petri Nets since all sub-configurations must be enumerated. Fortunately this algorithm can be specially tuned for sub-classes. In particular for the programming model of [13,16] it is tuned in an algorithm working in time $O(n^2 log(n))$, using the fact that events have a maximum of two causal predecessors, thus limiting the subsets to consider.

This section tunes the algorithm to our more complex model, using the fact that the amount of causal predecessors of events is also bounded. Next section shows how to incrementally compute $ex(C)$ to avoid recomputations. Figure 2 illustrates some aspects of an extension.

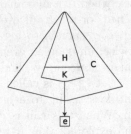

Fig. 2. A configuration C, extended by event e, its history H and maximal events K.

This section mandates some additional notations. Given a configuration C and an extension with action a, let $pre(a)$ denote the action right before a in the same actor, while $preEvt(a, C)$ denotes the event in C associated with $pre(a)$ (formally $e = preEvt(a, C) \iff e \in C, \lambda(e) = pre(a)$). Given a set F of events $F \subseteq E$, $Depend(a, F)$ means that a depends on all actions labeling events in F.

The definition of $ex(C)$ (set of extensions of a configuration C) $\{e \in E \setminus C : \lceil e \rceil \subseteq C\}$ can be rewritten using the definitions of Sect. 2 as follows: $\{e = \langle a, H \rangle \in E \setminus C : a = \lambda(e) \wedge H = \lceil e \rceil \wedge H \in 2^C \cap conf(E) \wedge a \in enab(H)\}$.

Fortunately, it is not necessary to enumerate all subsets H of C, that are in exponential numbers, to compute this set. According to the unfolding construction in Definition 4, an event $e = \langle a, H \rangle$ only exists in $ex(C)$ if the action a is dependant with the actions of all maximal events of H. This gives: $ex(C) = \{e = \langle a, H \rangle \in E \setminus C : a = \lambda(e) \wedge H = \lceil e \rceil \wedge H \in 2^C \cap conf(E) \wedge a \in enab(H) \wedge Depend(a, maxEvents(H))\}$. Now $ex(C)$ can be simplified and decomposed by enumerating Σ, yielding to: $ex(C) = \bigcup_{a \in \Sigma} \{\langle a, H \rangle : H \in S_{a,C}\} \setminus C$ where $S_{a,C} = \{H \in conf(E) : H \subseteq C \wedge a \in enab(H) \wedge Depend(a, maxEvents(H))\}$.

The above formulation of $ex(C)$ iterates on all actions in Σ. However, interpreting the persistence property (Lemma 1) for configurations entails that for two configurations H and C with $H \subseteq C$, an action a in $enab(H)$ is either in $actions(C)$ or $enab(C)$.

Therefore, $ex(C)$ can be rewritten by restricting a to $actions(C) \cup enab(C)$:

$$ex(C) = (\bigcup_{a \in actions(C) \cup enab(C)} \{\langle a, H \rangle : H \in S_{a,C}\}) \setminus C \qquad (3)$$

Now, instead of enumerating possible configurations $H \in S_{a,C}$, we can enumerate their maximal sets $K = maxEvents(H)$. Hence,

$$ex(C) = (\bigcup_{a \in actions(C) \cup enab(C)} \{\langle a, config(K) \rangle : K \in S_{a,C}^{max}\}) \setminus C \qquad (4)$$

with $S_{a,C}^{max} = \{K \in 2^C : K$ is maximal $\wedge a \in enab(config(K)) \wedge Depend(a, K))\}$ and K is maximal if $(\nexists e, e' \in K : e < e' \vee e \# e')$.

One can then specialize the computation of $ex(C)$ according to the type of action a. Due to space limitations, we only detail the computation for *AsyncSend* actions, the other ones being similar.

Computing Extensions for AsyncSend Actions. Let C be a configuration, and a an action of type $c = AsyncSend(m, \_)$ of an actor A_i. We want to compute the set $S_{a,C}^{max}$ of sets K of maximal events from which a depends.

According to independence theorems (see Sect. 3.3), a only depends on the following actions: $pre(a)$, all $AsyncSend(m, \_)$ actions of distinct actors A_j which concern the same mailbox m, and all *WaitAny* (resp. *TestAny*) actions that wait (resp. test) a *AsyncReceive* which concerns the same communication c. Considering this, we now examine the composition of maximal events sets K in $S_{a,C}^{max}$.

First, two events labelled by $AsyncSend(m, \_)$ actions cannot co-exist in K, formally $\nexists e, e' \in K : \lambda(e), \lambda(e')$ in $AsyncSend(m, \_)$: indeed, if two such events exist in a configuration, they are dependent but cannot conflict, thus are causality related and cannot be both maximal.

Second, if a *WaitAny(Com)* action concerns communication c, there are two cases: (i) either c is not the first *done* communication in *Com*, then *WaitAny(Com)* and the action a are independent. (ii) or c is the first *done* communication in *Com* and *WaitAny* is enabled only after a. Thus the only possibility for a maximal event to be labelled by a *WaitAny* is when $pre(a)$ is a *WaitAny* of the same actor. We can then write: $\nexists e \in K : \lambda(e)$ in *WaitAny* $\wedge \lambda(e) \neq pre(a)$.

Third, all *AsyncReceive* events for the mailbox m are causally related in configuration C, and c can only be paired with one of them, say c'. Thus a can only depend on actions $TestAny(Com')$ such that $c' \in Com'$ and c and c' form the first *done* communication in Com', and all those *TestAny* events are ordered. Thus, there is at most one event e labelled by *TestAny* in K such that $\lambda(e) \neq pre(a)$.

To conclude, K contains at most three events: $preEvt(a, C)$, some event labelled with an action *AsyncSend* on the same mailbox, and some *TestAny* for some matching *AsyncReceive* communication. There is thus only a cubic number of such sets, which is the worse case among considered action types. Algorithm 2 generates all events in $ex(C)$ labelled by an *AsyncSend* action a.

Algorithm 2. createAsyncSendEvt(a, C)

```
1   create e' = < a, config(preEvt(a, C)) >, and ex(C) := ex(C) ∪ {e'}
2   foreach e ∈ C s.t. λ(e) ∈ {AsyncSend(m,_), TestAny(Com)}
3   where Com contains a matching c' = AsyncReceive(m,_) with a do
4   │   K := ∅
5   │   - if ¬(e < preEvt(a, C) then K := K ∪ {e}
6   │   - if ¬(preEvt(a, C) < e) then K := K ∪ {preEvt(a, C)}
7   │   if  D(a, λ(e)) then
8   │   │   create e' = < a, config(K) > and ex(C) := ex(C) ∪ {e'}
9   foreach e_s ∈ C s.t. λ(e_s) = AsyncSend(m,_) do
10  │   foreach e_t ∈ C s.t. λ(e_t) = TestAny(Com)
11  │   where Com contains a matching c' = AsyncReceive(m,_) with a do
12  │   │   K := ∅
13  │   │   - if ¬(e_s < preEvt(a, C)) and ¬(e_s < e_t) then K := K ∪ {e_s}
14  │   │   - if ¬(e_t < preEvt(a, C) and ¬(e_t < e_s) then K := K ∪ {e_t}
15  │   │   - if ¬(preEvt(a, C) < e_s) and ¬(preEvt(a, C) < e_t) then
        │   │     K := K ∪ {preEvt(a, C)}
16  │   │   if  D(a, λ(e_t)) then
17  │   │   │   create e' = < a, config(K) >, and ex(C) := ex(C) ∪ {e'}
```

Example 1. We illustrate the Algorithm 2 by the example of Fig. 3. Suppose we want to compute the extensions of $C = \{e_1, e_2, e_3, e_4, e_5\}$ associated with a, the action $c2 = AsyncSend(m,\_)$ of $Actor_2$. First $e_6 = < AsyncSend, \{2\} > \in ex(C)$ because $preEvt(a, C) = e_2$ (line 1). We then iterate on all *AsyncSend* events in C, combining them with e_2 to create maximal event sets K (lines 2–8). We only have one *AsyncSend* event e_3. Since $\neg(e_2 < e_3)$ and $\neg(e_3 < e_2)$, we form a first set $K = \{e_2, e_3\}$, and add $e_7 = < AsyncSend, \{e_2, e_3\} >$ to $ex(C)$. Next all *TestAny* events that concern the mailbox m should be considered. Events e_2 and e_5 can be combined to form a new maximal event set $K = \{e_2, e_5\}$, but since a and $\lambda(e_5)$ are not related to the same communication, $D(a, \lambda(e_5))$ is not satisfied and no event is created. Finally combinations of e_2 with an *AsyncSend* event and a *TestAny* event are examined (lines 9–17). We then get $K = \{e_2, e_5, e_3\}$, and e_8 is added to $ex(C)$ since $D(a, \lambda(e_5))$ holds in the configuration $config(\{e_2, e_5, e_3\})$.

```
Actor₀:  c = AsyncReceive(m,_)
         c'= AsyncReceive(m,_)
         TestAny({c'})

Actor₁:  c1= AsyncSend(m,_)

Actor₂:  localComp
         c2 = AsyncSend(m,_)
```

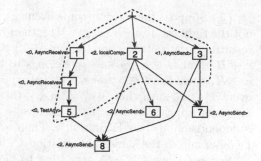

Fig. 3. The pseudo-code of a distributed program (left) and the configuration C.

4.3 Computing Extensions Incrementally

In the UDPOR exploration algorithm, after extending a configuration C' by adding a new event e, one must compute the extensions of $C = C' \cup \{e\}$, thus resulting in redundant computations of events. The next theorem improves this by providing an incremental computation of extensions.

Theorem 1. *Suppose $C = C' \cup \{e\}$ where e is the last event added to C by the Algorithm 1. We can compute $ex(C)$ incrementally as follows:*

$$ex(C) = (ex(C') \cup \bigcup_{a\,\in\,enab(C)} \{< a, H >: H \in S_{a,C}\}) \setminus \{e\} \tag{5}$$

where $S_{a,C} = \{H \in 2^C \cap conf(E) : a \in enab(H) \land Depend(a, maxEvents(H))\}$.

Proof. With the definition of $S_{a,C}$ as above, recall that

$$ex(C) = (\bigcup_{a\,\in\,actions(C)\cup enab(C)} \{\langle a, H \rangle : H \in S_{a,C}\}) \setminus C \tag{6}$$

Applying the same Eq. (6) to C' we get:

$$ex(C') = (\bigcup_{a\,\in\,actions(C')\cup enab(C')} \{\langle a, H \rangle : H' \in S_{a,C'}\}) \setminus C'$$

Now, exploring e from C' leads to C, which entails that $\lambda(e)$ belongs to $enab(C')$ and $actions(C') \cup \lambda(e) = actions(C)$, thus the range of a in $ex(C')$ which is $actions(C') \cup enab(C')$ can be rewritten $actions(C) \cup (enab(C') \setminus \lambda(e))$.

First, separating $action(C)$ from the root in both $ex(C)$ and $ex(C')$ we prove:

$$\bigcup_{a\,\in\,actions(C)} \{< a, H >: H \in S_{a,C}\} = \bigcup_{a\,\in\,actions(C)} \{< a, H' >: H' \in S_{a,C'}\} \tag{7}$$

$(\supseteq)$ This inclusion is obvious since $C \supseteq C'$, and thus $S_{a,C} \supseteq S_{a,C'}$.

($\subseteq$) Suppose there exists some event $e_n = < a, H >$ belonging to the left but not the right set. If $a = \lambda(e_n) = \lambda(e)$, then $H \in S_{a,C} \cap S_{a,C'}$, so e_n is in both sets, resulting in a contradiction. If $a = \lambda(e_n) \neq \lambda(e)$, there are two cases: (i) either $e \notin H$ then $H \in S_{a,C'}$ and e_n belongs to the right set, a contradiction. (ii) or $e \in H$, then $\lambda(e_n) \in actions(C) \setminus \{\lambda(e)\} = actions(C')$, thus there is another event $e' \in C'$ such that $\lambda(e') = \lambda(e_n)$, then e' cannot belong to H (one action a cannot appear twice in $\lceil e_n \rceil$). Besides, e is the last event explored in C, thus a depends on $\lambda(e)$ by Definition 4. Then, e' conflicts with e, contradicting their membership to the same configuration C. This proves (7).

Second, since $C' \subseteq C$, according to persistence of the programming model (Lemma 1), $(enab(C') \setminus \{\lambda(e)\}) \subseteq enab(C)$. We thus have:

$$\bigcup_{a \,\in\, enab(C') \setminus \{\lambda(e)\}} \{< a, H' >| \, H' \in S_{a,C'}\} \subseteq \bigcup_{a \,\in\, enab(C)} \{< a, H >| \, H \in S_{a,C}\}$$

$$(8)$$

Now, using Eqs. (7) and (8), $ex(C)$ can be rewritten as follows:

$$ex(C) = (\bigcup_{a \,\in\, actions(C) \cup (enab(C') \setminus \lambda(e))} \{\langle a, H' \rangle : H' \in S_{a,C'}\}$$

$$\cup \bigcup_{a \,\in\, enab(C)} \{\langle a, H \rangle : H \in S_{a,C}\}) \setminus (C' \cup \{e\})$$

$$(9)$$

But since no event in $\bigcup_{a \,\in\, enab(C)} \{\langle a, H \rangle : H \in S_{a,C}\}$ is in $(C' \cup \{e\})$, Eq. (9) can be rewritten as Eq. (5) in Theorem 1.

4.4   Experiments

We implemented the quasi-optimal version of UDPOR with k-partial alternatives [13] in a prototype adapted to the distributed programming model of Sect. 3, *i.e.* with its independence relation. The computation of k-partial alternatives is essentially inspired by [13]. Recall the algorithm reaches optimality when $k = |D| + 1$, while $k = 1$ corresponds to Source DPOR [1]. The prototype is still limited, not connected to the SimGrid environment, thus can only be experimented on simple examples.

We first compare optimal UDPOR with an exhaustive stateless search on several benchmarks (see Table 1). The first five benchmarks come from Umpire_Tests[5], while DTG and RMQ-receiving belong to [10] and [17], respectively. The last benchmark is an implementation of a simple Master-Worker pattern. We expressed them in our programming model and explored their state space with our prototype. The experiments were performed on an HP computer, Intel Core i7-6600U 2.60 GHz processors, 16 GB of RAM, and Ubuntu version 18.04.1. Table 1 presents the number of explored traces and running time for both an exhaustive search and optimal UDPOR. In all benchmarks UDPOR outperforms the exhaustive search. For example, for RMQ-receiving with 4 processes, the

---

[5] http://formalverification.cs.utah.edu/ISP-Tests/.

exhaustive search explores more than 20000 traces in around 8 s, while UDPOR explores only 6 traces in 0.2 s. Besides, UDPOR is optimal, exploring only one trace per Mazurkiewicz trace. For example in RMQ-receiving with 5 processes, with only 4 *AsyncSend* actions that concern the same mailbox, UDPOR explores exactly 24 (=4!) non-equivalent traces. Similarly, the DTG benchmark has only two dependent *AsyncSend* actions, thus two non-equivalent traces. Furthermore, deadlocks are also detected in the prototype.

We also tried to vary the value of k. When k is decreased, one gains in efficiency in computing alternatives, but looses optimality by producing more traces. It is then interesting to analyse, whether this can be globally more efficient than optimal UDPOR. Similar to [13], we observed that in some cases, fixing smaller values of k may improve the efficiency. For example with RMQ-receiving, $k = 7$ is optimal, but reducing to $k = 4$ still produces 24 traces (thus is optimal) a bit more quickly (2.3 s), while for $k = 3$ the number of traces and time diverge. We have to analyse this more precisely on more examples in the future.

Note that with our simple prototype, we do not yet make experiments with concrete programs (*e.g.* MPI programs), for which running time may somehow diverge. We expect to make it in the next months and then experiment the algorithms in more depth. However, we believe that the results are already significant and that UDPOR is effective for asynchronous distributed programs.

Table 1. Comparing exhaustive exploration and UDPOR. TO: timeout after 30 min; #P: number of processes; Deadlock: deadlock exists; #Traces: number of traces

Benchmarks	#P	Deadlock	Exhaustive search		UDPOR	
			#Traces	Time (second)	#Traces	Time (second)
Wait-deadlock	2	Yes	2	<0.01	1	<0.01
Complex-deadlock	3	Yes	36	0.03	1	<0.01
Waitall-deadlock	3	Yes	1458	1.2	1	<0.01
No-error-wait-any_src	3	No	21	0.02	1	0.01
Any-src-can-deadlock3	3	Yes	999	0.65	2	0.03
DTG	5	Yes	-	TO	2	0.07
RMQ-receiving	4	No	20064	8.15	6	0.2
	5	No	-	TO	24	2.52
Master-worker	3	No	1356444	1038	2	0.2
	4	No	-	TO	6	2.5

5   Conclusion and Future Work

The paper adapts the unfolding-based dynamic partial order reduction (UDPOR) approach [16] to the verification of asynchronous distributed programs. The programming model we consider is generic enough to properly model a large class of asynchronous distributed systems, including *e.g.* MPI applications, while exhibiting some interesting properties. From a formal specification of this model in TLA+, an independence relation is built, that is used by UDPOR to partly build the unfolding semantics of programs. We show that, thanks to the properties of our model, some usually expensive operations of UDPOR can be made efficient. A prototype of UDPOR has been implemented and experimented on some benchmarks, gaining promising first results.

In the future we aim at extending our model of asynchronous distributed systems, while both preserving good properties, getting a more precise independence relation, and implementing UDPOR in the SimGrid model-checker and verify real MPI applications. Once done, we should experiment UDPOR more deeply, and compare it with state of the art tools on more significant benchmarks, get a more precise analysis about the efficiency of UDPOR compared to simpler DPOR approaches, analysé the impact of quasi-optimality on efficiency.

Acknowledgement. We wish to thank the reviewers for their constructive comments to improve the paper.

References

1. Abdulla, P.A., Aronis, S., Jonsson, B., Sagonas, K.F.: Optimal dynamic partial order reduction. In: 41st Annual ACM SIGPLAN-SIGACT Symposium on Principles of Programming Languages, POPL 2014, San Diego, CA, USA, pp. 373–384, January 2014. https://doi.org/10.1145/2535838.2535845
2. Albert, E., Gómez-Zamalloa, M., Isabel, M., Rubio, A.: Constrained dynamic partial order reduction. In: 30th International Conference on Computer Aided Verification, CAV 2018, Oxford, UK, pp. 392–410, July 2018. https://doi.org/10.1007/978-3-319-96142-2_24
3. Aronis, S., Jonsson, B., Lång, M., Sagonas, K.: Optimal dynamic partial order reduction with observers. In: Beyer, D., Huisman, M. (eds.) TACAS 2018. LNCS, vol. 10806, pp. 229–248. Springer, Cham (2018). https://doi.org/10.1007/978-3-319-89963-3_14
4. Baier, C., Katoen, J.: Principles of Model Checking. MIT Press, Cambridge (2008)
5. Degomme, A., Legrand, A., Markomanolis, G.S., Quinson, M., Stillwell, M., Suter, F.: Simulating MPI applications: the SMPI approach. IEEE Trans. Parallel Distrib. Syst. **28**(8), 2387–2400 (2017). https://doi.org/10.1109/TPDS.2017.2669305
6. Esparza, J., Heljanko, K.: Unfoldings - A Partial-Order Approach to Model Checking. Monographs in Theoretical Computer Science. An EATCS Series. Springer, Heidelberg (2008). https://doi.org/10.1007/978-3-540-77426-6
7. Flanagan, C., Godefroid, P.: Dynamic partial-order reduction for model checking software. In: 32nd ACM SIGPLAN-SIGACT Symposium on Principles of Programming Languages, POPL 2005, Long Beach, California, USA, pp. 110–121, January 2005. https://doi.org/10.1145/1040305.1040315
8. Godefroid, P. (ed.): Partial-Order Methods for the Verification of Concurrent Systems. LNCS, vol. 1032. Springer, Heidelberg (1996). https://doi.org/10.1007/3-540-60761-7
9. Karp, R.M., Miller, R.E.: Parallel program schemata. J. Comput. Syst. Sci. **3**(2), 147–195 (1969). https://doi.org/10.1016/S0022-0000(69)80011-5

10. Khanna, D., Sharma, S., Rodríguez, C., Purandare, R.: Dynamic symbolic verification of MPI programs. In: 22nd International Symposium on Formal Methods, FM 2018, Oxford, UK, pp. 466–484, July 2018. https://doi.org/10.1007/978-3-319-95582-7_28

11. Lamport, L.: Specifying Systems. The TLA+ Language and Tools for Hardware and Software Engineers. Addison-Wesley, Boston (2002)

12. Landweber, L.H., Robertson, E.L.: Properties of conflict-free and persistent Petri Nets. J. ACM **25**(3), 352–364 (1978). https://doi.org/10.1145/322077.322079

13. Nguyen, H.T.T., Rodríguez, C., Sousa, M., Coti, C., Petrucci, L.: Quasi-optimal partial order reduction. In: 30th International Conference on Computer Aided Verification, CAV 2018, Oxford, UK, pp. 354–371, July 2018. https://doi.org/10.1007/978-3-319-96142-2_22

14. Palmer, R., Gopalakrishnan, G., Kirby, R.M.: Semantics driven dynamic partial-order reduction of MPI-based parallel programs. In: Proceedings of the 2007 ACM Workshop on Parallel and Distributed Systems: Testing and Debugging, PADTAD 2007, pp. 43–53. ACM (2007)

15. Pham, A., Jéron, T., Quinson, M.: Verifying MPI applications with SimGridMC. In: Proceedings of the 1st International Workshop on Software Correctness for HPC Applications, CORRECTNESS@SC 2017, Denver, CO, USA, pp. 28–33, November 2017. https://doi.org/10.1145/3145344.3145345

16. Rodríguez, C., Sousa, M., Sharma, S., Kroening, D.: Unfolding-based partial order reduction. In: 26th International Conference on Concurrency Theory, CONCUR 2015, Madrid, Spain, pp. 456–469, September 2015. https://doi.org/10.4230/LIPIcs.CONCUR.2015.456

17. Rosa, C.D., Merz, S., Quinson, M.: A simple model of communication APIs - application to dynamic partial order reduction. In: 10th International Workshop on Automated Verification of Critical Systems, AVOCS 2010, Düsseldorf, Germany, September 2010. http://journal.ub.tu-berlin.de/eceasst/article/view/562

18. Sharma, S., Gopalakrishnan, G., Bronevetsky, G.: A sound reduction of persistent-sets for deadlock detection in MPI applications. In: Gheyi, R., Naumann, D. (eds.) SBMF 2012. LNCS, vol. 7498, pp. 194–209. Springer, Heidelberg (2012). https://doi.org/10.1007/978-3-642-33296-8_15

Encapsulation and Sharing in Dynamic Software Architectures: The Hypercell Framework

Jean-Bernard Stefani[✉] and Martin Vassor[✉]

Univ. Grenoble-Alpes, Inria, CNRS, Grenoble INP, LIG, 38000 Grenoble, France
{jean-bernard.stefani,martin.vassor}@inria.fr

Abstract. We present in this paper a novel framework for the definition of formal software component models, called the Hypercell framework. Models in this framework (hypercell models) allow the definition of dynamic software architectures featuring shared components, and different forms of encapsulation policies. Encapsulation policies in an hypercell model are enforced by means of runtime checks that prevent a component, in a given context, to evolve in violation of these policies. We present the main elements of the framework, its operational semantics and the first elements of its behavioral theory. We give some results concerning its ability to express different forms of composition, and show by means of examples its ability to deal with sharing and different forms of encapsulation.

1 Introduction

Motivations. How do we formally model dynamic software architectures featuring both encapsulation and sharing? Can we define an operational semantics and behavioral theory for these architectures? These are the questions we deal with in this paper. By dynamic software architectures, we understand structured collections of software components and their inter-relations [3], that can evolve over time, either spontaneously, for instance to adapt to changing operating conditions, or following external intervention, for instance for purposes of fault correction or functional update. By encapsulation, we understand forms of confinement and isolation between components, typically coupled with information hiding and abstraction, that ensure capabilities offered, and information maintained by a component, can only be accessed through designated interaction points or interfaces. Examples include the many forms of encapsulation that have been studied under the topic of aliasing control and ownership types in object-oriented programming [14]. By architectures with sharing, we understand architectures where components can take part in different ensembles, compositions or aggregations, possibly with different attendant properties, e.g. in terms of encapsulation, lifetime and existential dependencies [2]. Examples include architectures featuring common services, such as databases or logs, that can be used

© IFIP International Federation for Information Processing 2019
Published by Springer Nature Switzerland AG 2019
J. A. Pérez and N. Yoshida (Eds.): FORTE 2019, LNCS 11535, pp. 242–260, 2019.
https://doi.org/10.1007/978-3-030-21759-4_14

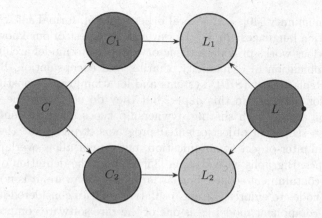

Fig. 1. Architecture with sharing: shared log service

by software components at different levels in a software structure, and architectures featuring shared resources such as virtual machines or operating system processes.

An example can illustrate the questions we are concerned with. Consider the architecture depicted in Fig. 1. In the figure, a composite component C has two subcomponents, C_1 and C_2, equipped with private log subcomponents L_1 and L_2, that are provided as client-specific logs by a composite log service component L (in the picture, components are depicted as circles, and an arrow from component X to component Y can be read as X *contains* Y, or Y *is a subcomponent of* X). The log service L is shared among the two subcomponents C_1 and C_2. One can argue that each private log component L_i ($i = 1, 2$) is participating to three different ensembles, C_i, C and L. C_i, because L_i is existentially dependent on C_i, and is partially encapsulated in C_i as only updates originating from C_i are possible (it is a partial encapsulation because not all communication between a component L_i and its environment is mediated or controlled by C_i). C because each C_i is a subcomponent of C, and C is supposed to encapsulate its subcomponents. L, because L_i is existentially dependent on L, has the same lifetime as L (if L is deleted so are L_1 and L_2), and relies on private functions (e.g. data storage) provided by L. These ensembles also correspond to encapsulation scopes, whose meaning is, roughly, that no communication outside the scope is possible without explicitly passing through the top component of each scope (C, L, C_1 or C_2), except for the communications between C_i and L_i.

Related Work. Over the past three decades, an abundant literature has developed that aims at formally modeling distributed, component-based, dynamic and adaptive software architectures, systems and services. One can cite notably: process calculi for distributed systems, such as π-calculi with localities [12,22,31], Ambient Calculi and their variants [10,11], and Milner's bigraphs [28,35]; process calculi and formal models for service-oriented computing and adaptive systems [9,17,19,20,37]; formal software component models such as BIP [6], Ptolemy [18],

Reo [23], Community [40], and several others [24,25]; formal software architecture description languages [26,32]. However, to the best of our knowledge, none of these previous works provide satisfactory support to model architectures featuring a combination of dynamicity, sharing and encapsulation. Synchronized Hyperedge Replacement (SHR) systems and location graphs constitute a direct inspiration for the work in this paper, but they do not allow the definition of encapsulation scopes with sharing. Ownership types allow the enforcement of encapsulation scopes in object-oriented programs, typically at the expense of restrictions in inter-object communication, but do not allow overlapping encapsulation scopes. Bigraphs with sharing [35] support the definition of nodes with overlapping containment scopes, but, as far as we are aware, it is not possible to use bigraph nodes to enforce the encapsulation policies considered in this paper. The Fractal component model [8] is one of the rare software component models that allows the description of component configurations with sharing, and that has been formally defined [27]. The architecture in Fig. 1 can readily be described in Fractal, with encapsulation scopes captured by Fractal composites. But we do not have a formal operational semantics for Fractal that would allow us to define the exact semantics of these scopes, nor do we have a proper behavioral theory for Fractal architectures. Interesting approaches to enforcing encapsulation policies are works that rely on dynamic access protection instead of aliasing control. These include notably the Siaam actor abstract machine [15], which relies on runtime checks to enforce actor encapsulation in a Java virtual machine, and access contracts [39] which provide dynamic access protection to Java objects that can support a wide range of encapsulation policies, including encapsulation policies with sharing as in the small architecture depicted in Fig. 1. However, Siaam and access contracts do not come with a formal behavioral theory, and the question of program equivalence in concurrent languages with Siaam-like or access contracts-like access protection mechanisms remains open.

Contributions. In this paper, we combine ideas from SHR systems [19], from location graphs [36], as well as Siaam [15] and access contracts [39] dynamic approaches to encapsulation enforcement, to define a formal operational framework, called the *Hypercell framework*. This framework allows the definition of different software component models (*hypercell models*), that support the modelling of dynamic component ensembles (*hypercells*) with sharing and encapsulation. The Hypercell framework can be seen as a conservative extension and generalization of the BIP and Fractal components models [6,8]. A main contribution of the Hypercell framework is how it handles encapsulation policies: to allow for maximum flexibility, they are enforced by runtime checks (*authorizations*), that prevent transitions of component ensembles that would violate the chosen policies. Defining a proper notion of authorization is not trivial however. In order to obtain a proper component theory (e.g. in the sense of [4]), we need a notion of hypercell equivalence that is a congruence for hypercell composition, and it is not clear how such a result can be obtained in presence of authorizations. The idea is to have authorizations operate only at the level of individual components (*cells*): this allows us to define a notion of hypercell bisimilarity where we can decouple the contribution of authorizations from the classical bisimulation game, which in turn allows us to obtain the required congruence result. However, this local form of authorization raises another problem: encapsulation policies are not local in nature, so how can we enforce them via such local checks, notably in presence of evolving component ensembles? We show, by means of examples, how this can be done via a combination of local but context-dependent authorization predicates and dynamic component types (*cell sorts*).

Outline. The paper is organized as follows. Section 2 is a brief informal introduction to hypercells. Section 3 presents the hypercell framework, and preliminary elements of a behavioral theory for hypercell models. Section 4 shows, by means of examples, how to enforce different forms of encapsulation using sorts and authorizations. Section 5 concludes the paper.

2   Informal Introduction

A hypercell is a finite set of *cells*. A cell has (we also say "offers") *roles* (a term we borrow from location graphs). A *role* is a point of attachment for cells, as well as a point of interaction between cells. A hypercell, much like a SHR system, constitutes a hypergraph, where the roles are vertices, and cells are the edges of the hypergraph. A role corresponds to a point of attachment and interaction between cells, and may be offered at most by two distinct cells. Hypercells are thus limited forms of hypergraphs, where hyperedges can connect any number of vertices, but a given vertex can only be connected by at most two edges. As in standard software component model ontology [16], roles are classified as *provided* or *required*: a provided role in a cell signals some service offered by the cell, whereas a required role signals some expected service. When a role belongs to two cells in a given hypercell (in required position in one cell, and in provided position in the other cell), we say that the role is *bound*, and that it *binds* the two cells that offer it. Otherwise, we say that the role is *unbound*.

A cell is a locus of computation, as are localities in process calculi such as the Distributed π-calculus [31], and Klaim [29]. One can understand a cell as a basic software component or as a connector, as in the component-and-connector view of software architecture [3] and in software component models [16]. A hypercell can be understood as a composite software component or component ensemble. In this sense, the hypercell concepts align well with the standard concepts of software component models [16] and software architecture, as present e.g. in the ACME [21] and Fractal [8] component models (cells and hypercells correspond to ACME and Fractal *components*, roles to ACME *ports* and Fractal *interfaces*, bound roles to Fractal *primitive bindings*).

Figure 1 depicts a small hypercell with roles drawn as black dots (or arrows when bound) and cells as ellipses. Interactions in a hypercell take the form of simple point-to-point bidirectional interactions between pairs of cells bound by some role. In Fig. 1, cells C_1 and L_1 can interact directly because they are bound, but C_2 cannot directly interact with C_1, nor C with L. In the architecture depicted in Fig. 1, the scopes discussed in the introduction are manifested by bound roles and the sorts adorning the different cells (hinted at by arrows).

The behavior of a hypercell is the result of the composition of the behavior of its cells. A cell evolves by transforming into some hypercell, in the process possibly interacting with, or removing, cells it is bound to. The evolution of a hypercell corresponds to the parallel firing of a number of such cell transitions. An interaction between two cells bound at a role r amounts to several binary rendez-vous on communication channels succeeding at role r. An interaction will typically result in the simultaneous exchange of values at each of the channels participating in the interaction.

For instance, a client-server interaction at role r between a client cell C and a server cell S, may, on the server side, take the form $\overline{r} : \{\text{op}\langle v, \text{resp}\rangle, \overline{\text{resp}}\langle w\rangle\}$, where r is the role which appears in provided position in the server (hence the overline $\overline{r}$), op is the channel on which the value v is sent, along with the return channel resp, and w is the value which is (instantly) returned by the server, in response to the request $\text{op}\langle v, \text{resp}\rangle$, on the requested return channel resp. On the client side, the interaction would take the conjugate form $r : \{\overline{\text{op}}\langle v, \text{resp}\rangle, \text{resp}\langle w\rangle\}$. Notice that we use an early form for interactions: this allows us, in the operational semantics of hypercell models, to abstract from syntactic details such as a distinction between sent values and receiving parameters (the latter typically under the scope of some binding constructs). Our operational semantics thus has no mention of substitution of values to formal parameters, but we do distinguish with channels between originating side (e.g. $\overline{\text{op}}$, on the client side) and receiving side (e.g. op, on the server side).

Interactions between cells can be higher-order. In particular cells can be exchanged as values on channels during interactions. This allows the removal or passivation of cells as in the Kell calculus [34], which in turns allows to model objective reconfigurations in software architectures, where certain components can exercize explicit control over other ones.

Interactions between bound cells in a hypercell can be guarded by priorities. Priorities are crucial for the expressive power of the framework and the definition of different forms of composition operators as cells or hypercells. A priority allows a cell to check for the presence or absence of a signal from another cell it is bound to, in the form of the ability or inability to communicate on a given channel. For instance the client side communication above could be guarded by the absence of communication on channel sig on role s, which we would write thus: $\langle \{s : \neg\overline{\text{sig}}\} \cdot \overline{r} : \{\text{op}\langle v, \text{resp}\rangle, \overline{\text{resp}}\langle w\rangle\}\rangle$. In effect, the possible emission of signal sig on role s preempts (takes priority over) the emission of the request op on role r.

Individual cell transitions are also guarded by authorizations. An authorization is a runtime check that determines whether a cell transition is licit or not. Authorizations rely on the hypercell context of an individual cell to make this determination. For instance, a cell within an encapsulation scope can be prevented from making a transition that would allow it to bind to a cell outside this scope, whereas the same transition of the cell outside of such a scope can be allowed to proceed.

3   The Hypercell Framework

We define in this section our Hypercell framework. This framework can be instantiated to yield different hypercell models. Each hypercell model must define the following sets: a set $\mathbb{P}$ of *processes*; a set $\mathbb{S}$ of *sorts*; an infinite set $\mathbb{R}$ of *roles*; a set $\mathbb{V}$ of *values*; an infinite set $\mathbb{A}$ of *names*; an infinite set $\mathbb{Ch}$ of *channels*; a set $\mathcal{T}_u$ of *unconstrained transitions*; and an authorization predicate $\mathtt{Auth}$. We require $\mathbb{R} \subset \mathbb{A}$, $\mathbb{Ch} \subset \mathbb{A}$, and that the sets $\mathbb{P}$, $\mathbb{S}$, and $\mathbb{A}$ be mutually disjoint. Values can comprise processes, sorts, and names as well as elements of other datatypes (booleans, integers, etc). Values can be exchanged between cells on channels at bound roles. We require that the set $\mathbb{Ch}$ contain the special channel $\mathtt{rmv}$, which is used in hypercell models with objective cell removal. We require the set of names $\mathbb{A}$ to be equipped with an involution, called the conjugate operation, which sends a name a to its conjugate $\overline{a}$. By definition, we have $\overline{\overline{a}} = a$, and we write $\widehat{a}$ to denote a or its conjugate $\overline{a}$.

We require that each of the sets above be equipped with an operation for swapping names: for any element x of the above sets, $(r\ s) \cdot x$ yields an element of the same set where names r and s have been permuted, i.e. where r is replaced by s. (in the long version of this paper, we require the datatypes above to be nominal sets [30], but for lack of space we do not go into details here). We also require the existence of an operation $\mathtt{supp}$ that extracts from an element the set of names it contains, and we write $a\#X$ for $a \notin \mathtt{supp}(X)$.

Formally, a cell in a hypercell model is a 4-tuple of the form $[P : \mathfrak{s} \vartriangleleft \mathbf{p} \bullet \mathbf{r}]$, where P is the process of the cell, $\mathfrak{s}$ is the sort of the cell, $\mathbf{p}$ and $\mathbf{r}$ are the sets of provided and required roles of the cell, respectively. If $C = [P : \mathfrak{s} \vartriangleleft \mathbf{p} \bullet \mathbf{r}]$, we have $C.\mathtt{process} = P$, $C.\mathtt{sort} = \mathfrak{s}$, $C.\mathtt{prov} = \mathbf{p}$, and $C.\mathtt{req} = \mathbf{r}$. Any cell C must meet the following constraints: $C.\mathtt{prov} \cap C.\mathtt{req} = \emptyset$. The set of cells in a hypercell model is noted $\mathbb{C}$. The process of a cell embodies its behavior; the fact that a process can be a value means that cells can potentially update their behavior dynamically. The sort of a cell is a dynamic type associated with the cell; sorts are used to enforce runtime constraints on cells, as is shown in Sect. 4.

A hypercell G is just a set of cells that meets the following constraints: for any partition G_1, G_2 of G ($G = G_1 \cup G_2$ and $G_1 \cap G_2 = \emptyset$), one must have $G_1.\mathtt{prov} \cap G_2.\mathtt{prov} = \emptyset$ and $G_1.\mathtt{req} \cap G_2.\mathtt{req} = \emptyset$, where the set $G.\mathtt{prov}$ of provided roles of hypercell G is defined as $\bigcup_{C \in G} C.\mathtt{prov}$ (and likewise for the set $G.\mathtt{req}$ of required roles of G). We note 0 the empty hypercell, and $\mathbb{H}$ the set of hypercells in a hypercell model. We define the set of roles, of bound roles and unbound roles of a hypercell G:

$$G.\mathtt{roles} \triangleq G.\mathtt{prov} \cup G.\mathtt{req} \qquad G.\mathtt{bound} \triangleq G.\mathtt{prov} \cap G.\mathtt{req}$$
$$G.\mathtt{unbound} \triangleq G.\mathtt{roles} \setminus G.\mathtt{bound}$$

When G and G' are two disjoint hypercells, we write $G \parallel G'$ to denote $G \cup G'$ when $G \cup G'$ is indeed a hypercell (i.e. a set of cells meeting the above constraints).

3.1   Operational Semantics of a Hypercell Model

The operational semantics of a hypercell model is defined as a set $\mathcal{T}$ of labelled (contextual) transitions. A transition is an element of $\mathbb{T} = \mathbb{E} \times \mathbb{H} \times \mathbb{\Lambda} \times \mathbb{H}$, where $\mathbb{E}$ is the set of *environments*, and $\mathbb{\Lambda}$ is the set of *labels*. A transition $t = \langle \Gamma, G, \Lambda, G' \rangle \in \mathbb{T}$ is noted $\Gamma \vdash G \xrightarrow{\Lambda} G'$, with $\Gamma \in \mathbb{E}$ the environment $t.\texttt{env}$ of the transition, $G \in \mathbb{H}$ the initial hypercell $t.\texttt{init}$ of the transition, $\Lambda \in \mathbb{\Lambda}$ the label $t.\texttt{label}$ of the transition, and $G' \in \mathbb{H}$ the final hypercell $t.\texttt{final}$ of the transition. Intuitively, if $\Gamma \vdash G \xrightarrow{\Lambda} G'$, then hypercell G, when placed in environment Γ, can evolve into hypercell G' provided the synchronizations in label Λ are met. The environment in a transition represents both the set of known names prior to the transition, and the hypercell context in which the initial hypercell of the transition is placed.

A *label* Λ is a pair $\langle \pi \cdot \sigma \rangle$, where π is a finite set of priorities, and σ is a finite set of interactions. We note ϵ the empty set of priorities or interactions. and we set $\langle \pi \cdot \sigma \rangle.\texttt{prior} = \pi$, $\langle \pi \cdot \sigma \rangle.\texttt{sync} = \sigma$.

An *interaction* corresponds to an exchange of a value V on a channel c at a role r. An interaction takes the form $r : \widehat{c}\langle V \rangle$ if the role r is provided, and $\overline{r} : \widehat{c}\langle V \rangle$ if the role is required. An interaction $\widehat{r} : c\langle V \rangle$ corresponds to a receipt on channel c at role r of value V, whereas an interaction $\widehat{r} : \overline{c}\langle V \rangle$ corresponds to the emission of value V on channel c at role r. An interaction $\widehat{r} : \widehat{c}\langle V \rangle$ succeeds when matched with its conjugate interaction $\overline{\widehat{r}} : \overline{\widehat{c}}\langle V \rangle$. Notice that the value V in a successful interaction must be the same on both emitter and receiver sides. For this reason, our presentation of an hypercell model transition relation can be said to follow an *early style* [33]. This allows us in the presentation of the hypercell framework to abstract away from syntactic details of interactions in hypercell models. We set $(r : \widehat{c}\langle V \rangle).\texttt{prov} = \{r\}$, $(r : \widehat{c}\langle V \rangle).\texttt{req} = \emptyset$, and the dual for $\overline{r} : \widehat{c}\langle V \rangle$. We set $(\widehat{r} : \widehat{c}\langle V \rangle).\texttt{roles} = \{r\}$ and $(\widehat{r} : \widehat{c}\langle V \rangle).\texttt{channels} = \{c\}$. The set of interactions in a hypercell model is noted $\mathbb{I}$.

A *priority* takes the following form: $\widehat{r} : \neg c$, where r is a role and c is a channel. Intuitively, a contraint $\widehat{r} : \neg c$ stipulates that the cell bound at role r is not ready to perform an interaction on channel c. The set of priorities is noted $\mathbb{\Pi}$. Priorities are inherited from location graphs and provide hypercell models with significant expressive power (see Proposition 1 below). We set $(\widehat{r} : \neg c).\texttt{roles} = \{r\}$.

An *environment* Γ is a pair $\Delta \cdot \Sigma$ comprising a set of known *names* (roles or channels) $\Delta \subseteq \mathbb{A} = \mathbb{R} \cup \mathbb{Ch}$, and a *skeleton hypercell* (or *skeleton*, for brevity) Σ. For $\Gamma = \Delta \cdot \Sigma$ we define $\Gamma.\texttt{names} = \Delta$ and $\Gamma.\texttt{graph} = \Sigma$. The set of known names in an environment corresponds intuitively to the set of already generated names during a hypercell execution. New names created in a transition are names that do not belong to this set. The skeleton in an environment gathers information about the hypercell that surrounds the initial hypercell in a transition. It is used in determining authorizations for individual cell transitions (see rule TRANS below). A skeleton cell is a triplet $[\mathfrak{s} \triangleleft \mathbf{p} \bullet \mathbf{r}]$. The set of skeleton cells in a hypercell model is noted $\mathbb{C}_s$. The set of skeleton hypercells in a hypercell model is noted $\mathbb{H}_s$. Essentially, a skeleton is a hypercell where one has erased all the

$$\text{TRANS} \quad \frac{\Gamma.\text{names} \cdot 0 \rhd C \xrightarrow{\Lambda} G \qquad \Sigma(C) \in \Gamma.\text{graph} \qquad \text{Auth}(\Gamma, C, \Lambda, G)}{\Gamma \vdash C \xrightarrow{\Lambda} G}$$

$$\text{(COMP)} \quad \frac{\begin{array}{c} \Gamma \vdash G_1 \xrightarrow{\langle \pi_1 \cdot \sigma_1 \rangle} G_1' \\ \Gamma \vdash G_2 \xrightarrow{\langle \pi_2 \cdot \sigma_2 \rangle} G_2' \qquad \text{Cond}_P(s, \pi, \pi_1, \pi_2, \Gamma, C_1, C_2) \\ \text{Cond}_I(\sigma, \sigma_1, \sigma_2, G_1 \parallel G_2) \qquad \text{Cond}(\Gamma, G_1 \parallel G_2) \end{array}}{\Gamma \vdash G_1 \parallel G_2 \xrightarrow{\langle \pi \cdot \sigma \rangle} G_1' \parallel G_2'}$$

$$\text{(CTX)} \quad \frac{\begin{array}{c} \Gamma \vdash G \xrightarrow{\langle \varpi \cdot \sigma \rangle} G' \\ \text{Ind}_P(s, \pi, \varpi, \Gamma, C, E) \qquad \text{Ind}_I(\sigma, E) \qquad \text{Cond}(\Gamma, G \parallel E, G' \parallel E) \end{array}}{\Gamma \vdash G \parallel E \xrightarrow{\langle \pi \cdot \sigma \rangle} G' \parallel E}$$

Fig. 2. Transition rules for a hypercell model

processes. The skeleton $\Sigma(G)$ of a hypercell G is defined inductively as follows:

$$\Sigma(0) = 0 \quad \Sigma([P : \mathfrak{s} \lhd \mathbf{p} \bullet \mathbf{r}]) = [\mathfrak{s} \lhd \mathbf{p} \bullet \mathbf{r}] \quad \Sigma(G_1 \cup G_2) = \Sigma(G_1) \cup \Sigma(G_2)$$

We denote by 0 the empty skeleton, and by $\mathbb{E}$ the set of environments in a hypercell model. We define $\Delta_1 \cdot \Sigma_1 \subseteq \Delta_2 \cdot \Sigma_2 \triangleq \Delta_1 \subseteq \Delta_2 \wedge \Sigma_1 \subseteq \Sigma_2$, and $\Delta_1 \cdot \Sigma_1 \cup \Delta_2 \cdot \Sigma_2 \triangleq \Delta_1 \cup \Delta_2 \cdot \Sigma_1 \cup \Sigma_2$.

An hypercell model must define the set $\mathcal{T}_u$ of unconstrained transitions of its individual cells, i.e. transitions that do not rely on any knowledge of the execution context of individual cells. This fits with the idea that software components can be reused in different contexts (in our case, hypercells), and that their behavior should be defined as independently as possible from their context of use. We write $\Gamma \rhd C \xrightarrow{\Lambda} G$ for $\langle \Gamma, C, \Lambda, G \rangle \in \mathcal{T}_u$. Environments in unconstrained transitions are of the form $\Delta \cdot 0$. An unconstrained transition $\Delta \cdot 0 \rhd C \xrightarrow{\Lambda} G$ for an individual cell C must obey the following conditions: (i) names in the support of C must be known names, i.e. names in Δ: $\text{supp}(C) \subseteq \Delta$; (ii) interactions and priorities in $\Lambda = \langle \pi \cdot \sigma \rangle$ must be offered at roles from C: $\sigma.\text{prov} \subseteq C.\text{prov} \wedge \sigma.\text{req} \subseteq C.\text{req}$ and $\pi.\text{roles} \subseteq C.\text{roles}$. In addition, we require $\mathcal{T}_u$ to be insensitive to name changes, namely: $\forall t \in \mathcal{T}_u, n, m \in \mathbb{A}, (n\ m) \cdot t \in \mathcal{T}_u$. An hypercell model can define cells that allow their removal by other cells they are bound to. A cell C that allows its removal on some role r must provide an unconstrained transition of the form $\Delta \cdot 0 \rhd C \xrightarrow{\langle \epsilon \cdot \{\hat{r}:\overline{\text{rmv}}\langle C \rangle\} \rangle} 0$.

A hypercell model must define an authorization predicate Auth. Predicate $\text{Auth} \subseteq \mathbb{E} \times \mathbb{C} \times \mathbb{A} \times \mathbb{H}$ determines whether an individual cell transition is possible in a given context (a surrounding hypercell). We require Auth to be name insensitive, namely: for all $n, m \in \mathbb{A}$, and cell transition $t \in \mathbb{E} \times \mathbb{C} \times \mathbb{A} \times \mathbb{H}$, we have $\text{Auth}(t) \iff \text{Auth}((n\ m) \cdot t)$.

Using terminology from [38], the operational semantics of a hypercell model is defined as the set of transitions $\mathcal{T} \subseteq \mathbb{T}$ that is the least well-suported model of the rules in Fig. 2.

Rule TRANS turns an unconstrained transition into a regular transition, provided that it be authorized in the current context.

The predicates $\text{Cond}, \text{Cond}_I, \text{Ind}_I$ in the premises of rules COMP and CTX are defined as follows:

$$\text{Cond}(\Gamma, G) \triangleq \text{supp}(G) \cdot \Sigma(G) \subseteq \Gamma$$

$$\text{Cond}_I(\sigma, \sigma_1, \sigma_2, G) \triangleq \sigma = \text{seval}(\sigma_1 \cup \sigma_2) \wedge \sigma.\text{roles} \subseteq G.\text{unbound}$$

$$\text{Ind}_I(\sigma, E) \triangleq \sigma.\text{roles} \cap E.\text{roles} = \emptyset$$

$$\text{seval}(\sigma) = \text{ if } \sigma = \{\widehat{r} : \widehat{c}\langle V \rangle, \overline{\widehat{r}} : \overline{\widehat{c}}\langle V \rangle\} \cup \sigma' \text{ then seval}(\sigma') \text{ else } \sigma$$

If C is a hypercell with $r \in C.\text{roles}$, such that there is a single cell $L \in C$ with $r \in L.\text{roles}$, then we note $(\!(C)\!)_r^s$ the hypercell $(s\ r) \cdot C$. For $\rho = \widehat{r} : \neg a$, we define $\rho.r = r$. We say that hypercell C, in environment Γ, satisfies the priority constraint $\rho = \widehat{r} : \neg a$, noted $C \models_\Gamma \rho$, if the following conditions hold:

$$\Sigma(C) \subseteq \Gamma.\text{graph} \wedge r \in C.\text{unbound}$$

$$\neg(\exists D \in \mathbb{H}, V \in \mathbb{V}, \Lambda \in \mathbb{A},\ \Gamma \vdash C \xrightarrow{\Lambda} D \wedge \overline{\widehat{r}} : \widehat{a}\langle V \rangle \in \Lambda.\text{sync})$$

The predicates Cond_P and Ind_P in the premises of the rules COMP and CTX are defined as follows:

$$\text{Cond}_P(s, \pi, \pi_1, \pi_2, \Gamma, C_1, C_2) \triangleq s \# \Gamma.\text{names}$$
$$\wedge\ \pi = \{\rho \in \pi_1 \cup \pi_2 \mid \rho.r \in (C_1 \parallel C_2).\text{unbound}\}$$
$$\wedge\ \bigwedge_{\rho \in \pi_1 \setminus \pi} (\!(C_1)\!)_{\rho.r}^s \parallel C_2 \models_\Gamma \rho \wedge \bigwedge_{\rho \in \pi_2 \setminus \pi} C_1 \parallel (\!(C_2)\!)_{\rho.r}^s \models_\Gamma \rho$$

$$\text{Ind}_P(s, \pi, \varpi, \Gamma, C, E) \triangleq s \# \Gamma.\text{names}$$
$$\wedge\ \pi = \{\rho \in \varpi \mid \rho.r \in (C \parallel E).\text{unbound}\}$$
$$\wedge\ \bigwedge_{\rho \in \varpi \setminus \pi} (\!(C)\!)_{\rho.r}^s \parallel E \models_\Gamma \rho$$

The predicate Cond_P expresses the fact that priorities that appear on roles that bind the hypercells C_1 and C_2 together must be verified. Priorities on roles that bind hypercells C_1 and C_2 are exactly those constraints ρ in the set $(\pi_1 \setminus \pi) \cup (\pi_2 \setminus \pi)$, where π is the set of priorities that appear on roles not bound in $C_1 \parallel C_2$ (since priorities that appear in a transition of a hypercell C are expected to adorn unbound roles in C). To check whether a priority ρ is satisfied, one considers a variant of configuration $C_1 \parallel C_2$ where the role $\rho.r$, in the hypercell from which the priority originates, is replaced by a fresh role. In effect, this replacement amounts to severing the binding $\rho.r$ between C_1 and C_2.

Remark 1. The definition of satisfaction for a priority by a hypercell is not entirely trivial because of cycles of constraints that may occur. As a sanity check, consider the two following examples, depicted in Fig. 3.

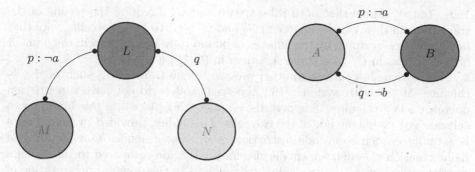

Fig. 3. Two hypercells with priorities

On the left, we are considering a hypercell $M \parallel L \parallel N$, and a transition from L of the form $\Gamma \vdash L \xrightarrow{\langle p:\neg a \cdot q:b \rangle} C$, where L can interact with N on channel b, provided M is not able to interact on a. Verifying the satisfaction of the priority on role p consists in checking whether $M \parallel (\!(L)\!)_p^s \parallel N$, where s is fresh, can interact on channel a on role p, which amounts to check that M can interact on channel a on role p.

On the right, we are considering a hypercell $A \parallel B$, with the following transitions:

$$t_A = \Gamma \vdash A \xrightarrow{\langle q:\neg b \cdot \{p:c,q:c\} \rangle} A' \qquad\qquad t_A' = \Gamma \vdash A \xrightarrow{\langle \epsilon \cdot p:a \rangle} A'$$

$$t_B = \Gamma \vdash B \xrightarrow{\langle p:\neg a \cdot \{p:c,q:c\} \rangle} B' \qquad\qquad t_B' = \Gamma \vdash B \xrightarrow{\langle \epsilon \cdot q:b \rangle} B'$$

In other terms, A can interact on channel c on roles p and q, provided B cannot interact on channel b on role q, and B can interact on channel c on roles p and q, provided A cannot interact on a on role p. To verify the satisfaction of the priority from A on role q, we have to check whether the graph $(\!(A)\!)_q^s \parallel B$, where s is fresh, can interact on channel b on role q, which amounts to check that B can interact on channel b on role q. This is the case because of transition t_B'. The priority from A on role q is thus not verified, and transition t_A cannot fire in this configuration. Likewise, the priority from B on role p is not satisfied and transition t_B cannot fire in this configuration.

In both examples, our rules give results that match the intuition: in the first case, we expect the priority on p to be satisfied merely if M cannot interact on channel a on role p, and in the second case we expect the hypercell $A \parallel B$ to deadlock.

Rule COMP stipulates that a hypercell $G_1 \parallel G_2$ can evolve by combining a transition from G_1 and a transition from G_2. The combination involves synchronizing interactions on roles that bind G_1 and G_2 (condition Cond$_I$) and verifying priorities on the roles that bind G_1 and G_2 (condition Cond$_P$). Rule CTX stipulates that in a hypercell $G \parallel E$, hypercell G can evolve independently of E, provided G's interactions and priorities do not involve roles from E (conditions

Ind_I, Ind_P). Notice that both rules COMP and CTX require the results of the transitions in their conclusion ($G'_1 \parallel G'_2$ and $G' \parallel E$) to be hypercells. Note that both rules are stratified by the number of bound roles in a hypercell: the number of bound roles in $C_1 \parallel C_2$ is one less than in $(\!(C_1)\!)^s_{\rho.r} \parallel C_2$.

Notice that, in contrast to other process calculi frameworks such as the ψ-calculus [5] and SHR systems [19], hypercell models do not have a restriction operator á la π-calculus. In hypercells, events taking place at a role binding two cells are not visible outside of the two cells. This hiding provided by bound roles is actually enough to encode restriction as in the π-calculus. Our handling of name creation via environments is also unusual, again compared to the use of a restriction operator á la π-calculus. It is related to the nominal presentation of the π-calculus in [13], but relies on name insensitivity instead of α-conversion. This is no way a limitation on the expressive power of the hypercell framework for the restriction operator, as well as any other composition operator definable by means of GSOS rules, i.e. structured operational semantics rules obeying the general format defined in [7]. More generally we can prove that any GSOS language (as defined in [7]) can be encoded as a hypercell model:

Proposition 1. *For any GSOS language $\mathcal{L}$, there exists a hypercell model and an encoding $[\![\cdot]\!] : \mathcal{L} \times \mathbb{R} \to \mathcal{P}(\mathbb{H})$, such that for any $P, Q \in \mathcal{L}, a \in \mathcal{A}, u \in \mathbb{R}$, we have $P \xrightarrow{a} Q$ if and only if there exist $\Delta \subseteq \mathbb{A}, \Lambda \in \mathbb{A}$ with $u : a \in \Lambda.\text{sync}$, $C \in [\![P]\!]_u$, and $D \in [\![Q]\!]_u$, such that $\Delta \vdash C \xrightarrow{\Lambda} D$.*

Similarly, we can prove that the π-calculus can be encoded as a hypercell model.

3.2   Behavioral Equivalence for Hypercell Models

We define in this section a strong notion of behavioral equivalence for hypercell models, in the form of a bisimilarity relation.

Definition 1 (Environment equivalence). *Two environments Γ, Γ' are said to be equivalent, noted $\Gamma \eqcirc \Gamma'$, if for all $\Upsilon \in \mathbb{E}$ such that $\Gamma \cup \Upsilon \in \mathbb{E}$ and $\Gamma' \cup \Upsilon \in \mathbb{E}$, for all $C \in \mathbb{C}, \Lambda \in \mathbb{A}, G \in \mathbb{H}$, we have $\text{Auth}(\Gamma \cup \Upsilon, C, \Lambda, G) = \text{Auth}(\Gamma' \cup \Upsilon, C, \Lambda, G)$. Two hypercells G and F are said to be environmentally equivalent, also noted $G \eqcirc F$, if $\text{supp}(G) \cdot \Sigma(G) \eqcirc \text{supp}(F) \cdot \Sigma(F)$.*

Definition 2 (Strong simulation). *A name insensitive binary relation on hypercells $\mathcal{R} \subseteq \mathbb{H} \times \mathbb{H}$ is a strong simulation if, for all $\langle G, F \rangle \in \mathcal{R}, G'' \in \mathbb{H}, \Lambda \in \mathbb{A}$, the following properties hold:*

1. *$G \eqcirc F$ and the unbound provided (resp. required) roles of G and F coincide.*
2. *For all $\Gamma \in \mathbb{E}$ such that $\Gamma \cup \Sigma(G) \in \mathbb{E}, \Gamma \cup \Sigma(F) \in \mathbb{E}$, if $\Gamma \cup \Sigma(G) \vdash G \xrightarrow{\Lambda} G'$, then there exists $F' \in \mathbb{H}$ such that $\Gamma \cup \Sigma(F) \vdash D \xrightarrow{\Lambda} F'$ with $\langle G', F' \rangle \in \mathcal{R}$.*

The main difference compared to the usual notion of strong simulation on labelled transition systems is the quantification on environments, which is necessary to take into account the effect of authorization functions. Note also that we require that a transition be simulated by a transition with the exact same label. This is a strong requirement but which can only be relaxed if one knows more about actions hypercells can take on values (e.g. if processes can only be exchanged and run – placed in a cell –, one may require only that they be similar, as in higher-order simulations).

Definition 3 (Strong bisimulation and bisimilarity). *A binary relation $\mathcal{R} \subseteq \mathbb{H}^2$ is a strong bisimulation if both it and its inverse relation $\mathcal{R}^{-1}$ are strong simulations.*

Strong bisimilarity, noted $\sim$, is defined by $\sim \triangleq \bigcup_{\mathcal{R} \in \mathsf{S}} \mathcal{R}$, where $\mathsf{S} \subseteq \mathcal{P}(\mathbb{H}^2)$ is the set of all strong bisimulations.

Crucially, in any hypercell model strong bisimilarity is a congruence (meaning our notion of bisimilarity is a reasonable notion of behavioral equivalence for hypercells):

Theorem 1. *In any hypercell model, for all $G, F \in \mathbb{H}$, if $G \sim F$, then for all $E \in \mathbb{H}$ such that $G \parallel E \in \mathbb{H}$ and $F \parallel E \in \mathbb{H}$, we have $G \parallel E \sim F \parallel E$.*

The proof of this is left out for lack of space but it proceeds by showing, by induction on the maximum number of bound names in $G \parallel E$ and $F \parallel E$, that the relation $\mathcal{R} = \{(G \parallel E, F \parallel E \mid G \sim F)\}$ is a strong bisimulation.

4 Encapsulation Policies

We show in this section how to enforce different encapsulation policies in hypercell models. Specifically, we present a form of strict encapsulation, inspired by *owner-as-dominator* policies studied in ownership types [14], and a weaker variant that allows software architectures with overlapping encapsulation scopes as in Fig. 1. The challenge is of course to enforce these policies in the highly dynamic and concurrent setting of hypercell evolutions. Some notations first. For $L, M \in \mathbb{C} \cup \mathbb{C}_s$, we write $L \frown M$ to mean L and M are bound, i.e. $(L.\mathsf{prov} \cap M.\mathsf{req}) \cup (L.\mathsf{req} \cap M.\mathsf{prov}) \neq \emptyset$. For $F, G \in \mathbb{H} \cup \mathbb{H}_s$, we write $F \parallel G$ to mean $F.\mathsf{roles} \cap G.\mathsf{roles} = \emptyset$.

4.1 Strict Encapsulation

In this form of encapsulation, cells come in three disjoint categories: *owner cells*, *owned cells*, and *free cells*. Owner cells can be understood as composite components. The cells they own – their owned cells – are their subcomponents. Free cells are neither owner nor owned. The encapsulation policy we consider here takes the form of a structural invariant which ensures an owned cell cannot directly interact with cells which do not belong to its owner's group - made by this owner cell and all its owned cells. For simplicity, we have only a single level of ownership (owner cells cannot be owned). It is relatively straightforward to extend this policy to allow multiple levels of ownerhsip.

To capture this, we consider a hypercell model (actually a class of models) with sorts that take the form of 4-tuples $\langle k, \mathbf{p}, \mathbf{o}, \mathbf{r} \rangle$, where $k \in \{\top, \bot\}$ is a flag and $\mathbf{p}, \mathbf{o}, \mathbf{r} \in \mathcal{P}_{\mathtt{fin}}(\mathbb{R})$. We set: $\mathfrak{s}.\mathtt{flag} = k$, $\mathfrak{s}.\mathtt{fprov} = \mathbf{p}$, $\mathfrak{s}.\mathtt{owned} = \mathbf{o}$, $\mathfrak{s}.\mathtt{freq} = \mathbf{r}$, and write $C.\mathtt{fprov}$ for $C.\mathtt{sort.fprov}$, $C.\mathtt{owned}$ for $C.\mathtt{sort.owned}$, $C.\mathtt{freq}$ for $C.\mathtt{sort.freq}$, $C.\mathtt{flag}$ for $C.\mathtt{sort.flag}$. Flags in sorts are used to avoid race conditions in the parallel evolution of owner and owned cells in a owner group, which would break the global structural invariant (for instance two owned cells being bound, while their owner is splitting itself in two).

A cell C in this model is assumed to maintain the following invariant:

$$C.\mathtt{prov} = C.\mathtt{fprov} \wedge C.\mathtt{req} = C.\mathtt{owned} \cup C.\mathtt{freq} \wedge C.\mathtt{owned} \cap C.\mathtt{freq} = \emptyset \quad (1)$$

We also require to identify in a transition label Λ the roles that are sent by the initial cell in the transition. We note $\Lambda.\mathtt{sent}$ the set of sent roles in Λ.

We define the following (these definitions apply to skeletons as well). For $L, M \in \mathbb{C}$, we write $L \multimap M$ for $L.\mathtt{owned} \cap M.\mathtt{prov} \neq \emptyset$ (intuitively, L owns M), and $M.\mathtt{up}_L$ for $L.\mathtt{owned} \cap M.\mathtt{prov}$ when $L \multimap M$. If $G \in \mathbb{H}$, we write $L \multimap G$ to mean that, for all $M \in G$, $L \multimap M$. For $G \in \mathbb{H}, L \in \mathbb{C}$, we define $\mathtt{scope}_G(L) = \{M \in G \mid L \multimap M\}$ (the set of cells owned by L), and $\mathtt{group}_G(L) = \{L\} \cup \mathtt{scope}_G(L)$. We write $\mathtt{scope}_\Gamma(L)$ for $\mathtt{scope}_{\Gamma.\mathtt{graph}}(L)$. We drop the subscript G to write $\mathtt{scope}(L)$ and $\mathtt{group}(L)$ when the hypercell or skeleton context G is clear. An *owner* is a cell L such that $L.\mathtt{owned} \neq \emptyset$ and we write L owner. We define: $G.\mathtt{owners} \triangleq \{M \in G \mid M.\mathtt{owned} \neq \emptyset\}$. An *owned* cell L in a hypercell G is a cell such that there exists $M \in G$ with $M \multimap L$. A *free* cell in a hypercell G is a cell which is neither owner nor owned.

The structural properties we expect are defined as follows. For any $G \in \mathbb{H} \cup \mathbb{H}_s$:

$$\forall L, M \in G, \ L \neq M \implies \mathtt{scope}_G(L) \parallel \mathtt{scope}_G(M) \wedge L.\mathtt{owned} \cap M.\mathtt{owned} = \emptyset \quad (2)$$

$$\forall L, M \in G, \ L \multimap M \implies M.\mathtt{owned} = \emptyset \quad (3)$$

$$\forall L, M, N \in G, \ L \multimap M \wedge M \multimap N \implies L \multimap M \vee L = N \quad (4)$$

Property (2) states that the encapsulation scopes of two owners L and M in the same hypercell are necessarily distinct and they are bound by no role. Property (3) states that there is only a single level of ownership: an owner cannot be owned. Property (4) states that cells in the encapsulation scope of an owner can only be bound to cells in the same scope or to the owner itself. We write $\mathtt{Inv}(G)$ if properties (2), (3), and (4) hold for G (hypercell or skeleton).

We assume the existence of a predicate $\mathtt{New} \subseteq \mathcal{P}(\mathbb{A}) \times \mathcal{P}_{\mathtt{fin}}(\mathbb{A}) \times \mathcal{P}_{\mathtt{fin}}(\mathbb{A})$ with the following properties ($\mathtt{New}$ can be defined constructively but we eschew this definition here for lack of space):

$$\mathtt{New}(\Delta, A, B) \implies B \cap (\Delta \cup A) = \emptyset$$

$$\mathtt{New}(\Delta, A, B) \wedge \mathtt{New}(\Delta, A', B') \wedge A \neq A' \implies B \cap B' = \emptyset$$

We define the following predicates, which are used in the definition of the authorization predicate. Predicate $\mathtt{Safe} \subseteq \mathbb{E} \times \mathbb{C} \times \mathbb{H}$ is such that $\mathtt{Safe}(\Gamma, M, G)$ holds if roles of G are new roles or are roles already used in the scope of M in the context Γ. It is defined as follows:

$$\texttt{Safe}(\Gamma, M, G) \triangleq \exists B \in \mathcal{P}_{\texttt{fin}}(\mathbb{R}), \texttt{New}(\Gamma.\texttt{names}, H.\texttt{roles}, B)$$
$$\wedge \; G.\texttt{roles} \subseteq B \cup \texttt{scope}_\Gamma(M).\texttt{roles}$$

Predicate $\texttt{Incl} \subseteq \mathbb{H}_s \times \mathbb{C}_s$ is such that $\texttt{Incl}(G, M)$ holds if M shares a role with a skeleton cell in G. It is defined as follows:

$$\texttt{Incl}(G, M) \triangleq M.\texttt{prov} \cap G.\texttt{prov} \neq \emptyset \vee M.\texttt{req} \cap G.\texttt{req} \neq \emptyset$$

We now define the authorization predicate for our class of hypercell models with strict encapsulation. Predicate $\texttt{Auth}$ is defined as follows. $\texttt{Auth}(\Gamma, L, \Lambda, G)$ is $\texttt{true}$ exactly in the cases below:

1. If $\exists M \in \Gamma$, $M \multimap \Sigma(L) \wedge M.\texttt{flag} = \top$, $G.\texttt{owned} = \emptyset \wedge M \multimap \Sigma(G) \wedge$ $\texttt{Safe}(\Gamma, M, G)$, and $\Lambda.\texttt{sent} \subseteq \texttt{supp}(L)$. If the flag of its owner is up, an owned cell can reconfigure into an hypercell G provided all the cells in G remain owned by the same owner, and the roles of G are either existing roles of cells in the owner scope, or brand new ones. If a cell is owned, the only constraint on its transitions labels is that sent roles in a label be roles already known by L (i.e. new roles created during a transition cannot be immediately sent).

2. If $L \texttt{ owner} \wedge L.\texttt{flag} = \bot$, $\texttt{Inv}(\texttt{H}(\Gamma, L, G)) \wedge \texttt{Osafe}(\Gamma, L, G)$ with:

$$\texttt{H}(\Gamma, L, G) \triangleq \Sigma(G) \cup (\texttt{scope}_\Gamma(L) \setminus \{M \in \texttt{scope}_\Gamma(L) \mid \texttt{Incl}(\Sigma(G), M)\})$$
$$\texttt{Osafe}(\Gamma, L, G) \triangleq \bigwedge_{K \in G.\texttt{owners}} \texttt{Safe}(\Gamma, L, \texttt{scope}_{\texttt{H}(\Gamma, L, G)}(K))$$

and $\Lambda.\texttt{sent} \subseteq \texttt{supp}(L) \wedge \overline{\texttt{rmv}} \notin \Lambda.\texttt{sync.channels}$. If its flag is down, an owner L can reconfigure into an hypercell G, provided G and the cells in L's
- scope remaining after the transition (those such that $\texttt{incl}(\Sigma(G), M)$ have been removed) respect the global invariant $\texttt{Inv}$, and the roles in the scope of owners in G are either ones already in its scope, or brand new ones. If a cell is an owner, the same constraint as above on sent roles apply, but in addition it cannot be removed by any other cell.

3. If $L \texttt{ owner} \wedge L.\texttt{flag} = \top$, $L.\texttt{owned} \subseteq G.\texttt{owned}$, $G \in \mathbb{C}$, and $\Lambda.\texttt{sent} \subseteq \texttt{supp}(L) \wedge \overline{\texttt{rmv}} \notin \Lambda.\texttt{sync.channels}$. If its flag is up, an owner can only change into a single owner cell, not losing any owned role, possibly adding some (e.g. to allow the reconfiguration of cells it owns).

4. If $L \texttt{ free}$, $\texttt{Inv}(G) \wedge \texttt{Fsafe}(\Gamma, L, G)$ where:

$$\texttt{Fsafe}(\Gamma, G) \triangleq G.\texttt{roles} \cap \Gamma.\texttt{owned} = \emptyset \wedge \bigwedge_{K \in G.\texttt{owners}} \texttt{Safe}(\Gamma, L, \texttt{scope}_G(K))$$

and $\Lambda.\texttt{sent} \subseteq \texttt{supp}(L)$. A free cell can reconfigure into a hypercell G provided it respects the global invariant $\texttt{Inv}$, it does not insert new cells in the scope of existing owners, and the roles of cells in the scope of new owners in G are safe. Also, since it is not an owner, new roles created during a transition cannot be immediately sent.

Note that, with the above definition of Auth, in an environment Γ where cell L is owned and the flag of its owner M is down, i.e. $\exists M \in \Gamma$, $M \multimap L \wedge M.\mathtt{flag} = \bot$, then L cannot evolve in environment Γ.

The authorization predicate is quite permissive in the kinds of evolutions owner cells can perform. Notice in particular that owner cells may split or dissolve during execution, allowing e.g. for the transfer of owned cells from one owner to another. Likewise, owned cells can be freed by their owner and become owner cells later on. The dynamicity and concurrency in the class of hypercell models obeying strict encapsulation is much bigger than that allowed in the computational models underlying ownership types (either strictly sequential or actor like).

Predicate Inv is indeed an invariant for the class of hypercell models equipped with these sorts and authorization functions:

Proposition 2 (Inv is an invariant). *For all* $\Gamma \in \mathbb{E}, G, G' \in \mathbb{H}, \Lambda \in \mathbb{A}$, *if* $\mathtt{Inv}(\Gamma)$, $\mathtt{Inv}(G)$ *and* $\Gamma \vdash G \xrightarrow{\Lambda} G'$, *then* $\mathtt{Inv}(G')$.

4.2   Selective Encapsulation

We extend the strict encapsulation policy of the previous section with a notion of *weak ownership*. Briefly, owner scopes of strict encapsulation are now allowed to include weakly owned cells. A cell may belong to only one owner, as previously, but may also belong to several weak owners. A cell can be weakly owned only if it has identified specific provided roles for this purpose (wprov roles below).

We extend sorts to 6-tuples $\langle k, \mathbf{p}, \mathbf{o}, \mathbf{r}, \mathbf{q}, \mathbf{w} \rangle$ with $\mathbf{q}, \mathbf{w} \in \mathcal{P}_{\mathtt{fin}}(\mathbb{R})$. We set $\mathfrak{s}.\mathtt{wowned} = \mathbf{w}$ and $\mathfrak{s}.\mathtt{wprov} = \mathbf{q}$. We write $C.\mathtt{wowned}$ for $C.\mathtt{sort.wowned}$, and $C.\mathtt{wprov}$ for $C.\mathtt{sort.wprov}$. $C.\mathtt{wowned}$ are required roles for binding to a weakly owned cell. $C.\mathtt{wprov}$ are provided roles for binding to a weak owner.

We adapt the invariant (1) as follows:

$$C.\mathtt{prov} = C.\mathtt{fprov} \cup C.\mathtt{wprov} \wedge C.\mathtt{fprov} \cap C.\mathtt{wprov} = \emptyset$$
$$\wedge\, C.\mathtt{req} = C.\mathtt{owned} \cup C.\mathtt{wowned} \cup C.\mathtt{freq} \qquad (5)$$
$$\wedge\, C.\mathtt{owned}, C.\mathtt{wowned}, C.\mathtt{freq}\ \text{mutually disjoint}$$

For $L, M \in \mathbb{C}$ (or $\mathbb{C}_s$), we write $L \rightharpoonup M$ for $L.\mathtt{wowned} \cap M.\mathtt{wprov} \neq \emptyset$.

Writing now $G.(\mathtt{roles} - \mathtt{wroles})$ for $G.\mathtt{roles} \setminus (G.\mathtt{wowned} \cup G.\mathtt{wprov})$, and $F \diamond G$ for $F.(\mathtt{roles} - \mathtt{wroles}) \cap G.(\mathtt{roles} - \mathtt{wroles}) = \emptyset$ he global structural invariant is now the conjunction of the following properties:

$$\forall L, M \in G, L \neq M \implies \mathtt{scope}_G(L) \diamond \mathtt{scope}_G(M) \wedge L.\mathtt{owned} \cap M.\mathtt{owned} = \emptyset \quad (6)$$
$$\forall L, M \in G, L \multimap M \implies M.\mathtt{owned} = \emptyset \qquad\qquad\qquad (7)$$
$$\forall L, M, N \in G,\ L \multimap M \wedge M \frown N \implies L \multimap N \vee L = N \vee M \rightharpoonup N \vee N \rightharpoonup M \quad (8)$$

Notice how the invariant (8) changes from the strict encapsulation policy. Cells in an owner scope are now allowed to bind to cells they weakly own, i.e. the weak ownership relation allows cells to bind roles across group boundaries.

The authorization predicate for this new policy is defined as in the previous section, with just a change in the definition of the Safe predicate. Safe is now defined as follows:

$$\texttt{Safe}(\Gamma, M, G) \triangleq \exists B \in \mathcal{P}_{\texttt{fin}}(\mathbb{R}), \texttt{New}(\Gamma.\texttt{names}, M.\texttt{roles}, B)$$
$$\land \ G.(\texttt{roles} - \texttt{wroles}) \subseteq B \cup \texttt{scope}_\Gamma(M).(\texttt{roles} - \texttt{wroles})$$
$$\land \ G.\texttt{wowned} \subseteq \Gamma.\texttt{wprov}$$

Using this policy, we can describe the architecture described in Fig. 1 as a hypercell with cells C, C_1, C_2, L, L_1, L_2, where C and L are owners of cells C_1, C_2 and L_1, L_2, respectively, and where C_1 and C_2 are weak owners of L_1 and L_2, respectively.

As it is, the selective encapsulation policy just allows for specifically identified roles to break the encapsulation policy, and for weakly owned cells to act as shared internal means of communication between different owner scopes. It is possible, however, to enforce additional constraints on weak ownership to reflect different aggregation semantics. For instance, one could enforce a lifetime dependency between weak owner and weak owned cell, preventing the removal of a weak owner if its weakly owned cells are still in place, or, one could ensure a cell has a single weak owner. We do not present these examples here, but our two examples in this section should provide a good taste of the possibilities offered.

5 Conclusion

We have presented the Hypercell framework for defining software component models (hypercell models). The basic ontology of any hypercell model agrees with the classical elements of software component models [16,21], but the combination of dynamicity, sharing and encapsulation an hypercell model can offer is, to the best of our knowledge, unique. The key points to retain are the following: (i) this combination is made possible by the use of contextual transitions, cell sorts and context dependent runtime checks that enforce encapsulation policies; (ii) a proper notion of equivalence between hypercells is obtained thanks to authorizations at the level of individual cells and a notion of bisimulation that decouples the effect of authorizations from the classical bisimulation game.

Our runtime approach to enforcing encapsulation policies seems more permissive, and able to express more forms of policies and aggregations semantics than possible with ownership types, as our examples suggest. However, we have at this time no formal proof of this. Also, how our approach compares with those combining static ownership discipline with dynamic ownership tests, as in the Mezzo permission-based language [1], remains to be seen. It is worth pointing out that in defining encapsulation policies in the Hypercell framework, we do have a choice between imposing static constraints on unconstrained transitions, and imposing dynamic constraints via authorization predicates. In this paper, we have opted in our examples for an approach that made maximal use of authorization, but other options are available that combine both. For expressivity, however, we believe some amount of run-time checking is inescapable.

A crucial question is of course whether our abstract Hypercell framework can be efficiently implemented and supported. An implementation of an abstract machine for object-based hypercells is currently under way, but is clear that enforcing encapsulation constraints via runtime checks is a viable option, as demonstrated by the work on Siaam [15]. This work showed, in the simpler context of the actor model, that the overhead of such checks can largely be mitigated by means of static analyses that can safely remove most unnecessary ones.

References

1. Balabonski, T., Pottier, F., Protzenko, J.: The design and formalization of Mezzo, a permission-based programming language. ACM Trans. Program. Lang. Syst. **38**(4), 14 (2016)
2. Barbier, F., Henderson-Sellers, B., Le Parc, A., Bruel, J.M.: Formalization of the whole-part relationship in the unified modeling language. IEEE Trans. Softw. Eng. **29**(5), 459–470 (2003)
3. Bass, L., Clements, P., Kazman, R.: Software Architecture in Practice SEI Series in Software Engineering, 3rd edn. Addison-Wesley, Boston (2013)
4. Bauer, S., et al.: Moving from specifications to contracts in component-based design. In: de Lara, J., Zisman, A. (eds.) FASE 2012. LNCS, vol. 7212, pp. 43–58. Springer, Heidelberg (2012). https://doi.org/10.1007/978-3-642-28872-2_3
5. Bengtson, J., Johansson, M., Parrow, J., Victor, B.: Psi-calculi: a framework for mobile processes with nominal data and logic. Log. Methods Comput. Sci. 7(1), 1–44 (2011)
6. Bliudze, S., Sifakis, J.: A notion of glue expressiveness for component-based systems. In: van Breugel, F., Chechik, M. (eds.) CONCUR 2008. LNCS, vol. 5201, pp. 508–522. Springer, Heidelberg (2008). https://doi.org/10.1007/978-3-540-85361-9_39
7. Bloom, B., Istrail, S., Meyer, A.R.: Bisimulation can't be traced. J. ACM **42**(1), 232–268 (1995)
8. Bruneton, E., Coupaye, T., Leclercq, M., Quema, V., Stefani, J.B.: The fractal component model and its support in Java. Softw. Pract. Exp. **36**(11–12), 1257–1284 (2006)
9. Bruni, R., Montanari, U., Sammartino, M.: Reconfigurable and software-defined networks of connectors and components. In: Wirsing, M., Hölzl, M., Koch, N., Mayer, P. (eds.) Software Engineering for Collective Autonomic Systems. LNCS, vol. 8998, pp. 73–106. Springer, Cham (2015). https://doi.org/10.1007/978-3-319-16310-9_2
10. Bugliesi, M., Castagna, G., Crafa, S.: Access control for mobile agents: the calculus of boxed ambients. ACM. Trans. Program. Lang. Syst. **26**(1), 57–124 (2004)
11. Cardelli, L., Gordon, A.: Mobile ambients. Theor. Comput. Sci. **240**(1), 177–213 (2000)
12. Castellani, I.: Process algebras with localities. In: Bergstra, J., Ponse, A., Smolka, S. (eds.) Handbook of Process Algebra, Elsevier (2001)

13. Cattani, G.L., Sewell, P.: Models for name-passing processes: interleaving and causal. Inf. Comput. **190**(2), 136–178 (2004)
14. Clarke, D., Östlund, J., Sergey, I., Wrigstad, T.: Ownership types: a survey. In: Clarke, D., Noble, J., Wrigstad, T. (eds.) Aliasing in Object-Oriented Programming. Types, Analysis and Verification. LNCS, vol. 7850, pp. 15–58. Springer, Heidelberg (2013). https://doi.org/10.1007/978-3-642-36946-9_3
15. Claudel, B., Sabah, Q., Stefani, J.B.: Simple isolation for an actor abstract machine. In: Graf, S., Viswanathan, M. (eds.) Formal Techniques for Distributed Objects, Components, and Systems, FORTE 2015. Lecture Notes in Computer Science, vol. 9039. Springer, Cham (2015). https://doi.org/10.1007/978-3-319-19195-9_14
16. Crnkovic, I., Sentilles, S., Vulgarakis, A., Chaudron, M.R.V.: A classification framework for software component models. IEEE Trans. Softw. Eng. **37**(5), 599–615 (2011)
17. Nicola, R.D., Loreti, M., Pugliese, R., Tiezzi, F.: A formal approach to autonomic systems programming: the SCEL language. ACM Trans. Auton. Adapt. Syst. **9**(2), 7 (2014)
18. Eker, J., et al.: Taming heterogeneity-the Ptolemy approach. Proc. IEEE **91**(1), 127–144 (2003)
19. Ferrari, G.L., Hirsch, D., Lanese, I., Montanari, U., Tuosto, E.: Synchronised hyperedge replacement as a model for service oriented computing. In: de Boer, F.S., Bonsangue, M.M., Graf, S., de Roever, W.-P. (eds.) FMCO 2005. LNCS, vol. 4111, pp. 22–43. Springer, Heidelberg (2006). https://doi.org/10.1007/11804192_2
20. Fiadeiro, J.L., Lopes, A.: A model for dynamic reconfiguration in service-oriented architectures. Softw. Syst. Model. **12**(2), 349–367 (2013)
21. Garlan, D., Monroe, R.T., Wile, D.: Acme: architectural description of component-based systems. Foundations of Component-Based Systems. Cambridge University Press (2000)
22. Hennessy, M., Rathke, J., Yoshida, N.: SAFEDPI: a language for controlling mobile code. Acta Inf. **42**(4–5), 227–290 (2005)
23. Jongmans, S.S.T.Q., Arbab, F.: Overview of thirty semantic formalisms for Reo. Sci. Ann. Comput. Sci. 22(1), 201–251 (2012)
24. Leavens, G., Sitaraman, M. (eds.): Foundations of Component-Based Systems. Cambridge University Press (2000)
25. Zhiming, L., He, J. (eds.): Mathematical Frameworks for Component Software - Models for Analysis and Synthesis. World Scientic (2006)
26. Magee, J., Kramer, J.: Dynamic structure in software architectures. In: 4th ACM symposium on Foundations of Software Engineering (FSE-4). ACM (1995)
27. Merle, P., Stefani, J.B.: A formal specification of the fractal component model in alloy. Research Report RR-6721, INRIA, France (2008)
28. Milner, R.: The Space and Motion of Communicating Agents. Cambridge University Press, Cambridge (2009)
29. De Nicola, R., Ferrari, G.L., Pugliese, R.: Klaim: a kernel language for agents interaction and mobility. IEEE Trans. Softw. Eng. **24**(5), 315–330 (1998)
30. Pitts, A.M.: Nominal Sets: Names and Symmetry in Computer Science. Cambridge University Press, Cambridge (2013)
31. Riely, J., Hennessy, M.: A typed language for distributed mobile processes. In: 25th ACM SIGPLAN-SIGACT Symposium on Principles of Programming Languages (POPL). ACM (1998)
32. Sanchez, A., Barbosa, L.S., Riesco, D.: Bigraphical modelling of architectural patterns. In: Arbab, F., Ölveczky, P.C. (eds.) FACS 2011. LNCS, vol. 7253, pp. 313–330. Springer, Heidelberg (2012). https://doi.org/10.1007/978-3-642-35743-5_19

33. Sangiorgi, D., Walker, D.: The π-calculus: A Theory of Mobile Processes. Cambridge University Press, Cambridge (2001)
34. Schmitt, A., Stefani, J.-B.: The kell calculus: a family of higher-order distributed process calculi. In: Priami, C., Quaglia, P. (eds.) GC 2004. LNCS, vol. 3267, pp. 146–178. Springer, Heidelberg (2005). https://doi.org/10.1007/978-3-540-31794-4_9
35. Sevegnani, M., Calder, M.: Bigraphs with sharing. Theor. Comput. Sci. **577**, 43–73 (2015)
36. Stefani, J.-B.: Components as location graphs. In: Lanese, I., Madelaine, E. (eds.) FACS 2014. LNCS, vol. 8997, pp. 3–23. Springer, Cham (2015). https://doi.org/10.1007/978-3-319-15317-9_1
37. Tutu, I., Fiadeiro, J.L.: Service-oriented logic programming. Log. Methods Comput. Sci. 11(3), 1–37 (2015)
38. van Glabbeek, R.J.: The meaning of negative premises in transition system specifications II. J. Log. Algebraic Program. **60–61**, 229–258 (2004). https://www.sciencedirect.com/journal/the-journal-of-logic-and-algebraic-programming/vol/60/suppl/C
39. Voigt, J.: Access contracts: a dynamic approach to object-oriented access protection. Technical report UCAM-CL-TR-880, University of Cambridge (2016)
40. Wermelinger, M., Fiadeiro, J.L.: A graph transformation approach to software architecture reconfiguration. Sci. Comput. Program. 44(2), 133–155 (2002)

Decentralized Real-Time Safety Verification for Distributed Cyber-Physical Systems

Hoang-Dung Tran[1]([✉]), Luan Viet Nguyen[2], Patrick Musau[1], Weiming Xiang[1], and Taylor T. Johnson[1]

[1] Institute for Software Integrated Systems,
Vanderbilt University, Nashville, TN, USA
trhoangdung@gmail.com
[2] Department of Computer and Information Science,
University of Pennsylvania, Philadelphia, PA, USA

Abstract. Safety-critical distributed cyber-physical systems (CPSs) have been found in a wide range of applications. Notably, they have displayed a great deal of utility in intelligent transportation, where autonomous vehicles communicate and cooperate with each other via a high-speed communication network. Such systems require an ability to identify maneuvers in real-time that cause dangerous circumstances and ensure the implementation always meets safety-critical requirements. In this paper, we propose a real-time decentralized safety verification approach for a distributed multi-agent CPS with the underlying assumption that all agents are time-synchronized with a low degree of error. In the proposed approach, each agent periodically computes its local reachable set and exchanges this reachable set with the other agents with the goal of verifying the system safety. Our method, implemented in Java, takes advantages of the timing information and the reachable set information that are available in the exchanged messages to reason about the safety of the whole system in a decentralized manner. Any particular agent can also perform local safety verification tasks based on their local clocks by analyzing the messages it receives. We applied the proposed method to verify, in real-time, the safety properties of a group of quadcopters performing a distributed search mission.

1   Introduction

The emergence of 5G technology has inspired a massive wave of the research and development in science and technology in the era of IoT where the communication between computing devices has become significantly faster with lower latency and power consumption. The power of this modern communication technology influences and benefits all aspects of Cyber-Physical Systems (CPSs) such as smart grids, smart homes, intelligent transportation and smart cities. In particular, the study of autonomous vehicles has become an increasingly popular

© IFIP International Federation for Information Processing 2019
Published by Springer Nature Switzerland AG 2019
J. A. Pérez and N. Yoshida (Eds.): FORTE 2019, LNCS 11535, pp. 261–277, 2019.
https://doi.org/10.1007/978-3-030-21759-4_15

research field in both academic and industrial transportation applications. Automotive crashes pose significant financial and life-threatening risks, and there is an urgent need for advanced and scalable methods that can efficiently verify a distributed system of autonomous vehicles.

Over the last two decades, although many methods have been developed to conduct reachability analysis and safety verification of CPS, such as the approaches proposed in [1, 4, 10, 11, 13, 15, 18], applying these techniques to *real-time distributed* CPS remains a big challenge. This is due to the fact that, (1) all existing techniques have intensive computation costs and are usually too slow to be used in a real-time manner and, (2) these techniques target the safety verification of a *single* CPS, and therefore they naturally cannot be applied efficiently to a *distributed* CPS where clock mismatches and communication between agents (i.e., individual systems) are essential concerns. Since the future autonomous vehicles systems will work distributively involving effective communication between each agent, there is an urgent need for an approach that can provide formal guarantees of the safety of distributed CPS in real-time. More importantly, the safety information should be defined based on the *agents local clocks* to allow these agents to perform "intelligent actions" to escape from the upcoming dangerous circumstances. For example, if an agent A knows based on its local clock that it will collide with an agent B in the next 5 s, it should perform an action such as stopping or quickly finding a safe path to avoid the collision.

In this paper, we propose a *decentralized real-time safety verification* approach for a distributed CPS with multiple agents. We are particularly interested in two types of safety properties. The first one is a *local safety property* which specifies the local constraints of the agent operation. For example, each agent is only allowed to move within a specific region, does not hit any obstacles, and its velocity needs to be limited to specific range. This type of property does not require the information of other agents and can be verified locally at run-time. The second safety property is a *global safety property* in which we want to check if there are any potential collision occurring between the agents.

Our decentralized real-time safety verification approach works as follows. Each agent *locally* and *periodically computes* the local reachable set from the current local time to the next T seconds, and then *encodes* and *broadcasts* its reachable set information to the others via a communication network. When the agent receives a reachable set message, it immediately *decodes* the message to read the reachable set information of the sender, and then performs *peer-to-peer collision checking* based on its current state and the reachable set of the sender. Additionally, the local safety property of the agent is verified simultaneously with the reachable set computation process at run-time. The proposed verification approach is based on an underlying assumption that is, all agents are time-synchronized to some level of accuracy. This assumption is reasonable as it can be achieved by using existing time synchronization protocols such as the Network Time Protocol (NTP). Our approach has successfully verified in real-time the local safety properties and collision occurrences for a group of quadcopters conducting a search mission.

2   Problem Formulation

In this paper, we consider a distributed CPS with N agents that can communicate with each other via an asynchronous communication channel.

Communication Model. The communication between agents is implemented by the *actions* of sending and receiving messages over an asynchronous communication channel. We formally model this communication model as a single automaton, Channel, which stores the set of in-flight messages that have been sent, but are yet to be delivered. When an agent sends a message m, it invokes a *send(m)* action. This action adds m to the *in-flight* set. At any arbitrary time, the Channel chooses a message in the in-flight set to either delivers it to its recipient or removes it from the set. All messages are assumed to be unique and each message contains its sender and recipient identities. Let M be the set of all possible messages used in communication between agents. The sending and receiving messages by agent i are denoted by $M_{i,*}$ and $M_{*,i}$, respectively.

Agent Model. The ith agent is modeled as a hybrid automaton [12,22] defined by the tuple $\langle \mathcal{A}_i = V_i, A_i, \mathcal{D}_i, \mathcal{T}_i \rangle$, where:

(a) V_i is a set of variables consisting of the following: (i) a set of continuous variables X_i including a special variable clk_i which records the agent's *local time*, and (ii) a set of discrete variables Y_i including the special variable $msghist_i$ that records all sent and received messages. A valuation $\mathbf{v}_i$ is a function that associates each $v_i \in V_i$ to a value in its type. We write $val(V_i)$ for the set of all possible valuations of V_i. We abuse the notion of $\mathbf{v}_i$ to denote a state of $\mathcal{A}_i$, which is a valuation of all variables in V_i. The set $Q_i \triangleq val(V_i)$ is called the set of *states*.

b) A_i is a set of *actions* consisting of the following subsets: (i) a set $\{send_i(m) \mid m \in M_{i,*}\}$ of send actions (i.e., output actions), (ii) a set $\{receive_i(m) \mid m \in M_{*,i}\}$ of receive actions (i.e., input actions), and (iii) a set H_i of other, ordinary actions.

(c) $\mathcal{D}_i \subseteq val(V_i) \times A_i \times val(V_i)$ is called the set of *transitions*. For a transition $(\mathbf{v}_i, a_i, \mathbf{v}'_i) \in \mathcal{D}_i$, we write $\mathbf{v}_i \xrightarrow{a_i} \mathbf{v}'_i$ in short. (i) If $a_i = send_i(m)$ or $receive_i(m)$, then all the components of $\mathbf{v}_i$ and $\mathbf{v}'_i$ are identical except that m is added to $msghist$ in $\mathbf{v}'_i$. That is, the agent's other states remain the same on message sends and receives. Furthermore, for every state $\mathbf{v}_i$ and every receive action a_i, there must exist a $\mathbf{v}'_i$ such that $\mathbf{v}_i \xrightarrow{a_i} \mathbf{v}'_i$, i.e., the automaton must have well-defined behavior for receiving any message in any state. (ii) If $a_i \in H_i$, then $\mathbf{v}_i.msghist = \mathbf{v}'_i.msghist$.

(d) $\mathcal{T}_i$ is a collection of trajectories for X_i. Each trajectory of X_i is a function mapping an interval of time $[0, t], t \geq 0$ to $val(V_i)$, following a flow rate that specifies how a real variable $x_i \in X_i$ evolving over time. We denote the *duration* of a trajectory as τ_{dur}, which is the right end-point of the interval t.

Agent Semantics. The *behavior* of each agent can be defined based on the concept of an *execution* which is a particular run of the agent. Given an initial state $\mathbf{v}_i^0$, an *execution* α_i of an agent A_i is a sequence of states starting from $\mathbf{v}_i^0$, defined as $\alpha_i = \mathbf{v}_i^0, \mathbf{v}_i^1, \ldots$, and for each index j in the sequence, the state update from $\mathbf{v}_i^j$ to $\mathbf{v}_i^{j+1}$ is either a transition or trajectory. A state $\mathbf{v}_i^j$ is *reachable* if there exists an executing that ends in $\mathbf{v}_i^j$. We denote $\mathsf{Reach}(A_i)$ as the reachable set of agent A_i.

System Model. The formal model of the complete system, denoted as System, is a network of hybrid automata that is obtained by parallel composing the agent's models and the communication channel. Formally, we can write, $\mathsf{System} \triangleq A_1 \| \ldots A_N \| \mathsf{Channel}$. Informally, the agent A_i and the communication channel Channel are synchronized through sending and receiving actions. When the agent A_i sends a message $m \in M_{i,j}$ to the agent A_j, it triggers the $send_i(m)$ action. At the same time, this action is synchronized in the Channel automaton by putting the message m in the *in-flight* set. After that, the Channel will trigger (non-deterministically) the $receive_j(m)$ action. This action is synchronized in the agent A_j by putting the message m into the $msghist_j$.

In this paper, we investigate two real-time safety verification problems for distributed cyber-physical systems as defined in the following.

Problem 1 (Local safety verification in real-time). The real-time local safety verification problem is to compute online the reachable set $\mathsf{Reach}(A_i)$ of the agent and verify if it violates the local safety property, i.e., checking $\mathsf{Reach}(A_i) \cap \mathcal{U}_i = \emptyset$?, where $\mathcal{U}_i \triangleq C_i x_i \leq d_i, x_i \in X_i$ is the unsafe set of the agent.

Problem 2 (Decentralized real-time collision verification). The decentralized real-time collision verification problem is to reason in real-time whether an agent A_i will collide with other agents from its current local time t_c^i to the *computable, safe time instance in the future* T_{safe} based on (i) the *clock mismatches*, and (ii) the *exchanging reachable set messages* between agents. Formally, we require that $\forall\ t_c^i \leq t \leq T_{safe}, d_{ij}(t) \geq l$, where $d_{ij}(t)$ is the distance between agents A_i and A_j at the time t of the agent A_i local clock, and l is the allowable safe distance between agents.

3   Real-Time Local Safety Verification

The first important step in our approach is, each agent A_i computes forwardly its reachable set of states from the current local time t^i to the next $(t^i + T)$ seconds which is defined by $\mathcal{R}_i[t^i, t^i + T]$. Since there are many variables used in the agent modeling that are irrelevant in safety verification, we only need to compute the reachable set of state that is related to the agent's physical dynamics (so called as *motion dynamics*) which is defined by a nonlinear ODE $\dot{x}_i = f(x_i, u_i)$, where $x_i \in \mathbb{R}^n$ is state vector and $u_i \in \mathbb{R}^m$ is the control input vector. The agent can switch from one mode to the another mode via discrete transitions, and in each mode, the control law may be different. When the agent computes its reachable set, the only information it needs are its current set of states $x_i(t^i)$ and the current control input $u_i(t^i)$. It should be clarified that although the control law may be different among modes, the control signal u_i is updated with the same control period T_c^i. Consequently, u_i is a constant vector in each control period.

Assuming that the agent's current time is $t_j^i = j \times T_c$, using its local sensors and GPS, we have the current state of the agent x_i. Note that the local sensors and the provided GPS can only provide the information of interest to some accuracy, therefore the actual state of the agent is in a set $x_i \in I_i$. The control signal u_i is computed based on the state x_i and a reference signal, e.g., a set point denoting where the agent needs to go to, and then computed control signal is applied to the actuator to control the motion of the agent. From the current set of states I_i and the control signal u_i, we can compute the forward reachable set of the agent for the next $t_j^i + T$ seconds. This reachable set computation needs to be completed after an amount of time $T_{runtime}^i < T_c^i$ because if $T_{runtime}^i \geq T_c^i$, a new u_i will be updated. The control period T_c^i is chosen based on the agent's motion dynamics, and thus to control an agent with fast dynamics, the control period T_c^i needs to be sufficiently small. This is the source of the requirement that the allowable run-time for reachable set computation be small.

To compute the reachable set of an agent in real-time, we use the well-known face-lifting method [3,6] and a *hyper-rectangle* to represent the reachable set. This method is useful for short-time reachability analysis of real-time systems. It allows users to define an allowable run-time $T_{runtime}^i$, and has no dynamic data structures, recursion, and does not depend on complex external libraries as in other reachability analysis methods. More importantly, the accuracy of the reachable set computation can be iteratively improved based on the *remaining allowable run-time*.

Algorithm 3.1 describes the real-time reachability analysis for one agent. The Algorithm works as follows. The time period $[t^i, t^i + T]$ is divided by M steps. The reach time step is defined by $h_i = T/M$. Using the reach time step and the current set I_i, the face-lifting method performs a *single-face-lifting operation*. The results of this step are a new reachable set and a *remaining reach time* $T_{remainReachTime}^i < T$. This step is iteratively called until the reachable set for the whole time period of interest $[t^i, t^i + T]$ is constructed completely, i.e., the remaining reach time is equal to zero. Interestingly, with the reach time step size h_i defined above, the face-lifting algorithm may be finished quickly after an amount of time which is smaller than the allowable run-time $T_{runtime}^i$ specified by user, i.e., there is still an amount of time called remaining run time $T_{remainRunTime}^i < T_{runtime}^i$ that is available for us to recall the face-lifting algorithm with a smaller reach time step size, for example, we can recall the face-lifting algorithm with a new reach time step $h_i/2$. By doing this, the conservativeness of the reachable set can be iteratively improved. The core step of face-lifting method is the single-face-lifting operation. We refer the readers to [3] for further detail. As mentioned earlier, the local safety property of each agent can be verified at run-time simultaneously with the reachable set computation process. Precisely, let $\mathcal{U}_i \triangleq C_i x_i \leq d_i$ be the unsafe region of the ith agent, the

Algorithm 3.1. Real-time reachability analysis for agent A_i.

Input: I_i, u_i, t^i, T, h_i, $T^i_{runtime}$, $\mathcal{U}_i$
Output: $\mathcal{R}_i[t^i, t^i + T]$, $safe = true$ or $safe = uncertain$

1: **procedure** INITIALIZATION
2:      $step = h_i$ % Reach time step
3:      $T^i_1 = T^i_{runtime}$ % Remaining run-time
4: **procedure** REACHABILITY ANALYSIS
5:      **while** $(T^i_1 > 0)$ **do**
6:          $\mathcal{CR} = I_i$ % Current reachable set
7:          $safe = true$
8:          $T^i_2 = T$ % Remaining reach time
9:          **while** $T^i_2 > 0$ **do**
10:             % Do Single Face Lifting
11:             $\mathcal{R}, T' = SFL(\mathcal{CR}, step, T^i_2, u_i)$
12:             $\mathcal{CR} = \mathcal{R}$ % Update reach set
13:             $T^i_2 = T'$ % Update remaining reach time
14:             **if** $(\mathcal{CR} \cap \mathcal{U}_i \neq \emptyset)$ **then**: $safe = uncertain$
15:             $\mathcal{R}_i[t^i, t^i + T] = \mathcal{CR}$
16:         % Update remaining runtime
17:         $T^i_1 = T^i_1 - (A_i.currentTime() - t^i)$
18:         **if** $T^i_1 \leq 0$ **then** break
19:         **else**
20:             $step = h_i/2$ % Reduce reach time step
21:         **return** $\mathcal{R}_i[t^i, t^i + T] = \mathcal{CR}, safe$

---

agent is said to be safe from t^i to $t^i + t \leq t^i + T$ if $\mathcal{R}_i[t^i, t^i + t] \cap \mathcal{U}_i = \emptyset$. Since the reachable set $\mathcal{R}_i[t^i, t^i + t]$ is given by the face-lifting method at run-time, the local safety verification problem for each agent can be solved at run-time. Since the Algorithm 3.1 computes an over-approximation of the reachable set of each agent in a short time interval, it guarantees the soundness of the result as described in the following lemma.

Lemma 1 [3,6]. *The real-time reachability analysis algorithm is sound, i.e., the computed reachable set contains all possible trajectories of agent A_i from t^i to $t^i + T$.*

4   Decentralized Real-Time Collision Verification

Our collision verification scheme is performed based on the exchanged reachable set messages between agents. For every control period T_c, each agent executes the real-time reachability analysis algorithm to check if it is locally safe and to obtain its current reachable set with respect to its current control input. When the current reachable set is available, the agent encodes the reachable set in a message and then broadcasts this message to its cooperative agents and listens to

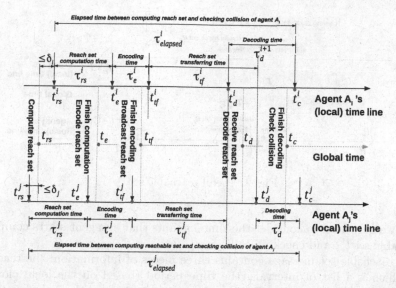

Fig. 1. Timeline for reachable set computing, encoding, transferring, decoding and collision checking.

the upcoming messages sent from these agents. When a reachable set message arrives, the agent immediately decodes the message to construct the current reachable set of the sender and then performs peer-to-peer collision detection. The process of computing, encoding, transferring, decoding of the reachable set along with collision checking is illustrated in Fig. 1 based on the agent's local clock.

Let t_{rs}^i, t_e^i, t_{tf}^i, t_d^i, and t_c^i respectively be the instants that we compute, encode, transfer, decode the reachable set and do collision checking on the agent A_i. Note that these time instants are based on the agent A_i's local clock. The actual run-times are defined as follows.

$$\tau_{rs}^i = t_e^i - t_{rs}^i, \% \ reachablet \ set \ computation \ time,$$
$$\tau_e^i = t_{tf}^i - t_e^i, \% \ encoding \ time,$$
$$\tau_{tf}^i \approx t_d^j - t_{tf}^i, \% \ transferring \ time,$$
$$\tau_d^i = t_c^i - t_d^i, \% \ decoding \ time.$$

Note that we do not know the exact transfer time τ_{tf}^i since it depends on two different local time clocks. The above transfer time formula describes its approximate value when neglecting the mismatch between the two local clocks. The actual reachable set computation time is close to the allowable run-time chosen by user, i.e., $\tau_{rs}^i \approx T_{runtime}^i$. We will see later that the encoding time and decoding time are fairly small in comparison with the transferring time, i.e., $\tau_e^i \approx \tau_d^i \ll \tau_{tf}^i$. All of these run-times provide useful information for selecting an appropriate control period T_c for an agent. However, for collision checking pur-

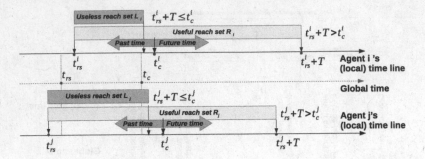

Fig. 2. Useful reachable set.

pose, we only need to consider the time instants that an agent starts computing reachable set t_{rs}^i and checking collision t_c^i.

A reachable set message contains three pieces of information: the reachable set which is a list of intervals, the time period (based on the local clock) in which this reachable set is valid, i.e., the start time t_{rs}^i and the end time $t_{rs}^i + T$ and the time instant that this message is sent. Based on the timing information of the reachable set and the time-synchronization errors, an agent can examine whether or not a received reachable set contains information about the future behavior of the sent agent which is useful for checking collision. The usefulness of the reachable sets used in collision checking is defined as follows.

Definition 1 (Useful reachable sets). *Let δ_i and δ_j respectively be the time-synchronization errors of agent A_i and A_j in comparison with the virtual global time t, i.e, $t - \delta_i \leq t^i \leq t + \delta_i$ and $t - \delta_j \leq t^j \leq t + \delta_j$, where t^i and t^j are current local times of A_i and A_j respectively. The reachable sets $\mathcal{R}_i[t_{rs}^i, t_{rs}^i + T]$ and $\mathcal{R}_j[t_{rs}^j, t_{rs}^j + T]$ of the agent A_j that are available at the agent A_i at time t_c^i are useful for checking collision between A_i and A_j if:*

$$t_c^i < t_{rs}^j + T - \delta_i - \delta_j,$$
$$t_c^i < t_{rs}^i + T. \tag{1}$$

Assume that we are at a time instant where the agent A_i checks if a collision occurs. This means that the current local time is t_c^i. Note that agent A_i and A_j are synchronized to the global time with errors δ_i and δ_j respectively. The reachable set $\mathcal{R}_j[t_{rs}^j, t_{rs}^j + T]$ is useful if it contains information about the *future behavior* of agent A_j under the view of the agent A_i based on its local clock. This can be guaranteed if we have: $t_{rs}^j + T \geq t_{rs}^j - \delta_j + T > t_c^i + \delta_i$. Additionally, the current reachablet set of agent A_i contains information about its future behavior if $t_c^i < t_{rs}^i + T$ as depicted in Fig. 2. We can see that if $t_c^i > t_{rs}^j + T + \delta_i + \delta_j$, then the reachable set of A_j contains a past information, and thus it is useless for checking collision. One interesting case is when $t_{rs}^j + T - \delta_i - \delta_j < t_c^i < t_{rs}^j + T + \delta_i + \delta_j$. In this case, we do not know whether the received reachable set is useful or not.

Algorithm 4.2. Decentralized Real-Time Collision Verification at Agent A_i.

Input: l,   % safe distance between agents

Output: $collision, T_{safe}$ % collision flag and safe time interval in the future

---

1: **procedure** PEER-TO-PEER COLLISION DETECTION
2:     **if** new message $\mathcal{R}_j[t_{rs}^j, t_{rs}^j + T]$ arrive **then**
3:        decode message
4:        $t_c^i = A_i.current\_time()$ % current time
5:        $t_{rs}^i = \mathcal{R}_i.t_{rs}^i$ % current reachable set start time
6:        **if** $t_c^i < t_{rs}^j + T - \delta_i - \delta_j$ and $t_c^i < t_{rs}^i + T$ **then**   % check usefulness
7:           compute possible minimum distance d_{min} between two agents
8:           **if** $d_{min} > l$ **then**
9:              Collision = false
10:              $T_{safe} = min(t_{rs}^j + T - \delta_i - \delta_j, t_{rs}^i + T)$
11:           **else**
12:              Collision = uncertain, $T_{safe} = [\,]$
13:        store the message

Remark 1. We note that the proposed approach does not rely on the concept of Lamport happens-before relation [17] to compute the local reachable set of each agent. If the agent could not receive reachable messages from others until a requested time-stamp expires, it still calculates the local reachable set based on its current state and the state information of other agents in the messages it received previously. In other words, our method does not require the reachable set of each agent to be computed corresponding to the ordering of the events (sending or receiving a message) in the system, but only relies on the local clock period and the time-synchronization errors between agents. Such implementation ensures that the computation process can be accomplished in real-time, and is not affected by the message transmission delay.

The peer-to-peer collision checking procedure depicted in Algorithm 4.2 works as follows: when a new reachable set message arrives, the receiving agent decodes the message and checks the usefulness of the received reachable set and its current reachable set. Then, the agent combines its current reachable set and the received reachable set to compute the minimum possible distance between two agents. If the distance is larger than an allowable threshold l, there is no collision between two agents in some known time interval in the future, i.e., T_{safe}.

Lemma 2. *The decentralized real-time collision verification algorithm is sound.*

Proof. From Lemma 1, we know that the received reachable set $\mathcal{R}_j[t_{rs}^j, t_{rs}^j + T]$ contains all possible trajectories of the agent A_j from t_{rs}^j to $t_{rs}^j + T$. Also, the current reachable set of the agent A_i, $\mathcal{R}_i[t_{rs}^i, t_{rs}^i + T]$, contains all possible trajectories of the agent from t_{rs}^i to $t_{rs}^i + T$. If those reachable sets are useful, then they contains all possible trajectories of two agents from t_c^i to sometime $T_{safe} = min(t_{rs}^j + T - \delta_i - \delta_j, t_{rs}^i + T)$ in the future based on the agent A_i clock.

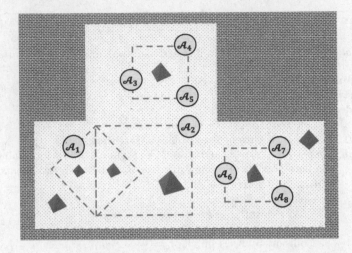

Fig. 3. Distributed search application using quadcopters.

Therefore, the minimum distance d_{min} between two agents computed from two reachable sets is the smallest distance among all possible distances in the time interval $[t_c^i, T_{safe}]$. Consequently, the collision free guarantee is sound in the time interval $[t_c^i, T_{safe}]$.

5 Case Study

The decentralized real-time safety verification for distributed CPS proposed in this paper is implemented in Java as a package called *drreach*. This package is currently integrated as a library in StarL, which is a novel platform-independent framework for programming reliable distributed robotics applications on Android [19]. StarL is specifically suitable for controlling a distributed network of robots over WiFi since it provides many useful functions and sophisticated algorithms for distributed applications. In our approach, we use the reliable communication network of StarL which is assumed to be asynchronous and peer-to-peer. There may be message dropouts and transmission delays; however, every message that an agent tries to send is eventually delivered with some time guarantees. All experimental results of our approach are reproducible and available online at: https://github.com/trhoangdung/starl/tree/drreach.

We evaluate the proposed approach via a distributed search application using quadcopters[1] in which each quadcopter executes its search mission provided by users as a list of way-points depicted in Fig. 3. These quadcopters follow the way-points to search for some specific objects. For safety reasons, they are required to work only in a specific region defined by users. In this case study, the quadcopters are controlled to operate at the same constant altitude. It has been

---

[1] A video recording is available at: https://youtu.be/YC_7BChsIf0.

shown from the experiments that the proposed approach is promisingly scalable as it works well for a different number of quadcopters. We choose to present in this section the experimental results for the distributed search application with eight quadcopters.

The first step in our approach is locally computing the reachable set of each quadcopter using face-lifting method. The quadcopter has nonlinear motion dynamics given in Eq. 2 in which θ, ϕ, and ψ are the pitch, roll, and yaw angles, $f = \Sigma_{i=1}^{4} T_i$ is the sum of the propeller forces, m is the mass of the quadcopter and $g = 9.81 \, \mathrm{m/s}^2$ is the gravitational acceleration constant. As the quadcopter is set to operate on a constant altitude, we have $\ddot{z} = 0$ which yields the following constraint: $f = \frac{mg}{cos(\theta)cos(\phi)}$. Let v_x and v_y be the velocities of a quadcopter along with x- and y- axes. Using the constraint on the total force, the motion dynamics of the quadcopter can be rewritten as a 4-dimensional nonlinear ODE as depicted in Eq. 3.

$$\ddot{x} = \frac{f}{m}(sin(\psi)sin(\phi) + cos(\psi)sin(\theta)cos(\phi)),$$
$$\ddot{y} = \frac{f}{m}(sin(\psi)sin(\theta)cos(\phi) - sin(\phi)cos(\psi)), \quad (2)$$
$$\ddot{z} = \frac{f}{m}cos(\theta)cos(\phi) - g,$$

$$\dot{x} = v_x,$$
$$\dot{v}_x = gtan(\theta),$$
$$\dot{y} = v_y, \quad (3)$$
$$\dot{v}_y = g\frac{tan(\phi)}{cos(\theta)}.$$

A PID controller is designed to control the quadcopter to move from its current position to desired way-points. Details about the controller parameters can be found in the available source code. The PID controller has a control period of $T_c = 200 \, \mathrm{ms}$. In every control period, the control inputs pitch (θ) and roll (ϕ) are computed based on the current positions of the quadcopter and the current target position (i.e., the current way-point it needs to go). Using the control inputs, the current positions and velocities given from GPS and the motion dynamics of the quadcopter, the real-time reachable set computation algorithm (Algorithm 3.1) is executed *inside* the controller. This algorithm computes the reachable set of a quadcopter from its current local time to the next $T = 2 \, \mathrm{s}$. The allowable run-time for this algorithm is $T_{runtime} = 10 \, \mathrm{ms}$. The local safety property is verified by the real-time reachable set computation algorithm at run-time. The computed reachable set is then encoded and sent to another quadcopter. When a reachable set message arrives, the quadcopter decodes the message to reconstruct the current reachable set of the sender. The GPS error is assumed to be 2%. The time-synchronization error between the quadcopters is $\delta = 3 \, \mathrm{ms}$. We want to verify in real-time: (1) local safety property for each quadcopter; (2) collision occurrence. The local safety property is defined by $v_x < 500$, i.e., the maximum allowable velocities along the x-axis of two arbitrary quadcopters are not larger than $500 \, \mathrm{m/s}$. The collision is checked using the minimum allowable distance between two arbitrary quadcopters $d_{min} = 100$.

quadcopter7 finishes computing reach set and stores the reach set
quadcopter6 finishes computing reach set and stores the reach set
quadcopter5 finishes computing reach set and stores the reach set
quadcopter1 finishes computing reach set and stores the reach set
quadcopter2 encodes its reach set to send out in 0.027134 milliseconds
quadcopter5 encodes its reach set to send out in 0.012657 milliseconds
quadcopter5 broadcasts its reach set to others
quadcopter2 broadcasts its reach set to others
quadcopter7 encodes its reach set to send out in 0.013169 milliseconds
quadcopter7 broadcasts its reach set to others
quadcopter0 encodes its reach set to send out in 0.012709 milliseconds
quadcopter0 broadcasts its reach set to others
quadcopter0 does not violate its local safety property
quadcopter1 encodes its reach set to send out in 0.012707 milliseconds
quadcopter1 broadcasts its reach set to others
quadcopter6 encodes its reach set to send out in 0.011081 milliseconds
quadcopter6 broadcasts its reach set to others
quadcopter1 does not violate its local safety property
quadcopter2 does not violate its local safety property
quadcopter5 does not violate its local safety property
quadcopter7 does not violate its local safety property
quadcopter6 may violates its local safety specification at time 2019-02-17 17:29:51.344
quadcopter7 finishes computing reach set and stores the reach set
quadcopter5 finishes computing reach set and stores the reach set
quadcopter6 finishes computing reach set and stores the reach set
Reach set (hull) of quadcopter0 that is valid from 2019-02-17 17:29:49.075 to 2019-02-17 17:29:51.074 of its local
time is:
dim = 0 -> [-263.98, 1034.28]
dim = 1 -> [-329.46, -287.49]
dim = 2 -> [129.36, 301.87]
dim = 3 -> [30.00, 58.48]
Current reach set (hull) of quadcopter1 that is valid from 2019-02-17 17:29:49.386 to 2019-02-17 17:29:51.383 of its
local time is:
dim = 0 -> [1959.99, 2040.00]
dim = 1 -> [-0.00, -0.00]
dim = 2 -> [-285.97, 395.76]
dim = 3 -> [-177.55, -149.38]
Current local time of quadcopter1 is 2019-02-17 17:29:49.423
Useful time for checking collision and global safety property for quadcopter1 is 1645 milliseconds
The received reachable set from quadcopter0 is useful
quadcopter1 will not collide with quadcopter0 in the next 1.645 seconds

Fig. 4. A sample of events.

Figure 4 presents a sample of a sequence of events happening in the distributed search application. One can see that each quadcopter can determine based on its local clocks if there is no collision to some known time in the future. In addition, the local safety property can also be verified at run-time. For example, in the figure, the quadcopter 1 receives a reachable set message from the quadcopter 0 which is valid from $17 : 29 : 49.075$ to $17 : 29 : 51.074$ of the quadcopter 0's clock. After decoding this message, taking into account the time-synchronization error δ, quadcopter 1 realizes that the received reachable set message is useful for checking collision for the next 1.645 s of its clock. After checking collision, quadcopter 1 knows that it will not collide with the quadcopter 0 in the next 1.645 s (based on its clock).

It should be noted that we can intuitively verify the collision occurrences by observing the intermediate reachable sets of all quadcopters and their interval hulls. The *intermediate* reachable sets of the quadcopters in every $[0, 2 s]$ time interval computed by the real-time reachable set computation algorithm (i.e., Algorithm 3.1) is described in Fig. 5. The zoom plot within the figure presents a very short-time interval reachable set of the quadcopters. We note that the

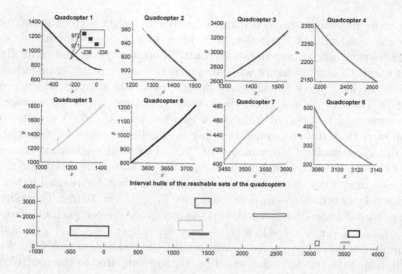

Fig. 5. One sample of the reachable sets of eight quadcopters in $[0, 2\,\mathrm{s}]$ time interval and their interval hulls.

intermediate reachable set of a quadcopter is represented as a list of hyper-rectangles and is used for verifying the local safety property at run-time. The reachable set that is sent to another quadcopter is the interval hull of these hyper-rectangles. The intermediate reachable set cannot be transferred via a network since it is very large (i.e., hundreds of hyper-rectangles). The interval hull of all hyper-rectangles contained in the intermediate reachable set covers all possible trajectories of a quadcopter in the time interval of $[0, 2\,\mathrm{s}]$. Therefore, it can be used for safety verification. One may question why we use the interval hull instead of using the convex hull of the reachable set since the former one results in a more conservative result. The reason is that we want to perform the safety verification online, convex hull of hundreds of hyper-rectangles is a time-consuming operation. Therefore, in the real-time setting, interval hull operation is a suitable solution. From the figure, we can see that the interval hulls of the reachable set of all quadcopters do not intersect with each other. Therefore, there is no collision occurrence (in the next 2 s of global time).

Table 1. The average encoding time τ_e, decoding time τ_d, transferring time τ_{tf}, collision checking time τ_c and total verification time VT of the quadcopters.

Time	Quad. 1	Quad. 2	Quad. 3	Quad. 4	Quad. 5	Quad. 6	Quad. 7	Quad. 8
Ecoding time τ_e (ms)	0.058	0.055	0.0553	0.0525	0.0557	0.0583	0.0584	0.0597
Decoding time τ_d (ms)	0.0169	0.0193	0.0197	0.019	0.0210	0.0181	0.0177	0.022
Transferring time τ_{tf} (ms)	2.64	2.48	1.42	1.11	1.12	1.08	1.05	1.13
Collision checking time τ_c (ms)	0.04	0.05	0.07	0.05	0.03	0.07	0.07	0.14
Total verification time VT (ms)	28.9363	27.9	20.6232	18.3055	18.2527	18.235	18.0223	19.1037

Since we implement the decentralized real-time safety verification algorithm inside the quadcopter's controller, it is important to analyze whether or not the verification procedure affects the control performance of the controller. To reason about this, we measure the average encoding, decoding, transferring and collision checking times for all quadcopters using 100 samples which are presented in Table 1. We note that the transferring time τ_{tf} is the average time for one message transferred from other quadcopters to the ith quadcopter. It can be seen that the encoding, decoding and collision checking times at each quadcopter constitute a tiny amount of time. The total verification time is the sum of the reachable set computation, encoding, transferring, decoding and collision checking times. Note that the allowable runtime for reachable set computation algorithm is specified by users as $T_{runtime} = 10$ ms. Therefore, the (average) total time for the safety verification procedure on each quadcopter is $VT_i = T_{runtime} + \tau_e^i + (N-1) \times (\tau_{tf}^i + \tau_d^i + \tau_c^i)$, where $i = 1, 2, \ldots, N$, and N is the number of quadcopters. As shown in the Table, the (average) total verification time for each quadcopter is small (<30 ms), compared to the control period $T_c = 200$ ms. Besides, from the experiment, we observe that the computation time for the control signal of the PID controller $\tau_{control}^i$ (not presented in the table) is also small, i.e., from 5 to 10 ms. Since $VT_i + \tau_{control}^i < T_c/4 = 50$ ms, we can conclude that the verification procedure does not affect the control performance of the controller.

Interestingly, from the verification time formula, we can estimate the range of the number of agents that the decentralized real-time verification procedure can deal with. The idea is that, in each control period T_c, after computing the control signal, the remaining time bandwidth $T_c - \tau_{control}$ can be used for verification. Let $\bar{\tau}_e(\underline{\tau}_e)$, $\bar{\tau}_{tf}(\underline{\tau}_{tf})$, $\bar{\tau}_d(\underline{\tau}_d)$, $\bar{\tau}_c(\underline{\tau}_c)$ be the maximum (minimum) encoding, transferring, decoding and collision checking times on a quadcopter, $\bar{\tau}_{control}(\underline{\tau}_{control})$ be the maximum (minimum) control signal computation time for each control period T_c, then the number of agents that the decentralized real-time safety verification procedure can deal with (with assumption that the communication network works well) satisfies the following constraint:

$$\frac{T_c - \bar{\tau}_{control} - T_{runtime} - \bar{\tau}_e}{\bar{\tau}_{tf} + \bar{\tau}_d + \bar{\tau}_c} + 1 \leq N \leq \frac{T_c - \underline{\tau}_{control} - T_{runtime} - \underline{\tau}_e}{\underline{\tau}_{tf} + \underline{\tau}_d + \underline{\tau}_c} + 1. \quad (4)$$

Let consider our case study, from the Table, we assume that $\bar{\tau}_e = 0.0597$, $\underline{\tau}_e = 0.0525$, $\bar{\tau}_{tf} = 2.64$, $\underline{\tau}_{tf} = 1.05$, $\bar{\tau}_d = 0.022$, $\underline{\tau}_d = 0.0169$, $\bar{\tau}_c = 0.14$, $\underline{\tau}_c = 0.03$ ms. Also, we assume that $\bar{\tau}_{control} = 10$ and $\underline{\tau}_{control} = 5$ ms. We can estimate theoretically the number of quadcopters that our verification approach can deal with is $64 \leq N \leq 168$.

6   Related Work

Our work is inspired by the static and dynamic analysis of timed distributed traces [8] and the real-time reachability analysis for verified simplex design [3]. The former one proposes a sound method of constructing a global reachable set for a distributed CPS based on the recorded traces and time synchronization errors of participating agents. Then the global reachable set is used to verify a global property using Z3 [7]. This method can be considered to be a *centralized analysis* where the reachable set of the whole system is constructed and verified by one analyzer. Such a verification approach is offline which is fundamentally different from our approach as we deal with online verification in a decentralized manner. Our real-time verification method borrows the face-lifting technique developed in [3] and applies it to a distributed CPS.

Another interesting aspect of real-time monitoring for linear systems was recently published in [5]. In this work, the authors proposed an approach that combines offline and online computation to decide if a given plant model has entered an uncontrollable state which is a state that no control strategy can be applied to prevent the plant go to the unsafe region. This method is useful for a single real-time CPS, but not a distributed CPS with multiple agents.

Additionally, there has been other significant works for verifying distributed CPS. Authors of [9,23,24] presented a real-time software for distributed CPS but did not perform a safety verification of individual components and a whole system. The works presented in [2,14,16] can be used to verify distributed CPS, but they do not consider a real-time aspect. An interesting work proposed in [21] can formally model and verify a distributed car control system against several safety objectives such as collision avoidance for an arbitrary number of cars. However, it does not address the verification problem of distributed CPS in a real-time manner. The novelty of our approach is that it can over-approximate of the reachable set of each agent whose dynamics are non-linear with a high precision degree in real-time.

The most related work to our scheme was recently introduced in [20]. The authors proposed an online verification using reachability analysis that can guarantee safe motion of mobile robots with respective to walking pedestrians modeled as hybrid systems. This work utilizes CORA toolbox [1] to perform reachability analysis while our work uses a face-lifting technique. However, this work does not consider the time-elapse for encoding, transferring and decoding the reachable set messages between each agent, which play an important role in distributed systems.

7   Conclusion and Future Work

We have proposed a decentralized real-time safety verification method for distributed cyber physical systems. By utilizing the timing information and the reachable set information from exchanged reachable set messages, a sound guarantee about the safety of the whole system is obtained for each participant based on its local time. Our method has been successfully applied for a distributed search application using quadcopters built upon StarL framework. The main benefit of our approach is that it allows participants to take advantages of formal guarantees available locally in real-time to perform intelligent actions in dangerous situations. This work is a fundamental step in dealing with real-time safe motion/path planing for distributed robots. For future work, we seek to deploy this method on a real-platform and extend it to distributed CPS with heterogeneous agents where the agents can have different motion dynamics and thus they have different control periods. In addition, the scalability of the proposed method can be improved by exploiting the benefit of parallel processing, i.e., each agent handles multiple reachable set messages and checks for collision in parallel.

Acknowledgments. The material presented in this paper is based upon work supported by the Air Force Office of Scientific Research (AFOSR) through contract number FA9550-18-1-0122 and the Defense Advanced Research Projects Agency (DARPA) through contract number FA8750-18-C-0089. The U.S. Government is authorized to reproduce and distribute reprints for Government purposes notwithstanding any copyright notation thereon. The views and conclusions contained herein are those of the authors and should not be interpreted as necessarily representing the official policies or endorsements, either expressed or implied, of AFOSR or DARPA.

References

1. Althoff, M.: An introduction to CORA 2015. In: Proceedings of the Workshop on Applied Verification for Continuous and Hybrid Systems (2015)
2. Bae, K., Krisiloff, J., Meseguer, J., Ölveczky, P.C.: Designing and verifying distributed cyber-physical systems using multirate PALS: an airplane turning control system case study. Sci. Comput. Program. **103**, 13–50 (2015)
3. Bak, S., Johnson, T.T., Caccamo, M., Sha, L.: Real-time reachability for verified simplex design. In: 2014 IEEE Real-Time Systems Symposium (RTSS), pp. 138–148. IEEE (2014)
4. Chen, X., Ábrahám, E., Sankaranarayanan, S.: Flow*: an analyzer for non-linear hybrid systems. In: Sharygina, N., Veith, H. (eds.) CAV 2013. LNCS, vol. 8044, pp. 258–263. Springer, Heidelberg (2013). https://doi.org/10.1007/978-3-642-39799-8_18
5. Chen, X., Sankaranarayanan, S.: Model predictive real-time monitoring of linear systems. In: 2017 IEEE Real-Time Systems Symposium (RTSS), pp. 297–306. IEEE (2017)
6. Dang, T., Maler, O.: Reachability analysis via face lifting. In: Henzinger, T.A., Sastry, S. (eds.) HSCC 1998. LNCS, vol. 1386, pp. 96–109. Springer, Heidelberg (1998). https://doi.org/10.1007/3-540-64358-3_34
7. de Moura, L., Bjørner, N.: Z3: an efficient SMT solver. In: Ramakrishnan, C.R., Rehof, J. (eds.) TACAS 2008. LNCS, vol. 4963, pp. 337–340. Springer, Heidelberg (2008). https://doi.org/10.1007/978-3-540-78800-3_24
8. Duggirala, P.S., Johnson, T.T., Zimmerman, A., Mitra, S.: Static and dynamic analysis of timed distributed traces. In: 2012 IEEE 33rd Real-Time Systems Symposium (RTSS), pp. 173–182. IEEE (2012)
9. Eidson, J.C., Lee, E.A., Matic, S., Seshia, S.A., Zou, J.: Distributed real-time software for cyber-physical systems. Proc. IEEE **100**(1), 45–59 (2012)
10. Frehse, G., et al.: SpaceEx: scalable verification of hybrid systems. In: Gopalakrishnan, G., Qadeer, S. (eds.) CAV 2011. LNCS, vol. 6806, pp. 379–395. Springer, Heidelberg (2011). https://doi.org/10.1007/978-3-642-22110-1_30

11. Girard, A., Le Guernic, C., Maler, O.: Efficient computation of reachable sets of linear time-invariant systems with inputs. In: Hespanha, J.P., Tiwari, A. (eds.) HSCC 2006. LNCS, vol. 3927, pp. 257–271. Springer, Heidelberg (2006). https://doi.org/10.1007/11730637_21

12. Henzinger, T.A.: The theory of hybrid automata. In: IEEE Symposium on Logic in Computer Science (LICS), p. 278. IEEE Computer Society, Washington, DC (1996)

13. Henzinger, T.A., Ho, P.-H., Wong-Toi, H.: HYTECH: a model checker for hybrid systems. In: Grumberg, O. (ed.) CAV 1997. LNCS, vol. 1254, pp. 460–463. Springer, Heidelberg (1997). https://doi.org/10.1007/3-540-63166-6_48

14. Johnson, T.T., Mitra, S.: Parametrized verification of distributed cyber-physical systems: an aircraft landing protocol case study. In: 2012 IEEE/ACM Third International Conference on Cyber-Physical Systems (ICCPS), pp. 161–170. IEEE (2012)

15. Kong, S., Gao, S., Chen, W., Clarke, E.: dReach: δ-reachability analysis for hybrid systems. In: Baier, C., Tinelli, C. (eds.) TACAS 2015. LNCS, vol. 9035, pp. 200–205. Springer, Heidelberg (2015). https://doi.org/10.1007/978-3-662-46681-0_15

16. Kumar, P., Goswami, D., Chakraborty, S., Annaswamy, A., Lampka, K., Thiele, L.: A hybrid approach to cyber-physical systems verification. In: Proceedings of the 49th Annual Design Automation Conference, pp. 688–696. ACM (2012)

17. Lamport, L.: Time, clocks, and the ordering of events in a distributed system. Commun. ACM **21**(7), 558–565 (1978)

18. Le Guernic, C., Girard, A.: Reachability analysis of hybrid systems using support functions. In: Bouajjani, A., Maler, O. (eds.) CAV 2009. LNCS, vol. 5643, pp. 540–554. Springer, Heidelberg (2009). https://doi.org/10.1007/978-3-642-02658-4_40

19. Lin, Y., Mitra, S.: StarL: towards a unified framework for programming, simulating and verifying distributed robotic systems. CoRR abs/1502.06286 (2015). http://arxiv.org/abs/1502.06286

20. Liu, S.B., Roehm, H., Heinzemann, C., Lütkebohle, I., Oehlerking, J., Althoff, M.: Provably safe motion of mobile robots in human environments. In: 2017 IEEE/RSJ International Conference on Intelligent Robots and Systems (IROS), pp. 1351–1357. IEEE (2017)

21. Loos, S.M., Platzer, A., Nistor, L.: Adaptive cruise control: hybrid, distributed, and now formally verified. In: Butler, M., Schulte, W. (eds.) FM 2011. LNCS, vol. 6664, pp. 42–56. Springer, Heidelberg (2011). https://doi.org/10.1007/978-3-642-21437-0_6

22. Lynch, N., Segala, R., Vaandrager, F., Weinberg, H.B.: Hybrid I/O automata. In: Alur, R., Henzinger, T.A., Sontag, E.D. (eds.) HS 1996. LNCS, vol. 1066, pp. 496–510. Springer, Heidelberg (1996). https://doi.org/10.1007/BFb0020971

23. Tang, Q., Gupta, S.K., Varsamopoulos, G.: A unified methodology for scheduling in distributed cyber-physical systems. ACM Trans. Embed. Comput. Syst. (TECS) **11**(S2), 57 (2012)

24. Zhang, Y., Gill, C., Lu, C.: Reconfigurable real-time middleware for distributed cyber-physical systems with aperiodic events. In: The 28th International Conference on Distributed Computing Systems, ICDCS 2008, pp. 581–588. IEEE (2008)

Short and "Journal First" Papers

On Certifying Distributed Algorithms: Problem of Local Correctness

Kim Völlinger[✉]

Humboldt University of Berlin, Berlin, Germany
voellinger@hu-berlin.de

Abstract. A *certifying* distributed algorithm (CDA) is a runtime verification method for distributed systems. Additionally to each output, a CDA computes a *witness* – a correctness argument for the particular output. If the witness is verified at *runtime*, the output is correct. The output is *distributed* over the system with each component holding its part of the distributed output.

In this paper, we investigate the case where the verification at runtime fails. Assume one component computes its part of the distributed output incorrectly. As a consequence, the distributed output is incorrect and the verification fails. Some components may still hold a correct part of the output. That is why we introduce the problem of *local correctness* of a component: *Is a component's part of the output correct?* As a case study, we investigate local correctness for a CDA computing shortest paths as used in distance-vector routing.

1 Introduction

A major problem in software engineering is assuring the *correctness* of a distributed system. A distributed algorithm runs on a distributed system where components communicate with each other in order to solve a common problem. The correctness of a distributed algorithm and of its implementation is crucial for the correctness of a distributed system. While formal verification is often too costly, testing is not sufficient if the system is of critical importance. Runtime verification tries to bridge this gap; it is not complete since verification at runtime can fail but it is a formal method based on mathematical reasoning.

Certifying Distributed Algorithms. A *certifying distributed algorithm* (CDA) is a runtime verification method. In order to verify its input-output pair (i, o), a CDA additionally computes a *witness* w such that if a *witness predicate* holds for the triple (i, o, w), the input-output pair (i, o) is correct [10]. A distributed *checker* algorithm decides the witness predicate at *runtime* [9]. To enable distributed checking, the witness predicate is *distributable*, i.e. a property in the system is expressed by stating properties for each component [7]. As an example of a witness, consider a distributed algorithm where the components of

© IFIP International Federation for Information Processing 2019
Published by Springer Nature Switzerland AG 2019
J. A. Pérez and N. Yoshida (Eds.): FORTE 2019, LNCS 11535, pp. 281–288, 2019.
https://doi.org/10.1007/978-3-030-21759-4_16

a network decide whether the network graph itself is bipartite. In case of a non-bipartite network graph, an odd cycle in the graph is a witness since an odd cycle is not bipartite itself. The witness predicate states that an odd cycle exists in the network. A distributable variant of this witness is given in [7]. With a CDA, a user does not have to trust the distributed algorithm, its implementation or execution but only the checker. With a well-chosen witness, the checker is simple and its verification feasible [8,9]. The idea of a CDA is to adapt the underlying algorithm of a program at design-time such that it verifies its input-output pair at runtime. In the typical setup of runtime verification, a system is instrumented to send outputs to a trusted monitor which decides if a given property holds [3]. Analogously, a CDA is instrumented to compute a witness and send it to the checker which decides if the input-output pair is correct.

Contribution of this Paper. The input, output and witness of a CDA are distributed over the system with each system's component holding its part. In this paper, we assume that one component computes its part of the output incorrectly. As a consequence, the distributed output is incorrect and verification fails at runtime, i.e. the checker rejects. However, the outputs of some components computed may still be correct. That is why we introduce the problem of *local correctness* of a component: *Is a component's part of the output correct?* As a case study, we investigate local correctness for a CDA computing shortest paths [10] as used in distance-vector routing [6].

Related Work. Certifying *sequential* algorithms are well established [5] but there is little work on certifying *distributed* algorithms [1,7–10]. However, CDAs can be classified as a distributed and choreographed runtime verification approach since the checker is a distributed algorithm, as well as a synchronous runtime verification approach since the system waits for the checker to accept [2]. To our knowledge, there is no work on the problem of local correctness.

2   Preliminaries: Certifying Distributed Algorithms

As distributed systems, we consider *networks* that are *asynchronous* (i.e. no global clock), *static* (i.e. unchanged topology) and *id-based* (i.e unique identifiers). We model the communication topology of a network as a connected undirected graph $N = (V, E)$: a vertex represents a component, an edge a channel. A *distributed algorithm* describes for each component a reactive algorithm such that all components together solve one problem (e.g. leader election or coloring) [4,6]. The input i of a distributed algorithm is distributed such that each component $v \in V$ has its input i_v and $i = \cup_{v \in V} i_v$; analogously for the output. A CDA computes a distributed *witness* w additionally to its input-output pair (i, o) such that if a predicate (the *witness predicate*) holds for the triple (i, o, w), the pair (i, o) is correct [10]. We call a predicate that is defined over a component's input, output and witness a *local predicate*. A predicate

Γ is *universally distributable* with a local predicate γ if for all triples (i, o, w) holds $(\forall v \in V : \gamma(i_v, o_v, w_v)) \longrightarrow \Gamma(i, o, w)$, and *existentially distributable* if $(\exists v \in V : \gamma(i_v, o_v, w_v)) \longrightarrow \Gamma(i, o, w)$. A predicate is *distributable* if one of the former applies, or if the predicate is implied by conjuncted and/or disjuncted universally/existentially distributable predicates [7]. The witness predicate is distributable, and can be decided by a distributed *checker* algorithm at runtime. Each component v has a checker algorithm that decides all local predicates over (i_v, o_v, w_v). Using a spanning tree, the checkers of the components aggregate the evaluated local predicates upwards and combine them by logical conjunction or disjunction depending on whether the according predicate is universally or existentially distributable; the root decides the witness predicate by combining the evaluated distributable predicates [9]. Hence, if the distributed checker accepts, the distributed input-output pair (i, o) is correct. The user of a CDA does not have to trust the actual algorithm but the distributed checker. The simplicity of the checker depends on the choice of the witness. Using the framework proposed in [8,9], an implemented distributed checker can be verified.

Certifying Distributed Shortest Path Computation. A certifying variant of the distributed Bellman-Ford Algorithm computing shortest paths in a network is described in [10]. We assume a network $N = (V, E)$ where the channels have positive costs $cost : E \to \mathbb{R}_{>0}$. The length of a path is the sum of the costs of its edges. We assume one special vertex, the source s. The length of a shortest path from the source to a vertex v is the *distance* of v. A function $D_s : V \to \mathbb{R}_{\geq 0}$ is a distance function for s iff [5]:

$$D_s(s) = 0 \tag{1}$$
$$\text{for each } (u, v) \in E : D_s(v) \leq D_s(u) + cost(u, v) \tag{2}$$
$$\text{for each } v \in V, v \neq s \text{ there exists } (u, v) \in E : D_s(v) = D_s(u) + cost(u, v) \tag{3}$$

The distributed Bellman-Ford algorithm [6] solves the shortest path problem; each component v computes its distance v_{Ds} to the source s. Note that we distinguish the computed distance v_{Ds} from the actual distance $D_s(v)$ since the computed distance could be incorrect. In the certifying variant, each component v additionally computes its part of the witness: the computed distances of its neighbors, and a neighbor with which the property (3) holds – its parent in the shortest path tree. The witness predicate is satisfied iff the properties (1)–(3) hold. The checker of each component v decides the properties (1)–(3) as local predicates for v. The witness predicate is universally distributable. Hence, if the checker of each component accepts, the distributed checker accepts and all computed distances are correct.

3   Problem: Local Correctness of a Component

We assume a CDA with a distributed checker for some problem. We know if the distributed checker accepts, the particular distributed input-output pair is correct. We assume that one component is faulty and computes its part of the output incorrectly. As a consequence, the distributed output is incorrect. Thereby, the witness predicate does not hold and the distributed checker rejects. Hence, the verification at runtime fails. A solution could be to repeat the whole computation or to use another distributed algorithm. However, while the output of some components may be affected by the incorrect output of the faulty component, other components may still hold a correct part of the output. That is why we introduce the problem of *local correctness* of a component: *Is the output of a component correct?* In some scenarios, it might be interesting to identify and keep correct parts of the output rather than repeating the computation. Hence, we think local correctness is worth to investigate. Note that local correctness requires that we know what correctness of a part of the distributed output means.

3.1   Case Study: Local Correctness in Shortest Paths Computation

We conduct a case study on local correctness for certifying shortest path computation as introduced in Sect. 2. We elaborate whether witness and checker are helpful in deciding local correctness. We assume that a component $v \neq s$ computes its output v_{Ds} incorrectly but with the right type (i.e. a positive number). Hence, $v_{Ds} \neq D_s(v)$, $v_{Ds} \geq 0$ and $v \neq s$. Each component $u \neq v$ computes its output u_{Ds} logically consistent to the faulty output v_{Ds}. Logically consistent means that for each component $u \neq v$ holds

$$u_{Ds} = 0 \; if \; u \; is \; the \; source \tag{4}$$

$$u_{Ds} \leq w_{Ds} + cost(u, w) \; for \; all \; neighbors \; w \; of \; u \tag{5}$$

$$u_{Ds} = w_{Ds} + cost(u, w) \; for \; at \; least \; one \; neighbor \; w \tag{6}$$

The properties (4)–(6) are equal to the properties (1)–(3) characterizing the distance function except that we are stating them for the *computed* outputs and only for the non-faulty components. The computed distances represent the distance function D_s iff the characterization properties hold for all components. Since v's output is incorrect, the output u_{Ds} can be correct ($u_{Ds} = D_s(u)$) or incorrect ($u_{Ds} \neq D_s(u)$) even though the properties (4)–(6) hold for u.

Identifying the Faulty Component Using the Checker. Since the witness predicate is universally distributable, the distributed checker rejects iff at least one checker of a component rejects. The checker of the faulty component v rejects. If $v_{Ds} > D_s(v)$, the inequality (5) does not hold. There exists a neighbor w of v such that $D_s(v) = D_s(w) + cost(v, w)$. Hence, $v_{Ds} > D_s(w) + cost(v, w)$. In case of $v_{Ds} < D_s(v)$, the equality (6) does not hold.

For each component $u \neq v$, the checker of u accepts. Since u's output is logically consistent, the properties (4)–(6) hold for u. We can identify the faulty component by the rejection pattern of the distributed checker since exactly the checker of v rejects. Moreover, the checker of v can even decide whether v computed its distance too great or too small.

Fault Propagation. In the following, we investigate the local correctness of a component by studying fault propagation into several subnetworks. To exemplify, we consider the network N and a partitioning in the subnetworks I-VI highlighted in gray boxes as shown in Fig. 1. For simplicity, we omit the cost of a channel in the illustration. We argue under which circumstances the components of a subnetwork hold a correct part of the output. For our reasoning, we use arguments about the checker, witness and topology. We chose the topology of the network such that we can illustrate all topology-based arguments. However, arguments depending on the checker and witness are topology independent.

Network N with
subnetworks I-VI:

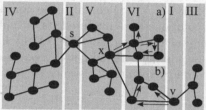

s is the source.
v is the faulty component.
↓ shows the parent relation
(only in subnetwork VI)
with the arrow pointing to a child.

Fig. 1. Example network to illustrate fault propagation into subnetworks. Costs of channels are omitted. The parent relation is shown only in subnetwork VI.

Subnetwork I and II. Subnetwork I contains only the faulty component v, and by assumption, v's output is incorrect. Moreover, v is not the source s which is the only component in subnetwork II. The source's output is logically consistent, and therefore the Eq. 4 holds. As a consequence, the source's output $s_{Ds} = 0$ is correct.

Subnetwork III. For each component u of the subnetwork III, the output u_{Ds} is incorrect since each path from s to u has to contain v. More precisely, a component u computes its distance to v correctly as $D_v(u)$. Hence, $u_{Ds} = D_v(u) + v_{Ds}$. If the output u_{Ds} would be correct, then $u_{Ds} = D_v(u) + D_s(v)$, and since each path from s to u contains v, it follows $v_{Ds} = D_s(v)$. A contradiction to our assumption $v_{Ds} \neq D_s(v)$. Thus, $u_{Ds} \neq D_s(u)$ for all components u of subnetwork III.

Subnetwork IV. For each component u of the subnetwork IV, the output u_{Ds} is correct. The output u_{Ds} could be only affected by the faulty output v_{Ds} if the shortest path from s to u would contain v. Such an s-u path would contain s at least twice. Since all costs of the channels and the faulty output v_{Ds} are positive, such a path would never be computed as a shortest path. Hence, the fault of v does not propagate into the subnetwork IV.

Subnetwork V. For each component u of the subnetwork V, its output u_{Ds} is correct if the component v computed its distance too great: $v_{Ds} > D_s(v)$. Note that $D_s(v) = D_x(v) + D_s(x)$, and hence, $v_{Ds} > D_x(v) + D_s(x)$. Moreover, for each component u holds $D_s(u) \leq D_s(x)$ due to the positive costs of channels.

Subnetwork VI. For the subnetwork VI, we additionally consider the computed shortest path tree indicated by the computed parent relation. Using the parent relation, we distinguish components which are non-descendants of component v from components which are descendants of v.

Subnetwork VI a. The subnetwork VI (a) contains the non-descendants of v of the subnetwork VI. If the component v computed its output v_{Ds} too small ($v_{Ds} < D_s(v)$), then all components of subnetwork VI (a) have the correct output. The reason is that these components did not choose the component v as ancestor even though v offered an even smaller distance than it actually has.

Subnetwork VI b. The subnetwork VI (b) contains the descendants of v. Hence, a component u of the subnetwork VI (b) has the output $u_{Ds} = D_v(u) + v_{Ds}$. Hence, the output u_{Ds} is potentially faulty. In contrast to the outputs of the components of the subnetwork III, $u_{Ds} = D_s(u)$ could still hold since there could be an s-u path without v which is a shortest and has the same sum u_{Ds}. Furthermore, note that, in the case of $v_{Ds} > D_s(v)$, the parent relation in subnetwork VI (b) is part of an actual shortest path tree since these components chose v as an ancestor even though v offered a greater distance than it actually has.

Cut Vertices. For the example network (Fig. 1), we draw some conclusions based on the topology. The components s, v and x are cut vertices, i.e. their removal increases the number of connected components. Those cut vertices are particularly interesting for fault propagation in our case study. Arguments using cut vertex x work for any cut vertex that separates the source and faulty component into different connected components. There are algorithms to detect cut vertices in a network [11]. However, for a static network, cut vertices could be known by initialization.

Arbitrary Topology. Some networks have no cut vertices. The arguments based on the computed parent relation are independent of the topology. The parent relation is part of the distributed witness. Moreover, the distributed checker identifies the faulty component v, and indicates whether v computed its distance too great or too small – both independent of the topology. Hence, the witness and the checker help in deciding local correctness for some components.

4   Discussion

We introduced the problem of *local correctness* of a component. We investigated local correctness in the context of a CDA where the runtime verification of a distributed input-output pair fails due to a faulty component. In particular, we conducted a case study of a CDA computing shortest paths, as for example used in distance-vector routing. In order to tackle local correctness, we investigated how a fault propagates through a network. We decided local correctness in subnetworks using the distributed checker, the distributed witness and the topology. We consider investigating local correctness in the context of a CDA promising since the distributed witness gives additional insight, being an argument for the correctness of an input-output pair.

Future Work. The case study could be extended by allowing the source to be faulty or by having several faulty components. Another direction is to study other problems. To study local correctness for a problem, there has to be a specification about the correctness of a component's output. Such a specification does not always come as natural as for the shortest path computation. Assume the problem of *leader election* where the components elect a unique leader among them. It is not straightforward what a correct leader election of a single component is since agreement on a leader is part of the problem. By relaxing local correctness of a component's output to the correctness of the outputs of a subnetwork, local correctness would be probably interesting for more problems.

References

1. Akili, S., Völlinger, K.: Case study on certifying distributed algorithms: reducing intrusiveness. In: Lecture Notes in Computer Science: 8th IPM International Conference on Fundamentals of Software Engineering. Springer (2019, to appear)
2. Francalanza, A., Pérez, J.A., Sánchez, C.: Runtime verification for decentralised and distributed systems. In: Bartocci, E., Falcone, Y. (eds.) Lectures on Runtime Verification. LNCS, vol. 10457, pp. 176–210. Springer, Cham (2018). https://doi.org/10.1007/978-3-319-75632-5_6
3. Hallé, S.: When RV meets CEP. In: Falcone, Y., Sánchez, C. (eds.) RV 2016. LNCS, vol. 10012, pp. 68–91. Springer, Cham (2016). https://doi.org/10.1007/978-3-319-46982-9_6
4. Lynch, N.A.: Distributed Algorithms. Morgan Kaufmann Publishers Inc., San Francisco (1996)
5. McConnell, R.M., Mehlhorn, K., Näher, S., Schweitzer, P.: Certifying algorithms. Comput. Sci. Rev. 5, 119–161 (2011)
6. Raynal, M.: Distributed Algorithms for Message-Passing Systems. Springer, Heidelberg (2013). https://doi.org/10.1007/978-3-642-38123-2
7. Völlinger, K.: Verifying the output of a distributed algorithm using certification. In: Lahiri, S., Reger, G. (eds.) RV 2017. LNCS, vol. 10548, pp. 424–430. Springer, Cham (2017). https://doi.org/10.1007/978-3-319-67531-2_29

8. Völlinger, K., Akili, S.: Verifying a class of certifying distributed programs. In: Barrett, C., Davies, M., Kahsai, T. (eds.) NFM 2017. LNCS, vol. 10227, pp. 373–388. Springer, Cham (2017). https://doi.org/10.1007/978-3-319-57288-8_27

9. Völlinger, K., Akili, S.: On a verification framework for certifying distributed algorithms: distributed checking and consistency. In: Baier, C., Caires, L. (eds.) FORTE 2018. LNCS, vol. 10854, pp. 161–180. Springer, Cham (2018). https://doi.org/10.1007/978-3-319-92612-4_9

10. Völlinger, K., Reisig, W.: Certification of distributed algorithms solving problems with optimal substructure. In: Calinescu, R., Rumpe, B. (eds.) SEFM 2015. LNCS, vol. 9276, pp. 190–195. Springer, Cham (2015). https://doi.org/10.1007/978-3-319-22969-0_14

11. Xiong, S., Li, J.: An efficient algorithm for cut vertex detection in wireless sensor networks. In: Proceedings of the 2010 IEEE 30th International Conference on Distributed Computing Systems, ICDCS 2010, pp. 368–377. IEEE Computer Society, Washington, DC (2010). https://doi.org/10.1109/ICDCS.2010.38

On a Higher-Order Calculus
of Computational Fields

Giorgio Audrito[1] , Mirko Viroli[2] , Ferruccio Damiani[1]([envelope]) ,
Danilo Pianini[2] , and Jacob Beal[3]

[1] Dipartimento di Informatica, University of Turin, Turin, Italy
{giorgio.audrito,ferruccio.damiani}@unito.it
[2] DISI, University of Bologna, Cesena, Italy
{mirko.viroli,danilo.pianini}@unibo.it
[3] Raytheon BBN Technologies, Cambridge, MA, USA
jakebeal@ieee.org

Abstract. Computational fields have been proposed as an effective
abstraction to fill the gap between the macro-level of distributed systems
(specifying a system's collective behaviour) and the micro-level (individual devices' actions of computation and interaction to implement that
collective specification), thereby providing a basis to better facilitate the
engineering of collective APIs and complex systems at higher levels of
abstraction. This approach is particularly suited to complex large-scale
distributed systems, like the Internet-of-Things and Cyber-Physical Systems, where new mechanisms are needed to address composability and
reusability of collective adaptive behaviour. This work introduces a full
formal foundation for field computations, in terms of a core calculus
equipped with typing, denotational, and operational semantics. Criti-
cally, we apply techniques for formal programming languages to collective adaptive systems: we provide formal establishment of a link between
the micro- and macro-levels of collective adaptive systems, via a result
of computational adequacy and abstraction for the (aggregate) denotational semantics with respect to the (per-device) operational semantics.

Keywords: Distributed computing · Core calculus · Type system ·
Denotational semantics · Operational semantics ·
Computational adequacy

1   Background

Aggregate computing [6] is a paradigm aiming to address the complexity of large-
scale distributed systems, by means of the notion of *computational field* [15] (or
simply *field*): this is a collective, distributed map from computational events
(when and where a device executes a computational action, also called a *round*)
to computational objects (data values of any sort, including higher-order objects
such as functions and processes) representing the result of computation at that

© IFIP International Federation for Information Processing 2019
Published by Springer Nature Switzerland AG 2019
J. A. Pérez and N. Yoshida (Eds.): FORTE 2019, LNCS 11535, pp. 289–292, 2019.
https://doi.org/10.1007/978-3-030-21759-4_17

event. Computing with fields means computing such global data structures, and defining a reusable block of behaviour means to define a reusable computation from fields to fields. This functional view holds at any level of abstraction, from low-level mechanisms of the language up to whole applications, which ultimately work by getting input fields from sensors and processing them to produce output fields for actuators. Most importantly, computing with fields is functional and hence declarative: *(i)* the designer focusses on the intended global goal of system behaviour, while the dynamics of interactions is left to the underlying platform (i.e., semantics); and *(ii)* one can scale with complexity by relying on functional composition: libraries of reusable building blocks can be constructed, and successive layering can be used to bottom-up derive whole applications.

The *field calculus* [11] is a tiny functional language providing basic constructs to work with fields.[1] It provides a unifying approach to understanding and analysing the wide range of approaches to distributed systems engineering that make use of computational fields [5,21]. The operational semantics of field calculus [11] can act as a blueprint for actual implementations where myriad devices interact via proximity-based broadcasts. More recently, the field calculus has been used to investigate formal properties of resiliency to environment changes [18,20] and to device distribution [7]. Its expressiveness has been investigated by introducing the *cone Turing Machine* [1].

The *higher-order field calculus* [12] combines self-organisation and code mobility by extending the field calculus with a semantics for distributed first-class functions. It allows self-organisation code to be naturally handled like any other data, e.g., dynamically constructed, compared, spread across devices, and executed in safely encapsulated distributed scopes. Ultimately, this calculus provides programmers with a novel first class abstraction, a "distributed function field". This is a dynamically evolving map from a network of devices to a set of executing distributed processes: in each space-time region where the proces is the same, devices form a coalition collectively carrying on that process in isolation.

2   Contributions of [3]

This paper presents syntax and operational semantics of the higher-order field calculus together with new contributions: a type system for the higher-order version of the calculus, a denotational semantics, and associated properties. The new, enhanced syntax is parametric in the set of the modeled data values (in [12] Booleans, numbers, and pairs were explicitly modeled). Moreover, the `if` construct has been removed by encapsulating its branching capability into function calls, which now take the form of a function field applied to arguments, implicitly enacting branching. Then, a novel key insight and technical result of this paper is that the notoriously difficult problem of reconciling local and global behaviour in a complex adaptive system [20] can be connected to a well-known problem in programming languages: correspondence between denotational and

---

[1] Much as λ-calculus [9] captures the essence of functional computation and FJ [14] the essence of class-based object-oriented programming.

operational semantics. On the one hand, denotational semantics can be used to characterise computations in terms of their collective effect across space (available devices) and time (device computation events)—i.e., the macro level. On the other hand, operational semantics gives a transition system dictating each device's individual and local computing/interactive behaviour—i.e., the micro level. Correspondence between the two, formally proved in this paper via *computational adequacy* and a form of *abstraction* (c.f. [10,19]) that we call *computational abstraction*, thus provides a formal micro–macro connection: one designs a system considering the denotational semantics of programming constructs, and an underlying platform running the distributed interpreter defined by the operational semantics guarantees a consistent execution. This is a significant step towards effective methods for the engineering of self-adaptive systems, achieved thanks to the standard theory and framework of programming languages.

3   Conclusions, Related and Future Work

The work presented in this paper builds on a sizable body of prior work, for which the field calculus can somewhat act as a lingua franca: foundational approaches to group interaction (ambients [8], shared-spaces [22]), device abstraction languages (TOTA [15], Hood [23]), pattern languages [16], information movement languages [17], and spatial computing languages (MGS [13] and Proto [4]). Accordingly, future plans include consolidation of this work to investigate variants of the field calculus [2], to support an analytical methodology and a practical toolchain for system development, and to isolate fragments of the calculus that satisfy behavioural properties such as self-stabilisation developed in [20].

References

1. Audrito, G., Beal, J., Damiani, F., Viroli, M.: Space-time universality of field calculus. In: Di Marzo Serugendo, G., Loreti, M. (eds.) COORDINATION 2018. LNCS, vol. 10852, pp. 1–20. Springer, Cham (2018). https://doi.org/10.1007/978-3-319-92408-3_1
2. Audrito, G., Damiani, F., Viroli, M., Casadei, R.: Run-time management of computation domains in field calculus. In: 2016 IEEE 1st International Workshops on Foundations and Applications of Self* Systems (FAS*W), pp. 192–197. IEEE (2016). https://doi.org/10.1109/FAS-W.2016.50
3. Audrito, G., Viroli, M., Damiani, F., Pianini, D., Beal, J.: A higher-order calculus of computational fields. ACM Trans. Comput. Logic 20(1), 5:1–5:55 (2019). https://doi.org/10.1145/3285956
4. Bachrach, J., Beal, J., McLurkin, J.: Composable continuous space programs for robotic swarms. Neural Comput. Appl. 19(6), 825–847 (2010)
5. Beal, J., Dulman, S., Usbeck, K., Viroli, M., Correll, N.: Organizing the aggregate: languages for spatial computing. In: Mernik, M. (ed.) Formal and Practical Aspects of Domain-Specific Languages: Recent Developments, chap. 16, pp. 436–501. IGI Global (2013). https://doi.org/10.4018/978-1-4666-2092-6.ch016
6. Beal, J., Pianini, D., Viroli, M.: Aggregate programming for the internet of things. IEEE Comput. 48(9) (2015). https://doi.org/10.1109/MC.2015.261

7. Beal, J., Viroli, M., Pianini, D., Damiani, F.: Self-adaptation to device distribution in the internet of things. ACM Trans. Auton. Adapt. Syst. **12**(3), 12:1–12:29 (2017). https://doi.org/10.1145/3105758
8. Cardelli, L., Gordon, A.D.: Mobile ambients. Theor. Comput. Sci. **240**(1), 177–213 (2000). https://doi.org/10.1016/S0304-3975(99)00231-5
9. Church, A.: A set of postulates for the foundation of logic. Ann. Math. **33**(2), 346–366 (1932). https://doi.org/10.2307/1968337
10. Curien, P.: Definability and full abstraction. Electromic Notes Theorerical Comput. Sci. **172**, 301–310 (2007). https://doi.org/10.1016/j.entcs.2007.02.011
11. Damiani, F., Viroli, M., Beal, J.: A type-sound calculus of computational fields. Sci. Comput. Program. **117**, 17–44 (2016). https://doi.org/10.1016/j.scico.2015.11.005
12. Damiani, F., Viroli, M., Pianini, D., Beal, J.: Code mobility meets self-organisation: a higher-order calculus of computational fields. In: Graf, S., Viswanathan, M. (eds.) FORTE 2015. LNCS, vol. 9039, pp. 113–128. Springer, Cham (2015). https://doi.org/10.1007/978-3-319-19195-9_8
13. Giavitto, J.L., Godin, C., Michel, O., Prusinkiewicz, P.: Computational models for integrative and developmental biology. Technical report, 72-2002, Univerite d'Evry, LaMI (2002)
14. Igarashi, A., Pierce, B.C., Wadler, P.: Featherweight Java: a minimal core calculus for Java and GJ. ACM Trans. Program. Lang. Syst. **23**(3), 396–450 (2001). https://doi.org/10.1145/503502.503505
15. Mamei, M., Zambonelli, F.: Programming pervasive and mobile computing applications: the TOTA approach. ACM Trans. Softw. Eng. Methodol. **18**(4), 1–56 (2009). https://doi.org/10.1145/1538942.1538945
16. Nagpal, R.: Programmable self-assembly: constructing global shape using biologically-inspired local interactions and origami mathematics. Ph.D. thesis, MIT, Cambridge, MA, USA (2001)
17. Newton, R., Welsh, M.: Region streams: functional macroprogramming for sensor networks. In: Workshop on Data Management for Sensor Networks, pp. 78–87. ACM, August 2004. https://doi.org/10.1145/1052199.1052213
18. Nishiwaki, Y.: Digamma-calculus: a universal programming language of self-stabilizing computational fields. In: 2016 IEEE 1st International Workshops on Foundations and Applications of Self* Systems (FAS*W). IEEE (2016). https://doi.org/10.1109/FAS-W.2016.51
19. Stoughton, A.: Fully abstract models of programming languages. Research Notes in Theoretical Computer Science, Pitman (1988)
20. Viroli, M., Audrito, G., Beal, J., Damiani, F., Pianini, D.: Engineering resilient collective adaptive systems by self-stabilisation. ACM Trans. Model. Comput. Simul. **28**(2), 16:1–16:28 (2018). https://doi.org/10.1145/3177774
21. Viroli, M., Beal, J., Damiani, F., Audrito, G., Casadei, R., Pianini, D.: From field-based coordination to aggregate computing. In: Di Marzo Serugendo, G., Loreti, M. (eds.) COORDINATION 2018. LNCS, vol. 10852, pp. 252–279. Springer, Cham (2018). https://doi.org/10.1007/978-3-319-92408-3_12
22. Viroli, M., Casadei, M., Montagna, S., Zambonelli, F.: Spatial coordination of pervasive services through chemical-inspired tuple spaces. ACM Trans. Auton. Adapt. Syst. **6**(2), 14:1–14:24 (2011). https://doi.org/10.1145/1968513.1968517
23. Whitehouse, K., Sharp, C., Brewer, E., Culler, D.: Hood: a neighborhood abstraction for sensor networks. In: Proceedings of the 2nd International Conference on Mobile Systems, Applications, and Services. ACM Press (2004). https://doi.org/10.1145/990064.990079

Semantically Sound Analysis of Content Security Policies

Stefano Calzavara[✉], Alvise Rabitti, and Michele Bugliesi

Università Ca' Foscari Venezia, Venice, Italy
{stefano.calzavara,alvise.rabitti,michele.bugliesi}@unive.it

Abstract. Content Security Policy (CSP) is a W3C standard designed to prevent and mitigate the impact of content injection vulnerabilities on websites. CSP is supported by all major web browsers and routinely used by thousands of web developers in the world to improve the security of their web applications. In this paper we review our formalization of a core fragment of CSP, which we fruitfully employed to reason on the security import of flawed CSP implementations and deployments, as well as to perform a longitudinal analysis of how existing policies are evolving as the result of maintenance operations.

Keywords: Content Security Policy · Formal methods · Web security

1 Introduction

Content injection is arguably one of the most severe threats on the Web. In a content injection attack, a malicious user manages to craft an attack payload, typically a script, which gets injected into a benign web application and becomes indistinguishable from legitimate web contents, thus inheriting their privileges. This way, the attack payload can steal confidential information from the web application or redress the user interface to fool the victim into unknowingly performing security-sensitive operations.

Content injection can be prevented by means of safe coding practices [4], yet it is now widely acknowledged that this is difficult in practice and thus security practitioners rely on a *defense-in-depth* approach against content injection, where protection is achieved by implementing mitigation at several different layers. One such layer is Content Security Policy (CSP), which is now supported by all major web browsers and routinely used by thousands of web developers in the world to improve the security of their web applications. CSP has undergone several authoritative studies as of now [2,5,6], with our article *Semantics-Based Analysis of Content Security Policy Deployment* being the latest research work on the topic [3]. The distinctive trait of our approach with respect to previous studies is the use of *formal methods* techniques to tackle a rigorous investigation of CSP. Specifically, we defined the *denotational semantics* of a significant

© IFIP International Federation for Information Processing 2019
Published by Springer Nature Switzerland AG 2019
J. A. Pérez and N. Yoshida (Eds.): FORTE 2019, LNCS 11535, pp. 293–297, 2019.
https://doi.org/10.1007/978-3-030-21759-4_18

fragment of CSP, called CoreCSP, which we fruitfully employed to reason on the security import of flawed CSP implementations and deployments, as well as to perform a longitudinal analysis of how existing policies are evolving as the result of maintenance operations.

2   Background on Content Security Policy

A content security policy is a list of *directives*, restricting content inclusion for web pages by means of a white-listing mechanism. Directives bind content types to lists of sources from which a CSP-protected web page is allowed to include resources of that type. For instance, the directive `img-src https://a.com` specifies that the web page is allowed to load images just from the host `a.com` using the HTTPS protocol. CSP is a client-server defense mechanism: content security policies are sent from the server to the browser by means of HTTP headers or `<meta>` elements in HTML pages, while their enforcement is performed at the browser side on a per-page basis. If a content security policy does not include an explicit directive for a given content type, the `default-src` directive is applied as a fallback. Allowed sources for content inclusion are defined using *source expressions*, a sort of regular expressions used to express sets of web origins in a convenient way. Content inclusion from a given URL is only allowed if the URL matches any of the source expressions specified for the appropriate content type.

To exemplify how CSP works, we show a very simple policy below:

```
script-src https://www.unive.it;
img-src https://*.unive.it;
default-src https://*
```

The policy above states that scripts can only be loaded from `www.unive.it`, images can be loaded from any sub-domain of `unive.it` and all the other contents, e.g., style-sheets, can be loaded from everywhere; in all cases, the HTTPS protocol must be used. Moreover, the policy automatically disables the execution of inline scripts, which are the most dangerous threats for content injection. This default restriction can be voided by including the `'unsafe-inline'` source expression in the `script-src` directive.

3   Research Summary

We used our CoreCSP model of the CSP semantics to:

1. reveal a *wrong implementation* of the CSP specification in Microsoft Edge, which was deemed dangerous and fixed after our report (CVE-2017-11863). Moreover, we identified a *subtle quirk* in all browser implementations, which deserved a careful security analysis using our semantics to be shown secure;
2. automatically analyze the security of existing content security policies against script injection. Our analysis showed that *91.6% of the existing policies are trivially bypassable and provide no protection at all*;

3. automatically track which changes to deployed content security policies have been performed in the name of security (more restrictive policies), to preserve compatibility (more permissive policies) and for maintenance reasons (unrelated policies). Our analysis showed that *less than 3% of policies changes were done to improve security*, which confirms that CSP is failing as a security mechanism against content injection.

In the next section, we provide an overview of our technical treatment.

4   Technical Overview

4.1   Syntax and Semantics of CoreCSP

We let *str* range over a denumerable set of strings. The syntax of policies is shown in Table 1, where we use dots (...) to denote additional omitted elements of a syntactic category. A policy p is either a single list of directives $d_1, \ldots, d_n$ or the conjunction of two policies $p_1 + p_2$, which requires both p_1 and p_2 to be enforced. Directives, in turn, bind content types t to directive values v; their syntax includes a default directive, applied to all the contents not restricted by other directives. Directive values are sets of source expressions $\{se_1, \ldots, se_n\}$.

Table 1. Syntax of CoreCSP (excerpt)

Content types	t	$::= \texttt{script} \mid \texttt{img} \mid \ldots$	$(t \neq \texttt{default})$
Schemes	sc	$::= \texttt{http} \mid \texttt{https} \mid \ldots$	
Policies	p	$::= d_1, \ldots, d_n \mid p + p$	$(n \in \mathbb{N})$
Directives	d	$::= t\texttt{-src}\ v \mid \texttt{default-src}\ v$	
Directive values	v	$::= \{se_1, \ldots, se_n\}$	$(n \in \mathbb{N})$
Source expressions	se	$::= h \mid \texttt{unsafe-inline}$	
Hosts	h	$::= sc \mid he \mid (sc, he)$	$(sc \neq \texttt{inl})$
Host expressions	he	$::= * \mid *.str \mid str$	

The formal semantics of CoreCSP is defined on top of three main entities: *locations* l are uniquely identifiable sources of contents, e.g., URLs; *subjects* s are HTTP(S) web pages enforcing the content security policy; and *objects* o are contents available to subjects for inclusion, e.g., images hosted at a given URL. The semantics follows the denotational style and is based on judgements like:

$$p \vdash s \hookleftarrow_t O,$$

reading as: the policy p allows the subject s to include as content of type t the set of objects O. It is possible to order policies using a subject-indexed binary relation $\leq_s$ such that, for all policies p_1 and p_2, we have $p_1 \leq_s p_2$ if and only if p_1 is no more permissive than p_2 when deployed at s. More formally, this means that $p_1 \vdash s \hookleftarrow_t O_1$ and $p_2 \vdash s \hookleftarrow_t O_2$ imply $O_1 \subseteq O_2$ for all the content types t.

4.2   Applications of CoreCSP

Wrong Implementations of CSP. We empirically observed a few inaccurate implementations of the CSP specification in major browsers by means of a set of test cases we manually crafted. To formally reason on the security import of such cases, we defined policy-to-policy compilations which embed the inaccurate behaviors of the browsers directly in the CoreCSP semantics. For example, we defined a compilation $| \cdot |$ which removes all the conjunctions (+) from policies, which captures the incorrect CSP implementation provided by Microsoft Edge. It is possible to prove that, for all policies p and subjects s, we have $p \leq_s |p|$, which formally shows that the CSP implementation of Microsoft Edge can only make policies more permissive than intended (and it actually does).

Vulnerability to Script Injection. We defined syntactic conditions on policies which capture their vulnerability to script injection and proved that such conditions are both sound and complete, i.e., they capture all and only the ways script injection might happen when CSP is deployed. We used such conditions to implement an automated security checker for existing content security policies, which we employed to show the insecurity of the very large majority of the policies deployed in the wild (91.6%).

Policy Changes. Since $p_1 \leq_s p_2$ if and only p_1 is no more permissive than p_2 when deployed at s, we can use the $\leq_s$ relation to capture the nature of policy changes in the wild, i.e., to understand whether observed policy changes lead to more restrictive or more permissive policies. We automated such analysis and performed it on a large scale, showing that only a tiny fraction of changes (less than 3%) is intended to improve security by making policies more restrictive.

5   Conclusion

Formal methods hold promise to support a more principled and rigorous analysis of the web platform, as shown by our analysis of the current CSP deployment. We encourage interactions between the formal methods community and the web security community on challenging research problems, which require both theoretical foundations and a practical point of view. We refer the interested readers to an extensive survey on formal methods for web security [1].

References

1. Bugliesi, M., Calzavara, S., Focardi, R.: Formal methods for web security. J. Log. Algebr. Method Program. **87**, 110–126 (2017)
2. Calzavara, S., Rabitti, A., Bugliesi, M.: Content security problems? evaluating the effectiveness of content security policy in the wild. In: CCS, pp. 1365–1375 (2016)
3. Calzavara, S., Rabitti, A., Bugliesi, M.: Semantics-based analysis of content security policy deployment. TWEB **12**(2), 10:1–10:36 (2018)

4. OWASP: XSS prevention cheat sheet (2017). https://www.owasp.org/index.php/ XSS_(Cross_Site_Scripting)_Prevention_Cheat_Sheet
5. Weichselbaum, L., Spagnuolo, M., Lekies, S., Janc, A.: CSP is dead, long live CSP! on the insecurity of whitelists and the future of Content Security Policy. In: CCS, pp. 1376–1387 (2016)
6. Weissbacher, M., Lauinger, T., Robertson, W.: Why is CSP failing? trends and challenges in CSP adoption. In: Stavrou, A., Bos, H., Portokalidis, G. (eds.) RAID 2014. LNCS, vol. 8688, pp. 212–233. Springer, Cham (2014). https://doi.org/10. 1007/978-3-319-11379-1_11

Author Index

Altisen, Karine 21
Åman Pohjola, Johannes 3
André, Étienne 39
Attiogbe, Christian 57
Audrito, Giorgio 289

Bao, Ran 57
Beal, Jacob 289
Bhardwaj, Chandrika 75
Bugliesi, Michele 293

Calzavara, Stefano 293
Carbone, Marco 129
Corbineau, Pierre 21

Damiani, Ferruccio 289
Debois, Søren 129
Delahaye, Benoît 57
Devismes, Stéphane 21

Ene, Cristian 93

Fournier, Paulin 57

Graf-Brill, Alexander 111
Groote, Jan Friso 185

Hermanns, Holger 111
Hildebrandt, Thomas T. 129
Hüls, Jannik 148

Jéron, Thierry 224
Johnson, Taylor T. 261

Lanese, Ivan 167
Laveaux, Maurice 185

Lime, Didier 39, 57
López, Hugo A. 129

Marmsoler, Diego 204
Mounier, Laurent 93
Musau, Patrick 261

Nguyen, Luan Viet 261

Palacios, Adrián 167
Pham, The Anh 224
Pianini, Danilo 289
Potet, Marie-Laure 93
Prasad, Sanjiva 75

Quinson, Martin 224

Rabitti, Alvise 293
Ramparison, Mathias 39
Remke, Anne 148

Slaats, Tijs 129
Stefani, Jean-Bernard 242

Tran, Hoang-Dung 261

Vassor, Martin 242
Vidal, Germán 167
Viroli, Mirko 289
Völlinger, Kim 281

Willemse, Tim A. C. 185

Xiang, Weiming 261

Printed in the United States
By Bookmasters